# A SACRED UNITY

## Also by Gregory Bateson

*Naven*
*Balinese Character* (with Margaret Mead)
*Communication* (with Jurgen Ruesch)
*Perceval's Narrative* (ed.)
*Steps to an Ecology of Mind*
*Mind and Nature*
*Angels Fear* (with Mary Catherine Bateson)

# A SACRED UNITY

*Further Steps to an Ecology of Mind*

Gregory Bateson

Edited by Rodney E. Donaldson

A Cornelia & Michael Bessie Book
*An Imprint of* HarperCollins*Publishers*

FIRST EDITION

**Library of Congress Cataloging-in-Publication Data**

Bateson, Gregory.
   A sacred unity: further steps to an ecology of mind / Gregory Bateson; edited by Rodney E. Donaldson.—1st ed.
        p.    cm.
"A Cornelia and Michael Bessie book."
  Includes bibliographical references and index.
    ISBN 0-06-250100-3 (alk. paper)
     1. Knowledge, Theory of.  2. Ethnology.  3. Evolution.
  I. Donaldson, Rodney E.  II. Title.
  BD161.B34 1991
  121—dc20

                       90-56469
                          CIP

91  92  93  94  95  HAD  10  9  8  7  6  5  4  3  2  1

This edition is printed on acid-free paper that meets the American National Standards Institute Z39.48 Standard.

# Contents

## Part I: Form and Pattern in Anthropology

## Part II: Form and Pathology in Relationship

## Part III: Epistemology and Ecology

## Part IV: Health, Ethics, Aesthetics, and the Sacred

# Acknowledgments

It may be true of all teachers worthy of the name that their written works are but, in Chuang Tzu's words, "the dust they left behind," and sometimes I find myself feeling that this is peculiarly so in the case of Gregory Bateson. Nevertheless, I personally would be a far poorer human being did I not have available to me the writings of William Blake, R. G. Collingwood, and others who have been of signal importance to my life and thinking; and so I have deemed it eminently worthwhile to devote nine years thus far to preserving the "dust" of my primary mentor.

In the midst of the work of creating Gregory Bateson's archive and editing his most important essays and correspondence for publication, I have acquired a number of debts, as any scholar must who undertakes such an enormous task.

First and foremost, I am grateful to Lois Bateson, Mary Catherine Bateson, and the Institute for Intercultural Studies (Bateson's literary executor) for entrusting me with the responsibility and privilege of saving, organizing, and editing Gregory Bateson's professional remains. Their unflagging faith, support, patience, and trust throughout the past nine years have been indispensable, and I acknowledge them with affection. I am also grateful to Mary Catherine for her meticulous reading of the original manuscript.

The many others who provided support, assistance, and encouragement during the years of my work on the Bateson Archive (which is now available to the public in the Special Collections section of the Library of the University of California, Santa Cruz) have received recognition in the Acknowledgments to my several-volume *Gregory Bateson Archive: A Guide/Catalog,* and I will therefore refrain from mentioning each by name again here. Nevertheless, the depth of my gratitude remains undiminished.

Among those whose support extends throughout the period of my work both on the archive and on the present volume, I would like to extend special acknowledgment to Heinz and Mai Von Foerster, without whose unwavering encouragement and wisdom I am not sure I could have endured the bumps along the way. My love and respect for these two friends and mentors is profound, and were it not improper to dedicate the work of another, I would have dedicated this volume to them.

It is also impossible to thank adequately two people who have stood by me for many years and whom I love deeply—my parents, Mr. and Mrs. E. L. Donaldson, Jr.

For financial assistance in aid of the present volume, I offer my heartfelt thanks to the W. Alton Jones Foundation, Howard Kornfeld and Dee Ann Naylor, Jay Haley, and Paul Herbert—as well as to the Institute for Intercultural Studies for its very generous loan of a word processor. Even more important has been the friendship and encouragement of Laurence D. Richards, Pete Becker, Humberto Maturana, Jean Taupin, the late Ronald J. Stebbins, Frederick Steier, Jane Jorgenson, Eric Vatikiotis-Bateson, David Lipset, and Melba Wallace. I am also deeply grateful for the constant nourishment I receive from the entire membership of the American Society for Cybernetics.

Two students, Mareen Lambert and Carl Childs, read the manuscript in its entirety and offered a number of valuable suggestions. The introduction benefited from the advice of Elaine Jessen and other friends already mentioned, as well as my editor, Tom Grady. Jenny Manes offered invaluable assistance in proofreading. And Cornelia Bessie and John Brockman Associates were kind enough to value the project from the start, as well as to provide me the breathing space to complete the volume in the midst of a host of interruptions of various kinds.

Finally, I am grateful for the friendship and support of Al Guskin, Gary Zimmerman, and the entire faculty and staff of Antioch University Seattle, especially my students and colleagues in the Whole Systems Design Graduate Program.

Overriding all of the above, however, is my debt to Gregory Bateson himself. My six years of working with him constitute an education of a breadth and depth all too rare in the twentieth century, and I am particularly appreciative of the years in which I enjoyed virtually daily interaction with him. It is a gift for which I am humbly grateful and for which I offer the present volume as the merest token.

# Introduction

*Now I a fourfold vision see,*
*And a fourfold vision is given to me;*
*'Tis fourfold in my supreme delight*
*And threefold in soft Beulah's night*
*And twofold Always. May God us keep*
*From Single vision & Newton's sleep!*

—*William Blake, Letter to Thomas Butts,*
22 *November 1802*

*For we now recognize the nature of our disease. What is wrong with us is*
*precisely the detachment of these forms of experience—art, religion, and the*
*rest—from one another; and our cure can only be their reunion in a*
*complete and undivided life. Our task is to seek for that life, to build up the*
*conception of an activity which is at once art, and religion, and science,*
*and the rest.*

—*R. G. Collingwood,* Speculum Mentis

Anthropologist, biologist, philosopher, student of behavior and experience in virtually every arena of human life, Gregory Bateson (1904–1980) was one of the most far-reaching thinkers of the twentieth century, an explorer who always saw the connections between the various objects and realms of his explorations. Bateson thus occupies a position uniquely suited to assist us in unifying our ever more fragmented lives and knowledges, as well as to teach us—between the lines—about love, elegance, clarity, and understanding.

## I. Bateson's Life and Work

Gregory Bateson's life covered considerable geographical and imaginative terrain. He took part in a biological expedition to the Galapagos Islands, did anthropological fieldwork in New Britain, New Guinea, and Bali, and taught at Cambridge, Sydney, Columbia, the New School for Social Research, Harvard, the University of California

Medical School, Stanford, the California School of Fine Arts, the University of Hawaii, and the University of California, Santa Cruz. He was a Guggenheim Fellow and a Fellow of the American Academy of Arts and Sciences. A teacher who always taught at the edge of his present thinking, his work has influenced scholars in a wide variety of fields and contributed much of the groundwork for the establishment of family therapy. Yet the range and depth of his thought has continued to render him an elusive figure even to many who profess to know his work.

Son of the English biologist William Bateson (who coined the word "genetics"), Gregory attended Cambridge University, where he earned a B.A. in Natural Science and an M.A. in Anthropology. In 1936 he established himself as a considerable theorist in the fields of anthropology and philosophy of science with his book *Naven: A Survey of the Problems Suggested by a Composite Picture of the Culture of a New Guinea Tribe Drawn from Three Points of View.* Over the next several years, Bateson went on to pioneer photographic field techniques with his first wife, Margaret Mead, resulting in their *Balinese Character: A Photographic Analysis* (1942) and a variety of ethnographic films of Bali and New Guinea. Following World War II, during which he served the U.S. Office of Strategic Services as a staff planner and regional specialist for Southeast Asia, Bateson became a primary figure in the birth of cybernetics and systems theory. About the same time, he moved to California and began exploring the field of psychiatry, resulting in two books, *Communication: The Social Matrix of Psychiatry* (1951) (with Jurgen Ruesch) and *Perceval's Narrative: A Patient's Account of His Psychosis, 1830–1832* (1961), and culminating in the double-bind theory of schizophrenia, for which he received the Frieda Fromm-Reichmann Award for Research in Schizophrenia. Moving from family psychotherapy to animal communication in search of wider abductive support for his theory, Bateson spent the next decade studying the behavior and social organization of dolphins in the Virgin Islands and at the Oceanic Institute in Hawaii, all the time refining his thinking about the role of logical typing in integrating all levels of biological communication— genetic, individual, cultural, and ecological.

*Steps to an Ecology of Mind* (1972) drew together all these strands to reveal a new epistemology of enormous power and beauty. Returning to California, Bateson spent his remaining years producing a final synthesis of his work, *Mind and Nature: A Necessary Unity* (1979), serving on the Board of Regents of the University of California, and striving in lectures and workshops to convey his ideas to other scholars and to anyone concerned about the future of Western thought and of our planet—his ideas having significant implications for such widely varying areas as nuclear proliferation, ecology, spiritual growth, aesthetics, ethics, and, above all, epistemology. Gregory died on July 4, 1980. A final work, *Angels Fear* (1987), was completed by his daughter, Mary Catherine Bateson.

None of this biographical data, however, manages to capture the significance of Gregory Bateson's work. Above all, he proposed a new way of looking, a new epistemology. In his wide-ranging work with patterns of progressive change in human relationships, the application of Russell's theory of logical types to human natural history and learning theory, the role of somatic change in evolution, the nature of play, the double-bind theory of schizophrenia, the effects of conscious purpose on human adaptation, the nature of addiction, the relationship between consciousness and aesthetics, the criteria of mental process, and the "metapattern" that eliminates the supposed dichotomy between mind and nature—in all this seemingly disparate work, Bateson sought continually to elucidate the basis of form and pattern in the living world. As a result, he is a primary harbinger of what may be a major shift in Western thought, a paradigmatic shift from a mindless biosphere to one arising in and through mental process. The implications of such a theoretical—and lived—unification of mind and body remain to be unfolded.

Bateson's work is unique. To paraphrase one of his own self-accounts: Using the findings of anthropology, cybernetics, and ecology, he worked forward from very simple principles to construct a view of the world relevant to current problems, providing a solid foundation for understanding what is wrong with current ways of thinking about humankind and nature.

Since he spent his entire life explicating how to think about mental process of whatever sort, Bateson's work is of value to scholars in virtually every field who are concerned with the epistemological bases of their disciplines and of their own research and thought in particular. His work also has many significant implications for the theoretical, social, ecological, ethical, educational, medical, and personal problems of our time.

## II. A Sacred Unity: Further Steps to an Ecology of Mind

Almost from the moment *Steps to an Ecology of Mind* appeared, Bateson was asked to publish a second volume of his essays, and as his reputation has widened, that demand has grown proportionally. As with *Steps to an Ecology of Mind,* the articles in *A Sacred Unity: Further Steps to an Ecology of Mind* have been published in a wide variety of journals and books, many obscure or out of print, and several have never been published at all.

Although I have selected and arranged the pieces, this book is Gregory Bateson's. Insofar as it was possible, I have separated my own voice from his, made selections that I believe he would have approved, and made fidelity to his words and meanings the foundation of my editorial principles. My nineteen years of familiarity with his work, including six years of personal apprenticeship with him and nine years of working with his archival materials, give me some hope that my editorial decisions might not be too greatly at variance with those that he might himself have made. In any case, because it is my intention that the book be Gregory Bateson's, and because it has been my experience that most of the people who speak or write about his work fail to comprehend the nature and texture of the totality toward which he was always working, I think it important to begin with Bateson's own accounts of what it was he was about.

The ultimate foundation of Bateson's work is the notion of "an ecology of mind," which he once defined as

a new way of thinking about the nature of order and organization in living systems, a unified body of theory so encompassing that it illuminates all particular areas of study of biology and behavior. It is interdisciplinary, not in the usual and simple sense of exchanging information across lines of discipline, but in discovering patterns common to many disciplines.

In *Steps to an Ecology of Mind,* he defined it as "a new way of thinking about *ideas* and about those aggregates of ideas which I call 'minds.'" By "ideas," Bateson meant something "much wider and more formal than is conventional"—ultimately, any "difference which makes a difference," traveling in a circuit.

It is important to note that the questions raised are not logical but ecological:

How do ideas interact? Is there some sort of natural selection which determines the survival of some ideas and the extinction or death of others? What sort of economics limits the multiplicity of ideas in a given region of mind? What are the necessary conditions for stability (or survival) of such a system or subsystem?

The ideas are joined not by logic but by *natural history.*

In *Mind and Nature: A Necessary Unity,* Bateson proposed "an indivisible, integrated meta-science whose subject matter is the world of evolution, thought, adaptation, embryology, and genetics—the science of mind in the widest sense of the word." What he wanted to investigate was "that *wider knowing* which is the glue holding together . . . the total biological world in which we live and have our being."

The method of this meta-science is "double or multiple description," the juxtaposition of mental processes (aggregates of ideas) to disclose the underlying patterns and economics of patterning embodied in them, as well as the complex richnesses and increments of insight produced by their combination.

Such a method is *necessary,* since

> evolutionary process [of whatever sort] must depend upon such double increments of information. Every evolutionary step is an addition of information to an already existing system. Because this is so, the combinations, harmonies, and discords between successive pieces and layers of information will present many problems of survival and determine many directions of change.

In perhaps his clearest and most concise statement of the task of the new field—now interchangeably referred to as ecology of mind or Epistemology (the latter increasingly capitalized to differentiate it from the study of "local epistemologies")—Bateson concluded that "[t]he comparing of . . . thought with evolution and epigenesis with both . . . is the *manner of search* of the science called 'epistemology.'" Alternatively, he added, "we may say that epistemology is the bonus from combining insights from all these separate genetic sciences."

Finally and perhaps most importantly, it is a central aim of this science "to propose *a sacred unity* of the biosphere [emphasis added] that will contain fewer epistemological errors than the versions of that sacred unity which the various religions of history have offered." Bateson firmly believed that we are parts of a living world and that our loss both of a sense of unity of biosphere and humanity and of the notion that that ultimate unity is *aesthetic* is a disastrous epistemological error: "I surrender to the belief that my knowing is a small part of a wider integrated knowing that knits the entire biosphere or creation."

The subtitle of the present volume, *Further Steps to an Ecology of Mind,* is meant to indicate three things:

(1) that it contains "further" steps to an ecology of mind in the form of additional essays by Bateson that may be added to the

      previously anthologized essays to provide greater elucidation of the pathways by which he arrived at his synthesis;

(2)    that it contains more properly "further" steps that date from the years following the 1972 publication of *Steps to an Ecology of Mind;* and

(3)    that it attempts to explicate and enrich "further" the notion of an ecology of mind and its implications for critical problems confronting humankind.

I take it as my editorial task to tie together these three uses of the word "further" and to suggest ways in which readers may enrich their appreciation of the overall epistemology that Bateson offers, steering carefully between the twin founderings of our age, trivialization and ossification (vulgarization and the creation of dogma).

* * *

And perhaps it is appropriate to use these last two notions as a wedge into the nature of the total epistemology. At the end of *Mind and Nature,* Bateson makes the assertion, "To be conscious of the nature of the sacred or of the nature of beauty is the folly of reductionism." To understand the profound truth of that assertion, and then to contemplate that understanding in the light of an ecology of mind entailing an economics of flexibility, is to have entered the heart of the epistemology.

To spell out this last point, without vulgarizing it, is not simple. To me there seems to be value in taking the experience of trying to be conscious of that which to be merely conscious of, is to kill it, and placing that experience side by side with a formal description of cybernetic systems. To experience the former is to experience being the sort of mental organization described in the latter. And the nature of beauty and of the sacred has something to do with the *integration* of the total organization, unconscious as well as conscious, which we are. It is this acute and perspicacious critique of the conscious which renders Bateson particularly difficult, and valuable, to many readers.

Try the following exercise. Close your eyes, and imagine growing yourself (a feat that you in fact once achieved, though this is perhaps an unfamiliar use of the pronoun "you"). Imagine all the branchings, the self-differentiations, that necessarily take place in the process, and imaginatively identify with this process.

If you take the exercise seriously, you may discover that it is somehow illuminating to get in touch with this "you." Why? And what does this experience tell us about what it means to say "I"?

Now entertain the notion that the "you" that grew yourself has analogues in all living things, in ecologies of living things, and in the whole of biological evolution, as well as in the evolution of ideas in the narrower and more conventional sense of the word.

This exercise can help trigger the beginnings of a deeper understanding of some of the implications of Bateson's epistemology. It can also provide an experiential ground from which to discuss "embodied knowing" (vs. "knowing about"), the possibility of empathy with other creatures and even with biological and ecological processes, the potential humility that such a widened understanding of self can provide for the narrower conscious "self," and, most important of all, the notion of *integrating* many parts and levels of mind.

Taking seriously the notion of an ecology of parts and levels of mental process—all the way from a single "difference which makes a difference," to the largest possible instances of what Bateson called an evolving "ecological tautology" (e.g., the total interconnected planetary ecology, including human thought and social systems, seen in the perspective of time)—permits us to glimpse in all its complex simplicity the nature of the epistemology that Bateson offers us. Ultimately, this way of looking discloses a world of habits, of details of behavior within the parameters imposed by those habits, and of still further parameters imposed by still deeper habits (frequently older, frequently embedded in larger gestalts, and always dealing with propositions of still higher degree of abstraction or generality)—until we arrive at the most abstract patterns-in-time (habits) of all, including the very possibility of such patterns-in-time. As Bateson explains it in the third essay in Part III of the present volume, "[W]hat we were doing in 1955–1960 was the beginning of a formal science which would study the forms of interaction among explicit, implicit, and embodied ideas."

It is crucial to notice that in this proposed formal science (as he points out in the fourth essay in the same section), "We deal not with an energy budget but with budgets of entropy, negentropy, available pathways and patterns"—in short, with an economics of flexibility (see "The Role of Somatic Change in Evolution" and the first essay in Part II of the present volume). In "The Message of Reinforcement," Bateson hints at the implications of this last point by observing that

> information of higher type . . . is under certain circumstances most useful when least "conscious." This suggests that not only the logical typing of a piece of information but also its location and status in the circuitry of the organism may affect its usefulness in learning.

In other words, there is an economics that would seem to govern the relations between the habits and the behaviors that fall within the parameters (or contexts) that the habits impose, as well as between and among the habits themselves.

The way of looking called ecology of mind consists in taking a piece of mental process and its relations to the wider mental ecology in which it resides, and comparing it and its ecological relations to ecologies of mental process in a different region of Mind—ultimately, "comparing . . . thought with evolution and epigenesis with both."

I therefore advise the reader to read each essay in the present volume as though it were primarily about regions of an evolving ecological tautology, and only secondarily about the more immediate matters that the essay addresses and that keep its analysis of an ecology of ideas grounded in experience.

To reground the present discussion, I invite the reader to consider a point that Bateson seems to me to be making in "The Case Against the Case for Mind/Body Dualism." When he says, "Perhaps the people who leave their bodies could stay with their bodies if they once could grasp the fundamental truth that religion is unifying and ancient, where magic is divisive, degenerate, and late," and when he adds that "to be fully present in the present, here and now, and of the Body, is strangely difficult," he can be heard as suggesting that mind/body unity or dualism is, ultimately, not only a question of "fact" but also a question of ethics, of *integrity* (using the word both in its usual sense and in the sense of *integrating* all aspects of oneself or of one's experience). As Bateson's "'Last Lecture'" puts it: "It seems to me important for our notions of responsibility . . . that we accept very firmly that body and mind are one."

The reader may at this point usefully recall that pregnant phrase in the first chapter of *Mind and Nature: A Necessary Unity:* "to unify and thereby sanctify."

If, as Bateson asserts, all we can know is difference, then it becomes at least plausible that the bulk of our personal, interpersonal, international, and ecological problems arise ultimately from the simple turning of a distinction into a separation, and the separation into an opposition. It is obvious enough that an opposition presupposes a separation, and that a separation presupposes a distinction. It is less obvious, though readily grasped once the effort is made, that a distinction cleaves a ground of some sort in which the two halves of the distinction were previously joined. One can even gain a glimmer of the idea that this ground is in some sense oneself-in-interaction, or at least that the distinction is in some sense a distinction within one's own experiencing. All this is not to propose and espouse what a world of logic would tend to deduce: a void wherein there are no distinctions whatever. This, while true within its own terms, is too simple. Rather, what is being proposed is a dance: a dance of, for lack of a better word, *integrating*. The dance of an evolving ecological tautology.

"It's a matter of how to keep those different levels . . . *not* separate . . . and *not* confused," as Bateson says of the Protestant-Catholic argument over whether the bread "is" or "stands for" the body (see "Ecology of Mind: The Sacred").

* * *

We are perhaps now prepared to discuss the suggestion implicit in the title I have selected for the final section of the present volume: "Health, Ethics, Aesthetics, and the Sacred."

It is clear to me that Bateson's work contains the seeds of our liberation from what Blake refers to as "Newton's sleep." Not, let it be said, "the answers"—just the seeds: any "answer" being intrinsically wrongheaded.

In what do I think these seeds consist?

(1)  in the rectification of what I would term an incorrect or incomplete relation to consciousness, effected by a realization that our conscious-purpose "self" is but a tiny portion of the fuller life which is our birthright;

(2)  in the rectification of what I would term an incorrect or incomplete relation to language, effected by a realization that language is primarily injunctive and only secondarily descriptive;

(3)  in an escape from the overwhelmingly prevalent error of projecting models of conscious mental process onto preconscious mental process—an error from which even cybernetics itself is only slowly emerging;

(4)  in a rectification of the errors of the nineteenth century, during which (as Bateson wrote in an unfinished metalogue) "[t]he biologists worked hard to un-mind the body; and the philosophers disembodied the mind";

(5)  in the substitution of a temporalized "eco-logic" for the timeless "logic" which previously served as a model or image of mind;

(6)  in the integration of intellect and emotion (which brings to mind another of Blake's gems: "Thought without affection makes a distinction between Love & Wisdom as it does between body and Spirit");

(7)  in the understanding that learning is a stochastic process, formally paralleling phylogenetic processes under natural selection;

(8)  in an emphasis on knowing, as opposed to knowledge; and,

(9)  in the assertion "that our loss of the sense of aesthetic unity was, quite simply, an epistemological mistake."

In short, in the very possibility of an ecology of mind.

\* \* \*

And from the perspective of an ecology of mind, it seems to me a nontrivial exercise to inquire into the nature of optimally functioning wholes. Are health, ethics, aesthetics, and the sacred somehow related, or even, in some sense, "the same"? By what right could they be said to be "the same," and what would be the resulting implications for each of them as separate fields of inquiry as well as for the fields of medicine, education, social change, and so on?

It would seem to me that if we were to see health, ethics, aesthetics, and the sacred all from the standpoint of a whole functioning organism-in-its-environment, that is, as being defined operationally as opposed to prescriptively,[1] we could conceivably arrive ourselves at a vision of each of these seemingly separate categories as pointing toward a complex dynamic state of an evolving ecological tautology.

To return to the place from which we started: "To be conscious of the nature of the sacred or of the nature of beauty is the folly of reductionism."

I leave the relation between health, ethics, aesthetics, and the sacred as a genuine question, and invite the reader to explore it.

For my part, I will be content if the reader bears in mind that there is a way of understanding which all the "further" "steps" in the present volume go together to integrate—a sacred unity necessarily richer than

---

1. See William Blake's "If Morality was Christianity Socrates was the Savior," and "Jesus was all virtue, and acted from impulse: not from rules," as well as Lewis Carroll's "'I wish *I* could manage to be glad!' the Queen said. 'Only I never can remember the rule.'"

any description of it. Finally, it is my hope that the book will serve as a springboard for those who are able to explore . . . further.

I give Gregory the final word:

> And last, there is death. It is understandable that, in a civilization which separates mind from body, we should either try to forget death or to make mythologies about the survival of transcendent mind. But if mind is immanent not only in those pathways of information which are located inside the body but also in external pathways, then death takes on a different aspect. The individual nexus of pathways which I call "me" is no longer so precious because that nexus is only part of a larger mind.
>
> The ideas which seemed to be me can also become immanent in you. May they survive—if true.

—Rodney E. Donaldson

Seattle, Washington
July 4, 1991

# Editor's Note on the Selection and Arrangement of Material

The contents of the present volume were selected from over a hundred published and unpublished articles. Constraints on the length of the book made it necessary to omit a number of items worthy of inclusion, and, inevitably, some readers will regret the omission of this or that favorite article. I was guided in my selection by a desire to represent all aspects of Bateson's work and by a determination to choose those essays that contribute to ongoing theory.

Above all, since I have observed a tendency on the part of many to take pieces out of Bateson's work and miss the nature and texture of the whole, I have selected articles with an eye to pushing the reader gently in the direction of that larger whole toward which Gregory was always working. Like its predecessor, *Steps to an Ecology of Mind,* the present volume's overarching aim is to point the reader toward the total epistemology and not merely a portion or portions of Bateson's work.

The titles of the first three sections of the present volume are the same as the titles for the second, third, and fifth sections of Bateson's *Steps to an Ecology of Mind.* They represent the successive overlapping periods in his life in which anthropology, psychiatry, and the new epistemology arising out of systems theory and ecology were his dominant concerns. Unfortunately, there was no really suitable available essay dealing solely with evolutionary theory, an omission which I regret. I was sorely tempted to reprint from *Steps to an Ecology of Mind* "The Role of Somatic Change in Evolution," and were I to recommend a single additional article for the reader to explore, it would be that one, an essay that I have increasingly come to regard as pivotal to Bateson's epistemology, providing it be read at a sufficiently metaphoric level. The perceptive reader will, however, observe an early version of that essay's argument in "The New Conceptual Frames for Behavioral Research," printed herein.

Within each section, the essays are in chronological order, with two exceptions made for stylistic reasons.

At the beginning of each article, I have placed an introductory footnote indicating the occasion on which the article was written or the lecture delivered, as well as the date of actual writing or delivery (as opposed to the date of publication, which may be found in the Bibliography at the end of the volume). Having thus indicated the context of the remarks, I have then left the words and phrases which refer to the particular occasion unexplained in the body of the text.

Following Bateson's own practice in *Steps to an Ecology of Mind,* I have omitted extraneous introductory and discussion material, and have silently corrected minor errors. Articles receiving more than ephemeral editing are referred to in the Bibliography as being "reprinted, edited," in the present volume.

Finally, this volume includes a mix of written and spoken material, providing the reader an experience of both the formal and informal Gregory Bateson. Readers who find Bateson's earlier writings heavy going might temporarily pass them by and move ahead to his later essays and informal talks, returning to the earlier material at a subsequent time, fortified with an appreciation of the direction in which his work was moving. Although there is some repetition, the fact that a number of important ideas appear in different contexts and juxtapositions may stimulate the reader to a depth of understanding which could never be derived from a single encounter with the point in question.

I hope the reader derives as much joy from the following pages as I have.

# PART I

Form and Pattern in Anthropology

# 1

# *Cultural Determinants of Personality**

When we think of the multitudinous variety of the special cases of human behavior, when we watch a native of New Guinea doing this, a native of New York doing that, a native of Samoa doing something else, we are faced, as scientists, with a very serious difficulty—the difficulty of trying to imagine what order of general statement will cover these very diverse phenomena—and many different scientific approaches have been devised in the effort to solve this problem. In this book [*Personality and the Behavior Disorders*] we have, for example, the theories which have been devised by physiologists and neurologists, and other theories devised by those who studied the phenomena of experimental learning; other theories, again, devised by those who studied mental pathology; and so on. The basic presumption of such a symposium as this is that these various theories, no matter how diverse, are not necessarily mutually contradictory; that there is a possibility of translating, in the end, from the theories devised by psychoanalysts into terms of the theories derived from physiology; and those again into terms derived from experimental learning.

In spite of this great hope of ultimate translation, we have the fact that the theories have originated among workers using different kinds of data. This chapter is intended to give some general statement of the theories which have been reached by those who worked with a very curious kind of data, namely, observations upon preliterate people, and we shall endeavor to build up this picture inductively, starting from the various different threads in cultural anthropological work. But before we do this, it is necessary to make one negative statement about "cultural determinism," which needs to be kept clearly in the mind of the reader. We do *not* suggest that culture fully "determines" anything. The phrase

*Reprinted from *Personality and the Behavior Disorders: A Handbook Based on Experimental and Clinical Research*, Vol. 2, edited by Joseph McV. Hunt, 1944, by permission of John Wiley & Sons, Inc. Copyright © 1944 by the Ronald Press Company. Written 1942.

"economic determinism" has, unfortunately, become a slogan of those who believe that economic "factors" are more "basic" than, perhaps, any others. In the opinion of the writer, this view is disastrous, and I should like to see substituted for it the notion that, at best, an economic approach to human behavior is rewarding, perhaps very rewarding, for the insight which it gives. This is a very different position, and implies that economics is something that scientists do, not something that exists in the world as a determinative or "basic" cause. Similarly, we shall use the phrase "cultural determinism" to imply that "culture" is an abstraction—a ready label for a point of view built up by a number of scientists—a point of view from which those scientists have achieved some insight.

## Origin of the Concept of Cultural Determinism

The early days of anthropology were concerned chiefly with the business of description, and especially the early anthropologists were struck by outstanding bizarre features of the cultures which they studied. In their attempts to generalize, they were concerned chiefly to find identities or close similarities between phenomena in one place and phenomena in another. This is perhaps always the first step in a new science—the search, not for an abstract regularity, but for a concrete, episodic similarity between what occurs here and what occurs elsewhere; or between something which occurs now and something which occurs at some other time. Correspondingly, the theories of these early anthropologists were chiefly oriented to explaining such similarities, and naturally, since the similarities searched for were episodic, the type of theory which was devised was episodic or historical theory. Controversy raged, for example, between those who believed that resemblance between far-separated cultures ought to be accounted for in terms of similar evolutionary process and those others who believed that all such resemblance could only be accounted for by processes of cultural contact and diffusion. In the latter half of the nineteenth century and the beginning of the twentieth, cultural anthropologists were very seriously influenced by ways of thinking which they believed were in line with the Darwinian theory of evolution, and indeed it is perhaps fair to blame upon Darwin some of the errors of this period in anthropology. The Darwinian theory, in the form in which it was popularized, gave great emphasis to problems of origin. It was assumed that the way to account for some biological phenomenon—especially for some anatomical detail—was to seek for the phylogenic origin of that anatomical detail. Similarly, the anthropologists concerned themselves with looking for cultural phylogenies, and their controversies were parochial squabbles within the general assumption that phylogeny was the answer.

In the biological field, the ways of thought have changed very much since 1900. Biologists have focused more and more upon the *processes* of evolutionary change and less and less upon the actual history or phylogenic "tree" of any given species. In place of phylogeny, biologists nowadays talk about genetics and growth. The same change has been taking place in the field of cultural anthropology. We may have lagged a bit behind the biologists, but the direction of change in our ways of thinking has been the same. Nowadays, in place of arguing points of cultural phylogeny, we discuss the fine details of cultural change, and still more the fine details of internal organization within a culture at a given time. We have developed a sort of cultural "physiology" in place of the former groping after isolated details of cultural anatomy, and a sort of cultural "genetics" in place of the former cultural phylogeny. It is this sort of cultural "genetics" and cultural "physiology" which I have tried to sum up with the phrase "cultural determinism."

The basic shift in our ways of thinking, from this episodic-historical approach which looks for similarities toward a more orthodox scientific approach which looks for *regularities* in human behavior, has taken place gradually over the last twenty years, and those who contributed most to the shift often scarcely realized what order of contribution they were making. The shift from one approach to another means that, in place of investigating one set of variables, we turn to another set, and the first step was, perhaps, the establishment by Boas (1938) of the concept of "culture area," which enabled us to dismiss one set of variables and to start paying attention to others. According to this theory, it is possible to delimit areas within which so much contact has occurred between the various cultures that every one of the cultures in the area can be presumed to have had access by contact to every one of the principal cultural motifs which occur in the area. The delimitation of these areas is done by a careful study of the *resemblances* between the neighboring cultures and is oriented to testing the bare fact of their relationship rather than to any sort of speculative reconstruction of their history. This theory, when it appeared, was regarded as a historical approach to culture, and the preliminary inspection of the cultures in order to determine whether they constituted such a "culture area" and to determine the limits of the area was, in fact, historical. The theory was safe against historical attack because of this preliminary spade work, but the implicit rider—that we could say of any given culture: "this culture or this community has had access, by way of diffusion, to all the main motifs current in this area"—set us free to think about differences between cultures within such a cultural area. We could dismiss the problem of diffusion within a general "other things being equal" clause and proceed to investigate the cultures in terms of variables other than the episodic-historical details of diffusion and contact.[1]

When we looked at two neighboring cultures, say the Zuñi pueblos and the Indians of the Southwest, we could stop asking "What similarities are there which show that these two cultures are related?"—because this question had been answered by the preliminary spade work with a general affirmative—"Yes, the two cultures are related." And we could go on to ask: "Why, then, is the one so very different from the other?" and we could try to reduce these differences to generalizations, e.g., by showing that the internal emphases of Zuñi imply so much dislike of loss of self-control that, no matter how much contact that culture might have with neighboring tribes who base religious cults on the use of the peyote drug or with Europeans who base conviviality on the use of alcohol, the Zuñi will at most only adopt extremely denatured versions of these cultural traits.

A second trend in modern anthropological thinking, almost as important as the escape from the episodic and historical, has been the gradual recognition of the fallacy of "misplaced concreteness" (Whitehead, 1920), and this recognition came, not from epistemology, but from careful factual demonstration that theories which ascribed causal effectiveness to "religion," "geography," "language," and the like, would not fit the facts. Boas (1938) again was a leader in this discovery. He showed that the family of language which a people has does not determine other aspects of their culture, that the geographic circumstances under which they live similarly do not determine the other aspects of their culture, and so on. In fact, Boas first freed us from examining two unprofitable sets of variables, and then went on to demonstrate that certain other variables were not profitable subjects of inquiry.

Overlapping with the main period of Boas's work, there were other anthropologists similarly engaged in developing a nonhistorical and abstract approach to the phenomena of culture. Malinowski (1927a), with a team of well-trained, careful fieldworkers, showed that the behavior patterns in any community formed an interlocking, interdependent

1. In this connection, there is an interesting polemic book (Radin, 1933) in which the author attacks Boas for not being a historian, without realizing the implications for further and more scientific development of anthropological theory which are implicit in Boas's breakaway from conventional historical thinking. See also Kroeber (1939).

unity; that the "culture" of any people is not to be seen as a set of parts, each separately investigable, but rather that we should see the whole mass of behavior and artifacts and geographical circumstances as an interlocking functional system, such that, if we started from, say, the food-getting behavior—the system of agriculture, hunting, fishing, and the rest—and examined that system carefully, we should find that the functioning—the effective, continual working of the agricultural sys-tem—interlocks at every step with the religion of the people, with their language, with their magic, with the geographic circumstances of their life, etc., and, similarly, that their religion interlocks with all other phases of their behavior; their economics likewise; and their kinship likewise. Malinowski, in fact, laid a basis for an organismic approach to cultural phenomena. While Boas had demonstrated that language is not a cause of religion or magic, Malinowski demonstrated that everything in a cul-tural system was, if not a cause, at any rate a necessary condition for everything else. He showed that, in describing a culture, it was possible to start with any institutional category of behavior and from that to work outward in ever-widening circles of relevance, until the whole cultural system appears as relevant background for the particular set of data from which we started.

While Malinowski and his fellow workers were engaged in demon-strating the enormous complexity and mutual interdependence of all the parts of a culture, working out, like a fine patchwork quilt, the conti-nuity and ramifications of all these relationships, Radcliffe-Brown (1931, 1940) approached the problem from a different angle. He accepted, as a matter of course, this enormous interdependence within a culture and regarded the system of behavior in any community as organic in this sense. Then he went on to ask: "What is the bony structure, what are the salient features of this fine, intricate design?" And his answer was what he called "social structure." Running through the whole variety of seri-ous anthropological field work from the time of Morgan (1871) to that of Radcliffe-Brown, there was a very strong emphasis upon the study of the kinship systems of preliterate peoples, and these very profound and conspicious differences between one cultural system and another had stimulated a very wide variety of speculation. The data were then inter-preted in evolutionary terms. The peculiarities of differentiation between mother's brother and father's brother were regarded as symp-toms of a former matriarchy. The same peculiarities of preliterate cultures have also been interpreted by diffusion theories. When Radcliffe-Brown was working, the central theme, the central problem of ethnography, was kinship. Thus, Radcliffe-Brown's work developed as a study of the interrelationship between kinship structure and what he called "social structure." By "social structure" he meant the system of sub-groups—clans, moieties, age-grades, factions, classes, castes, and the like, in the community. Radcliffe-Brown's classical work was done on the Australian tribes, and he succeeded in demonstrating the functional interplay between the totemic system and the highly complex system of behavior roles toward various kin. The totemic system is unilateral and "closed," which meant that the position of any given relative—say, a mother's brother, or a father's sister's husband—in the totemic system, is fixed relative to ego, so that all ego's brothers-in-law are necessarily of the same generation and the same totemic group. There is not space to go into the fine details of the Australian system. Basically, if we consider only two exogamous divisions of the community, e.g., Eagle Hawk and Crow, with membership determined either by matrilineal or patrilineal descent, it is clear that if everybody obeys the rule of exogamy, every Eagle Hawk man will have relations-in-law in the Crow group and, even before his marriage, he might logically classify all Crow people together as "potential relatives-in-law." Australian systems have carried this principle much further by superposing more dichotomous divisions which define generations, as well as lineal descent, until it is possible for every individual to classify all the other people in the community by equating subgroup membership with potential kinship to himself.

Such a system could be analyzed as working on two levels of abstraction. We have first the enjoined behavior patterns between kin, e.g., between wife's brother in Eagle Hawk and sister's husband in Crow; and, second, the whole symbolism of myth and ceremony which defines the major group relationship between Eagle Hawk and Crow.

Radcliffe-Brown was concerned to show that the psychological presumptions within the family—the patterns of behavior between man and wife, between parent and child—were related to the whole pattern of this totemic system, which also governs the pattern of behavior of clan members.

The clans and other subdivisions of an Australian tribe are parts of a very complex system of opposition and allegiance. The ambivalent tensions which are culturally induced between affinal relatives are expressed again in the relationship between groups which are potentially related by affinal ties, and the whole functioning of the society depends upon these ambivalences and the nice balance between positive and negative components of hostility and love (just as our own society depends, in a laissez-faire period, upon nice balance between competition and cooperation, production and consumption, etc.). Thus, Radcliffe-Brown's work led, finally, to some general notion of how opposition and allegiance can be balanced against each other in a stable community, and this work of Radcliffe-Brown's was perhaps the first push which deflected the study of culture and society toward a study of psychology.[2] He did not himself regard his work as psychological, but implicit in it were assumptions about the human personality, about the psychological nature of maleness and femaleness, parenthood and childhood, opposition and allegiance, love and hate, which were a first step toward that later development in cultural anthropology which has diverted more and more attention to the tracing of the characterological aspects of human behavior.[3]

In Radcliffe-Brown's work there is still an assumption that peoples are psychologically alike, that there are certain basic psychological traits within individuals. The task of the anthropologist was to ask about the structure and the functioning of human society, "other things being equal"; and within this phrase "other things being equal" was a presumption that human personality is, in some measure, constant.

The next great change in anthropological approach came with the attempt to explore yet other variables. It was demonstrated that human personality is *not* constant, and this was accomplished largely under the influence of Boas's students, Ruth Benedict (1934a) and Margaret Mead (1928a). The latter went to Samoa to study the phenomena of adolescence at the behavioral level. It had been tacitly assumed that the psychological impact of puberty "naturally" caused behavior to be intense and erratic during the period of adjustment to the new physiological equilibrium. It followed from this assumption that, if human character and human physiology were essentially alike the world over, we ought to expect a similar period of maladjustment to occur in all cultures. Margaret Mead showed, however (1928a), that this was not true of Samoa, and, further, that the smooth, easy adjustment of the Samoan adolescent could be referred to peculiarities of the Samoan family organization. Whereas in Western cultures family organization is such that very intense ties are established between the child and one or two adults, in Samoa the ties of affection are slighter and are diffused over a large number of adults and child nurses. The capacity for intense emo-

---

2. It is difficult, in this connection, to estimate the contributions of Radcliffe-Brown's teacher, W. H. R. Rivers. Rivers was originally a psychologist and physiologist, but later became a historically minded anthropologist (1923).

3. For further development of Radcliffe-Brown's approach, see Warner (1941), and Dollard (1937).

tional behavior is, in fact, a variable which depends on the cultural milieu.

Since that time, cultural anthropology has devoted itself more and more to unraveling the very complex problems which arise when we regard as variable not only the whole structure of social groupings, the whole system of behavior, but also, as equally variable, the human individual who exhibits these various forms of behavior.

This research into problems of culture and human behavior has developed along many different lines, all of them ultimately contributing one to another, but as yet imperfectly synthesized together. And since this synthesis is still not achieved, it will be necessary for us to consider each one of these lines separately.

## Typology and Psychiatric Syndromes

For all anthropologists who regard personality as a variable which must be taken into account, the crucial technical problem is that of *describing* the personality. It is no use to recognize a variable until salt can be put upon its tail. The problem of handling a new variable, or rather such a complex of variables as is denoted by the word "personality," at once forces us to try to find either numerical statements—dimensions which can be measured—in terms of which personality can be evaluated, or failing such a quantitative approach, we must develop adjectives which will describe personality. It is natural, therefore, that anthropology has turned to psychology, and especially to those schools of psychology which have tried to define or to discriminate different *types* of personality. The earliest work on these lines was done by Seligman (1931), who used the typology suggested by Jung, of "introvert" and "extravert" types of personality. Seligman attempted to describe cultures according to whether they produced, in the individuals, a more introvert or a more extravert personality structure.

Seligman's work was very little followed up by other psychologists, and the next major attempt to describe culture in terms of personality types was made by Ruth Benedict (1934a). Benedict was stimulated, not by Jung, but rather by the Dilthey and Spengler school of historians. She attempted to apply the "Apollonian" and "Dionysian" dichotomy[4] to the

---

4. Benedict does not follow Nietzsche in the finer details of his description of this typology. The sense in which she uses the terms "Apollonian" and "Dionysian" can best be conveyed in her words: "The Dionysian pursues them (the values of existence) through the 'annihilation of the ordinary bounds and limits of existence'; he seeks to attain in his most valued moments escape

contrast between the Zuñi, a quiet Apollonian group in the Southwest pueblo, and two groups of violently Dionysian people, the Plains Indians and the Mexican Penitentes, with whom the Zuñi were in contact. It is significant that this technique of describing cultural contrast was most successful in Benedict's hands when applied to cultures which were actually in contact. She was able to show, for example, that a very high valuation was placed upon various forms of dissociated excitement by the Plains Indians and the Penitentes. The Plains Indians achieve mystic experience when seeking for a vision either through drastic self-torture or self-repression; or they may achieve it by the use of drugs. Among the Zuñi all these things were either absent, or—more significantly—if present, were practiced in such a way that they no longer had any Dionysiac quality. Where the Plains Indians use peyote, a drug, for the achievement of a high degree of disassociation, the Zuñi, with the same drug, living close to the area where peyote is obtained, have never accepted the peyote cult as part of their religious practices, with the exception of one, small, deviant group. Similarly, the Zuñi have resisted alcohol, to which every other group of American Indians has, to some extent, succumbed. In general, where the Plains Indians seek for ecstasy, for the extremes of religious experience, the Zuñi practice their religion with decorum and precision. Their dancing is exact, a following of a careful pattern; it is not ecstatic. Benedict was able to follow this contrast through the whole gamut of Zuñi and Plains Indian cultures, and to show that these cultures had consistently specialized in these particular forms of expression in all their fields and institutions.

In addition to using this dichotomy, Benedict (1934a) also used concepts derived from psychiatry. She analyzed two cultures, that of Dobu in the Western Pacific, and that of the Kwakiutl in the Northwest of America, and showed how paranoidal suspicion runs through Dobuan culture, while a more megalomaniac paranoidal tendency is characteristic of the Northwest.

This use of terminology derived from psychiatry raises at once certain problems and difficulties. We, in Western civilization, regard paranoidal

---

from the boundaries imposed upon him by his five senses, to break through into another order of experience. The desire of the Dionysian, in personal experience or in ritual, is to press through it toward a certain psychological state, to achieve excess. . . . The Apollonian distrusts all this, and has often very little idea of the nature of such experiences. He finds means to outlaw them from his conscious life. He 'knows but one law, measure in the Hellenic sense.' He keeps the middle of the road, stays within the known map, does not meddle with disruptive psychological states. In Nietzsche's fine phrase, even in the exaltation of the dance he 'remains what he is, and retains his civic name.'"

trends as pathological, and our picture of the paranoiac is of a deviant living among other people who are not compelled strongly by paranoia. Benedict's picture of Dobu or of the Northwest is of a community in which paranoidal trends are normally developed in all, or in a great majority of individuals. The norms of these cultures are only understandable if we suppose that these trends are either present in all individuals or in so many individuals that the trends appear as the normal stuff of social life. In such a community, the paranoidal constructs, instead of being the illusions of a few, become the knowledge and vision—the correct assumptions—of the many. The paranoidal suspicion which every Dobuan has for every other Dobuan is not an unreal figment; it is a legitimate generalization from his experience that the other Dobuan is out to do him in, to beat him in one way or another—to sorcerize him or to steal his yams by magical attack on his garden. So that while, to us, the term "paranoid" is descriptive of a relationship to other nonparanoid individuals, the term as applied to the Dobuans refers to relationships *between* paranoid individuals.

This raises in very serious form the problem of cultural deviance, and Benedict's (1934b) contribution to this problem is to point out that deviance is a culturally relative phenomenon—that a character structure which is normal among us may be deviant among the Kwakiutl or the Dobuans, while a structure which is normal and highly respected among them would be looked on as dangerous and disruptive in our community.

This typological approach to cultures has been criticized on the lines that, presuming some degree of standardization, it makes no allowance for deviance. To this type of criticism, the reply is, first, that the term "deviance" implies standardization; and, second, that deviance *is* allowed for and expected to occur in all cultures, though it is not expected that deviance will occur in the same directions in all cultures. Indeed, if similar distribution of *sorts* and frequency of deviance in all cultures could be demonstrated, the whole theoretical approach would have to be abandoned. Such demonstration has, however, not been achieved. Some work has gone into statistical study of the frequency of various forms of psychopathology in different parts of the world, but as yet this work has given only very inconclusive results. The methods of diagnosis and especially the methods of selecting deviants for commitment to institutions vary so widely from country to country and function so irregularly in those parts of the world where European medicine is in contact with preliterate peoples, that none of the statistical data is fit for comparative study.

There is, however, some indirect evidence to show that, in fact, the forms and frequencies of deviance do depend upon cultural circumstances. This evidence is derived from our communities. We find, for example, that considerable changes in frequency of psychosomatic and other psychopathological deviance occur from one period to another. One of the most striking of these demonstrations concerns the sex distribution of perforated peptic ulcer. It has been shown repeatedly (Alstead, 1939; Jennings, 1940; Mittelmann et al., 1942) that, in the latter half of the nineteenth century this condition affected more females than males, in Western cultures. Mittelmann et al. give the ratio for New York as six males to seven females for the years 1880 to 1900. The corresponding figures for the years 1932 to 1939 are twelve males to one female. In the same paper, the authors examine the case histories of a number of recent New York cases and show that perforated peptic ulcer follows a definite type of psychological history and character formation; that this background is at least as much a cause as it is an effect of the ulceration; and that the cultural changes in sex roles in the last fifty years have been such as would fit the striking change in sex distribution.

It may be argued that the differences between New York of 1900 and New York of 1935 are, at most, only of "subcultural" order. But from this we would predict that, *a fortiori*, still greater differences in form and frequency of psychosomatic deviance ought to occur between basically different cultural milieux.

Another reply which might be made to those who criticize the typological and psychiatric approach for its handling of the problem of deviance would be based on the notion of configuration. The theories are built upon a gestalt level of abstraction, rather than upon notions of simple cause and effect. They presume that the human individual is endlessly simplifying and generalizing his own view of his own environment; that he constantly imposes upon this environment his own constructions and meanings; and that it is these constructions and meanings which are regarded as characteristic of one culture, as over against another. This means that, when we approach a context of extreme deviance—when we look, for example, at the melting-pot communities of our own culture—we must be willing to see that heterogeneity itself may be a positive standardizing factor.

Granted that, in such a community, individual experience is infinitely various, and that each individual in New York City is, in this sense, a unique product, we can still say that all individuals are alike in so far as all have experienced the heterogeneity of the city; and, in terms of this common experience, we may look forward to finding certain psychological resemblances among them. We can even find these resemblances institutionalized in the cultures of such communities. Such poems as John Latouche's *Ballad for Americans,* which rejoices in the richness of a heterogeneous background, the quiz programs of the radio, and the infinite disconnected variousness of Ripley's *Believe It or Not,* are all symptomatic of this standardization due to heterogeneity. Even in the institutionalized curricula of higher education we can trace the analogous tendencies toward the dissection of knowledge into separate bits. We find that high value is placed upon factual information and that the student's progress is judged largely by the percentage of disconnected factual questions which he is able to answer correctly. He is, in fact, being fitted to live in a heterogeneous world in which generalizations are hard to apply, and he is being taught a way of thinking suited to such a world.

In fact, if we are willing to think at a rather high gestalt level, the phenomena of deviance fall into place very simply, and support, rather than conflict with, notions of cultural standardization. Extreme heterogeneity becomes a factor of standardization, and the isolated accident of a single individual's upbringing equally falls into place. Human individuals do not live in a cultural vacuum, and the isolated accidental deviant is faced with the problem of either accepting the norms of his culture, or reacting against them. Moreover, to react against one norm can usually only be done by accepting many of the premises upon which the norm is based. The individual who resists a hierarchical structure usually does so by attempting to rise in that structure; he accepts the major premise that human life in his cultural milieu is structured in hierarchical terms. So far as his character is concerned, it is molded to fit the cultural emphases, even though he fight against those emphases.

In this sense, and at this level of abstraction, the attempt to describe cultures in terms of the types of individuals which they foster is, I believe, sound; but a greater difficulty in the way of such an approach is that the typologies upon which it is based are still very unclear.

The syndromes of introversion, extraversion, Apollonian and Dionysian character, paranoia, etc., have not been critically and operationally defined. This criticism, of course, is not one which the anthropologist can be expected to answer. We have only taken the terms from other disciplines and adopted them as a convenient tool, and it is not for us, in this chapter, to examine the validity of these typologies. We may, however, express an opinion that the general notion of syndromes of personality is sound even though the study of these syndromes is not yet sufficiently advanced for us, in another science, to use them as tools. Since various other methods of approach are available to us, we need not delay our investigations because one descriptive technique is not completely satisfactory. Our solution is to supplement this technique with others.

## Description of Personality in Terms of the Socialization Process

Since the description of syndromes of character is still in a somewhat unsatisfactory condition, we have to proceed to use other descriptive methods of relating character to the cultural milieu in which it occurs. Of these, the most rewarding is the study of the socialization process by which the child is educated to become a typical member of the community into which he was born. This method is, in a sense, historical, rather than scientific. It assumes that a description of personality can be arrived at in terms of the experiences through which the individual has lived. The method accepts the fact that we have virtually no vocabulary for describing what people *are* like, and substitutes for such description statements about their past.

The great pioneer of this method was, of course, Sigmund Freud. For the present chapter, it is sufficient only to note certain peculiarities of the classical approach. First and foremost, Freud was a therapist, and his contribution was a science and technique of therapy. For this purpose, what we have noted as a conceptual failing in the method, namely, the indirect description of the present through the invocation of the past, was a positive advantage. The therapeutic procedure was based upon communication between the therapist and the patient, and for such communication an enormous new vocabulary of technical terms descriptive of present personality would have been exceedingly inconvenient. All that was necessary was that the patient should understand *himself*; it was not necessary that he should understand a general science of personality structure; and this understanding of himself could best be conveyed in a language provided by the patient himself. The incidents in the patient's anamnesic material provided such a rich variety of illustrative and immediately relevant material that a more precise terminology was unnecessary. In these circumstances, a whole massive science of human behavior and character has been built up around less than a hundred technical terms, and these, for the most part, are imperfectly defined.[5]

When we try to examine Freud's contribution to our understanding of culture, we very soon find that the preoccupation with therapy and the resulting poverty of critical terminology makes it almost impossible to arrive at any clear picture of Freud's opinions about the role of

---

5. The much younger science of stimulus-response psychology, dealing with a very much simpler gamut of phenomena, has already between one hundred and two hundred technical terms, many of them carefully defined.

culture, or his opinions as to whether human personality should be regarded as fundamentally "the same" all over the world. That he believed that similar processes (e.g., repression, displacement, introjection, projection, etc.) operated to produce human character in all communities is clear, but it is not clear whether Freud believed that the *products* were everywhere comparable or that the various processes have the same relative importance in all cultures.

"Totem and Taboo" (Freud, 1904) is an attempt to dissect the products of these processes in Central Australia. Freud shows, for example, that the whole gamut of Central Australian ritual dealing with the animal which is regarded as a clan ancestor or totem can be seen as an expression of ambivalent attitudes toward the father, and this analysis satisfactorily covers both the general taboo on killing the totem and the special ritual occasions on which the totem is killed, eaten, and mourned for.

Freud, however, goes further than this and constructs a tentative picture of the original patricidal act, by way of illustrating his hypothesis. He suggests that the young men freed themselves from the tyranny of a father, and even says: "Perhaps some advance in culture, like the use of a new weapon, had given them the feeling of superiority."[6]

This early attempt on the part of Freud to account for cultural phenomena in terms of the psychological past raises, in dramatic form, the problems of method and meaning upon which subsequent work has been focused. Broadly, we may classify the various subsequent attempts to use the incidents of the past as a descriptive vocabulary into three groups, according to the sources for data upon past events.

For the practicing psychoanalyst, the principal source of information about the past is the patient's anamnesic material, the picture which he is now able to give us of what he thinks happened at some past time. This picture is, no doubt, a doubly distorted version of the real past events, first distorted in terms of the interpretation which the patient put upon the events when they occurred, and distorted again by the patient's mood at the time when he relates them to the analyst. But in spite of this distortion, the anamnesic picture is undoubtedly a true source, in so far as we use its contents solely as a means of describing the patient's character and personality *today* in the consulting room.

---

6. In a footnote to another part of the same paragraph, Freud gives an extract from Atkinson's *Primal Law*, in which, long before Freud, Atkinson says of the young men: "A horde as yet weak in their impubescence they are, but they would, when strength was gained with time, inevitably wrench by combined attacks renewed again and again, both wife and life from the paternal tyrant" (Atkinson, 1903, pp. 220–21). Freud does not comment on the parallel between pubescence and the "new weapon."

Like the analyst, the field anthropologist uses an indirect source for his information about the psychological past. It is not possible for him to record the experience and behavior of the same individual year in and year out, from birth through adolescence to adult life, which, though cumbersome, would perhaps be the ideal genetic approach. Instead of doing this, he argues that the adult natives whom he can observe today presumably had childhood experiences similar to those of the children of today. He therefore endeavors to describe the adults whom he sees in terms of the way the children of today are treated and the way the children behave under that treatment. (For an examination of this method, see Lasswell, 1937.)

To those who are familiar only with rapidly changing communities, where the cultural norms vary from year to year and a craze for putting babies on schedules may rise and fall in a decade, the basic presumption that a native culture may be stable for over thirty years may seem incredible. In general, however, it is justified. Before contact with the white man, the cultures of preliterate peoples were changing much more slowly than European cultures and their norms were much more clearly defined than ours; and further, it is not difficult for the ethnologist in the field to form an estimate of the degree of disruption which the culture has suffered since contact began.

Using this method, we have come to a new evaluation of the role of culture in shaping the personality and character of the individual. The original Freudian position, which gives maximal importance to the family constellation, still stands unchallenged, and there is no doubt that it will continue to stand. We have, however, come to realize that the family constellations—the behavior patterns between the members of the family and the attitudes which underlie these patterns—differ very profoundly from culture to culture. At the physiological level, we can, of course, refer to the processes of sex and reproduction as universal, but when we come to use these terms as counters in psychological discussion, we find that they may mean very different things in different cultural systems. Sexual initiative may come typically either from the male or from the female (as among the Iatmul of New Guinea), and the sexual act may be conceived of as aggressive (as among the Mundugumor), or as affectionate (as among the Arapesh). The relationship between man and wife may be predominantly tinged with dominance-submission, or with succoring-dependence, or with exhibitionism-spectatorship, or with any of the many variants of competition or cooperation; and these characteristics may be relatively standardized in the most varied ways in different communities.

This means that the constellation into which the child is born, the Oedipus situation which he encounters, varies profoundly from culture to culture. When the child is added to a previously existing relationship involving the two parents, the behavior of the latter toward the child will inevitably be a function of their relationship to each other.[7] Their relationship to each other was in large measure shaped in terms of the conventions of their culture, and where it deviated from those norms the parents were, consciously or unconsciously, influenced by the fact of deviation. Similarly, their behavior toward the child is in large measure conventionalized, and both they and the child, when they deviate from the conventions, deviate not in a vacuum but with conscious or unconscious recognition of deviation.

Thus, in healthy cultures, we find that a very high degree of uniformity of character is passed on from generation to generation, and in unhealthy cultures we find sometimes no less uniformity. Among the Mundugumor (Mead, 1935) we find that deviance and the guilt of deviance are passed on, rather than simple conformity. The marriage system of these people is so complex and so demanding that, as a matter of fact, no marriages at the present time follow the native convention. In spite of this, all are alike in suffering from their deviation from the cultural standard.

So far, we have considered only what might be called the "content" of character and personality, and we have noted that very profound differences occur in what patterns of behavior are passed on to the child. If we go on from this to ask *how* these patterns are passed on, we find that here again differences occur from culture to culture. It is common in Western cultures to find that the growing child builds up a set of intrapsychic habits of self-approval and self-disapproval. This superego is modeled upon the child's impressions of the character of one or the other parent. This valuational system may or may not be consistent with other intrapsychic systems in the same individual, and where discrepancies occur we observe the phenomena of guilt. The superego system may even be differentiated to such a point that it can be hallucinated as a scolding voice or the like.

This whole system clearly depends upon a very specific set of circumstances. For the establishment of an organized and more or less personified superego, such as we are familiar with in Western cultures: (a) the inculcation of cultural norms must be predominantly reinforced by punishment (including threats of withheld affection under this term);

---

7. I understand that Dr. Kurt Lewin has recently initiated studies of such triangular relationships, first observing the patterns of behavior between two children and then adding a third child and observing the readjustments which follow this addition (Unpublished).

(b) the punishing role must be played by some individual adult (a parent or parent substitute); and (c) the behavior of this punishing parent must be such that some species of close affective tie is established between the child and the parent. These three conditions may be varied in many ways, according to local convention. The punishment may be intense or mild, regular or irregular; it may be done in anger or in cold blood; the introjected parent may be male or female (as in Manus); the affective tie may be strong or weak; it may have various characteristics and may be broken in various ways. But, provided these three conditions are somehow fulfilled, we may expect to find some structure in the native personality which we can recognize as a "superego."

These three basic conditions for this type of character structure are, however, by no means universal. Indeed, it is probably rather rare to find them all in combination. In a very large number of cultures (Samoa, Lepcha, Bali), the baby spends the greater part of its time in the care of some little girl, so that if any strong affective tie is developed (and in such cases the baby is often treated more as a bundle than as a person), the introjected personality will be, not that of an adult, but rather that of a juvenile.

In other cases, punishment is very rare (Samoa); or it may be carried out by some person *other* than the parents. Among many American Indian tribes, punishment is done by masked dancers. Unknown to the child, the parents call in these punishing agencies. When these dancers arrive, the parents go through an appearance of pleading with them, asking them to spare the child. Or, again, the inculcation of cultural norms may be done by invocation of "what other people will say," establishing a proneness to shame rather than to guilt, and introjecting a vague multitude rather than a single personality. (For a general discussion of these variants, see Mead, 1940b.)

Of special interest are the variants of character structure which depend upon the type of affective tie established between the parent and the child. In English-speaking cultures, this tie, in childhood, contains many complementary components. These are patterns of behavior in which the roles of parent and child are differentiated one from the other and mutually complementary (e.g., dominance-submission, succoring-dependence, exhibitionism-spectatorship, etc.). But the business of growing up consists largely in substituting more symmetrical patterns of behavior. In both England and America, we find strong insistence that the child, as he grows up, shall not react with overt dominance or submission in relationships with people stronger or weaker respectively than himself. But while in England the remodeling of these ties is often done by drastic separation between parents and child, such as sending the child to boarding school, in America the same function is usually performed by the parents themselves, who respond with admiring spectatorship to any signs of independence and self-sufficiency which the child may exhibit. Thus, in both cultures, we develop a character structure in which symmetrical patterns are superposed on a complementary base. These cultures differ, however, in the relationship between these two layers (see Bateson, 1942a).

In some of the other cultures of the world, there is no reversal of this sort, and we know of still other possibilities:

(a) The behavior of the parents may be such that from the very beginning, symmetrical patterns are emphasized. Among the Iatmul of New Guinea, the mother behaves as if the child were as strong as she (Mead, 1940a). She first resists the child's demands for food, and later gives way to them in response to the child's temper: "the child was too strong." Any sort of punishment is preceded by a chase, and usually the child is "too quick" to be caught.

(b) The behavior of the parents may be such that any tendency which the child may have toward developing close affective ties is discouraged from the very beginning. The Balinese mother (and the child nurse) very much enjoys the responsiveness of her child, and often prompts the child to respond, either by small teasings or by affectionate advances. She was, herself, once a Balinese child and had a Balinese mother, and so she herself is not responsive in the same way as the young child. The child responds to her advances either with affection or temper, but the response falls into a vacuum. In Western cultures, such sequences lead to small climaxes of love or anger, but not so in Bali. At the moment when the child throws its arms around the mother's neck or bursts into tears, the mother's attention wanders (Bateson, 1941).

Thus, by using the details of childhood experience as a vocabulary for describing character structure, and studying the parent-child relationship in various cultures, it is possible to show that the cultural milieu is relevant to character and personality at many different levels. It may contribute to determining the content; the list of behaviors which are passed on from generation to generation is different for every culture. More fundamental than this determination of content, the cultural milieu may, by altering the contexts of learning, contribute to shaping the interpretation which the child habitually places upon his own acts and upon the universe in which he lives. The child who has learned by punishment will see one sort of world, and the child who has learned by reward will see a different world. Finally, at a still more fundamental level, the cultural milieu may determine the manner of organization of the learned behaviors. In some cultures, these are elaborately organized into an image of a parent, but it is clear that other types of intrapsychic organization may occur.

## The Study of Interpersonal and Intergroup Attitudes

The strong tendency in science to look for cause has led us to try to describe adult character in terms of childhood experience; and, indeed, this approach has so far proved rewarding. But this is not the only scientific method, and several attempts have been made to use adult behavior itself as a descriptive medium. One can build a systematic *classification* of behaviors rather than a systematic accounting for behaviors.

This method is necessarily very cumbersome and exacting, and progress in it will depend more and more upon the use of strict operational definitions and the techniques of mathematics and symbolic logic. When we put adult behavior beside childhood experience, it is not necessary to be very precise in our description of either set of observations, since some extra clarity is given by the juxtaposition. But when we have only a single set of phenomena and must somehow deal with them in their own terms, a very much greater stringency is necessary, not only in our recording of the phenomena, but also in the formulation of the problems which we hope to solve and the analytic procedures which we apply to our collected data.

We have noted, above all, that all the details of behavior and circumstance which go to make up what we call a culture are interrelated, and very little thought is sufficient to show that various sorts of interrelationship occur in every culture. We have, for example, all the relationships which must be considered if we want to understand the integration of the community at a strictly sociological level, and if this is the sort of problem which we set out to solve, we have to put side by side the details of how the community is subdivided into groups and the factors which make for union or dissension among these groups. This particular type of functional approach will, however, scarcely help us toward a psychological picture of the individual in that society.

For such a psychological picture, there are various possible ways of arranging our data, according to the sort of psychological insight which we are seeking.

*View of the World.* The data can be arranged to give us information about such matters as native orientation in space and time, among objects and among people; native systems of cause and effect; the natives' view of the universe in which they live; the sorts of logic and illogic which they follow. This has not yet been done systematically for any culture, though a real beginning has been made by the gestalt psychologists and especially the topological school, in experimental studies of individuals of European and American background. At the preliterate level, we have not been able to approach this degree of precision, but from the crude survey work which has been done, it is evident that marked differences among cultures can be revealed by this approach. We find, for example, that in some cultures the whole ceremonial life is geared to a calendar, so that the precipitating stimulus for any ceremonial celebration is the date. In other cultures, again, we find that the date is ignored, and ceremonial is precipitated by events at the human level, such as birth and death, victories, harvests, quarrels, etc. Even among calendric cultures we find variation. Our own calendar is a double system, with the week as a simple cyclic motif, while the days and months are built into an endless ongoing system. For us, the cyclical motif is comparatively unimportant; we forget the day of the week on which we were born but remember the day of the month, and the serial number attached to the year. In Bali, on the other hand (Bateson and Mead, 1942), the cyclical motif is all-important, and any individual can tell you that he was born "on the third day of the five-day week and the sixth day of the seven-day week," and he will probably be able to tell in which month he was born in the twelve-month sequence. He will *not* be able to tell in what year he was born and is not interested in this question.[8]

Differences of this order are more than mere details of the calendar, and if we examine the rest of the culture, we find that the same type of difference in the perceived pattern goes through the whole of life. Our world is shaped in terms of the notion that the past was different from the present and that the future will be different again. The Balinese world is based on a presumption that the present is only a repetition of the past and the future will continue in the same circular fashion. The two cultures are, however, alike in using spatial metaphors in referring to temporal sequences.

---

8. There is, in Bali, a system which gives serial numbers to the years, but this is not used except by the most pedantic. The majority of the Balinese scholars are content to date their everlasting manuscripts with the day of the week and the name of the month.

*Goal Orientation.* A second method of arranging the data will give us, instead of a cognitive[9] picture, a picture of goal orientation. We noted above that the Balinese child is continually frustrated in the climaxes which should follow his sequences of love and hate behavior, and when we examine the adult behavior we find that there are no sequences of mounting tension in interpersonal relations, no factions, and no oratory. Equally, there is no mounting tension in efforts to deal with impersonal barriers. The Balinese have no word for "to try hard," and their goal orientation is not strengthened by any appreciation of the sequence of contrasts in which mounting tension is followed by release. They do not purposely increase their intrapsychic tensions in order to increase the ultimate satisfaction of release, as we do with apéritifs or by deliberate abstemiousness.

*Affective and Postural Patterns.* The data may also be arranged to give an "affective" picture of the system of linked responses. At a very simple postural level, we may observe that, in our own culture, people tend to leave their fingers, when at rest, in regular positions. If the fingers are flexed, they will either be all flexed to the same extent, or, if differentially flexed, the differences will follow some regular system of progression, commonly each flexed a little more than its neighbor on the radial side. The Balinese, very much more often, leave their fingers in what appear to us to be distorted positions, as though each finger were a separate entity or a separate sense organ. True, in our culture, it is polite in certain sections to extend the little finger when holding a teacup, but in Bali this sort of thing is enormously developed, and photographic records show that the tendency to disharmonic finger postures *increases* in the extreme excitement of rioting over the body at funerals (Bateson and Mead, 1942).

Building further on this picture, we find that in witchcraft the emphasis on discrepancy between body parts reaches its height. We find play with fantasies of one-footed balance, and evil spirits consisting of single body parts, personified legs, arms, heads, and even spirits which have a face at every joint.

With this sort of synthesis we arrive at a culturally limited description of "fear," putting together a study of postures and contexts in which certain postures are exhibited. And there is no doubt that comparative

---

9. The old terms, cognitive, affective, and conative, are here used to refer not to artificially isolated processes which are supposed to occur in organisms, but to different sorts of generalization which we arrive at by different methods of arranging our data.

studies of different cultures on these lines will show very profound differences in the organization of emotion.

*Interpersonal Behavior.* Lastly, we can arrange our data to give a picture of interpersonal behavior sequences. Here, again, our main difficulty is with the operational definition of our concepts and units, and progress will be delayed until we have clear operational definitions of dominance, submission, dependence, exhibitionism, narcissism, climax, identification, and the like. One very significant attempt, however, has been made by Chapple (1939, 1940). Using a small machine with a recording drum, Chapple obtains a record of the duration of all overt behaviors in a conversation between two or more individuals. He ignores completely the verbal content and "meaning" of the behavior, and concentrates attention entirely on the time properties. This simplification gives him the chance to define "initiative" operationally in terms of time relationships, and his data are such that he can proceed to a statistical study of "initiating behavior," "interruptions," "duration of responses," etc. The results show very marked differences between individuals and especially marked peculiarities in the case of deviant and psychopathic personalities.

We may expect that application of these methods to individuals from cultures other than our own will show marked differences, and that this method will give us useful abstractions for the handling of cultural characteristics.

## Conclusion

We may sum up our knowledge of cultural determinants of personality by saying that, while culture is not by any means the only determinant, it is very important. The whole of human behavior as we know it (with the possible exception of some reflexes) is either learned or modified by learning, and learning is, in large measure, an interpersonal process. The contexts in which it occurs vary from culture to culture, as also do the methods of reinforcement. Thus, not only *what* is learned is, in some measure, culturally determined, but also the role of the learned behavior in the psychic life of the individual. Eating may mean nearly the same thing to a starving man in whatever culture, but in the ordinary course of everyday life, apart from the extremes of deprivation, we must expect every one of the simple physiological behaviors, such as eating, defecation, copulation, and even sleep, to have special meaning for the individual, and this meaning will be culturally determined and will vary from culture to culture. Our task, as anthropologists or psychologists, is to recognize and define the regularities in this complex tangle of phenomena.

## References

Alstead, G. 1939. *The Changing Incidence of Peptic Ulcer.* London: Oxford University Press.

Atkinson, J. J. 1903. *Primal Law.* Bound with Lang, A., *Social Origins.* London: Longmans, Green.

Bartlett, F. C. 1937. "Psychological Methods in Anthropological Problems." *Africa* 10:400–29.

Bateson, G. 1935. "Culture Contact and Schismogenesis." *Man* 35:178–83. [Reprinted in *Steps to an Ecology of Mind.*]

—. 1936. *Naven.* London: Cambridge University Press.

—. 1941. "The Frustration-Aggression Hypothesis and Culture." *Psychol. Rev.* 48:350–55.

—. 1942a. "Morale and National Character." In Watson, G., *Civilian Morale.* Boston: Houghton Mifflin. [Reprinted in *Steps to an Ecology of Mind.*]

—. 1942b. Comment on Margaret Mead's "The Comparative Study of Culture and the Purposive Cultivation of Democratic Values." In *Science, Philosophy and Religion; Second Symposium.* New York: Country Life Press. [Reprinted in *Steps to an Ecology of Mind* as "Social Planning and the Concept of Deutero-Learning."]

Bateson, G., and M. Mead. 1942. *Balinese Character: A Photographic Analysis.* New York: New York Academy of Sciences.

Benedict, R. 1934a. *Patterns of Culture.* Boston: Houghton Mifflin.

—. 1934b. "Anthropology and the Abnormal." *J. Gen. Psychol.* 10:59–82.

—. 1938. "Continuities and Discontinuities in Cultural Conditioning." *Psychiatry* 1:161–67.

Boas, F. 1938. *The Mind of Primitive Man.* New York: Macmillan.

Chapple, E. D. 1939. "Quantitative Analysis of the Interaction of Individuals." *Proc. Nat. Acad. Sci., Wash.* 25:58–67.

—. 1940. "'Personality' Differences as Described by Invariant Properties of Individuals' Reactions." *Proc. Nat. Acad. Sci., Wash.* 26:10–16.

Dennis, W. 1940. *The Hopi Child.* New York: Appleton-Century.

Dollard, J. 1937. *Caste and Class in a Southern Town.* New Haven: Yale University Press.

DuBois, C. 1937a. "Some Anthropological Perspectives on Psychoanalysis." *Psychoanal. Rev.* 24:246–73.

—. 1937b. "Some Psychological Objectives and Techniques in Ethnography." *J. Soc. Psychol.* 8:285–300.

Erikson, E. H. 1939. "Observations on Sioux Education." *J. Psychol.* 7:101–56.

Fortes, M. 1938. "Social and Psychological Aspects of Education in Teleland." *Africa* 11, Suppl.: 4–64.

Fortune, R. F. 1932. *Sorcerers of Dobu.* London: Routledge.

—. 1935. "Manus Religion." *Mem. Amer. Phil. Soc.* 3.

Frank, L. K. 1931. "The Concept of Inviolability in Culture." *Amer. J. Sociol.* 36:607–15.

—. 1938. "Cultural Control and Physiological Autonomy." *Amer. J. Orthopsychiat.* 8:622–26.

—. 1939. "Cultural Coercion and Individual Distortion." *Psychiatry* 2:11–27.

Freud, S. 1904. "Totem and Taboo." In *The Basic Writings of Sigmund Freud.* New York: Modern Library, 1938.

Fromm, E. 1932. "Die Psychoanalytische Characterologie und ihre Bedeutung für die Sozialpsychologie." *Z. SozForsch.*

Gorer, G. 1938. *Himalayan Village.* London: Michael Joseph.

Hambly, W. 1926. *Origins of Education Among Primitive Peoples: Comparative Study in Racial Development.* London: Macmillan.

Henry, J. 1936. "The Personality of the Kaingang Indian." *Character & Pers.* 5:113–23.

—. 1940. "Some Cultural Determinants of Hostility in Pilaga Indian Children." *Amer. J. Orthopsychiat.* 10:111–12.

Homburger, E. H. 1937. "Configurations in Play—Clinical Notes." *Psychoanal. Quart.* 6:138–214.

Horney, K. 1937. *The Neurotic Personality of Our Time.* New York: Norton.

Jennings, D. 1940. "Perforated Peptic Ulcer: Changes in Age-Incidence and Sex Distribution in the Last 150 Years." *Lancet* 238: 395–98, 444–47.

Kardiner, A. 1939. *The Individual and His Society.* New York: Columbia University Press.

Klineberg, O. 1935. *Race Differences.* New York: Harper.

Kluckhohn, C. 1939. "Theoretical Bases for an Empirical Method of Studying the Acquisition of Culture by Individuals." *Man* 39:98–103.

Kohler, W. 1937. "Psychological Remarks on Some Questions of Anthropology." *Amer. J. Psychol.* 59:271–88.

Kroeber, A. L. 1935. "History and Science in Anthropology." *Amer. Anthrop.* 37:539ff.

—. 1939. "Totem and Taboo in Retrospect." *Amer. J. Sociol.* 45:446–51.

Landes, R. 1938. *The Ojibwa Woman.* New York: Columbia University Press.

Lasswell, H. D. 1935. "Collective Autism as a Consequence of Culture Contact." *Z. SozForsch.* 4:232–47.

—. 1937. "The Method of Interlapping Observation in the Study of Personality and

Culture." *J. Abnorm. Soc. Psychol.* 32:240–43.

—. 1939. "Person, Personality, Group, Culture." *Psychiatry* 2:533–61.

Lee, D. D. 1940. "A Primitive System of Values." *J. Phil. Sci., N.Y.* 7:355–78.

Levy, G. 1939. "Sibling Rivalry Studies in Children of Primitive Groups." *Amer. J. Orthopsychiat.* 9:203–14.

Lindgren, E. J. 1935. "Field Work in Social Psychology." *Brit. J. Psychol.* 26:177–82.

Malinowski, B. 1927a. *Sex and Repression in Savage Society.* New York: Harcourt, Brace.

—. 1927b. *The Father in Primitive Psychology.* New York: Norton.

—. 1929. *Sexual Life of Savages in Northwestern Melanesia.* New York: Liveright.

Mead, M. 1928a. *Coming of Age in Samoa.* New York: Morrow.

—. 1928b. "The Role of the Individual in Samoan Culture." *J. R. Anthrop. Inst.* 53:481–95.

—. 1928c. "A Lapse of Animism Among a Primitive People." *Psyche* 9:72–79.

—. 1930a. "Adolescence in Primitive and Modern Society." In Calverton, F. V., and S. D. Schmalhausen, *The New Generation; Symposium.* New York: Macaulay.

—. 1930b. *Growing Up in New Guinea.* New York: Morrow.

—. 1930c. "An Ethnologist's Footnote to 'Totem and Taboo.'" *Psychoanal. Rev.* 17:297–304.

—. 1931. "The Primitive Child." In Murchison, C., *Handbook of Child Psychology.* Worcester, Mass.: Clark University Press.

—. 1932. "Investigation of the Thought of Primitive Children, with Special Reference to Animism." *J. R. Anthrop. Inst.* 62:173–90.

—. 1934. "The Use of Primitive Material in the Study of Personality." *Character & Pers.* 3: 1–16.

—. 1935. *Sex and Temperament in Three Primitive Societies.* New York: Morrow.

—. 1937. *Cooperation and Competition Among Primitive People.* New York: McGraw-Hill.

—. 1939. "Researches in Bali and New Guinea." *Trans., N.Y. Acad. Sci.* 2:1–8.

—. 1940a. "Character Formation in Two South Seas Societies." *Trans. Amer. Neurol. Assn.* 66:99–103.

—. 1940b. "Social Change and Cultural Surrogates." *J. Educ. Sociol.* 14:92–109.

Mekeel, S. 1936. "An Anthropologist's Observations on American Indian Education." *Progr. Educ.* 13:151–59.

Miller, N. E., and J. Dollard. 1941. *Social Learning and Imitation.* New Haven: Yale University Press.

Mittlemann, B., H. G. Wolff, and M. P. Scharf. 1942. "Emotions and Gastroduodenal Function: Experimental Studies on Patients with Gastritis, Duodenitis, and Peptic Ulcer." *Psychosom. Med.* 4:5–61.

Morgan, L. H. 1871. *Systems of Affinity and Consanguinity.* Washington: Smithsonian Instn.

Nadel, S. F. 1937a. "The Typological Approach to Culture." *Character & Pers.* 5:267–84.

—. 1937b. "Experiments on Cultural Psychology." *Africa* 10:421–35.

—. 1937c. "A Field Experiment in Racial Psychology." *Brit. J. Psychol.* 28:195–211.

Nissen, H. W., S. Machover, and E. F. Kinder. 1935. "A Study of Performance Tests Given to a Group of Native African Children." *Brit. J. Psychol.* 25:308–55.

Radcliffe-Brown, A. R. 1931. *The Social Origin of Australian Tribes.* Melbourne: Macmillan.

—. 1940. "On Social Structure." *J. R. Anthrop. Inst.* 70, Part 1:1–12.

Radin, P. 1933. *The Method and Theory of Ethnology.* New York: McGraw-Hill.

Rivers, W. H. R. 1923. *Conflict and Dreams.* London: International Library of Psychology, Philosophy, and Scientific Method.

Róheim, G. 1934. *The Riddle of the Sphinx.* London: Hogarth.

—. 1939. "Racial Differences in the Neuroses and Psychoses." *Psychiatry* 2:386ff.

Sapir, E. 1934. "Emergence of the Concept of Personality in the Study of Culture." *J. Soc. Psychol.* 5:408–15.

Schilder, P. 1940. "Cultural Patterns and Constructive Psychology." *Psychoanal. Rev.* 27:158–70.

Seligman, C. G. 1931. "Japanese Temperament and Character." *Trans. Japan Soc., Lond.* 28:124–38.

Spitz, R. A. 1935. "Frühkindliches Erleben und Erwachsenkultur bei den Primitiven. Bemerkungen zu Margaret Mead, 'Growing Up in New Guinea.'" *Imago, Lpz.* 21:367–87.

Warner, W. L. 1941. *Color and Human Nature.* Washington, D.C.: American Council on Education.

Whitehead, A. N. 1920. *The Concept of Nature.* Cambridge: Cambridge University Press.

Whiting, J. W. M. 1941. *Becoming a Kwoma.* New Haven: Yale University Press.

Whiting, J. W. M., and S. Reed. 1938. "Kwoma Culture." *Oceania* 9:197–99.

# 2

## *Human Dignity and the Varieties of Civilization*\*

When you ask me as an anthropologist to take the words "human dignity" and try those words against the great variety of cultures and civiliza-
tions which exist in the world, I must first pause to clarify what I mean
by the phrase "human dignity." I will start with the premise that some
sort of acceptance of the self is a prerequisite not only of self-respect but
of mutual respect between two or more people, and I shall go on to discuss what phenomena in social life, what sequences of behavior between
persons, tend to promote such a generous acceptance of self. I shall consider as promoting human dignity:

(a) Those sequences of interpersonal behavior which increase the
self-respect of one participant without diminishing it in the others;
(b) those sequences which enhance self-respect in all participants; and
(c) those general notions and presumptions about life which help us to
see our own roles with self-respect.

That is the limit of tightness with which I can define the concept of
human dignity, and, as you see at once, this defining frame still leaves
the individual free to accept or value himself for the most diverse characteristics; and this is perhaps the greatest difficulty inherent in the
question which you have set. We know, for example, that human beings,
as a result of special cultural milieu, family background, religious affilia-
tion, etc., can come to an extreme repudiation of the self. But man is an
extraordinarily versatile creature: he can continually shift his point of
view, he can, like a mathematician, put brackets around any juxtaposition of factors, and those who have learned an extreme repudiation of

\*This paper was delivered at the Third Symposium of the Conference on Science,
Philosophy and Religion, held August 27–31, 1942, in New York. Reprinted from *Science,
Philosophy and Religion; Third Symposium,* edited by Lyman Bryson and Louis Finkelstein, 1943.
An appendix consisting of discussion material has been deleted.

self can still achieve a generous self-acceptance by including their repudiation within the brackets. After they have learned the repudiation, they
can respect themselves the more for repudiating themselves. Even self-
repudiation can, under certain circumstances, be built up into a coher-
ent pattern whose whole gives self-acceptance; and, if this be so, if the
opposite of self-respect can be built up into self-respect, then we can presume that there is available infinite variety of characteristics, any of
which can conceivably be included in the organized and accepted picture of the self. No listing of such characteristics will help us. We have
always to think in terms of how the picture of the self is organized.

It is possible, however, without attempting to define a list of characteristics, to give something like a listing of the ways in which the picture
may be organized:

(a)  Acceptance of the self may depend upon seeing oneself repro-
     ducing the picture that one formed of a parent (father or
     mother). This would be to some extent true of the English cul-
     tural emphases. In that culture a person can accept himself
     (or herself) if he comes up to his own estimate of his parent's
     role and adequacy (unless, perhaps, the parent has been defi-
     nitely deviant or stigmatized by the community in which he
     lived).

(b)  Acceptance of the self may depend upon realizing the parent's
     image of the child's future. This criterion for self-valuation is
     probably more congenial in America than in England. Here
     the presumption is that the child's role in life will be dif-
     ferent from, and superior to, the role played by his parents.
     Americans set themselves (as a result partly of the frontier tra-
     dition, partly of the history of immigration and assimilation)[1] a
     much more ambitious task than the English. The parental
     image of the child's success and advancement may be vague,
     and in the case of foreign-born parents their picture of the
     child's American success can have extraordinarily little relation
     to reality; but still the picture is there, and the picture is con-
     ventionally brighter than the child's picture of the parent's own
     achievement.

(c)  Acceptance of the self may depend upon conformity—upon
     knowing that there is no conspicuous difference between one-

---

1. See Margaret Mead, *And Keep Your Powder Dry* (New York, 1942), for a fuller analysis of
these themes in American culture.

self and one's fellows. This, too, is perhaps more an American than an English scale of valuation. Again as a result of immigration and assimilation, the American necessarily learns to take his cues from his siblings, other boys on the block, his schoolmates, etc., and his power to accept himself may be diminished by an anxious feeling that he himself is perhaps not quite like his fellows.

(d) Acceptance of the self, curiously enough, may even depend upon idiosyncrasy. I was asked the other day what my feelings as an Englishman were about the English titled aristocracy. My first reply was: "They are not our sort of people," and under further pressure as to what I would expect of a man with a hereditary title, I said that I would expect him to have something special, which might be looks (specially good or specially ugly), bearing (specially graceful or specially awkward)—some conspicuous characteristic, which could be either plus or minus. I think it would be fair to say that, for the English generally, acceptance of self is enhanced by feeling that one is a little different from one's fellows, and reciprocally, an individual is accepted by his fellows a little more easily if he is labeled as rather different.

(e) Acceptance of the self may be increased by drastic repudiation of the parent. This gives, of course, a cultural picture very sharply at variance with either the American or the English. It gives a system in which the self is seen as a revolutionary, a Hitler, who fought his parents and won the battle against growing up and becoming a customs officer, and became instead a leader of revolutionary perpetual adolescents.

In addition to these different frames within which the self may be judged, we have a varied set of notions which may promote or limit self-respect. If, for example, we take a culture which has made self-respect conditional upon success greater than that of the parent (<b> above) and add to that pattern the notion that only a limited amount of success is available, so that A's success must always be depriving B, then we get a picture which must necessarily reduce the total of human dignity. The American valuation of success will increase mutual respect between Americans so long as the historic circumstances allow them to see themselves as living in a perpetually expanding frontier, but with the end of the physical frontiers and the cramping of economic depression, the contrary notion—that only a limited amount of success is available—will always find a foothold and will always diminish dignity. The frontier need not, of course, be a physical one, but the task seen ahead must be infinite. Perhaps this war, and the reconstruction after it, may give sufficient space for this psychological expansion.

Then there are the notions of the defined personal role. One of the most interesting generalizations which appear in American comment on England and English comment on America is the fact that employees in England appear to Americans to be subservient, while a great many employees in America appear either truculent or subservient to English eyes. I know that I, as an Englishman, am continually disoriented by this, especially by what seems to my English eye to be the overobsequiousness of American hotel servants. Now the point in all this is the notion which we have in England of the defined role. Crude dominance-submission sequences—in which A commands or forbids; B obeys; and A rewards or punishes—are perhaps necessarily undermining to the self-respect of B. But, as we noted above, man is a remarkably versatile animal, and he can put brackets around sequences of this sort and rephrase them in other terms. Something of this sort has occurred in England, so that I, a member of the professional or middle class, do not feel myself inferior to the aristocracy but different from them, and am able to grant positive value to both sides of those differences.

Still more extreme, and therefore more useful as an illustration, is the Balinese caste system. This is a system in which dominance and submission as we know them virtually do not exist, since the patterns of behavior between individuals of higher and lower status are conceived of not as enforced by the individuals of higher status, but rather as inevitable grooves or tramlines in the structure of the universe; and these grooves are not merely limiting in their functions, they provide an idiom and a tone of voice in which very full and free communication can occur between one sort of people and another.

The English patterning of life has something of the same sort of impersonal structure. The conventions and idioms used by people of lower status in addressing people of higher status (and vice versa) are not seen as directly enforced by the superior person (though the superior is rather sharply conscious of being put back in his place by the inferior if he should deviate from the pattern), and it is certainly significant that the learning of these patterns is indirect. In the upper and middle classes, the child learns deference to his parents, chiefly from instruction which the nurse gives him in how he should behave, and to a much slighter extent, in face-to-face relation with the parent; and similarly, with the lower status levels, deference to those of higher status is indirectly taught. The lower status child is taught by lower status parents how to behave toward higher status people; he does not learn this in a harsh face-to-face relationship with the latter; and when the patterns are learned, a very great deal of initiative and criticism can come from the lower to the higher without ever overstepping the conventions.

More subtly, when we look at the sequences of behavior we find that here, too, we have to deal not simply with relative frequencies of different sorts of behavior, but with more intricate combinations. We are too liable to think that dominance-submission is bad for human dignity. Only at a very crude level is this true, and we would do better, I believe, to think of a whole series of themes—dominance-submission, exhibitionism-spectatorship, succoring-dependence, etc.—as pan-human elements in behavior which may be recombined to give the most various resulting products, some poisonous and some beneficial. In England, for example, in the parent-child relationship the parents are on the whole dominant, succoring, and exhibitionist, while the children practice submission, dependence, and spectatorship. But what is learned is the combination of these things, not each element separately, and if you put an Englishman in an exhibitionistic role—if, for example, he comes to America and gives lectures—his tone of voice will inevitably echo that early training in which dominance and exhibitionism were linked together on the same side of the picture. He will lecture as if it were for him to decide what is good for that audience.

In the corresponding American pattern, the parents show dominance (slightly), succoring, and spectatorship, while the children show submission, dependence, and exhibitionism. The exhibitionism-spectatorship is reversed in its combination with the other themes, and indeed this reversal seems to be an essential component of American upbringing. In England the child's dependence is drastically broken (in the upper and middle classes) by sending him to school; in America, the analogous psychological weaning is done by the parents themselves, who act as approving spectators whenever the child shows off independence or self-sufficiency.

What I am trying to say is that all our thinking on such a subject as human dignity has got to be done in terms of rather complex gestalten; and that in the postwar world—even already, in the relations between the United Nations—we ought to be thinking about the problems which these patterns present. In the event of Allied victory, we shall, I hope, not see a world in which one set of cultural patterns is ineffectually forced upon all other cultures and communities. Some of the talk about democracy, of course, sounds as though we proposed to set up Demo-Quislings in all the nondemocratic patches of the world—a procedure which would be contrary to all the basic premises of democracy, a procedure necessarily ineffectual and one which I think would be wasteful even if it were practical. I myself attach a great deal of value to the diversity of cultural patterns which variegate the world. They are beautiful things, and the fact of their diversity I feel to be beautiful. The problem, as I see it, will be one of ordering this diversity, not by eliminating all the patterns except one, but by devising patterns of communication which will transcend the differences. Just as nobody is proposing a nonstratified or undifferentiated community, but rather communities in which the differentiation tends toward self-acceptance in all parts of the society, so also on an international level we ought to plan for differentiation, with acceptance and understanding of the differences.

At the present moment, we do not know what patterns exist. I have tried to give a few thumbnail comments on England and America, but no serious study of English character and English patterns of behavior has ever been carried out. I hope what I have told you is a little truer and a little simpler than what you could get from studying the American stereotype of England, or the English stereotype of America.

One thing is certain: that you cannot establish a stable relationship between two peoples with different cultural patterns unless the stereotypes in terms of which they see each other have some approach to the truth. You can boost up good relations for a short time with a false stereotype, or you may wreck the relationship for a long time with a false stereotype; but for any sort of permanent good relationship the pictures which you draw have got to be acceptable to both nations, and something like the truth is more likely to fulfill this condition. You can love or hate the English for their arrogance (by which I suppose we mean the compound of dominance with exhibitionism instead of spectatorship) or you can love or hate them for their habit of understatement (whose psychological roots I do not know), but I believe really that all these simplified statements fall short of understanding, and that probably mutual understanding should be counted as a basic condition for self-acceptance and mutual respect.

# 3

## *Sex and Culture**

It is certainly too early to try to introduce rigor into those anthropological hypotheses which mention sex as a causal factor, or which seek to explain the diversities of sexual behavior by referring to the cultural milieu. Even the word, *sex*, is used by us in a series of different senses, varying from observable and definable copulatory behaviors to a hypothetical drive, or drives, which are believed to influence a very wide and undefinable category of behaviors. It is even doubtful whether we should, at this time, attempt to sharpen our definitions, and not rather wait until some clarity begins to appear, as we amass more data. Definitions and abstractions are, after all, only "right" or "wrong" in so far as they form part of hypotheses which experience can test. Such hypotheses as we have today, relating sex to culture, are still so vague that very much more exploratory work will be needed before the abstractions involved can be sharply defined.

There is, however, a serious drawback to such a laissez-faire attitude toward theory. It is, unfortunately, easy to construct hypotheses with vague concepts, and such hypotheses are usually impossible to prove or to disprove. The current theories of personality and character formation already contain an excessive number of parentheses (compensation, bisexuality, etc.), any one of which can be invoked to explain why behavior in a given case does not conform to hypothetical expectation. This building up of parenthetical variables has reached such a point that today it is almost unkind to demand of any theorist: "What conceivable fact could disprove your hypothesis?"

---

*The original paper, as read before the Conference on Physiological and Psychological Factors in Sex Behavior, New York Academy of Sciences, Sections of Biology and Psychology (March 1, 1946), was illustrated by a film of Balinese trance behavior, and by a series of Balinese carvings. These materials were used to demonstrate the wide ramifications, in human behavior, of effects which are in part traceable to "sex." The present summary examines more fully than was possible at the conference the theoretical implications of the sorts of data which were then presented. Reprinted by permission of the New York Academy of Sciences.

There are, however, two possible approaches which may be of use: not to introduce rigorous hypotheses before the science is ready for them, but rather to suggest the sorts of question which we ought to be asking; and to delimit the orders of hypothesis to which we should look forward.

The first of these approaches will only be mentioned at this stage. It consists in asking metascientific questions about that order of hypothesis which would relate a concept or set of phenomena derived from one scientific field (physiology) to concepts and phenomena derived from another field (cultural anthropology). We are attempting to argue from a narrower sphere of relevance, the individual's internal environment, to a wider sphere which includes almost the whole of human behavior and the external environment. All such transitions from a narrower to a wider sphere of relevance are known to be fraught with difficulty, and we may expect a priori that very simple alterations in the narrower sphere will be represented by excessively complex changes in the wider. A small change in atomic structure may denote a total change at the molecular level. Similarly, even so simple a matter as a difference in physical stature might determine very complex differences of culture or society. Physiological sex is known to have causally powerful and complex ramifications within the individual, and, a priori, we may expect the social and cultural ramifications of this set of phenomena to be so complex that "sex" will almost cease to be a useful category for the ordering of phenomena at this wider level. Indeed, we know already that those social extensions of "sex" which anthropologists call the "family" and the "kinship system" are crucial to the whole of culture, in the sense that all behavior can be related back to these concepts, just as the same whole can be related back to hunger and the economics of food.[1, 2, 3] This fact, that the effects of any phenomenon within the narrow sphere ramify throughout the *whole* of the wider sphere, indicates that we may not make much headway in attempting to trace the manifold cultural expressions of physiological sex. It is possible, however, that we might make advances by an inverse approach: that, from cultural data, we might be able to derive hypotheses about the narrower physiological sphere. This inverse procedure has an advantage, in that our hypotheses are the more

1. B. Malinowski, *The Sexual Life of Savages* (London: George Routledge & Sons, Ltd., 1929).

2. B. Malinowski, *Coral Gardens and Their Magic*, 2 vols. (London: George Allen and Unwin, Ltd., 1935).

3. Audrey Richards, *Hunger and Work in a Savage Tribe* (London: George Routledge & Sons, Ltd., 1932).

likely to be subject to experimental testing.

The second approach to hypotheses which will relate sex and culture, consists in asking what sorts of data anthropologists do, in fact, collect. This can be followed up with the question: "What types of verifiable hypothesis can be suggested or tested by data of this kind?"

Actually, there appears to be considerable confusion among other scientists, and among anthropologists themselves, about the nature of the data with which the cultural anthropologist works. Therefore, this matter must be made categorically clear. We too often think that the abstractions which we draw are a part of the data from which they are drawn and regard ourselves as studying "culture," or "social organization," or "diffusion," or "religion," or "sex." The creatures which we study are talking mammals and, whether they be natives of New York or of New Guinea, their talk is filled with abstract terms. Thus, we easily fall into the fallacy of assigning a false concreteness to these same abstractions. It is, therefore, salutary, at times, to leave all these abstractions aside for the moment and look at the actual objective data from which all the abstractions are drawn.

There are, I believe, only three types of data in cultural anthropology:

(1) *An identified individual in such-and-such a recorded context said such-and-such, and was heard by the anthropologist.* More than half of all our data take this form, and our main effort in fieldwork goes into the astonishingly difficult task of collecting such items. We do not always succeed, for various reasons. Sometimes, the individual is imperfectly identified. We may have insufficient information about his past experience and position in the kinship system and social organization. Still more often, we may have only an incomplete understanding of the context in which he spoke. But this remains our ideal type of datum.

(2) *An identified individual in such-and-such a recorded context was seen by the anthropologist to do so-and-so.* Here again, the ideal record is not always complete. The identification of the individual and the recording of the context present the same difficulties as in (1), above. In addition, we face very serious technical difficulties when we attempt to record bodily movements. Even with photographic or cinematic techniques, this is almost impossible, and the record, when obtained, can only with very great difficulty be translated into a verbal form for analysis and publication.

(3)  *Artifacts (tools, works of art, books, clothes, boats, weapons, etc.),
     made and/or used by such-and-such individuals in such-and-such
     contexts.* These are, in general, the easiest data to collect, and
     the most difficult to interpret.

There are, at present, no other types of objective data in cultural
anthropology.[4]

From inspection of this list of types of data, certain traps in anthropological deduction appear. The most serious of these is baited with the
temptation to confuse verbal with behavioral data. Objectively, we may
know that an individual said such-and-such about himself, or about some
other individual; but we do not know, objectively, whether what he said is
true. The objective fact—the only basis upon which we can build—is that
he *said* such-and-such. Whether his statement is true or false must be
immaterial to any hypotheses which we may construct, unless (as sometimes, though rarely, happens) we have other objective data bearing
upon the truth or falsity of the original statement. The importance of this
point can scarcely be overemphasized when we are considering the validity
of hypotheses relating to sex—a matter about which human beings are not
only reticent and dishonest, but even totally unable to achieve an objective
view of their own behavior or that of others.

An example may help to make clear how the anthropologist must
proceed in such a case, and how he may construct hypotheses without
assuming the objective truth of the verbal datum. Let us suppose that the
anthropologist hears and records, verbatim, the statement of a man who
claims: "I copulate with my wife $n$ times every night." This may be an
important objective datum, because within it are implicit numerous indications about the psychology of boasting and the psychological role of
sex in that man's life. The next question which the anthropologist asks

---

4. In defining the contexts of human behavior, many types of nonanthropological information may be necessary. For this purpose, the field anthropologist may have to borrow from
almost any of the other sciences. In practice, the "context" of behavior is usually limited to a nar-
ration of those factors which the anthropologist deems important and is able to describe. Merely
permissive circumstances are usually omitted. For example, meteorological and geophysical circumstances always play a part in permitting an interview to take place, but these factors will usually not be mentioned in the record, unless the anthropologist believes that the shape and content
of the conversation was thereby affected. More serious is the common omission of physiological
circumstances: the appetitive state of both subject and interviewer, and so on. It is usually imprac-
tical to record these in anthropological fieldwork. However, the related sciences of psychoanalysis and experimental psychology are already benefiting from their closer association with the
physiological laboratory, and we should certainly look forward to a time when physiologists will
collaborate in anthropological fieldwork and amplify the scope of the available data.

himself will not be: "Is the man's statement objectively true?" He will rather seek for those data which will enable him to place the man's statement in the cultural setting. He will want to know whether boasting and the use of sex activity for the enhancement of self-esteem are culturally acceptable. He will want to know whether such behavior is felt to be aggressive, and against whom the aggression is probably directed, and so on. He will therefore note, first and foremost, who is present on the occasion, and how these other people react to the boasting. He will look to see whether any of those present are markedly superior or inferior in status to the speaker, and whether any women are present; and he may later try to draw comments from the bystanders, after the original speaker has left the group. But in all this, he will not be trying to verify the truth of the original statement, and he will not, in general, care whether that statement is true. At most, he may carry a little suspended query in the back of his mind, a note that this is something about which he does not know, just to remind himself that every hypothesis suggested by the recorded statement must be so constructed that the truth or untruth of the statement will be irrelevant to the hypothesis.

The cultural anthropologist, in fact, is in the peculiar position of studying mammals which talk, and it is necessary to underline this fact to the minds of those who study less articulate and, therefore, less deceptive creatures. The circumstance that our subjects can talk to us, and to each other, is the great advantage which we have over the animal experimenter. However, it is very important not to abuse this advantage. To avoid such errors, stringent precautions must be observed, and these precautions necessarily limit the nature of the hypotheses which we can construct and verify.

Another peculiarity of the data collected by cultural anthropologists is the extreme complexity of each individual datum. The requirement that each datum include full identification of the individual and description of the context, is perhaps never fully met in practice. The fact remains, however, that a very large number of circumstances are always relevant, in the sense that a small change in any one of them might reverse, or drastically change, the form of the behavior which we are recording. There is, therefore, almost no possibility of handling the data statistically. The contexts, the individuals, and the behaviors are too various for their combinations and permutations to be handled in this way. The unit data of which any sample is composed are too heterogeneous to be legitimately thrown together into a statistical hopper. Moreover, the data are not selected at random, but according to circumstances which are forced upon the anthropologist rather than contrived by him.

Anthropological informants, of which we do not use very many, are not a random sample of any population. Rather, they are carefully selected and carefully trained individuals, and the characteristics (accuracy, intelligence, articulacy, special interests, special social status, etc.) which make a man a good informant are not statistically normal in any population. Moreover, the selection is performed by the informants at least as much as by the anthropologist. The man who is in some way deviant, psychologically, sexually, physically, or by social experience, is more likely to want to talk to the anthropologist, and is likely to withstand such interviews with a minimum of boredom. The normal, nondeviant individual rarely, if ever, becomes a regular informant.[5]

The fact that our data are not suitable for statistical analysis means that they must be handled in other ways. This can be done, just because the unit datum is so complex. It is not necessary to discover hundreds of specimens of *Archaeopteryx lithographica,* in order to satisfy the scientific world that this creature existed and had a number of phylogenetically significant features. The existing samples, consisting of one nearly perfect skeleton, one imperfect skeleton, and one single feather, are more than sufficient, simply because an *Archaeopteryx* skeleton is a complex object. In the same way, the data of the cultural anthropologist, if they are a valid base for theory, are so because they are complex. "This given complex pattern of events occurred"; and this unique occurrence is one of the bricks which must form the material for our theoretical constructions.

This peculiarity of our data, like the unreliability of verbal statements, is a factor which must limit our hypotheses. Neither the single *Archaeopteryx*, nor any number of single specimens of different species, would suffice to demonstrate whether evolution is a continuous or discontinuous process, nor to answer the many sorts of questions which can only be answered by statistical analysis of random or representative samples. Similarly, anthropological data will not suffice to test hypotheses which would require statistical validation, and we must, therefore, avoid hypotheses of this kind. Ideally, we should concentrate upon those hypotheses of which it may be expected that the single exception will disprove the rule.

Within the limitations outlined above, cultural anthropologists have a vast mass of objective data directly relevant to sex. We cannot report, of

---

5. There is some variation among cultures in this respect. Among the Iatmul, where verbal articulacy is highly developed, my informants were certainly more culturally normal than among the Balinese, where verbal skill is rare.

course, anything about frequency or characteristics of "normal" sexual intercourse, because such behavior is only accessible to observation under circumstances so exceptional as to preclude use of the term, normal, e.g., copulation on orgiastic occasions, or specially staged for the observer and distorted by his presence, or included in traditional dramatic performances.

On the other hand, we have a large mass of information about native notions and psychological attitudes toward sex behavior, and we have information about how these various native attitudes and notions compare, and fit in, with other ideas which the same natives have on other subjects, such as achievement, sadism, humor, prestige, caste, etc. We know a great deal about the stylization of the differences between the sexes, and the roles of the two sexes in daily life and parenthood. We have collected hundreds of fantasies about copulation, love, homosexuality, incest, and so on. Then again, we have a mass of information on the economic aspects of sex behavior: dowries, bride prices, affinal exchanges, prostitution, etc. And masses of gossip about so-and-so's reputed sexual or courtship behavior, data which reflect on the culturally conventional attitudes toward various types of sexual normality and abnormality, and data on the sanctions which the people carry out (or say that they would carry out) in certain types of deviant circumstances.

The problem is to introduce theoretical order into this confused jumble of data, arbitrarily separated from the remainder of our data by their evident relevance to the concept of "sex" which is derived from the physiological sphere of relevance.

Two generalizations can be drawn from all this material: first, that cultures differ markedly among themselves and, second, that a high degree of consistency obtains among the data on any one culture.[6]

---

6. Operationally, it is probably necessary to define a "culture" as an aggregate of collected objective data of the kinds mentioned above. This definition may later be amplified, if necessary, by inclusion of some references to the type of order imposed on the data by the scientist. If, however, we limit ourselves to the minimum operational definition, the demarcation between one "culture" and another will have to be defined in terms of causal integration. If we fall into the error of defining this demarcation in terms of homogeneity, saying that culture A shall be separated from culture B if the data included under A differ markedly from the data included under B, then we shall have great difficulty in dealing with the differentiation of occupational, age, and sex groupings within the single culture. Still more serious, the generalization in the text above will be a mere endowing of our data with a characteristic of our own operations. If, on the other hand, we delimit our cultures by saying, "Data shall be assigned to a single culture so long as causal interdependence among the data can be recognized," ignoring for the moment the problem of the delimitation of cultures in the time dimension and the related problems of culture contact, we shall, at least, postpone these troubles.

These two generalizations suggest that the regularities which occur within one society[7] are of a different order from those which occur within an individual organism, and the matter can, perhaps, best be made clear by discussing this difference. If a biologist were allowed to make an exhaustive study of several different tissues derived from a single species of animal, and then were presented with another tissue differing from all those which he had so far studied, it would be almost impossible for him to determine whether this last specimen was or was not taken from the same animal species. The cultural anthropologist, on the other hand, if presented first with data upon several sorts of individuals in a given society, will probably be able to recognize that the data referring to other sorts of individuals in that same society do, in fact, have that provenience. Moreover, in their attempts to solve this problem, the biologist and the anthropologist will look for clues of quite different sorts. The biologist will look for characteristics of the cells so basic that they persist even through tissue differentiation. For example, he may attempt to count the chromosomes. The anthropologist, on the other hand, will look first for details of language and other very superficial learned characteristics, and if details of this sort are not available, he will look for more basic patterns and regularities which will be diagnostic of the *acquired* character structure of the individuals. It is significant that the biologists talk about "differentiation" of cells and tissues, while the anthropologists talk about the "acculturation" of individuals. The problem stressed by the biologist is: "How do genetically similar cells become different one from another, and how do they maintain these differences in spite of a homogeneous environment internal to the individual organism?" The problem for the cultural anthropologist, on the other hand, is: "How do individuals, who presumably differ among themselves in innate characteristics, become similar and remain sufficiently similar to understand each other, in spite of very evident differences in individual experience?"

In fact, to the cultural anthropologist, man appears not mainly as a physiological mechanism, nor yet as a creature endowed with instinctive urges and innate patterns of response. He appears to us, above all, as a creature which *learns*. The fact of human flexibility under environmental experience determines the major focus of our scientific attention.

Let us now return to the problems of "sex." If learning is the basic concept for the cultural anthropologist, then we can take a first step in

7. Operationally, the "society" may be defined as an aggregate of those individuals actually mentioned in the data which constitute a single culture, *plus* those others about whom data can be presumed to belong to the same aggregate.

relating "sex" to "culture," by examining the relations between sex and learning, bearing in mind that the phenomena connected with learning are to give us the definition of those sorts of regularity and homogeneity which we observe to be characteristic of each single culture. This definition still remains to be drawn.

To the anthropologist, it appears that all human sexual behavior is, in some degree, learned. The human infant apparently develops, at a very early age, a considerable reflex equipment. Its genitalia are erectile in response to various physical stimuli, and this tumescence is early associated with specifically interpersonal stimuli. This reflex equipment is precocious in the sense that the neural connections are present before the infant has the muscular development necessary to put the whole mechanism to work.

In this, there is nothing peculiar about sexuality, and the same sort of precocity is recognizable in other sorts of behavior. The infant also shows what appear to be inherited reflex arcs for walking, swimming, arboreal suspension, and balance in an upright posture. For all of these activities, it appears that neural connections are established before the muscular development is adequate, and the rudimentary responses, which indicate the existence of these neural connections, fade out. A period of "latency" occurs not only in regard to sexual, but also locomotor, behavior.[8]

Now, the crucial question about sexual latency is: "*Is it learned?*" Is the change from genital responsiveness to unresponsiveness to be ascribed to topological changes in the neural network, induced in that network by impulses which pass through it? The obvious alternative to such a hypothesis would be to ascribe the change in responsiveness to changes in the endocrine system and to hope that a fuller knowledge of maturation will enable us to account for these changes in endocrine balance without again being pushed back upon a theory of changes in the neural network induced by experience.[9]

---

8. We have, unfortunately, no comparative data about the occurrence of these various types of latency in different cultures, where different methods of handling, carrying, and exercising the baby occur. Even for sexual latency, the data are very poor, and it is perfectly possible that, in some cultures, the potentiality for genital tumescence does not disappear in childhood. It is, however, to be expected that, in all cultures, there is a period during which the child ceases to show specifically sexual desires directed toward adults.

9. A third possibility (that all types of latency are due to topological changes in the neural network, but that these changes are a function of maturation and not brought about by the passage of neural impulses) would also be tenable. This hypothesis will, however, differ somewhat from conventional notions about maturation, in that it must account for the breaking or inhibition of previously existing arcs.

From what little we know, it appears to me that we must assume that
latency is learned, rather than due to a hypothetical endocrine change.
The necessary shift in endocrine balance has not been observed,[10] and it
appears, rather, that concentrations of androgens and estrogens in children's urine show a progressive rise through childhood to a peak at
puberty. Moreover, the hypothesis that latency is learned will have the
additional recommendation that it can be applied not only to sexual but
also to locomotor latency, for which an endocrine theory can less readily
be imagined.

Granting that learning probably plays a part in causing latency, the
next question must be: "What are the stimuli or contexts which determine this learning?" Here we know, from anthropological data, that
marked differences exist between cultures. In American and English cultures, we know that, among adults, even the notion of infantile sexuality
is strongly resisted; masturbation of the child by parents or nurses is
strongly deprecated (and, therefore, probably accompanied by guilt
reactions on the part of the adult, when it occurs); and masturbatory
behavior on the part of the child is sharply discouraged. Therefore, for
these cultures, we must expect that latency will be induced not only by
experience of own muscular insufficiency, but also by positive extinction
or inhibition of tumescence. In sharp contrast to this, we know of cultures in which masturbation of the child by the parent is common and
not deprecated. Even among these cultures, we may expect sharp differences which will be significant for the character formation of the child.
The reason given by Italian peasants for this masturbation of the child is
"to put it to sleep," and we may presume that, in Italy, the child is given
some sort of sexual climax or other satisfactory experience. In Bali, on
the other hand, our observations show that the child is not given satisfaction and, instead of going to sleep, becomes more restive. Indeed, from
the mother's evident enjoyment both of the baby's responsiveness and of
the temper tantrum which often follows, it would appear that the purpose of the masturbation is rather to wake it up. It is easy to see that
the Anglo-Saxon and Balinese systems of handling may induce latency,
though very different types of latency in the two areas. What sort of latency, if any, is induced by the Italian system, is not so clear.

These contrasts indicate very clearly that the social contexts which
accompany the onset of latency are important for sexual learning. They
may determine the individual's attitude toward sexual behavior and the

10. R. Neustadt and A. Myerson. "Quantitative Sex Hormone Studies in Homosexuality,
Childhood, and Various Neuropsychiatric Disturbances." *Am. J. Psychiat.* 97 (1940): 542–51.

part which these behaviors will play in his character. The matter becomes still more complex when we go on to consider the culturally stylized sexual play, masturbation, and courtship behaviors of the latency period, and the rewards and punishments which determine the role of these behaviors in the individual's character. These experiences will label the sexual patterns as safe or dangerous, approved or disapproved, as important sources of self-esteem and prestige, or as important sources of sensual pleasure.

Still later, the onset of puberty can be seen as a further set of learning and character-forming contexts, and the problems are analogous to those which we discussed in connection with latency. Here, the case for ascribing the change in responsiveness to endocrine factors is perhaps a little stronger, but it is possible that the importance of these factors has been exaggerated. There are, in addition, a host of interpersonal and social factors which push the individual into puberty. The sexual initiative of other persons; the value which the individual himself has been trained to place upon sexual adequacy and sexual conformity; his desire to acquire the respect of his fellows of the same sex and of possible sexual partners; all of these, in addition to his endocrines, may push him toward puberty. Further, the psychology of that puberty, when attained, will be determined by the specific qualities of the latency which has been broken down, and by the dynamics of the beginning of puberty. The individual who is pushed into active sexual life, by his physiological needs, at a period when he still feels that social pressures are on the side of latency, will learn something very different from what is learned by the individual who enters upon sexuality in an attempt to conform to social pressures before he is driven to this by physiological need.

The role played by sexual behavior and experience in determining character structure, and the inverse role of experience in determining sexual behavior, could be elaborated almost ad infinitum. To relate human sexual behavior to learning is easy, though at every turn we come upon new problems and new hypotheses requiring data for their verification. However, there is still another order of hypothesis which must be considered before we can be said to have related sexual behavior to culture.

It was suggested, above, that the data on a given culture show an internal regularity, or consistency, not simply deducible from the operation which we performed in defining the limits of the single culture in terms of causal interdependence of all events within this margin. We noted, also, that there is a contrast between physiology and cultural anthropology in that, though both sciences deal with spheres of relevance definable in terms of causal interdependence of events within the sphere, the physiologist is preoccupied with differentiation, while the anthropologist is preoccupied with acculturation. Our next step will be to define more sharply these regularities within the single culture, and to relate them to the theory of learning.

What has so far been said about learning could be deduced from any learning theory, such as that of *association*, which will describe learning as the setting up of a classification of perceived objects and events, linked to a classification of responses and to a rudimentary linear value system which will discriminate the pleasant from the unpleasant. Such a system will, for example, account for the simple forms of sexual symbolism. Balinese carvings, for instance, illustrate a large number of types of symbolic distortion of the human body. The breasts may be equated with buttocks; the head may be equated with male genitalia; the mouth may be equated with the vulva; and so on.[11] All of these distortions can be seen as due to simple associational learning.

We find, however, in our cultural data, something more than this. If we take the data from a given culture and sort them by subject matter, putting all the data which refer to sex in one heap, the data referring to initiation in another, the data referring to death in another, and so on, we get a very remarkable result.[12] We find that similar types of order are recognizable in every heap. We find that, whether we are looking at the sex data, or the initiation data, or the death data, the system of classification of perceived objects and events (the *eidos* of the culture) is still the same. Similarly, if we analyze the heaps of data to obtain the system of linked responses and values (the *ethos*) of the culture, we find that the ethos is the same in each heap. Briefly, it is as if the same sort of person had devised the data in all the heaps.

Two obvious hypotheses which might account for this finding can, I believe, be ruled out. We cannot assume that these ethological and eidological regularities are simply due to innate human characteristics, because very different kinds of ethos and eidos have been analyzed out of different cultures. And we cannot say that the ethological and eidological uniformities are due to the uniform working of peculiarities of the mind of the analyst, because in different cultures the same analyst obtains different results.

---

11. Specimens of these carvings, collected by the writer, were exhibited at the conference. The collection of about 1,200 carvings has been deposited at the American Museum of Natural History, New York, New York.

12. G. Bateson, *Naven*. (Cambridge: Cambridge University Press, 1936). (This book is an experiment in analyzing a New Guinea culture, on these lines.)

It would, I believe, be impossible to deduce these results, the uniformity within one culture and the contrast between cultures, from the simple associational learning theory from which we started.[13]

However, these ethological and eidological uniformities within the single culture, and the corresponding contrasts between cultures, are precisely what we would expect if, in addition to the processes postulated in simple learning, there is a carryover from learning in one context which will influence later behavior in quite different contexts. Various theories of this type have been put forward [14, 15, 16] and, in general, the experimental findings indicate that some such postulate may be necessary even at the animal level. At the human level, the carryover from one context to others can be demonstrated in the phenomena of "transfer" of learning, and especially in the experimental increase in learning proficiency from one context to another of similar formal structure.[17]

Such a postulated carryover from one context of learning to another will give us a theoretical system which will permit us to speak of changes in *character*, instead of limiting us to the mere addition or subtraction of associational links. We can very easily see how such a theory would give precision to qualities of the order of "optimism," "pessimism," "fatalism," "initiative," "level of aspiration," and the like, and lead us to expect that qualities of this sort, learned by experience in one sort of context, will be carried over into other contexts of very various types. This, I suggest, is the explanation of the ethological and eidological uniformities characteristic of each human culture.

We are driven, I believe, to conclude that what is learned in contexts associated with sex will be carried over into contexts associated with quite different spheres of life—initiation, death, trade, etc.—and that, vice versa, what is learned in these other contexts will be carried over into specifically sexual life.

---

13. The logical proof of this assertion is, however, beyond my powers, and probably not feasible until the concepts of *eidos* and *ethos* and, indeed, the whole of gestalt psychology have been much more critically defined than is possible today.

14. L. K. Frank, "The Problems of Learning," *Psych. Rev.* 33 (1926): 329–51.

15. N. R. F. Maier, "The Behavior Mechanism Concerned with Problem Solving." *Psych. Rev.* 47 (1940): 43–58.

16. G. Bateson, Comment on M. Mead's "The Comparative Study of Culture and the Purposive Cultivation of Democratic Values." In *Science, Philosophy and Religion; Second Symposium*, New York, New York, 1942. ["Social Planning and the Concept of Deutero-Learning." In *Steps to an Ecology of Mind.*]

17. C. Hull, *Mathematico-Deductive Theory of Rote Learning* (New Haven: Yale University Press, 1940). (This book gives experimental curves for increase in proficiency in rote learning, but does not deduce this increase from a postulate system.)

Such a conclusion will reduce the title of the present paper to non-sense, by indicating that *sex* is scarcely a useful concept for the analysis of human cultures—a conclusion which was foreshadowed in our a priori metascientific examination of any attempt to relate phenomena in the physiological sphere of relevance to phenomena in the cultural sphere.

Our excursion into theory has not, however, been fruitless, because it has lent anthropological support to a type of hypothesis connected with learning, and this type of hypothesis is such that it can be tested and made more precise by further anthropological work, and by laboratory experiments. In addition, we have demonstrated that, in the psychological analysis of anthropological data, it is not useful to classify these data according to the sorts of physiological need to which they appear relevant. It is, however, very rewarding to classify these data according to the formal characteristics of the contexts of behavior. It is important to note that the Balinese baby is subjected to the same formal sequence, both when the mother refuses to respond to its temper tantrum and when she cheats it of sexual climax, and that the mother's behavior in both these contexts is an effect of her own past character formation, as determined by experiences similar to those to which she is now subjecting the child. From such a beginning, we can go on to look at other types of Balinese data, and recognize that the same formal sequence recurs in certain ceremonials in which young men attack a masked figure representing the Witch. They are powerless against her, and fall into a state of disassociation in which they symbolically turn their aggression against themselves, thus achieving an introverted climax.[18]

From such a systematic analysis of the contexts of learning and the native interpretations of context which are implicit in cultural data, we may hope to build a formal science of culture.

---

18. For photographs of the ceremonial, see G. Bateson and M. Mead, *Balinese Character: A Photographic Analysis.* Special Pub., No. 2 (1942), N.Y. Acad. Sci.

# 4

# Naven: *Epilogue 1958*\*

There is a well-known story about the philosopher Whitehead. His former pupil and famous collaborator, Bertrand Russell, came to visit Harvard and lectured in the large auditorium on quantum theory, always a difficult subject, and at that time a comparatively novel theory. Russell labored to make the matter intelligible to the distinguished audience, many of whom were unversed in the ideas of mathematical physics. When he sat down, Whitehead rose as chairman to thank the speaker. He congratulated Russell on his brilliant exposition "and especially on leaving . . . *unobscured* . . . the vast darkness of the subject."

All science is an attempt to cover with explanatory devices—and thereby to obscure—the vast darkness of the subject. It is a game in which the scientist uses his explanatory principles according to certain rules to see if these principles can be stretched to cover the vast darkness. But the rules of the stretching are rigorous, and the purpose of the whole operation is really to discover what parts of the darkness still remain, uncovered by explanation.

But this game has also a deeper, more philosophic purpose: to learn something about the very nature of explanation, to make clear some part of that most obscure matter—the process of knowing.

In the twenty-one years that have elapsed since the writing of this book [*Naven*], epistemology—that science or philosophy which has for subject matter the phenomena which we call knowledge and explanation—has undergone an almost total change. Preparing the book for republication in 1957 has been a voyage of discovery backward into a period when the newer ways of thought were only dimly foreshadowed.

*Naven* was a study of the nature of explanation. The book contains of course details about Iatmul life and culture, but it is not primarily an ethnographic study, a retailing of data for later synthesis by other

---

*Reprinted from *Naven*, Second Edition, by Gregory Bateson, with the permission of the publishers, Stanford University Press. © 1958 by the Board of Trustees of the Leland Stanford Junior University.

scientists. Rather, it is an attempt at synthesis, a study of the ways in which data can be fitted together, and the fitting together of data is what I mean by "explanation."

The book is clumsy and awkward, in parts almost unreadable. For this reason: that, when I wrote it, I was trying not only to explain by fitting data together but also to use this explanatory process as an example within which the principles of explanation could be seen and studied.

The book is a weaving of three levels of abstraction. At the most concrete level there are ethnographic data. More abstract is the tentative arranging of data to give various pictures of the culture, and still more abstract is the self-conscious discussion of the procedures by which the pieces of the jigsaw puzzle are put together. The final climax of the book is the discovery, described in the epilogue—and achieved only a few days before the book went to press—of what looks like a truism today: that ethos, eidos, sociology, economics, cultural structure, social structure, and all the rest of these words refer only to scientists' ways of putting the jigsaw puzzle together.

These theoretical concepts have an order of objective reality. They are *really* descriptions of processes of knowing, adopted by scientists, but to suggest that "ethos" or "social structure" has more reality than this is to commit Whitehead's fallacy of misplaced concreteness. The trap or illusion—like so many others—disappears when correct logical typing is achieved. If "ethos," "social structure," "economics," etc., are words in that language which describes how scientists arrange data, then these words cannot be used to "explain" phenomena, nor can there be any "ethological" or "economic" categories of phenomena. People can be influenced, of course, by economic theories or by economic fallacies—or by hunger—but they cannot possibly be influenced by "economics." "Economics" is a *class* of explanations, not itself an explanation of anything.

Once the fallacy has been detected, the way is open for growth of an entirely new science—which has in fact already become basic to modern thought. This new science has as yet no satisfactory name. A part of it is included within what is now called communications theory, a part of it is in cybernetics, a part of it in mathematical logic. The whole is still unnamed and imperfectly envisioned. It is a new structuring of the balance between Nominalism and Realism, a new set of conceptual frames and problems, replacing the premises and problems set by Plato and Aristotle.

One purpose, then, of the present essay is to relate the book to these new ways of thought which were dimly foreshadowed in it. A second more specific purpose is to relate the book to current thinking in the field of psychiatry. While the climate of epistemological thought has been changing and evolving throughout the world, the thinking of the author has undergone changes, precipitated especially by contact with some of the problems of psychiatry. I have had the task of teaching cultural anthropology to psychiatric residents, and have had to face such problems as are raised by the comparison between the variety of cultures and those hazily defined "clinical entities," the mental diseases which have their roots in traumatic experience.

This narrower purpose, to make the book relevant to psychiatry, is easier to achieve than the wider one of placing it in the current epistemological scene. And therefore I will attempt the psychiatric problem first, with this reminder to the reader—that the problems of psychiatry are after all shot through with epistemological difficulties.

*Naven* was written almost without benefit of Freud. One or two reviewers even complained about this, but I think that the circumstance was fortunate. My psychiatric taste and judgment were at that time defective, and probably a greater contact with the Freudian ideas would only have led me to misuse and misunderstand them. I would have indulged in an orgy of interpreting symbols, and this would have distracted me from the more important problems of interpersonal and intergroup process. As it was, I did not even notice that the crocodile jaw which is the gate to the initiatory enclosure is called in Iatmul *tshuwi iamba*—literally, "clitoris gate." This piece of data would really only confirm what is already implied when the male initiators are identified as "mothers" of the novices, but still the temptation to analyze the symbolism could have interrupted the analysis of the relationship.

But the fascination of symbol analysis is not the only pitfall in psychiatric theory. Perhaps even more serious are the distractions of psychological typology. One of the great errors in anthropology has been the naive attempt to use psychiatric ideas and labels to explain cultural difference, and certainly the weakest part of the book is that chapter in which I tried to describe ethological contrast in terms of Kretschmer's typology.

No doubt more modern approaches to the problem of typology, such as Sheldon's work on somatotypes, are a great improvement upon the crudely dualistic system of Kretschmer. But this is not the point which concerns me. If Sheldon's typology had been available to me in 1935, I would have used it in preference to that of Kretschmer, but I would still have been wrong. As I see it today, these typologies, whether in cultural anthropology or in psychiatry, are at best heuristic fallacies, culs-de-sac, whose only usefulness is to demonstrate the need for a fresh start. Fortunately, I separated my dalliance with psychiatric typology into a single chapter; if this were not so, I would hardly permit the republication today.

But still the status of typology is undefined and crucial. Psychiatrists still hanker after classifications of mental disease; biologists still hanker for genera and species; and physiologists still hanker after a classification of human individuals which shall show a coincidence between classes defined by behavioral criteria and classes defined by anatomy. Lastly, be it confessed, I myself hanker for a classification, a typology, of the processes of interaction as it occurs either between persons or between groups.

This is a region in which problems of epistemology become crucial for the whole biological field, including within that field both the Iatmul culture and psychiatric diagnosis. There is an area of comparable uncertainty in the whole theory of evolution: Do species have real existence or are they only a device of description? How are we to resolve the old controversies between continuity and discontinuity? Or how shall we reconcile the contrast which recurs again and again in nature between continuity of change and discontinuity of the classes which result from change?

It seems to me, today, that there is a partial answer to these problems in the processes of schismogenesis[1] which are analyzed in this book [*Naven*], but this partial answer could hardly have been extracted from that analysis when the book was written. These further steps had to wait upon other advances, such as the expansion of learning theory, the development of cybernetics, the application of Russell's Theory of Logical Types to communications theory, and Ashby's formal analysis of those orders of event which must lead to parametric change in previously steady-state systems.

A discussion of the relationship between schismogenesis and these more modern developments of theory is therefore a first step toward a new synthesis. In this discussion I shall assume that formal analogies exist between the problems of change in all fields of biological science.

The process of schismogenesis, as described in the book, is an example of progressive or *directional* change. And a first problem in evolution is that of direction. The conventional stochastic view of mutation

---

1. [*Editor's Note:* "I would define schismogenesis as *a process of differentiation in the norms of individual behaviour resulting from cumulative interaction between individuals.*" (From *Naven*, p. 175.)]

assumes that change will be random, and that direction is only imposed upon evolutionary change by some phenomenon like natural selection. Whether such a description is sufficient to explain the phenomenon of orthogenesis—the long process of continuous directional change shown by the fossil record in ammonites, sea urchins, horses, asses, titanotheres, etc.—is very doubtful. An alternative or supplementary explanation is probably necessary. Of these the most obvious is climatic or other progressive change in the environment, and this type of explanation may be appropriate for some of the orthogenic sequences. More interesting is the possibility that the progressive environmental change might occur in the *biological* environment of the species concerned, and this raises questions of a new order. Marine organisms like ammonites or sea urchins can hardly be supposed to have much effect upon the weather, but a change in the ammonites might affect their biological environment. After all, the most important elements in the environment of an individual organism are (a) other individuals of the same species and (b) plants and animals of other species with which the given individual is in intense interactive relationship. The survival value of a given characteristic is likely to depend in part upon the degree to which this characteristic is shared by other members of the species; and, vis-à-vis other species, there must exist relationships—e.g., between predator and prey—which are comparable to those evolving interactive systems of attack and defense so grievously familiar in armaments races at the international level.

These are systems which begin to be closely comparable to the phenomena of schismogenesis with which this book [*Naven*] is concerned. In the theory of schismogenesis, however (and in armaments races), an additional factor to account for the directedness of change is assumed. The direction toward more intense rivalry in the case of symmetrical schismogenesis, or toward increasing differentiation of role in complementary schismogenesis, is assumed to depend upon phenomena of learning. This aspect of the matter is not discussed in the book, but the whole theory rests upon certain ideas about processes of character formation—ideas which are also latent in most psychiatric theory. These ideas may be briefly summarized.

The order of learning to which I refer is that which Harlow has called "set-learning," and which I myself have called "deutero-learning." I assume that in any learning experiment—e.g., of the Pavlovian or the Instrumental Reward type—there occurs not only that learning in which the experimenter is usually interested, namely, the increased frequency of the conditioned response in the experimental context, but also a more abstract or higher order of learning, in which the experimental subject improves his ability to deal with contexts of a given type. The subject comes to act more and more as if contexts of this type were expectable in his universe. For example, the deutero-learning of the animal subjected to a sequence of Pavlovian experiences will presumably be a process of character formation whereby he comes to live as if in a universe where premonitory signs of later reinforcements (or unconditioned stimuli) can be detected but nothing can be done to precipitate or prevent the occurrence of the reinforcements. In a word, the animal will acquire a species of "fatalism." In contrast, we may expect the subject of repeated Instrumental Reward experiments to deutero-learn a character structure that will enable him to live as if in a universe in which he can control the occurrence of reinforcements.

Now, all those psychiatric theories which invoke the past experience of the individual as an explanatory device depend necessarily upon some such theory of high-order learning, or learning to learn. When the patient tells the therapist that, in her childhood, she learned to operate a typewriter, this is of no particular interest to him unless he happens to be a vocational counselor as well as therapist. But when she starts to tell him about the context in which she learned this skill, how her aunt taught her and rewarded her or punished her or withheld reward and punishment, then the psychiatrist begins to be interested; because what the patient learned from formal characteristics or *patterns* of the contexts of learning is the clue to her present habits, her "character," her manner of interpreting and participating in the interaction between herself and others.

This type of theory which underlies so much of psychiatry is also fundamental to the idea of schismogenesis. It is assumed that the individual in a symmetrical relationship with another will tend, perhaps unconsciously, to form the habit of acting as if he expected symmetry in further encounters with that other, and perhaps, even more widely, in future encounters with all other individuals.

The ground is thus laid for progressive change. As a given individual learns patterns of symmetrical behavior he not only comes to expect this type of behavior in others, but also acts in such a way that others will experience those contexts in which they in turn will learn symmetrical behavior. We have here a case in which change in the individual affects the environment of others in a way which will cause a similar change in them. This will act back upon the initial individual to produce further change in him in the same direction.

But this picture of schismogenesis cannot be true of Iatmul society as I observed it. Evidently, what has been achieved is only a one-sided picture of processes which, *if permitted,* would lead either in the direction of excessive rivalry between symmetrical pairs or groups of individuals or in the direction of excessive differentiation between complementary pairs. At a certain point, if these were the only processes involved, the society would explode. Of this difficulty I was already aware when I wrote the book, and I made an effort to account for the presumed dynamic equilibrium of the system by pointing out that the symmetrical and complementary processes are in some sense opposites of each other (*Naven,* p. 193) so that the culture containing both of these processes might conceivably balance them one against the other. This, however, was at best an unsatisfactory explanation, since it assumed that two variables will, *by coincidence,* have equal and opposite values; but it is obviously improbable that the two processes will balance each other unless some functional relationship obtains between them. In the so-called dynamic equilibrium of chemical reactions, the rate of change in one direction is a function of the concentration of the products of the inverse change, and reciprocally. But I was not able to see any such functional dependence between the two schismogenic processes and had to leave the matter there when the book was written.

The problem became totally changed with the growth of cybernetic theory. It was my privilege to be a member of the Macy Conference which met periodically in the years following the end of World War II. In our earlier meetings the word "cybernetics" was still uncoined, and the group was gathered to consider the implications for biology and other sciences of what we then called "feed-back." It was immediately evident that the whole problem of purpose and adaptation—the teleological problem in the widest sense—had to be reconsidered. The problems had been posed by the Greek philosophers, and the only solution they had been able to offer was what looked like a mystical idea: that the end of a process could be regarded as a "purpose," and that this end or purpose could be invoked as an explanation of the process which *preceded* it. And this notion, as is well known, was closely connected with the problem of the *real* (i.e., transcendent rather than immanent) nature of forms and patterns. The formal study of feedback systems immediately changed all this. Now, we had mechanical models of causal circuits which would (if the parameters of the system were appropriate) seek equilibria or steady states. But *Naven* had been written with a rigorous taboo on teleological explanation: the end could never be invoked as an explanation of the process.

The idea of negative feedback was not new; it had been used by Clerk Maxwell in his analysis of the steam engine with a governor, and by biologists such as Claude Bernard and Cannon in the explanation of physiological homeostasis. But the power of the idea was unrecognized. What happened at the Macy meetings was an exploration of the enormous scope of these ideas in the explanation of biological and social phenomena.

The ideas themselves are extremely simple. All that is required is that we ask not about the characteristics of lineal chains of cause and effect but about the characteristics of systems in which the chains of cause and effect are circular or more complex than circular. If, for example, we consider a circular system containing elements A, B, C, and D—so related that an activity of A affects an activity of B, B affects C, C affects D, and D has an effect back upon A—we find that such a system has properties totally different from anything which can occur in lineal chains.

Such circular causal systems must in the nature of the case either seek a steady state or undergo progressive exponential change; and this change will be limited either by the energy resources of the system, or by some external restraint, or by a breakdown of the system as such.

The steam engine with the governor illustrates the type of circuit which may seek a steady state. Here the circuit is so constructed that the faster the piston moves the faster the governor spins; and the faster the governor spins the wider the divergence of its weighted arms; and the wider the divergences of these arms the *less* the power supply. But this in turn affects the activity of the piston. The self-corrective characteristic of the circuit as a whole depends upon there being within the circuit at least one link such that the more there is of something, the less there will be of something else. In such cases the system may be self-corrective, either seeking a steady rate of operation or oscillating about such a steady rate.

In contrast, a steam engine with a governor so constructed that a wider divergence of the arms of the governor will *increase* the supply of steam to the cylinder affords an instance of what the engineers would call "runaway." The feedback is "positive," and the system will operate faster and faster, increasing its speed exponentially to the limit of the available supply of steam or to the point at which the flywheel or some other part must break.

For the present purposes it is not necessary to go into the mathematics of such systems except to notice that the characteristics of any such system will depend upon timing. Will the corrective event or message reach the point at which it is effective at an appropriate moment and will the effect be sufficient? Or will the corrective action be excessive? Or too little? Or too late?

Substituting the notion of self-correction for the idea of purpose or adaptation defined a new approach to the problems of the Iatmul culture. Schismogenesis appeared to promote progressive change, and the problem was why this progressive change did not lead to a destruction of the culture as such. With self-corrective causal circuits as a conceptual model, it was now natural to ask whether there might exist, in this culture, functional connections such that appropriate controlling factors would be brought into play by increased schismogenic tension. It was not good enough to say that symmetrical schismogenesis happened by coincidence to balance the complementary. It was now necessary to ask, is there any communicational pathway such that an increase in symmetrical schismogenesis will bring about an increase in the corrective complementary phenomena? Could the system be circular and self-corrective?

The answer was immediately evident (*Naven*, p. 8). The *naven*[2] ceremonial, which is an exaggerated caricature of a complementary sexual relationship between *wau*[3] and *laua*,[4] is in fact set off by overweening symmetrical behavior. When *laua* boasts in the presence of *wau*, the latter has recourse to *naven* behavior. Perhaps in the initial description of the contexts for *naven* it would have been better to describe this as the primary context, and to see *laua's* achievements in headhunting, fishing, etc., as particular examples of an achieved ambition or vertical mobility in *laua* which place him in some sort of symmetrical relationship with *wau*. But the Iatmul do not think of the matter this way. If you ask a Iatmul about the contexts for *naven*, he will first enumerate *laua's* achievements and only as an afterthought mention the less formal (but perhaps more profoundly significant) contexts in which *wau* uses *naven* to control that breach of good manners of which *laua* is guilty when he presumes to be in a symmetrical relationship with *wau*. Indeed, it was only on a later visit to Iatmul that I discovered that when *laua* is a baby and is being held in *wau's* lap, if the baby urinates, the *wau* will threaten *naven*.

It is also interesting that this link between symmetrical and complementary behavior is doubly inverted. The *laua* makes the symmetrical

---

2. [*Editor's Note: naven*, a Iatmul ritual involving transvesticism and offering of the buttocks, performed on the occasion of a sister's child's first performance of specified adult deeds.]

3. [*Editor's Note:* "*wau*, mother's brother, son's wife's brother, and other relatives classified with them. Cf. p. 94." (From *Naven*, p. 312.)]

4. [*Editor's Note:* "*laua*, sister's child, sister's husband's father (m.s.), and other relatives classified with them. Cf. p. 94." (From *Naven*, p. 309.)]

gesture and *wau* responds not by overbearing complementary dominance but by the reverse of this—exaggerated submission. Or should we say the reverse of this reverse? *Wau*'s behavior is a caricature of submission?

The sociological functions of this self-corrective circuit cannot be so easily demonstrated. The questions at issue are whether excessive symmetrical rivalry between clans will in fact increase the frequency with which *laua*s act symmetrically vis-à-vis their *wau*s, and whether the resulting increase in frequency of *naven* will tend to stabilize the society. This could only be demonstrated by statistical study and appropriate measurement, which would be extremely difficult. There is, however, a good case for expecting such effects inasmuch as the *wau* is usually of a different clan from *laua*. In any instance of intense symmetrical rivalry between two clans, we may expect an increased probability of symmetrical insult between members, and when the members of the pair happen to be related as *laua* and *wau*, we must expect a triggering of the complementary rituals which will function toward mending the threatened split in society.

But if there exists a functional relationship such that excess of symmetrical rivalry will trigger complementary rituals, then we should expect to find also the converse phenomenon. Indeed, it is not clear that the society could maintain its steady state without an excess of complementary schismogenesis touching off some degree of symmetrical rivalry.

This too can be demonstrated with ethnographic data:

(1) In the village of Tambunum, when two little boys exhibit what looks to their age mates like homosexual behavior, the others put sticks in their hands and make the two stand up against each other and "fight." Indeed, any suggestion of passive male homosexuality is exceedingly insulting in Iatmul culture and leads to symmetrical brawling.

(2) As discussed in the book, while the *wau*'s transvesticism is a caricature of the female role, the transvesticism of father's sister and elder brother's wife is a proud exhibition of masculinity. It looks as though these women are stating a symmetrical rivalry vis-à-vis the men, compensating for their normally complementary role. It is perhaps significant that they do this at a time when a man, the *wau*, is stating his complementarity vis-à-vis *laua*.

(3) The extreme complementarity of relationship between initiators and novices is always counterbalanced by extreme rivalry between

initiatory groups. Here again complementary behavior in some way sets the scene for symmetrical rivalry.

Again we may ask the sociological question, whether these changes from complementarity to symmetry can be regarded as effective in the prevention of social disintegration; and, again, to investigate this question with the available examples is difficult. There is, however, another aspect of the matter which justifies us in believing that this oscillation between the symmetrical and the complementary is likely to be of deep importance to the social structure. What has been demonstrated from the data is that Iatmul individuals recurrently experience and participate in such shifts. From this we may reasonably expect that these individuals *learn,* besides the symmetrical and the complementary patterns, to expect and exhibit certain sequential relations between the symmetrical and the complementary. Not only must we think of a social network changing from moment to moment and impinging upon the individuals, so that processes tending toward disintegration will be corrected by activation of other processes tending in an opposite direction, but also we have to remember that the component individuals of that network are themselves being trained to introduce this type of corrective change in their dealings with each other. In one case we are equating the individuals with the *A, B, C,* and *D* of a cybernetic diagram; and in the other, noting that *A, B, C,* etc., are themselves so structured that the input–output characteristics of each will show appropriate self-corrective characteristics.

It is this fact—that the patterns of society as a major entity can by learning be introjected or conceptualized by the participant individuals—that makes anthropology and indeed the whole of behavioral science peculiarly difficult. The scientist is not the only human being in the picture. His subjects also are capable of all sorts of learning and conceptualization and even, like the scientist, they are capable of errors of conceptualization. This circumstance, however, leads us into a further set of questions posed by communications theory, namely, those questions which concern the *orders* of event which will trigger corrective action, and the order of that action (considered as a message) when it occurs.

Here I use the word "order" in a technical sense closely resembling the sense in which the word "type" is used in Russell's Theory of Logical Types. This may be illustrated by the following example. A house with a thermostatically controlled heating system is a simple self-corrective circuit of the sort discussed above. A thermometer appropriately placed in the house is linked into the system to control a switch in such a way that when the temperature goes above a certain critical level the furnace is switched off. Similarly, when the temperature falls below a certain level the furnace is switched on. But the system is also governed by another circumstance, namely, the setting of the critical temperatures. By changing the position of a dial, the owner of the house can alter the characteristics of the *system as a whole* by changing the critical temperatures at which the furnace will be turned on and shut off. Following Ashby, I will reserve the word "variables" for those measurable circumstances which change from moment to moment as the house oscillates around some steady temperature, and shall reserve the word "parameters" for those characteristics of the system which are changed for example when the householder intervenes and changes the setting of the thermostat. I shall speak of the latter change as of higher order than changes in the variables.

The word "order" is in fact here used in a sense comparable to that in which it was used earlier in this essay to define orders of learning. We deal as before with metarelationships between messages. Any two orders of learning are related so that the learning of one order is a learning *about* the other, and similarly in the case of the house thermostat the message which the householder puts into the system by changing the setting is *about* how the system shall respond to messages of lower order emanating from the thermometer. We are here at a point where both learning theory and the theory of cybernetic systems come within the realm of Russell's Theory of Types.

Russell's central notion is the truism that a class cannot be a member of itself. The class of elephants has not got a trunk and is not an elephant. This truism must evidently apply with equal force when the members of the class are not things but names or signals. The class of commands is not itself a command and cannot tell you what to do.

Corresponding to this hierarchy of names, classes, and classes of classes, there is also a hierarchy of propositions and messages, and within this latter hierarchy the Russellian discontinuity between types must also obtain. We speak of messages, of metamessages, and meta-metamessages; and what I have called deutero-learning I might appropriately have called metalearning.

But the matter becomes more difficult because, for example, while the class of commands is not itself a command, it is possible and even usual to give commands in a metalanguage. If "Shut the door" is a command, then "Listen to my orders" is a metacommand. The military phrase, "That is an order," is an attempt to enforce a given command by appeal to a premise of higher logical type.

Russell's rule would indicate that as we should not classify the class of elephants among its members, so also we should not classify "Listen to my orders" among such commands as "Shut the door." But, being human, we shall continue to do so and shall inevitably be liable to certain sorts of confusion, as Russell predicts.

Returning to the theme which I am trying to elucidate—the general problem of the continuity of process and the discontinuity of the products of process—I will now consider how we might classify the answers to this general problem. Of necessity, the answers will be in the most general terms, but still it is of some value to present an ordering of thoughts about change as it must, a priori, occur in all systems or entities which either learn or evolve.[5]

First, it is necessary again to stress the distinction between change in the variables (which is, by definition, within the terms of the given system) and change in the parameters, i.e., change in the very terms which define the system—remembering always that it is the observer who does the defining. It is the observer who creates messages (i.e., science) about the system which he is studying, and it is these messages that are of necessity in some language or other and must therefore have *order*: they must be of some or other Logical Type or of some combination of Types.

The scientist's task is only to be a good scientist, that is, to create his description of the system out of messages of such logical typology (or so interrelated in their typology) as may be appropriate to the particular system. Whether Russell's Types "exist" in the systems which the scientist studies is a philosophic question beyond the scientist's scope—perhaps even an unreal question. For the scientist, it suffices to note that logical typing is an inevitable ingredient in the relationship between any describer and any system to be described.

What I am proposing is that the scientist should accept and *use* this phenomenon, which is, in any case, inevitable. His science—the aggregate of his messages about the system which he is describing—will be so constructed that it could be mapped in some more or less complex diagram of logical types. As I imagine it, each message of the description

---

5. This is not the place to discuss the controversies which have raged over the relation between learning and evolutionary process. Suffice it that two contrasting schools of thought are in agreement on a fundamental analogy between the two genera of process. On the one hand, there are those who, following Samuel Butler, argue that evolutionary change is a sort of learning; on the other hand, there are those who argue that learning is a sort of evolutionary change. Notable among the latter are Ashby and Mosteller, whose models of learning involve stochastic concepts closely comparable to the concepts of natural selection and random mutation.

would have its location on this map, and the topological relationship
between various locations would represent the typological relationship
between messages. It is of the nature of all communication, as we know
it, that some such mapping be possible.

But in describing a given system, the scientist makes many choices.
He chooses his words, and he decides which parts of the system he will
describe first; he even decides into what parts he will divide the system in
order to describe it. These decisions will affect the description as a whole
in the sense that they will affect the map upon which the typological relations between the elementary messages of the description are represented. Two equally sufficient descriptions of the same system could
conceivably be represented by utterly different mappings. In such a case,
is there any criterion by which it would be possible for the scientist to
choose one description and discard the other?

Evidently an answer to this question would become available if scientists would use, as well as accept, the phenomena of logical typing. They
are already scrupulous about the precise coding of their messages and
insist upon singularity of referent for every symbol used. Ambiguity at
this simpler level is abhorred and is avoided by rigorous rules for the
translation of observation into description. But this rigor of coding could
also be useful on a more abstract level. The typological relations between
the messages of a description could also be used, subject to rules of coding, to represent relations within the system to be described.

After all, any modification of the signal or change in relationship
between modifications of the signal can be made to carry a message; and
by the same token any change in relationship between messages can
itself carry a message. There is then no inherent reason why the various
species of metarelationship between the messages of our description
should not be used as symbols whose referents would be relationships
within the system to be described.

Indeed, something like this technique of description is already followed in certain fields, notably in the equations of motion. Equations of
first order (in $x$) denote uniform velocity; equations of second order (in
$x^2$) imply acceleration; equations of third order (in $x^3$) imply a change in
acceleration; and so on. There is moreover an analogy between this hierarchy of equations and the hierarchy of Logical Types: a statement of
acceleration is *meta* to a statement of velocity. The familiar Rule of
Dimensions is to physical quantities what the Theory of Logical Types is
to classes and propositions.

I am suggesting that some technique of this sort might be used in
describing change in those systems which either learn or evolve, and

further that if such a technique were adopted, there would then be a natural basis upon which to classify answers to the problems of change in these systems: the answers would fall into classes according to the typology of the messages which they contain. And this classification of answers should coincide both with a classification of systems according to their typological complexity and with a classification of changes according to their *orders*.

In illustration of this, it is now possible to go back over the whole body of description and argument contained in this book [*Naven*] and to dissect it on a generalized typological scale or map.

The book starts with two descriptions of Iatmul culture, in each of which relatively concrete observations of behavior are used to validate generalizations. The "structural" description leads to and validates eidological generalization, and a corpus of ethological generalization is validated by observations of expression of affect.

In the 1936 Epilogue [to *Naven*], it is demonstrated that ethos and eidos are only alternative ways of arranging data or alternative "aspects" of the data. This, I believe, is another way of saying that these generalizations are of the same order or Russellian type. I needed, for obscure reasons, to use two sorts of description, but the presence of these two descriptions does not denote that the system described actually has a complexity of this dual nature.

One significant duality has however already been mentioned in this brief survey, namely, the duality between observations of behavior and generalization, and this duality, I believe, here reflects a special complexity in the system: the dual fact of learning and learning to learn. A step in Russellian typology inherent in the system is represented by a corresponding step in the description.

A second typological contrast in the description, which I believe represents a real contrast in the system described, is that between ethos–eidos on the one hand and sociology on the other. Here, however, the matter is less clear. Insofar as the total society is represented in native thought and communication, clearly this representation is of higher type than the representations of persons, actions, and so on. It would follow that a segment of the description should be devoted to this entity, and that the delimiting of this segment from the rest of the description would represent a real typological contrast within the system described. But, as the matter is presented in the book, the distinctions are not perfectly clear, and the idea of sociology as a science dealing with the adaptation and survival of societies is mixed up with the concept "society" as a gestalt in native thought and communication.

It is appropriate next to ask about the concept "schismogenesis." Does the isolating and naming of this phenomenon represent an extra order of complexity in the system?

Here the answer is clearly affirmative. The concept "schismogenesis" is an implicit recognition that the system contains an extra order of complexity due to the combination of learning with the interaction of persons. The schismogenic unit is a two-person subsystem. This subsystem contains the potentialities of a cybernetic circuit which might go into progressive change; it cannot, therefore, be conceptually ignored and must be described in a language of higher type than any language used to describe individual behavior—the latter category of phenomena being only the events in one or another arc of the schismogenic subsystem.

It is necessary, next, to note that the original description contained a major error in its typological mapping. The description is presented as "synchronic,"[6] which in more modern terminology may be translated as "excluding irreversible change." The basic assumption of the description was that the system described was in a steady state, such that all changes within it could be regarded as changes in variables and not in the parameters. In self-justification, I may claim that I stated that there must exist factors which would control the runaways of schismogenesis—but still I overlooked what is crucial from the present point of view: that the system must contain still larger *circuits* which would operate correctively upon the schismogeneses. In omitting to make this deduction, I falsified the whole logical typology of the description by not depicting its highest level. This error is corrected in the earlier part of the present Epilogue.

It is thus possible, at least crudely, to examine the scientific description of a system and to relate the logical typology of the description to the circuit structure of the system described. The next step is to consider descriptions of change preparatory to asking how a classification of such descriptions may be related to problems of phenomenal discontinuity.

From what has already been said, it is clear that we must expect statements about change to be always in a language one degree more abstract than the language which would suffice to describe the steady state. As statements about acceleration must always be of higher logical type than statements about velocity, so also statements about cultural change must be of higher type than synchronic statements about culture. This rule

---

6. There is also a second sense in which anthropologists use the word "synchronic": to describe a study of culture which ignores progressive change by considering only a brief (or infinitesimal) span of time. In this usage, a *synchronic* description differs from a *diachronic* almost as differential calculus differs from integral calculus.

will apply throughout the field of learning and evolution. The language for the description of character change must always be of higher type than the description of character; the language to describe psychiatric etiology or psychotherapy, both of which impute change, must always be more abstract than the language of diagnosis. And so on.

But this is only another way of saying that the language appropriate for describing change in a given system is that language which would also be appropriate for describing the top typological level in a steady-state system having one more degree of complexity in its circuits. If the original description of Iatmul culture, as put forward in the body of the book, had been a sufficient and correct description of a steady state, then the language of the additional statements about the larger circuits would have been precisely that language appropriate to describe *change* or disturbance in that steady state.

When the scientist is at a loss to find an appropriate language for the description of change in some system which he is studying, he will do well to imagine a system one degree more complex and to borrow from the more complex system a language appropriate for his description of change in the simpler.

Finally it becomes possible to attempt a crude listing of types of change and to relate the items of this listing to the general problem from which I started—that of the contrast between continuity of process and discontinuity of the products of process.

Take for a starting point a system $S$ of which we have a description with given complexity $C$, and observe that the absolute value of $C$ is for present purposes irrelevant. We are concerned with the problem of *change* and not at all with absolute values.

Consider now events and processes within $S$. These may be classified according to the orders of statement which must be made in the description of $S$ in order to represent them. The crucial question which must be asked about any event or process within $S$ is: Can this event or process be included within a description of $S$ as a *steady state* having complexity $C$? If it can be so included, all is well and we are not dealing with any change that will alter the parameters of the system.

The more interesting case, however, is that in which events or processes are noted in $S$ which cannot be comprised within the steady-state description of complexity $C$. We then face the necessity of adding some sort of metadescription to be chosen according to the type of disturbance which we observe.

Three types of such disturbance may be listed: (a) Progressive change, like schismogenesis, which takes place in the values of relatively superficial and fast–changing variables. This, if unchecked, must always disrupt the parameters of the system. (b) Progressive change which, as Ashby has pointed out, must always occur in the more stable variables (or parameters?) when certain of the more superficial variables are *controlled*. This must happen whenever limitation is imposed upon those superficial and fast-changing variables which previously were essential links in some self-corrective circuit. An acrobat must always lose his balance if he is unable to make changes in the angle between his body and his balancing pole.

In either of these cases, the scientist is driven to add to his description of *S* statements of higher order than those included within the previous description *C*.

(c) Lastly there is the case of "random" events occurring within the system *S*. These become especially interesting when a degree of randomness is introduced into the very signals upon which the system depends for its self-corrective characteristics. The stochastic theories of learning and the mutation-natural-selection theory of evolution both invoke phenomena of this kind as basis for description or explanation of change. The stochastic theories of learning assume random changes of some kind in the neurological net, while the mutation theory assumes random changes in the chromosomal aggregate of messages.

In terms of the present discussion neither of these theories is satisfactory because both leave undefined the logical typing of the word "random." We must expect, a priori, that the aggregate of messages which we call a *genotype* must be made up of individual messages of very various typology, carried either by individual genes or by constellations of genes. It is even likely that, on the whole, more generalized and higher-type messages are more frequently carried by constellations of genes, while more concrete messages are in general carried by individual genes. Of this, there is no certain knowledge, but still it seems improbable that small "random" disturbances can alter with equal frequency messages of whatever logical type. We must ask, then: What distribution of disturbance among the messages of various types do the proponents of these theories have in mind when they use the word "random"? These, however, are questions more specific than the broad terms of the present discussion and are introduced only to illustrate the problems which are posed by the new epistemology which is now evolving.

The problem of discontinuity now falls into place in the sense that it is possible to classify the principal types of process and explanation which crystallize around this phenomenon. Consider still the hypothetical system, *S*, and the description of this system whose complexity I am calling *C*.

The first type of discontinuity is that relatively trivial case in which the state of the system at a given time is observed to contrast with its state at some other time, but where the differences are still such as can be subsumed within the terms of the given description. In such cases, the apparent discontinuity will be either an artifact resulting from the spacing of our observations in time, or will be due to the presence of on-off phenomena in the communicational mechanism of the system studied.

A less trivial case is proposed in considering two similar systems $S_1$ and $S_2$, both of them undergoing continuous changes in their variables such that the two systems appear to be diverging or becoming more and more different one from the other. Such a case becomes nontrivial when some extra factor is involved which may prevent later convergence. But any such factor will of course have to be represented in the description of the systems by messages of higher logical type.

The next category of discontinuity will include all those cases which involve parametric contrast. I have considered briefly above the types of ongoing process which must lead to parametric disruption and have noted that these are all instances in which the description of the system undergoing change must be of higher logical type than would have been the case in absence of such processes. This I believe to be true even in that vast majority of instances where the parametric disturbance leads to gross simplification of parameters after the disruptive change. Most commonly such disruptions will—in accordance with laws of probability—result in the "death" of the system. In a few cases some simplified version of $S$ may persist, and, in still fewer cases, the parametric disruption will lead to the creation of a new system, typologically more complex than the original $S$.

It is this rare possibility that is perhaps most fascinating in the whole field of learning, genetics, and evolution. But, while in the most general terms it is possible to state with some rigor what sort of changes are here envisaged and to see the results of such progressive discontinuous change in, for example, the telencephalization of the mammalian brain, it is still totally impossible to make formal statements about the categories of parametric disturbance which will bring about these positive gains in complexity.

Here is the central difficulty which results from the phenomenon of logical typing. It is not, in the nature of the case, possible to predict from a description having complexity $C$ what the system would look like if it had complexity $C + 1$.

This formal difficulty must in the end always limit the scientific understanding of change and must at the same time limit the possibilities of planned change—whether in the field of genetics, education, psychotherapy, or social planning.

Certain mysteries are for formal reasons impenetrable, and here is the vast darkness of the subject.

## References

Ashby, W. R. 1952. *Design for a Brain.* New York: Wiley.

—. 1956. *Introduction to Cybernetics.* New York: Wiley.

Bateson, G. 1949. "Bali: The Value System of a Steady State," in M. Fortes, ed., *Social Structure.* New York: Oxford University Press. [Reprinted in *Steps to an Ecology of Mind.*]

—. 1956. "The Message 'This Is Play,'" in *Second Conference on Group Processes.* New York: Josiah Macy, Jr. Foundation. Pp. 145–242.

Bateson, G., D. D. Jackson, J. Haley, and J. H. Weakland. 1956. "Toward a Theory of Schizophrenia." *Behavioral Science* 1: 251–64. [Reprinted in *Steps to an Ecology of Mind.*]

Bush, R. R., and F. Mosteller. 1955. *Stochastic Models for Learning.* New York: Wiley.

Butler, S. 1878. *Life and Habit.* London: Fifield.

—. 1887. *Luck or Cunning.* London: Fifield.

Foerster, H. von, ed. 1949–1953. *Cybernetics.* 5 vols. New York: Josiah Macy, Jr. Foundation. (Transactions of the 6th, 7th, 8th, 9th, and 10th Conferences.)

Martin, C. P. 1956. *Psychology, Evolution, and Sex.* Springfield, Ill.: Charles C. Thomas.

Richardson, L. F. 1939. "Generalized Foreign Politics." *British Journal of Psychology Monograph Supplements,* no. 23.

Ruesch, J., and G. Bateson. 1951. *Communication: The Social Matrix of Psychiatry.* New York: W. W. Norton.

Russell, B. 1956. Introduction to Wittgenstein, *Tractatus Logico-Philosophicus.* New York: Harcourt.

Shannon, C. E., and W. Weaver. 1949. *The Mathematical Theory of Communication.* Urbana: University of Illinois Press.

Waddington, C. H. 1957. *The Strategy of the Genes.* London: Allen & Unwin.

Weyl, H. 1949. *Philosophy of Mathematics and Natural Science.* Princeton, N.J.: Princeton University Press.

Whitehead, A. N., and B. Russell. 1910. *Principia Mathematica.* Cambridge: Cambridge University Press.

Wiener, N. 1948. *Cybernetics.* New York: Wiley.

# 5

## *Distortions Under Culture Contact**

Culture contact seems to be one of the most difficult things to talk about that we attempt. As we talk about it here in this room and focus preponderantly upon cultural exchange and contact between various Oriental cultures and various Occidental cultures, we are actually dealing with our subject on two levels. That is, we are not quite in the position that we would be in if we were discussing contact between two New Guinea tribes, or even, I think, two Oriental nations, though my comparative knowledge of Oriental cultures isn't good enough for me to say that. What we face is contact between a culture-contact culture and other cultures. Linguists have said that the English language has many of the characteristics of a pidgin or lingua franca, and the history of our civilization is that of multiple culture contact, of rapid change; and in a sense, what you Orientals are contacting is a civilization that is already to a very large extent molded by the phenomena of culture contact. This is worth taking a look at. What sort of phenomena do we expect? What are the characteristics? What happens? What's it like?

I'd like to introduce that subject by describing an experience I had in England a couple of years ago, when I went out to the South Downs. These are rounded chalk hills, which when I was a boy were covered with grass, maybe at the most two inches high, a high turf that you could practically roll a golf ball over, except that it was all rounded and sloped. About fifty species of plants were growing in that turf in a very complicated ecology, the limits of which were maintained by two organisms— the rabbits and the sheep who grazed the grass and kept it so short.

With the coming of the automobile, the sheep got onto the road and attacked the automobiles, and the sheep had to be removed because it

* This talk was delivered at the Third Conference on Culture and Mental Health in Asia and the Pacific, held March 15–19, 1971, in Honolulu. Reprinted by permission of University of Hawaii Press from *Youth, Socialization, and Mental Health,* Vol. 3 of *Mental Health Research in Asia and the Pacific,* edited by William P. Lebra, 1974.

was too expensive to fence the Downs. Shortly after that a virus disease was discovered that would kill rabbits. For some reason, it was thought desirable to exterminate the rabbits of the Downs, and for some weeks the roads of England stank with dead rabbits. Then the turf grew. When I revisited those hills two years ago, the turf was something on the order of three feet high and contained, of course, only those plants of the original population that could live in both conditions—one-inch turf and three-foot turf.

So you've got a fractionation. Every time you get change in a complex ecosystem or culture, you are likely to get a fractionation in which only the ideas or those modes, etc., that can survive in both "before" and "after" conditions are likely to remain.

Culture contact is, first, a simplification. Especially a simplification of ideas. Dr. Yeh has talked about the adjectives that Chinese students apply to themselves and to Americans. To apply these adjectives at all is a perfectly fantastic and monstrous thing to do in human relations. Really! But we all do it. When do we do it? We do it in culture-contact situations, you see. Then the Chinese are patient, wise, shrewd, etc., etc., etc. What you get, perhaps even more extreme than an oversimplification of people by applying adjectives to them, is a quantification. What is above all understandable from one culture to another is quantity. And of all quantities, that which is easiest to understand is quantity of money. And after the initial corruption of a culture, money becomes the royal road to cross-cultural . . . I was going to say understanding. That's how it goes.

Now, this being so, we haven't looked carefully at what goes on. We're interested in mental health, and I suppose in the sort of mental health that can be based upon an extreme simplification of life. Personally, I prefer mental healths that are based upon complexities. All sorts of things happen. For example, you have a rain dance, and you look at this as culture change or culture contact. Obviously culture change and culture contact are much alike. In both you get interfaces between people who think differently—in one case we call it generation gap, in another case we call it culture gap, and so on. You have a complex religious phenomenon and you look at it through the narrowing prism of culture contact, and you see instead a magical phenomenon. Obviously rain dances are to make the rain come, you know. Now, in general, religious phenomena are not like that. I suspect that a good many Indians who have rain dances think they are supposed to make the rain come and have fallen into the same sort of vulgarity that anthropologists are subject to from time to time.

The real point of things like rain dances is to affirm a total complex relationship between oneself and the weather and the supernatural

powers that control oneself and the weather and so on. Instead you get
the vulgarity of looking at the religious phenomenon as a magical phenomenon.

Then, another thing you can do, of course, is to take the custom of
one place and put it into the context of another. The hula dance, for
example, is obviously a magical ceremony for the removal of money from
the pockets of tourists into the pockets of Occidentals who organize hula
dances. Now if you do that, if you take somebody's action patterns or
symptoms, whatever, and pin them down—not pin them down, but give
them the context of another culture, another set of values—this is called
psychotherapy. You see, what the psychotherapist always does is take the
patient's symptoms and ask him to exhibit those symptoms under the
therapist's approval. The symptoms in most cases were designed to
annoy people, you know. Then the therapist *asks* for them. This sort of
takes the wind out of their sails. This is the sort of thing that happens
when you take customs or dances or whatever and try to transplant them
and give them a cross-cultural . . . you know, appreciate these people
whose sense of rhythm is so wonderful, and so they end up as entertain-
ers. We do this with the porpoises, not only Orientals, Negroes, and so
forth—wonderful sense of rhythm—constructing cross-cultural contexts
for the behavior of the other culture.

Lastly, I mentioned the idea of quantity, and how quantification is
after all the royal mode of exchange cross-culturally. Man lives in a very
strange world, with trees, and fishes, and oceans, and what not, and he
has a sort of culture contact with this strange world and tries to understand it. The first thing he does is try to quantify it, you know, and that's
what science is about. Science is a piece of bastard culture contact studying between man and nature in which the complexities of nature get
simplified as far as possible into measurements of one kind or another,
preferably meter readings of little things in machines, and we count the
storms, the raindrops, the frosts, the vegetation, how many inches high
the turf is, and so on.

What I want to get across this afternoon is the idea that the culture-
contact situation is one that itself shapes the thinking of those who
study it, not merely because they happen to be on one side or the other
of a culture-contact situation, but because as human beings scientists
are in a culture-contact situation already. This whole matter has a depth
to it. We can't really do very well skating on the top of it and avoid looking down into the depths, which I would hope some of us here will manage to do.

# 6

## *Some Components of Socialization for Trance**

Let me be clear from the beginning that by "components" I do not mean events or pieces of events that can be counted to become members of a statistical sample. I am doubtful whether in human behavior there are any such. In certain games, such as baseball and cricket, the named actions of the players appear to be repeated many times over and upon the samples so created a sort of statistic can be computed, assigning "batting averages" and the like to the various players; and such "averages" are indeed a rough indication of "better" and "worse." But it is clear that every play of the game is unique and that every ball pitched or bowled is conceptually inseparable from others, forming with them a larger strategy. The most elementary requirement of statistics—uniformity of sample—is therefore not met.

"Into the same river no man can step twice," not because the universe is in flux, but because it is organized and integrated.

The behavioral stream of events, like baseball or cricket, is segmented in time; and this segmentation is not to be violated by treating its numbers as quantities. As in the segmentation of an earthworm, each segment can have an ordinal name from "first" to "last," but no cardinal number can be applied. The total number of segments, whether in the worm or the game, is the name of a pattern. Segmentation is itself not a quantity; it is a component or premise of the morphology of the worm.

But still there is an economy, a parsimony of description to be gained by recognizing the repetitive character of the segments, whether these be of life or of game or of worm. We shall require fewer words and phrases, fewer linguistic bits, in our description if we take advantage of the repetitive and rhythmic nature of what is to be described.[1] In seeking for components of socialization, it is such a parsimony that I would

*This essay was written in 1974. Reproduced by permission of the American Anthropological Association from *Ethos* 3: 2, 1975. Not for further reproduction.

1. In the wide biological field, where description must be passed on from one generation to another, a similar parsimony is de rigeur. This necessity explains (for me) the phenomena of *homology*, both phylogenetic and metameric.

hope to achieve. My ultimate goal is simple and not very ambitious. It is merely to discover a few notions, a few categories, which can be used over and over again.

But in the whole realm of behavioral science, our ignorance is perhaps most conspicuously medieval when we pose questions about the classification of sequences of behavior. We have a whole host of words which name *classes* of action without identifying the members of the class. For some unknown reason, we cannot spell out the characteristics of any of these classes: What is "play"? What is "aggression"?

"He picked up his pen," "the cat scratched him," "he was hurrying," "she ate the steak," "he sneezed," "they quarreled," etc., etc. Not one of these descriptive statements can be classified without more information.

Here is an exercise: Consider for each of the above statements what you would need to know in order to say "that was play" or "that was exploration" or "practice" or "histrionics" or "humor" or "somnambulism" or "aggression" or "art" or "courtship" or "love" or "mourning" or "exploration" or "manipulation" or even "accident." "Ritual" or "magic"? Or was it mere "spinal reflex"?

And are any of these categories mutually exclusive?

It is not too much to say that a science of psychology might begin here. If we only knew what that rat or that graduate student was doing while he was "acting" as "subject" of our "experiment"! And what are those men with masks in New Guinea doing? Is it "dancing"? Is that actor "pretending" to be Hamlet?

The exercise is nontrivial.

Note first of all that such exercises concern how we, the observers, shall classify the items of behavior. How shall *we* structure our description? And what, if you please, is an "item" of behavior?

But these primary questions turn on another more difficult. What we are watching are not the impacts of billiard balls but of organisms, and they in turn have their own classification and structuring of the events in which they participate. The rat has surely a much more complex structure than the earthworm, and the structure is, surely, more complex again for the graduate student, though he, at least, will try to help the observer by trying (and seeming) to do what is asked of him. Our first task is to learn how the subject structures his living. Only after that is done can we build a "psychology," a science of biological categories.

This indeed is the trap of the laboratory in which the experimenter is caught: that the units of behavior are defined by the *structure of the experiment,* which structure is unilaterally determined by only one of the participants . . . and that the wrong one. Under such circumstances, the only units that can be investigated must always be simpler, smaller, and of lower logical type than the structure of the experiment. It is all very well to perform an experiment with a "naive" rat. When he becomes "test wise," the sophistication of the experiment will have to transcend that test wisdom.

This need to transcend, that is, to use in the explanations, propositions of higher logical type than the descriptive proposition used in the explanandum, has a logical corollary in the familiar rule that no scientific hypothesis can ever be verified by inductive procedure. The proposition of lower type can contradict but never verify that of high type. This rule is especially cogent when the explanandum contains propositions such as ideas in the heads of rats and people.

Finally, what about cultural contrast? How, if at all, can the anthropologist recognize "play," "manipulation," and so on, among people of another culture? And what about dolphins and octopuses?

All of these questions are embarrassing and all must be faced to make sure that we do not claim insight to which we are not entitled by our experience, but I, personally, do not believe that the gross difficulty of these questions makes invalid all attempts to understand what goes on in other cultures and among nonhuman organisms.

As it seems to me, there are several components of our problem which suggest that it may be not insoluble and which, conversely, suggest that research which ignores all these advantageous components is likely to be a tilting at epistemologically monstrous windmills. First, "socialization" (by definition) requires *interaction*, usually of two or more organisms. From this it follows that, whatever goes on below the surface, inside the organisms where we cannot see it, there must be a large part of that "iceberg" showing above surface. We, biologists, are lucky in that evolution is always a co-evolution and learning is always a co-learning. Moreover, this visible part of the process is no mere by-product. It is precisely that production, that set of appearances, to produce which is supposedly the "goal" of all that learning which we call "socialization." Moreover, this aggregate of externally observable phenomena, always involving two or more "persons,"[2] contains not only what has been learned but also all the imperfect attempts of both persons to fit together in an ongoing process of interchange.

Above all, out there and imaginable for the scientist, are the *contexts* of all those failures and successes that mark the process of "socialization."

---

2. The "person," after all, is the *mask*. It is what is perceivable of a human organism. It is a unilateral view of the interface between one organism and another.

In other words, the scientist who would investigate "socialization" is lucky in that nature displays before him phenomena that are already *ordered* in two ways that should be of interest to him. He can observe "out there" both the *actions* of the interacting persons and, by a sort of inductive perception, the *contexts* of these actions.

Clearly a first step in defining units or parts of the process of socialization will be the explication of these two levels of order: the "actions" and the "contexts."

Before illustrating this program, however, a word must be said about those phenomena that are only *subjectively* observable.

I can know something of the inner determinants of my own actions, and something of what the *contexts* of my actions look like to me. But how much egomorphism should I allow myself in interpreting the actions and contexts of others? No final answer can be given, since both internal and external sources of information are certainly valuable—especially as corrective of each other. The excesses of "behaviorism" can only be corrected by empathy, but the hypotheses that empathy proposes must always be tested in the external world.

Without identification of context, nothing can be understood. The observed action is utterly meaningless until it is classified as "play," "manipulation," or what not. But contexts are but categories of the mind. If I receive a threat from him, I can never get empirical validation of my interpretation of his action as "threat." If his threat is successful and deters me from some action, I shall never be sure that he was really threatening. Only by calling his bluff (and was it "bluff"?) can I get an indication of how he *now*, at this later moment and in this new context of my "calling his bluff," classifies his potential threat. *Only* by use of introspection, empathy, and shared cultural premises—the products of socialization—can anybody identify how context appears to another.

One form of habitual error can, however, be pilloried. This is the trick of drawing a generalization from the world of external observation, giving it a fancy name, and then asserting that this named abstraction exists *inside* the organism as an explanatory principle. Instinct theory commonly takes this monstrous form. To say that opium contains a dormitive principle is no explanation of how it puts people to sleep. Or do the people contain a dormitive instinct that is "released" by the opium?

What is important is that the conscious use of introspection and empathy is always to be preferred to their unconscious use. When all is said and done, we are still human and still organisms, and it is silly not to compare what we personally know about being human with what we can see of how other people live, and silly not to use what we humans know of living as a background for thinking about the being of other species. The *difference* between man and planarian must be enlightening because these two creatures resemble each other more than either resembles a stone.

What is disastrous is to claim an objectivity for which we are untrained and then project upon an external world premises that are either idiosyncratic or culturally limited. Biology, alas, is still riddled with hypotheses that are unconscious projections upon the biosphere of social philosophies generated by the Industrial Revolution. It was right—and inevitable—for Darwin and the others to create hypotheses out of the climate of their own culture and epoch, but disastrous to not see what they were doing.

The danger inherent in the use of subjective insights is not that these are necessarily wrong. The subjective view is, in 1974, still the richest and most rewarding source of understanding in biology. (So little do we know of the nature of life!) The danger arises from what seems to be a fact of natural history: that the insights given by introspection and empathy seem irresistibly true. Like the axioms of Euclid, the premises of subjective insight seem "self-evident."

With this caveat regarding the subjective, I now return to the two species of order—the actions and the contexts of action—which characterize the observable part of socialization, and I ask what clues to the understanding of this external order can be derived from my own internal experience of living. As I see it, the fundamental idea that there are separate "things" in the universe is a creation of and projection from our own psychology. From this creation, we go on to ascribe this same separateness to ideas, sequences of events, systems, and even persons.[3] I therefore ask whether this particular psychological habit can be trusted as a clue to understanding the order or sorts of order that are (expectably)[4] immanent in the socialization process; and the answer is not what naive positivism might lead us to suspect. The more complex entities—ideas, sequences, persons, and so on—seem to be suspiciously

---

3. Opinions differ as to which separating line was primary. Some suppose that the first distinction is that between self and notself.

4. Note that already the psychological habit of isolating and naming processes as if they were things creeps in with this word "expectably" and with my reference to *the* socialization process. But are there any total divisions between things? Is there a place or time where one thing begins and another ends? If so, then clearly there could be no causal or logical interaction between them!

intangible and suspiciously devoid of limiting outlines, and we might therefore be led to suppose them illusory, creations only of the mind and, therefore, to be distrusted in scientific analysis.

But, precisely at this point, there is a paradoxical reversal: the socialization that we try to study is a *mental* process and therefore only the productions and processes of mind are relevant. The dissection of experience into ideas, sequences, and events may be "really" invalid but certainly the occidental mind really thinks in terms of such separations. If, therefore, we are to analyze processes of socialization we must examine and map these separations and, by this act of separating a group of phenomena, I commit myself to natural history. My aim is to study those separations (valid or not) that characterize the thought of those whom I study, of whom "I" am one.

This leaves conspicuously unanswered the analogous question about the organization of mind in the Orient and elsewhere. From an external view of what is reported, it seems that there are several arduous pathways by which experience of other ways of knowing can be achieved. Some of these other epistemologies are also accessible to Westerners by pathways not less arduous. What is reported by East and West alike is that, in these special states of mind, the way of knowing is precisely *not* organized in separate or separable gestalten.

In the jargon of this essay, it seems that for these states there are no separable components of socialization and possibly no meaning attachable to "socialization." Or perhaps such words could refer only to some buzzing of irrelevant memory, recalling other more prosaic states.

For the mystic shares with the pragmatist that fact of natural history—whereby the premises of mind, in whatever state it be, seem self-evident. His thoughts may be more abstract and perhaps more beautiful. From where the mystic sits, the premises of the pragmatic and the ego-centered will appear parochial and arbitrary, but his own premises are, for him, completely self-evident.

In sum, what can be said about the mystics defines our upper limit, an upper level of abstraction into which we need not pursue the search for data, since socialization is not there, but *from* which we can look out at the data generated in other levels. The epistemology onto which we map the facts of socialization must be more abstract than the facts to be mapped.

Gradually the outlines of how to think about components of socialization or about any sort of mental change begin to appear. We are to concern ourselves with the psychologically "self-evident" and with a premise that the psychologically self-evident is divisible into components.

This latter premise, is, itself, self-evident at the psychological level where the components appear to be (and therefore *are*) separable. But at a higher level of abstraction, where the mystics live, it is claimed that such separation is not only not self-evident, it is almost inconceivable. It is some traveler's tale from the world of illusion or *maya*. The mystic may laugh at us but still the task of the anthropologist is to explore the world of illusion, perhaps with the eyes and ears of the mystic.

To be "self-evident," a proposition or premise must be out of reach and unexaminable: it must have defenses or roots at unconscious levels. Similarly, to be "self-evident," a proposition or premise must be either self-validating or so general as to be but rarely contradicted by experience.

Enough has now been said to be background for considering a cluster of cultural phenomena in an attempt to recognize components that shall compose the socialization "behind" those cultural phenomena.

The most direct approach is that of looking at sequences of interchange between parents or other teachers and children in which the former are "socializing" the latter. Margaret Mead and I have provided data for such a study on a rather large scale in *Balinese Character,* where data in actual socialization are set side by side with other Balinese material. In this book, the plates, each with from five to nine pictures, were built according to what we thought or felt were cultural and characterological themes. These themes do not appear, however, in the naming of the plates, which is done in terms that appear to be episodic or concrete: "Cremation," "Cock Fighting," "Eating Snacks," "A Bird on a String," "Fingers in Mouth," and so on. But, in fact, every plate is a complex statement, illustrating either different facets of some quite abstract theme or the interlocking of several themes.

Each picture is raw data except for the fact of selection—the aiming of the camera and the choice of the particular print for reproduction. Beyond that, of course, the juxtaposition of the various pictures on the plate is, necessarily, ours. It is our first step toward computing some sort of theory from the data. The method is comparative but not statistical, reticulate rather than lineal.

Faced with these data, I ask again whether there is a useful species of component of culture? Are the themes useful in the formal sense that by recognition of them we can describe the Balinese culture and socialization in a more economical manner?

Consider plate 17, which is entitled "Balance." The two preceding plates[5] (15* and 16) are called "Visual and Kinaesthetic Learning I" and

---

5. [*Editor's Note:* Items followed by an asterisk (*) are not reproduced here.]

"Visual and Kinaesthetic Learning II." The three plates following "Balance" are called "Trance and *Beroek* I," "Trance and *Beroek* II," and "Trance and *Beroek* III." The whole series of six plates from plate 15* to plate 20 are interrelated. (In addition, plate 17 in my copy has on it a penciled note in my handwriting: "This plate should more appropriately follow the series on 'Elevation and Respect' and point up the balance problems of the elevated. Cf. also 'Fear of Space' (plate 67*) and 'Fear of Loss of Support' and 'Child as (elevated) God' (plate 45*)."

In a word, the book is built in such a way that the interlocking nature of the themes is stressed and their separateness as "components" is made most difficult to disentangle. I have chosen the "Balance" plate for this essay because it illustrates a point of meeting of many different themes.

The context of plate 17 is described in the book as follows:

> Plates 14*, 15*, and 16 taken together give us indications about the Balinese body image. We have, on the one hand, the fantasy of the inverted body with its head on the pubes; and on the other, the Balinese method of learning through their muscles, the discrepant muscular tensions which are characteristic of their dancing, and the independent movement and posturing of the separate fingers in dance. We have, in fact, a double series of motifs—indications that the body is a single unit as perfectly integrated as any single organ, and contrasting indications that the body is made up of separate parts, each of which is as perfectly integrated as the whole.
>
> This plate illustrates the motif of the perfectly integrated body image, while Plates 18, 19*, and 20 illustrate the fantasy that the body is made up of separate parts and may fall to pieces (*beroek*).

The nine pictures which make up "Plate 17, Balance," are as follows:

Two frames of a small boy learning to stand and walk while holding on to a horizontal bamboo. In the second picture he holds onto his penis in addition to the bar. (Other records not reproduced in this book support the proposition that male toddlers hold onto their penes when balance is precarious.)

One frame of a small girl, with hands holding each other in front of her belly.

One frame of a child nurse stooping to pick up a baby and one of an adolescent girl stooping to pick up an offering.

One frame shows a small boy scratching his knee. He simply stands on the other leg and lifts the knee to within reach of his hand. (Again

Plate 16. Visual and Kinaesthetic Learning II (Bateson and Mead, 1942)

Plate 17. Balance (Bateson and Mead, 1942)

Plate 18. Trance and Beroek I (Bateson and Mead, 1942)

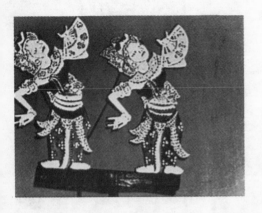

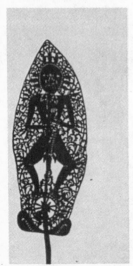

*Plate 20. Trance and* Beroek *III (Bateson and Mead, 1942)*

there is massive support in the data for saying that Balinese movement is extremely economical. They contract just those muscles needed for each action.)

The three remaining frames are of works of art representing witches in different stages of transformation. It seems that to embark upon a horrendous "trip" in the realms of altered consciousness a woman should go out in the night with a small altar, a live chicken, and small offerings (*segehan*) for the chthonic demons. All alone she will then dance with her left foot on the chicken and her right hand on the altar. As she dances she will gradually assume the shape and appearance of the witch (*Rangda*).

In other words, whether or not the Balinese "know" what they are doing and intend this outcome, they somehow sense and recognize in art that their kinesthetic socialization prepares the individual for altered consciousness—for a temporary escape from the ego-organized world.

The use of dance as an entry into ecstasy and an ego-alien world is ancient and perhaps worldwide, but the Balinese (and perhaps every people) have their particular version of this pathway. Plates 15* and 16 together with 18, 19*, and 20 illustrate the matter.

Balance is a partly involuntary and unconscious business, dependent on "spinal reflexes." When provided with appropriate context, these reflexes go into oscillation that is called "clonus," a phenomenon that is familiar to everybody and which is easily produced. (While sitting, place the leg with thigh horizontal and foot supported on the floor. Move the foot inward toward you so that the heel is off the floor and the ball of the foot supports the weight of the leg. When the weights and angles are correctly adjusted, an oscillation will start in the muscle of the calf with a frequency of about six to eight per second and an amplitude of about half an inch at the knee. This oscillation is called *clonus* in neurophysiology and is a recurrent series of patellar reflexes, generated in a feedback circuit. The effect of each contraction is fed back as a modification of tension to the calf muscle. This change of tension triggers the next patellar reflex.)

The process of clonus involves three propositional or injunctional components: two of these are the usual paired components of any cybernetic oscillation which generate the sequential paradox in, for example, a buzzer circuit. In words: "If the circuit is 'on,' then it shall become 'off.'" And "if it is 'off,' then it shall become 'on.'" But, in addition to these two contradictory components, there is a process that sets values for the parameters of the whole system. The thresholds or other components of the oscillation can be changed by "meta" injunctions that presumably come from the brain. The two contradictory components are immanent in spinal cord and muscle.

The potentially ego-alien nature of such action is basic. Anybody, by ignoring (repressing the perception of) the meta-injunctions that control the parameters, can have the reflexive experience of seeing his or her leg engage in involuntary movement; and this oscillatory trembling can serve the same function as that of involuntary hand movements in the induction of hypnotic trance. The involuntary movement is first a detached object of perception: "I" see my leg move but "I" did not move it.

This detachment of the object proposes then two lines of development: (1) the possibility of "out-of-body experience," and (2) the possibility of integrating to perceive the body as an autonomous, ego-alien entity. Either the detached "I" or the detached "body" can become the focus of elaboration. Of these paths, it is the second that Balinese follow so that, by a curious inversion, the word "*raga*," which seems to have the primary meaning of "body," comes to mean "self."

By extension from the experience of clonus, the various perceivable parts of the body become, in fantasy or mystic experience, each separately animated. If the arm or the leg can act of its own accord—(and, indeed, clonus is a completed self-corrective circuit; it is a true aliveness)—then a similar separate aliveness can be expected and can be found in any limb.

The Balinese cemetery is haunted not by whole ghosts but by the ghosts of separate limbs. Headless bodies, separate legs, and unattached arms that jump around and sometimes a scrotum that crawls slowly over the ground—these are the boggles of Balinese fantasy.

From this it is a small step to perceiving the body as a puppet or to imagining such supernaturals as *Bala Serijoet* (plate 20, fig. 4), the "Multiple Soldier" whose every joint—shoulders, elbows, knees, ankles, and so on—is separately animated and provided with an eye.

These fantasies generate or are generated by a paradox, a dialectic between integration and disintegration. Is there a whole? Or is it only parts? Or are the parts combined into a whole? And this paradox of disintegration-integration proposes a whole spectrum of entities, ranging from separated animated limbs to such supernaturals as *Sangiang Tjintjia* or *Betara Tunggal* (plate 20, fig. 6). This is the totally detached, totally integrated, "God of god," (*Dewaning Dewa*). He is completely integrated, sexless, enclosed within his own effulgence and totally withdrawn.

It is my impression, though I do not recall any Balinese telling me this, that as the woman by occult practices can cause her own transformation into the form of the Witch of witches (*Rangdaning Durga*), so also by occult practices the adept becomes transformed into a supernatural of the *Sangiang Tjintjia* genus.

Plates 16 and 18 illustrate another aspect of the character formation that centers in balance. In both of these plates the kinesthetic integration of the individual is invaded. His or her individuation is violently destroyed to achieve a new integration.

In plate 16, the famous dancer, Mario, teaches a preadolescent boy to dance, forcibly guiding the pupil's hands and body into the correct postures and almost throwing him across the dancing space.

In plate 18, two little girls are put into the trance state in which they will dance. The procedure is a little complicated: two dolls, weighted with bells, are threaded on a string about fifteen feet long which is strung between two vertical bamboo sticks. The sticks are held by two men in such a way that clonus in their biceps will change the tension in the string causing the dolls or *dedari* (angels) to dance up and down, while the weighted dolls provide a feedback promoting the clonus in the men's arms. When the *dedari* are dancing fast, the girl who is to go into trance takes hold of the shaking stick so that she is violently shaken by the man's clonus.

Meanwhile the crowd around is singing songs about *dedari*. The girl's action in holding the stick breaks the rhythm of the clonus and she takes control of the stick beating with its end upon the wooden stand that supports it. She beats out a few bars of the song that the crowd is singing and then falls backward into trance. She is then dressed up by the crowd and will dance as *dedari*.

Curiously enough, a conspicuous element of the dance is the balancing feat of dancing while standing on a man's shoulders (plate 10*, fig. 3).

In sum, the business of explanation and the business of socialization turn out to be the same. To make a premise "self-evident" is the simplest way to make action based upon that premise seem "natural." To illustrate this, data from Bali have been adduced.

A large part of Balinese behavior is based upon paradigms of experience which are, for the Balinese, unquestionable. These are the paradigms of balance and of the interaction between the moving human body and the gravitational field in which it must move. This interaction is rooted in the unquestionable on both sides. On the one side are the reflexes of balance of which surely many components are genetically determined and, on the other side, are the universal characteristics of bodily mass and earth's gravity. These are combined to make it "self-evident" that the cemeteries would be haunted by autonomous parts of bodies.

And yet there is no universal cross-cultural imperative that would insist that everywhere in the world these generalities of balance and gravity shall become major cultural premises; or even that the synthesis of gravity and spinal reflex shall take the particular shape that is characteristic for Balinese culture.

## Reference

Bateson, Gregory, and Margaret Mead. 1942. *Balinese Character: A Photographic Analysis* (Special Publications of the New York Academy of Sciences, 2). New York: New York Academy of Sciences.

# 7

## *From Anthropology to Epistemology**

For many anthropologists, even today, the bare data are sufficient to justify the labor. Perhaps because the roots of our science are preponderantly in literary and humanistic fields; perhaps because the early theories were so naive and "explained" so little; perhaps because literary people have distaste for "materialism"; perhaps because the fashionable biological theories of the first quarter of the century denied the usefulness of *mind* as an explanatory principle. . . .

For whatever reason, anthropologists are chary of theory.

I came into anthropology in 1925, bouncing out of the sterile academic zoology of that date into British anthropology and the controversies between "evolution" and "diffusion."

I was not much happier in anthropology than I had been in zoology, and I tried vaguely to apply in anthropology the sorts of thinking that had seemed most interesting in biology—a combination of morphogenesis and genetics. (Of course, nobody knew then that these were branches of informational science!)

On my second trip to New Guinea I met Margaret Mead and Reo Fortune, as she has described in *Blackberry Winter*. She says I was "sophisticated" at that time—but not so. I was still deeply puzzled about what I could do in anthropology.

Into this puzzlement came the manuscript of Ruth Benedict's *Patterns of Culture* and the first suggestion of a field of theory where I might contribute. It took some years to develop the linkage between character of persons and configuration of cultures. Margaret's first big contribution in that area was *Sex and Temperament;* mine was *Naven.*

But in *Naven*, I was already moving away from typology to process. "Schismogenesis"—the word itself—marked the idea of evolutionary change. The idea was *change with direction*, but it was still a long way from

---

*These remarks were delivered to a Symposium of the American Association for the Advancement of Science entitled "Fifty Years of Anthropology," honoring Margaret Mead, held February 1976, in Boston. Previously unpublished.

the coining of the word to realizing in a deep sense that, of course, all directional change must depend upon interaction between organisms.

"Orthogenesis," as it had been called in biology—whether of ammonites, horses, Echinocardium, or culture—was the outward and visible sign of interactive process. The whole theory of Darwinian adaptation was shifting—as many of us knew it surely had to shift.

From the 1940s to the present has been an exciting time. Let me list some of the high points:

1939 was the year of publication of Richardson's equations for armaments races.

In the early years of the war, the basic cybernetic and systems ideas were developed in half a dozen different electronic labs. I had early contact with that development through McCulloch and Bigelow.

By the end of the war, our heads were full of "feedback" and "teleological mechanisms." The logjam of "purpose" was broken.

For me, an exciting move forward was the formulation of deutero-learning theory—in my discussion of a paper of Margaret's.

Later, after the war, came the Macy cybernetic meetings and the linking of the levels of learning to Russell's "logical types."

After that, the next big shift for me was the rise of ecology. That science is still stuck in energy budgets and fear of mental explanation. But in principle we know where it has to go and anthropology has to go with it.

We (a thin line of thinkers, from Lamarck, to Fechner, to Samuel Butler, to William Bateson) knew that mind must in some way enter into the larger schemes of explanation. We knew that ultimately the theory of evolution must become identical with a resolution of the body/mind problem.

Today both evolution and body/mind are linked in *epistemology,* and this last is no longer a branch of philosophy. It has become, largely under McCulloch's leadership, a branch of experimental and observational science.

# PART II

# Form and Pathology in Relationship

# 8

# *The New Conceptual Frames for Behavioral Research*\*1

*. . . May God us keep*
*From Single vision & Newton's sleep!*
*—W. Blake, Letter to Thomas Butts.*

To relieve your anxiety I want to make you a promise that I will ultimately talk about behavioral research, and even specifically, about psychiatric research. But before I come to this I shall have to go the long way around Robin Hood's barn, and lay out for you something of the conceptual framework of the Theory of Games. I shall do this not as a mathematician but as a biologist, and I shall find it necessary to modify the conceptual framework which the mathematicians offer us, and to modify the whole theory of biological evolution and natural selection. That is, I shall try to achieve a synthesis between evolutionary theory and the theory of games, modifying both these bodies of theory in order to bring them into alignment. When that is accomplished, at least to my temporary satisfaction, I will go on to apply the resulting theoretical system to the formal problems presented by schizophrenia and those family constellations in which schizophrenic behavior is an appropriate strategy for one or more of the family members.

The Theory of Games initiated by Von Neumann and Morgenstern (1944) and since elaborated by many others, is the most complex and elegant—perhaps also the most significant—theoretical advance that has

*This paper is reprinted from *Proceedings of the Sixth Annual Psychiatric Institute* (held September 17, 1958, at the New Jersey Neuro-Psychiatric Institute, Princeton, New Jersey).

1. The ideas in this paper represent the combined thinking of the staff of the Project for the Study of Schizophrenic Communication. The staff consists of Gregory Bateson, Jay Haley, John H. Weakland, Don D. Jackson, M.D., and William F. Fry, Jr., M.D. The project is financed by the Josiah Macy, Jr. Foundation, administered by the Department of Anthropology at Stanford University, and functions at the Veterans Administration Hospital, Palo Alto, California.

yet been achieved in the whole field of behavioral science. In their great book Von Neumann and Morgenstern observe that the social sciences are in a stage of development equivalent to that of pre-Newtonian physics. They asserted that what these sciences lack is some conceptually simplified paradigm around which theory might crystallize. Newton's artificially simplified concept, the free-falling body, was such a seminal idea in the field of physics. It was a myth, a fictitious ideal around which physical theory could take shape and, when the Theory of Games was first initiated, it appeared that the social sciences had no such artificial simplified concept.

Personally I believe that the very book in which this comment was made will be found to contain something like this abstract and simplified paradigm which the social sciences need.

The Theory of Games deals with a complex family of conceptual models, and the achievement of the mathematicians has been to enumerate, classify, and analyze these models. This achievement I do not propose to criticize. Indeed for a nonmathematician to do so would be impertinent and, for me to do so, would be ungrateful. The Theory of Games has given me pleasure whenever I have forced myself to follow some of its intricacies.

I observe, however, that current attempts to apply these models are usually based on naive premises regarding the biological nature of man and his place in the universe. These premises I propose to examine.

The models—the so-called games—are constructed according to certain principles which have been chosen with great care and for profound reasons. If we are to use these models as explanatory devices in the business of describing any category of interactional phenomenon, it is necessary to understand these principles of simplification and the reasoning upon which the principles are based.

Broadly, there are four groups of simplifying ideas:

(1) The premise that the rules of the given game shall be stable within the limits of any given theorem about that game. This assumption prevents us from any loose use of the models which would regard them as analogous to any of those "games" whose character depends upon the emergence of new rules in the process of play. For example, such interactional processes or games as courtship, politics, psychotherapy, differ profoundly from Von Neumannian games in that an essential characteristic of the interaction is a process in which new rules and patterns of interaction are continually being evolved.

(2) The premise that the problem-solving equipment of the players shall be similarly stable. Von Neumann's phrasing of the matter is simply to posit that all players have from the start all the equipment necessary to solve all the problems which can be presented by the rules. This premise excludes from loose analogy all interactional phenomena which involve learning how to play or learning the rules of the game. Incidentally, it also excludes from the play of Von Neumannian games all *detectable* tricks. No player can hope that his opponent will make an error resulting from failure to consider some possibility of the situation.

(3) The premise that the players act as if motivated by constant, monotone, and transitive preferences. They attempt to maximize some single quantity or variable, referred to as "utility." This premise and indeed the whole of utility theory has been subject to much argument, probably because this is the bridge which connects the theory of games with the phenomena of economics. While, however, the "utility" of games theory and of theoretical economics has close analogies with money—or with whatever it is that money can buy—it is still not clear that utility or any concept like utility is a fundamental determinant of the behavior of any known organism. Rats may select an optimum diet under experimental conditions, but it is not clear that they are guided to this by any single transitive preference. And human beings notoriously lack this basic wisdom which rats seem to possess. It is not impossible that the value system derivative from the Occidental concept of money plays an important part in diminishing our strategic skill when faced with dietary and other basic problems. It is possible that "money" is an epiphenomenon imposed by cultural contexts upon an organism ill equipped to operate in terms of such a notion, foreign to the nature of the beast.

Be all that as it may, it is clear that the utility premise excludes certain types of application of games theory to the explanation of behavior. In the two-person zero-sum game, utility may be gained by one player, but his gains are only equal to his opponent's losses. There is no overall gain and therefore, within the theory, no explanation for the two players' participation in the game. *If* two players are engaged in a zero-sum two-person game, and these hypothetical players have the characteristics enumerated above, *then* certain theorems about their strategies follow. But the characteristics of the players expressly exclude all explanation of why they would ever engage in such a game. There is no "utility" to be gained from a lottery in which the player stands an even chance of winning twice the price of his ticket. And, conversely, if for one player the ratio, prize : ticket price, is *greater* than the probability of winning the prize, this player will never find an opponent willing to play with him. Such an opponent could only be some entity ill equipped to solve the problems presented by the game.

Similarly the utility premise excludes from consideration all appeals from one player to another which would attach value to the continuance of the game. "The game cannot go on unless you do such and such" or "I won't play with you unless you do such and such." No move is made in a games-theoretical game for the sake of keeping the game going; and by the same token, no player can act upon a desire to stop the game. To do either would be to act as if motivated by *meta*utility, and it is precisely this possibility that is excluded by the simplified utility premise.

Indeed, if we examine these three simplifying premises we find that each of them is carefully designed to exclude a family of *meta*possibilities. The whole edifice of games theory is constructed in such a way that it shall be investigable by mathematical tools. The mathematicians who constructed it were wise enough to recognize the limitations of their exploratory tools and therefore limited the structure within premises which would permit the use of these tools.

This procedure is certainly tautological, and perhaps this has made games theory difficult for scientists to accept. But all can agree that it is elegant, and after all, there would be no sense in inventing a fictitious universe which could *not* be investigated by the tools of the inventors.

Games theory, then, is characterized by these simplifying assumptions which systematically exclude all possibilities which could only be described in some language having a metarelationship to the language of games theory. There shall be no talk about the evolution of the rules of the game. There shall be no talk about acquisition or loss of skill in play, and there shall be no metamotivation: neither value set upon the experience of play as such, nor value set upon changes in motivational structure. There shall, in fact, be no such changes.

(4) There is, however, a fourth simplifying assumption quite different in nature from the other three. These three already may seem sufficiently unreal in that they totally depersonalize the

players. The fourth assumption unexpectedly seems to *personify* the environment. In non–zero–sum games, the players are pitted against nature, from whom they may gain or to whom they may lose. And the fourth simplifying assumption is simply that this overall antagonist—the environment—shall be considered as another "player." Indeed, what objection can there be to the premise that the environment is to be equated with the already depersonified participants in the "game"? The poets and religionists have often personified Nature more completely than this.

However, if Nature—or the environment—is to be simply the nth person in a non–zero–sum n–1 person game, she must conform to the rigor and symmetry of the theory as a whole. In a word, she must fit in with the other three simplifying assumptions: no evolution of rules; no learning to play; and complete determination of choices by a utility premise.

Conversely, whatever meaning we attach to these simplifying assumptions when we apply them to the environment must, in fact, be the meaning attaching to them in our descriptions of the other players. We can critically investigate what we mean by "rules," "learning," and "utility" by asking what we would mean by these words in applying them to Nature, the nth player.

It does not immediately shock us to say that Nature never "learns" how to play and never changes the rules by which she plays. Let us therefore assume for the moment that we know roughly what these statements might mean and proceed at once to the more puzzling statement that nature or the environment makes choices which are governed by a simple utility premise.

What, if anything, does this mean?

What variable does Nature seek to maximize?

This is a question which must be faced and, if we are to preserve the elegance and symmetry of the whole theoretical system, we must expect that the answer will suggest new and more generalized meanings of the word "utility" when this word is applied to the other n–1 players in the non–zero–sum game. It would make nonsense of the whole system of models to suppose the nth player to be motivated by some sort of "utility" different from that which motivates the others.

But we actually know something about Nature's preferences:

She prefers the probable to the improbable, and if she were guided only by this single preference, called the Second Law of Thermodynamics, the universe would be simple—if rather dull. But she has clearly another preference: she prefers the stable to the unstable. This preference, also, by itself would lead to a dull universe. It is the combination of—the conflict between—these two preferences which leads to the highly complex and strangely unexpectable universe in which we live. There would be no surprises in a universe governed either by probability alone or by stability alone. Indeed, there would be no evolution and no organisms to be surprised in either of these universes.

The whole fantastic, agitated "game" in which all the organisms and indeed all the particles of the universe are engaged depends upon this dual preference system which seems to be characteristic of Nature.

At this point it is necessary to examine rather closely what I have called "probability" and what I have called "stability." I invited you just now to consider two imaginary worlds. One in which only probability would obtain, and the other which would be governed only by stability. The first would rapidly end in total entropy, the *Warmetodt,* while the other would rapidly end up with all atoms combined into the most stable possible molecular forms.

Both of these worlds are impossible fictions. In the world in which we live, there is always a combination between the trend toward probability and the trend toward stability. In many cases, even, this combination can be described in mathematical form and predictions can be based upon the resulting equations. When, for example, we mix in solution two inorganic salts, AX and BY, we can predict the proportions of each of these substances which will break down to its component ions, A and X, B and Y. We can predict the encounters between these ions and the probability of formation of new substances, AY and BX, by what used to be called "double decomposition." If all four substances, AX, BY, AY, and BX, are soluble, all will coexist in a dynamic equilibrium in solution. If, however, one of the resultant substances happens to be insoluble—suppose, for example, we had mixed silver nitrate with calcium chloride, so that one of the products would be the almost insoluble substance, silver chloride—then the insoluble substance will be withdrawn from the system by precipitation, and will therefore be stable. A dynamic equilibrium will not occur and the probabilities of impact between the remaining molecules will result in *directional* change toward an end state characterized by silver chloride at the bottom of the test tube, and calcium nitrate in solution.

There are many other instances in which the conceptual framework used to predict events combines in a single phrasing both the notions of probability and the notions of stability. The "half-life" of an atom of some radioactive substance is a familiar instance of such a combination.

All that I am saying is that there are two frames of reference within which we may consider events. One of these frames allows for consideration of only the *sequential* aspects of time. The other makes allowance also for time in its *durational* aspects. The purely probabilistic statement can tell us about direction of change, e.g., toward entropy, but the statement which makes allowance for stability and duration will often contradict the statement which ignores this aspect. The classic instance of such a contradiction is in the field of evolution, and has fascinated men's minds for many thousands of years. In terms of the Second Law of Thermodynamics, we would expect the particles of matter to become more and more homogenized—as the milkman would say. And if this was so, pasteurization would never be necessary because nothing so complex as a bacterium could ever be evolved. But throughout biological evolution we see the innovation of complexity and differentiation, and this unexpected "progress" has, for the last hundred years, been explained by the theory of "natural selection." A theory which invokes stability as an explanatory principle. Evolution, it is argued, is likely to occur in the direction of those organic forms which are most likely to endure or survive.

Be it noted in passing that it is we who invent the descriptive language. It is we who define classes of events and say that certain of these classes shall be called "differentiation," and others "homogenization." When we shuffle a pack of cards, we expect the result to be a randomization of the pack, and would be surprised if on inspecting the pack after shuffling we found it sorted for suits. But it was we who invented the limited category of arrangements of cards which we call "sorted for suits," and actually no single member of this category is more improbable than any single member of the much larger category which we would call "randomized." It is only that the categories differ in size, and that we arbitrarily selected a category which we called "sorted" and which happens to be much smaller than the other.

Similarly with stability. That which is "stable" is *our* statement about a system. If these continue to be true, we say that the system is "stable." And it is usually necessary to specify what descriptive statement we are thinking of when we make this assertion.

To some of you what I am saying will seem irrelevant. To others it may seem elementary. What I am trying to develop is the notion that science is a language and, because it is a language, it necessarily deals with the universe as though that universe were composed of gestalten (which may indeed be the case, but about that we can have no knowledge). And further, that in describing events we impose two types of frames of reference upon them. One frame of reference, the probabilistic, which ignores the durational aspects of time, and another frame which includes this aspect of the matter.

Now let me invite you to consider some organism, pitted in a sort of game vis-à-vis a larger environment called Nature and consisting of all the other organisms and the physical conditions of existence. It does not much matter for my purpose whether you think of what is conventionally called a single organism, or a species, or a whole ecological system, like a redwood forest or a human community. By stochastic process this entity will choose certain courses of behavioral, physiologic, or anatomical change which will adapt it to the status quo.

But our organism is faced with very difficult problems of strategy.

The status quo has temporal characteristics that may be subject to change of various kinds, and while we may presume that any organism which exists has already survived those changes which have occurred in the status quo in the recent past, it cannot, in the nature of the case, predict other changes which may occur. Plants whose habitat is the talus of rolling stones on a mountain slope may be expected to have the sort of root system which can survive the frequent disturbances of the soil in which they live. Indeed, without such adaptation they could not be there. But the status quo may change. Some invading organism may bind the talus or some change in humidity may alter its characteristics. (The actual variable which caused the plant to develop and enormously elongate its root system may have been the aridity of the location. With increased humidity, the plant might not have this characteristic which happened to be adaptive also to the rolling environment.)

Moreover, there is a whole mass of changing characteristics of the environment which are brought about by the organism itself or by the total population of members of its species. A predator may almost exterminate its prey. Or there may be interactive changes so that as the prey evolves new methods of escape, the predator must evolve new methods of attack. The *system* in which prey and predator are combined may undergo progressive change. Each step of this change may be adaptive so far as the individual species is concerned, but the overall change in the larger system may be an increasing mutual dependence from which neither can escape. What I am suggesting is that the strategy for survival of a species or an ecological community can only be immediately *governed* by contingency, but is continually being *tested* in terms of longer time spans, larger gestalten, and unpredictable changes which cannot be foreseen.

Up to this point I have only been talking orthodox Darwinism. There is however a point to be added. Evidently, from what I have said already, the fight is not only to the strong or to the well adapted, it is also to the *flexible*. If we are to compute the probability of survival for a given organism which at this moment is prospering in a given environment, we must include in our computation some factor which shall represent the ability of that organism to survive under change and possibly adverse conditions. But we do not know what changes or what adverse difficulties the organism should be prepared for.

The creative, nonstatic characteristic of living things is precisely due to the capricious nature of their environment. And I use the word *caprice* advisedly.

What seems to happen is that the longer an adaptive characteristic continues to have positive survival value, the more this characteristic becomes entrenched in the organization of the creature. I am not speaking of a crude inheritance of acquired characteristics, but of an analogy deeper than this between evolutionary process and individual learning. Perhaps I may make the matter clear by pointing out that the phenomenon of habit is economical. If repeated experience of a certain type of context shows that a certain type of response is regularly success-ful, this response becomes habitual, and there results an economy of mental process whereby the habitual response can be immediately pro-duced without expenditure of effort upon those internal or external tri-als and errors which would be necessary if the situation were treated as unfamiliar. The phenomenon of habit is an economical shortcut to adaptation. It sets free for the solution of other problems those parts of the mind which are most flexible and are, if you like, the organs of adap-tive behavior.

In the same sort of way there is evidently in the evolutionary process a progressive incorporation of adaptation. Experimentally,[2] it appears that *if* the environment both causes the development of a given charac-teristic and is selective of those individuals which show this characteristic in most pronounced form, then there will be a tendency for this charac-teristic to appear in the genotype. We might say for example that the environment selects for the *potentiality* to produce this characteristic with minimum disturbance of adaptive function. As it is more economical to hand over a behavior pattern to habit, so also it appears to be more eco-nomical to hand over an acquired anatomical peculiarity to the deep-seated corpus of embryological instructions contained in the chromosomes.

---

2. C. H. Waddington, "Genetic Assimilation of an Acquired Character," *Evolution* 7, no. 2 (June 1953). C. H. Waddington, "The Integration of Gene-Controlled Processes and its Bearing on Evolution." *Caryologia*, vol. suppl., 1954.

When this has occurred the word *capricious* becomes appropriate to describe the sort of dirty trick that Nature plays upon the well-adapted organism. For many generations she has let this organism act on the assumption that some characteristic of hers could be relied upon. The organism has been led up the garden path until it has incorporated into its deeper structure those factors which produced the adaptation. And now, the characteristic of the environment undergoes change. This is, in a sense, most unfair. Nature encourages the organism to rely upon her and then shifts her tactics and says, "You see. You relied on me. Now look at you. You are a mess." But in another sense, or looked at in a wider perspective, this unfairness is the recurrent condition for evolutionary creativity.

This discussion of the evolutionary problem and the relationship between organism and environment is offered here as an introduction to a discussion of the problems of method in research in the field of schizophrenia.

It has been the hypothesis of our research at Palo Alto that schizophrenia has a formal etiology, very closely comparable to the sort of double bind which I have imagined as imposed upon the organism by the total environment in the long eons of the evolutionary process. We have predominantly thought of the double bind as a destructive experience—a trauma. But, if the analogy which I have been drawing is sound, then it is evident that while the experience of the double bind must always be partly unpleasant, it is also possible that this type of experience is an integral part of what we may vaguely call characterological growth. Without it, the individual would be in some sense static; even though with too much of it, he may be driven to schizophrenia. It looks as if differentiation and creativity—whatever these words mean—occur when the environment is neither too consistent nor too capricious.

Now, if the picture I have drawn is anything like right, the theory of games as it stands is only applicable to organisms of whatever kind at those infinitesimal moments when conditions are static and evolution is stationary. Precisely because all organisms including man are in process of evolution, and because this process is never completed, organisms can never have the simplicity or single-mindedness of the player in a Von Neumannian game. They are never equipped to solve all the problems which the rules can present and will never, by learning, achieve this complete equipment. They do not live in a universe in which the rules of the game are constant and above all they can never be motivated by simple "utility," of whatever sort.

This last point requires some examination. If two organisms, A and B, are engaged in a game from which neither can escape, the strategy of each will initially be determined by his "utility." If both are motivated by the same sort of utility, the position can be simple and static. If, however, A and B are differently motivated, an unstable position must result because the strategies which A will follow are of necessity contexts of learning for B. And, vice versa, B's strategies will provide learning contexts for A. There will therefore be a tendency toward a sharing of "values." This process evidently may proceed toward an intermediate uniformity or toward an end point in which either A's or B's values dominate the interchange. Notoriously, it is difficult to fight the philosophy of another individual without adopting the latter's philosophy as a determinant of one's own strategy. Proverbially, we are advised to fight fire with fire, and anybody who has ever engaged in psychotherapy—that battle of personal philosophies and "values"—will know how difficult it is for either of the two individuals to maintain the "game" without adopting the value premises of the other.

We are, I believe, very far from any mathematics which would be applicable to these phenomena. But, the phenomena must be systematically allowed for in our thinking about organisms in evolution, and in our thinking about the psychodynamics of family systems and the etiology of such conditions as schizophrenia. If the vis-à-vis adopts strategies which are not determined by any simple utility, but are in fact inconsistent in the sense that the frame within which the organism must choose a strategy is being continually changed, then we must expect the organism also to acquire something of these inconsistent characteristics of the vis-à-vis. Therefore, expectably, organisms, for systematic reasons, will be governed by utility systems much more complex than any which conventional games theory would posit. Specifically, we must expect the utility systems of real organisms to be labile or to have partially labile contextual frames.

If now we turn to what is known of the anatomy, physiology, and behavior of organisms, this is precisely what we find. Our a priori prediction is supported over and over again by the data. Over and over again we find organisms whose entire strategy will change from one period of time to another. In one phase the major preoccupation will be food, in another phase the animal may even cease to eat during a season of courtship or rutting. With the beginning of pregnancy the strategy may change again toward setting maximum value upon the next generation. And so on. Even among Protozoa there are shifts of this sort—periods of growth and fission, periods of sexual activity, periods of encystment, and so on.

We know very little about what determines the sequence of these periods or their duration, or precipitates the change from one period to another. Indeed, these phenomena are difficult to investigate except in those cases where some simple environmental variable precipitates change. Evidently, however, this is not the whole story. There are many cases in which the change is a function of inner physiologic rhythms.

Again, if we look at the broader sweep of the evolutionary series, it would appear that, insofar as we can say that evolution is progressive from the simple to the more complex, we can also say that there is a progressive increase in the particular sort of flexibility which I am discussing. The astonishing phenomenon of telencephalization which has been characteristic of the evolution of the brain, from such organisms as Amphioxus through to Man, has consisted, at each step, in adding new circuits on top of those previously existing. Now what we know of servomechanisms and control systems indicates that the addition of new circuits on top of old ones must always (if adaptive) be an addition of metacontrols. The new circuits are in a metarelationship to the old. The information which enters the new circuit is information *about* what is happening in the old, and the output of the new circuits is either a modification of what is occurring in the old, or is a modification of the output of the old circuits.

Again, the same pattern of increased complexity is recognizable in the evolutionary sweep from unicellular organism through cell colony, to metazoan organism with differentiated organs, and on to the evolution of highly complex and differentiated communities of metazoan individuals. The highest products of such an evolution, the complex communities, demand of their component parts precisely the sort of flexibility which I have discussed above, namely the ability to compromise between a utility based upon the smaller gestalt, the individual, and a utility system derived from the larger unit, the community.

In sum, the inner functional topology of the circuits which determine behavior comes to be a reflexion of, or a microcosmic diagram of, the total matrix, nature, in which the microcosm is embedded and of which it is a part. It used to be said that the organism, Man, was created in the image of God. And it was perhaps an error to reverse this statement and say that Man created God in his own image. It looks as if, in truth, every organism is of necessity created in the image of nature, or should we say creates itself in an image of nature under her strict jurisdiction.

Some of you may think that this rather wide canvas of speculation upon which I have been working is irrelevant to the pragmatic and immediate questions of research method. I do not think so. Research plans and methods are, of necessity, determined by the scientist's opinions—and often only half-conscious opinions—about what sort of thing he is dealing with. And I have tried to answer for you in the first half of my speech the question—"What seems to be the epistemological structure of the field in which we propose to do research?" If you think that the field of communicational behavior is structured in lineal chains of cause and effect, you will do certain sorts of research, and I believe that your research will be stultified by the epistemological error in your premise. I have tried to give you a more sophisticated premise, but we shall hardly know for another fifty years whether it will stand. If, however, you adopt it as an epistemological hypothesis, it will determine the questions you ask and the procedures which you follow.

Let me now talk about the problem of how to study the communicational homeostasis of a family constellation. Grossly, it seems to us that the families which contain known schizophrenic members appear to be narrowly homeostatic. Every living system undergoes changes from moment to moment and from day to day, and these changes could conceivably be represented by the wanderings of a curve in a multidimensional graph (or "phase space"), in which each variable necessary to the description of the states of the system would be represented by one dimension of the graph. And specifically, when I say that these families are *narrowly* homeostatic, I mean that the roaming of this graph, or the wandering of this point in phase space, will cover a comparatively limited volume. The system is homeostatic in the sense that when it approaches the limits of its areas of freedom, the direction of its path will change so that the wandering will never cross the limits. And for these families these limits are narrow. As the small boy said of his crib: "The sides are too near the middle."

But the task of the research man is not to make generalizations of this sort, it is to demonstrate the actual processes by which this homeostasis is maintained, and this is a formidable task for which he will need to travel light.

Let him first throw out the window as epistemologically inappropriate all the conventional ideas which derive from lineal chains of causation. I mean, for example, any expectation that the etiology of schizophrenia might be based upon some identifiable characteristic of some identifiable individual in the triad father–mother–child. Schizophrenia is not caused by "overprotective mothers," or by overstrong fathers, or by weak fathers, or by any psychological characteristic of any given individual—if indeed individuals have psychological characteristics, which I rather doubt. My suspicion is that they have only *patterns* which determine how they will learn in certain constellations of interaction with other individuals.

Be that as it may, we assume that we are looking for *circuits* of causation and interaction and that all phrasings, as that schizophrenia is caused by overprotective mothers, refer at best only to segments of such circuits. So that the overprotective mother can only be an effective cause of schizophrenia if she happens to be a part of a larger constellation which will determine the schizophrenic response to this overprotectiveness.

Now, we have shifted the gestalt of our thinking; we have discarded questions about the action of one part upon another and have substituted questions about the system as a whole. And we find ourselves in a rather unusual situation because our point of observation is *inside* the system which we are seeking to study. Almost the whole of science has been devoted to trying to explain the external characteristics of entities by creating hypotheses about what is inside them and, historically, the progress of this activity has been from the smaller to the larger. It was inevitable that sooner or later we would face the problem of studying systems which we would be unable to view from the outside.[3]

We are in the position of certain electronic engineers during the war, whose task it was to dissect electronic "black boxes" which had been captured from the enemy and to determine from the internal circuit structure of these boxes what functions they were intended to perform and with what degrees of accuracy they might perform these functions. We are to determine, from what happens between the component individuals—the parts of the family constellation—what the total characteristics of the system may be. This involves methodological problems of no mean order.

However, to help us think about these problems we have a good deal that is already known about systems theory, and especially some of the things which I said earlier when the systems which I was discussing were organisms or communities of organisms vis-à-vis "nature." We know for example that any characteristic be it anatomical, physiological, or behavioral will, if it continue to be adaptive over considerable periods of time, be sunk deeper and deeper in the organizational structure of the system. That is, the constellation of causes which bring about the adaptive characteristic will gradually change in such a way that, when this process reaches its later stages, a gross disruption of the total system may be necessary to prevent the production of the previously adaptive characteristic. Moreover, the dilemma in which the system then finds itself will be formally comparable with what we call the double bind. It will appear to the system (again personifying) as if it can only achieve external adaptation at the price of internal disruption.

---

3. When systems become astronomically large, it is again easy for us to do a partial study from what seems to us to be an external position—we being so very small.

But a similar dilemma seems to beset the individuals of whom the family constellation is composed. They, too, and especially the identified schizophrenic patient, feel that external adaptation could only be achieved at the price of internal disruption and, to this view of the family environment, the patient *adapts* by forms of communicational behavior in which either the internal world, or the external, or both, is implicitly or even explicitly denied.

What we are studying is a whole (the family) made up of parts (the individuals) such that both the whole and the parts of which it is made have similar formal characteristics, and our task is to test and substantiate this description. In the course of this process, as the description gathers substance, it will undoubtedly undergo modification and correction.

Let me first try to give substance to the idea that families which contain identifiable schizophrenics are narrowly homeostatic. It is characteristic of these families that they are unable to reach decisions. No individual in the constellation will take responsibility for settling any matter in a decisive manner. We might suppose from this that the family would as a result lack rigidity and be free to undergo profound changes. This, however, is not the case. We might almost say that the family as a unit is rigidly indecisive.

In terms of what I have said earlier about the economics of flexibility, this makes a great deal of sense. As long as indecision is maintained the family unit can roam within a limited list of states, $S_1 \ldots$ to $S_n$, but is limited to this list of states. If one of these states were decisively selected and sunk to the level of a parameter of the system the available states would then not include $S_1$ to $S_n$, (of which all but one are now excluded), but would include a new set which can come into being the moment a choice is made among the first set. The act of decision is, as it were, a parametric change and from then on a new set of choices exist which were not formerly accessible. Freedom to wander into new regions of phase space follows only when some choice has been made among the alternatives in the old region.

This is the converse of what I said above. I said that an organism achieves an economy of its more flexible apparatus by "sinking" its adaptive processes to deeper parts of its organization. Conversely, if it does not sink its adaptive mechanisms, these must be continually occupied in solving and re-solving the old problems.

At the individual level, we already have some natural history knowledge of the types of behavior in individual A which will prevent habit formation in individual B. These are in fact the patterns of double binding.

What I have called habit formation or the sinking of adaptive mechanisms into the deeper organization is synonymous with the development of self. But at the family level, we do not as yet have this natural history knowledge, and I must go out on a limb to predict the sort of phenomena which this approach leads me to expect.

We are concerned with a question which can be summarized as "What would be the dynamics of group indecision?," and when put in this way we have at least hints of an answer. Again, the most sophisticated answer is the complex analysis in Von Neumann and Morgenstern's book on the theory of games and economic behavior, in which it is demonstrated that in all those games where coalition between players is of the essence of the game, the total group of players (if more than three in number) will be unable to reach any stable pattern of coalition. A less complex case will however suffice for the present discussion.

Let us consider the case of three voters, A, B, and C, who are to choose between three alternatives, x, y, and z. Now let us suppose that A's preference order is x, y, z; while B's preference order is y, z, x; and C's preference order is z, x, y.

Now we offer the three alternatives to the three voters. A will vote for x. B will vote for y. But, what C does will depend upon whether he knows what A and B have voted for. If he has no knowledge about A and B, he will vote for z, which is his preferred alternative. The group as a whole will then be unable to reach a decision since one vote each has been cast for each alternative.

If, on the other hand, C has information about how A and B voted, then he will observe that he can get his second preference by voting the way B did. The system can then make a stable decision. We may make the general statement that where the three persons vote in a sequence, and there is information about the previous voting, the third person in such a system can always obtain his second preference and the system will settle to this alternative.

Now let us consider the diagrammatic three-person family, father–mother–child. This unit is characterized by two different orders of communication. There is bi-polar communication between each pair of individuals, father–mother, mother–child, and father–child. But there is also a more complex set of inputs for each individual because each receives information about what goes on between the other two. Father observes what happens between mother and child. Mother observes what happens between father and child. Child observes what happens between father and mother.

Every message, in this sense, exists in two contexts. If father is speaking to child, his message is not only part of the relationship father–child, but also has to be seen as part of the relationship father–mother–child. And such a double contextual frame is ideal for the creation of double binds.

We are discussing the dynamics of group indecision, and I must answer the question "indecision about what?" The two diagrammatic examples which I briefly outlined—the case of the many-person game involving coalition and the case of the population of three persons voting for one of three alternatives—these examples were both instances of indecision about patterns of coalition. I submit that this is the essence of the matter. For formal purposes it is irrelevant to ask about the content of the matter to be decided. If, for example, the family is undecided as to where it will go for a vacation, this indecision must of necessity be reducible to indecision about coalitions. If some member of the family proposes a holiday at the beach and this suggestion can neither be followed by the other members nor can it be discarded, then this characteristic group behavior can always be described so as to be reducible to statements about coalitions. No pair of individuals can make their coalition, as implied by their joint preference, stick against the criticisms of the third person; and no single individual can make his opinion stick—he cannot maintain his isolated stand against the other two.

If then the characteristic of these families which we call group indecision is synonymous with a statement about the instability of their coalitions, it should follow that any change in family communication which will favor the formation of coalitions or will hinder their breakup should make it easier for the family as a whole to reach decisions.

Under experimental conditions, communication within the family can be restricted in various ways, and at this point I would like to go out on the limb which I mentioned earlier to make some predictions about experiments which we hope to perform in Palo Alto with the aid of Dr. Alexander Bavelas, but which have not yet been performed. Be it understood that these are of necessity highly abstract predictions and must be hedged by some precautionary clause: "*If* we can construct the appropriate experimental conditions, we predict such and such results."

It seems to me that an important condition of family life is the fact that when the three persons are together, every interchange between two persons is cross-monitored by the third, and that this cross-monitoring could be rather easily restricted under experimental conditions. It would therefore be possible to find out which families are most able to function with cross-monitoring, and which families are most able to function when cross-monitoring is excluded. My prediction would be that appropriate experimental conditions can be devised in which the schizophrenic families will be able to perform better with exclusion of cross-monitoring than they can with freedom of cross-monitoring. And further, that under these conditions normal families will do better *with* cross-monitoring and worse with exclusion of cross-monitoring.

This prediction, however, is offered only as an illustration of a method and I want to stress in conclusion that this method which I have tentatively offered grows out of what I earlier called an epistemology—a set of premises regarding what sort of objects these are which we propose to study. Or, if you wish me to translate the word epistemology more precisely, let me say that what I have offered you are premises regarding the sort of knowledge which can be appropriately called an understanding of these systems.

## References

Von Neumann, John, and Oskar Morgenstern. 1944. *Theory of Games and Economic Behavior.* Princeton, N.J.: Princeton University Press.

Waddington, C. H. 1957. *The Strategy of the Genes.* London: George Allen and Unwin Ltd.

# 9

# *Cultural Problems Posed by a Study of Schizophrenic Process*[*][1]

## The Steady State in Anthropology and Psychiatry

In the years immediately following World War II, there occurred a significant change in the whole structuring of theory in the behavioral sciences. These were the years during which cybernetics, information theory, and the theory of games provided us with entirely new and much more rigorous models for thinking about social and interpersonal processes. The rather crude concepts of *equilibrium* which we had developed before the war were replaced by the more rigorous and more flexible ideas associated with the words *steady state,* which will be used to refer to those equilibria which are maintained by homeostatic mechanisms.

To illustrate this change: fieldwork in a New Guinea community had shown us two processes at work. On the one hand, various sorts of symmetrical rivalry among individuals and groups were observed and it was evident that such rivalrous sequences of interaction could be progressive and therefore ultimately pathogenic. If A's rivalrous behavior provokes rivalry in B and vice versa, then unless some corrective phenomenon

*This lecture was delivered to the Symposium on Schizophrenia, American Psychiatric Association symposium of the Hawaiian Divisional Meeting, 1958, in San Francisco. Reprinted from *Schizophrenia: An Integrated Approach,* edited by Alfred Auerback, 1959. Discussion material has been deleted.

1. The ideas in this lecture represent the combined thinking of the staff of the Project for the Study of Schizophrenic Communication. The staff consists of Gregory Bateson, Jay D. Haley, John H. Weakland, Donald D. Jackson, M.D., and William F. Fry, M.D. The project is financed by the Josiah Macy, Jr. Foundation, administered by the Department of Anthropology at Stanford University, and functions at the Veterans Administration Hospital, Palo Alto, California.

occurs, the system must go on to disruption. On the other hand, the second process observed involved complementary themes such as dominance-submission, exhibitionism-spectatorship, and succoring-dependence, where the behavior of B fit in with but was not the same as that of A.

It appeared, moreover, that these complementary themes of action were in some sense the psychological opposites of the symmetrical themes. In a symmetrical relationship, if A is ahead of B in some psychological direction, B will respond by trying to catch up, whereas in a complementary relationship, B, if he is already behind, will lag further behind. Or, we may put it this way: in a symmetrical relationship B's strength is a stimulus for A's aggression; whereas in a complementary relationship A's aggression will appear when he sees B's weakness.

This psychological contrast between two themes of human relationship presented the beginnings of a hypothesis which would account for the fact that in a culture where both themes were highly developed, neither theme could progress to such an intensity as to disrupt the system. The hypothesis was that the culture maintained psychological equilibrium by a balancing of these two contrary processes, either of which by itself would lead to disruption. But there was no way of explaining why these two trends should happen to be of equal strength.

When the data were reexamined in terms of steady-state theory, it became evident that the culture does not depend upon mere coincidence to balance the two contradictory trends, but that, in fact, an excess of symmetrical behavior touches off rituals which emphasize complementarity, and vice versa.

The details of this example have been published elsewhere (Bateson, 1936, 1958). Here it suffices to present two ideas connected with the concept *steady state:* (a) that progressive change in whatever direction must of necessity disrupt the status quo; and (b) that a system may contain homeostatic or feedback loops which will limit or redirect these otherwise disruptive processes.

All steady states, of course, are not desirable nor is all irreversible change undesirable. And if the discussion so far has come close to suggesting this, it is because the presentation is deliberately oversimplified by exclusion of the larger gestalten or contexts, and especially those which involve long epochs of time. The homeostasis of the New Guinea culture which has been briefly dissected here may well be such as to prevent that culture from undergoing adaptive change under the impact of twentieth-century conditions, and the steady state which in one sense is so beautifully balanced may in a wider context contribute to the death of the system. The norms of a culture may be such that in the long run that culture cannot live with its neighbors or cannot live within the wider framework of an embracing industrial civilization. In such a case we would have to say that the homeostasis is undesirable in terms of this wider setting.

To illustrate more concretely: in New Guinea the actual rituals of complementary behavior, which correct for excess of symmetrical rivalry, involve sexual transvestism. It is easily conceivable that these rituals might be prohibited by missionaries or the Occidental government. In such a case, to obey the government would be to risk internal disruption.

This general theoretical approach seems immediately applicable to the problems of schizophrenia. What we have done above is to imagine a culture placed in a double bind. From its own point of view, the culture faces either external extermination or internal disruption, and the dilemma is so constructed as to be a dilemma of *self*-preservation in the most literal sense. Under no circumstances can the preexisting "self" survive. Every move seems to propose either extermination by the larger environment or the pains of inner disruption. Even if the culture elects for external adaptation and by some feat achieves the necessary inner metamorphosis, that which survives will be a different "self."

This brief personification of the cultural system will indicate how it happens that the double-bind paradigm is specifically destructive of self-identification.

## The Steady State of the Schizophrenic Family

Following is outlined in formal terms the sort of interaction which we find to be characteristic of the natural history of families which contain schizophrenic or near schizophrenic individuals. First and foremost, that which is characteristic is a very tough stability which Jackson has referred to as *homeostasis* (1957). We are not yet in a position to say exactly what variables touch off the corrective processes of this homeostasis, but still the behavior of the system as a whole justifies the use of the word. When the identified patient begins to get well, we observe all sorts of subtle pressure being exerted to perpetuate his illness. However, as is well known, there are many cases in which, as the patient gets well, some other member of the family starts to show symptoms of psychiatric stress. It follows that these families are not simply homeostatic around the invalid status of the particular identified patient. It would seem then that the variables which must at all costs be kept constant are somewhat more abstract or more secret in nature. It is not that at all costs the identified patient must be kept confused; rather it seems as if the patient himself is an accessory—even a willing sacrifice—to the family homeostasis. If he ceases to play this role, there is a likelihood that some other member of the family will assume it in his place. Like many complex homeostatic systems, the pathogenic family seems to be able, like a newt, to regenerate a missing limb.

This type of phenomenon is of course very familiar in the wider field of group dynamics (Redl, 1959). But its nature and mechanisms are in general obscure except in those cases where definite procedures exist for the regenerative process. We know something of how a committee regenerates a new chairman in place of one who has been lost, but we know virtually nothing of the process which occurs when the same committee loses a member who had inconspicuously performed certain catalytic functions in its meetings. Sometimes "spontaneously" another member who had previously been inactive takes over those functions.

Analogous phenomena also occur in many biological systems. If, for example, the apical shoot of a Christmas tree is cut off, *one* of the first whorl of branches below the cut will bend upward and replace the lost apex. This branch will then lose its former bilateral symmetry and become radially symmetrical like any other apical shoot. Such systems are perhaps best thought of as, in some sense, competitive. The various individuals (in this case, branches) of which the system is composed would seem to be so mutually related that, by their interactions, one will always be selected as the "winner" or as the "loser." This individual then becomes specialized in the functions of this position and in performing these functions actively prevents the other individuals from taking over this specialized role.

The "identified" patient has been mentioned and also the replacement of this individual by another, but it is sometimes not as easy as we politely assume to identify one member of such a family as more specifically sick than the others. If we define schizophrenia not in terms of the ability to meet the outside world but more formally in terms of the distortions of communication, then we get a picture of three or four individuals, all with distorted habits of communication but all fitting as differentiated members of a family subculture.[2] This pathogenic subculture is no doubt idiosyncratic or deviant from the subculture of other families in the community, but the problem of homeostasis in this particular family is perhaps not fundamentally different from problems of cultural homeostasis in general.

------

2. For a study of subcultural contrast between families in the normal range see the film "Communication and Interaction in Three Families" by G. Bateson and W. Kees.

The members of the pathogenic family are differentiated in their roles and form an interacting and self-maintaining system within which it is scarcely possible to point to one member as causative for the characteristics of the system as a whole. Indeed, the assigning of cause or blame to one or other member of such a plexus presents problems rather similar to those presented by the question: "Who is most sick?" The identified patient is most overtly sick, but the family system itself is undoubtedly strange and the strangeness may be specifically located not in the individuals but in the premises governing the differentiation of their roles.

What we observe is homeostatic limitation of change to a narrowly circumscribed region. In fact, in many cases, it looks as if the schizophrenogenic family can only be *stable*, i.e., stay within its restricted limits of change, in the presence of a *reductio ad absurdum* of that philosophy which underlies the role differentiation of the members, and as if this function is supplied by the identified patient.

A philosophy of human relationships which to be viable needs the presence of its own confutation?

The idea is not exactly new. We know, for example, that the philosophy of the police state can be maintained only in the presence of ostensible criminals and that such a state, if it lacks or cannot detect the real article, will focus attention upon innocent scapegoats. Sometimes even the *myth* of subversive attack may contribute to stabilizing such a philosophic system.

"Prisons are built with the stones of law and brothels with bricks of religion"—and so on. And it is significant that the sociological system—the police state—chosen here to exemplify those philosophies which are stable only in the presence of their own confutation, is in fact a system which promotes paranoid and other schizophrenic symptoms among its members.

It is significant also that this philosophic system, in spite of its ruthlessness, insists upon a superficial benevolence and may even call itself a "Welfare State."

These, however, are only analogies and poetic images. What is needed first from the anthropologists is a general theory of family homeostasis. This will be, no doubt, an abstract theoretical model, deductive from some set of axioms. It will probably owe much to the modern theory of games and perhaps as much to recent developments in the field of genetics and embryology. Already anthropologists and others are beginning to work on this and related problems (Bavelas, 1959; Romney, 1956; Von Neumann and Morgenstern, 1955; and Waddington, 1957), but it will be several years before they give us much help. For the present we have to concentrate our thinking about family subcultures within the more narrow field of the pathogenic family.

## The Family System as Seen by Two Individuals

A composite picture of the interactions in such families, derived from our film recordings of their behavior and our attempts at family therapy, here follows. The schizophrenic communication of the identified patient is appropriate to his perception of what goes on between himself and the other members of the family. He "sees" himself as continually placed in contexts of a certain sort, and it is only fair to say that the context at any given moment is in part determined by his own previous behavior. The other members of the family act and communicate in ways which reinforce the patient's perception and behavior, but they, too, like him, are acting appropriately in the contexts as they perceive them and are themselves contributing by their own previous action to determine the context at any given moment. From the point of view of the patient, the contexts have the following formal structure: a parent whom he intensely both loves and hates emits signals of an incongruent nature. This incongruence is perhaps most clear when one half of the parent's behavior precedes an act of the patient and the other half follows. The parent will, for example, invite the patient to express a courageous opinion, and when that opinion is expressed, will disparage it as unloving, disloyal, disobedient, etc. Characteristically, the first half of the parent's behavior will appear to be set in a certain mode or philosophy of interpersonal relations, while the second half is a denial of this mode and the substitution of another. The first might, for example, be joking (or serious). The patient gives an appropriate response to this mood and finds that the mood has been switched on him. The preliminary smile was only a trap, or the preliminary seriousness was only a trap preceding mockery.

From the patient's point of view his response, sandwiched between these two modalities, can only be destructive of self. *He* is eliminated in the same sense that the "self" is destroyed in the example given earlier of a culture faced with a double bind. The self which responded seriously to the parental signal must be revised in favor of another self when that serious response is received by the parent as something other than what it was.

If I say something which I intend to be serious and the audience laughs, I may be tempted toward an image of myself as a humorous speaker, but this self-image also may be later destroyed in the same sort of way. If the group here assembled is nonpathogenic, I shall have a chance to settle down to a consistent image of self. If this group is pathogenic, it will never permit this settling down to occur—and I, in turn, will not allow the group to permit it to occur!

There are other features of the context which must also be mentioned. From the point of view of the identified patient, there is, or appears to be, an absolute prohibition upon calling attention to the parent's incongruity in any overt way. It was said that the patient "sees" himself as in a bind, but this must now be qualified to say that the prohibition upon comment may be so strong as to result in something like a repression of his perception of the bind. Neither the parent nor the patient is able to act as if fully aware of the incongruities.

There is also a prohibition upon escaping from the field, and, in addition, an insistence on the part of the parent that the patient respond. There shall be no nonresponding and no not caring. And all these prohibitions are linked together. After all, to leave the field or to express "not caring" would be to point a finger at the incongruities.

## The Typical Schizophrenic Message

Under these circumstances, the human being will appropriately protect himself by emitting messages which cannot be maltreated. Characteristically, this is done by stripping the message of all explicit or implicit metacommunicative material. For instance, if you look at a Western Union telegraph blank, you will see that it has a space for the text of the message and a number of other spaces for material which will label this text, classifying the message under such categories as to whom, from whom, date, place, time, priority, codes used, and so forth. All this latter material—the procedural part of his message—the schizophrenic will omit or distort. In addition, he will distort the text itself at precisely those points where procedural or metacommunicative inferences might be drawn. For example, pronouns will be avoided, and similarly he will avoid all indications of what sort of relationship might obtain between himself and the person he is addressing. He will falsify the priorities of his utterance, indicating a high importance for a relatively trivial message or denying the importance of a message which he feels to be vital. In addition, he may code the message in a metaphoric form without indicating that such a code is being used. Even a second metaphoric code may be superposed upon the first. Lastly, the message, so distorted, may be made to simulate an objective message about some other subject in the real world. The schizophrenic may even make very small changes in a straightforward message, changes just sufficient to enable him to tell himself secretly that this is not *his* message. He may, for example, call himself W. Edward Jones, when his real name is Edward W. Jones—like a child who crosses his fingers behind his back while telling a fib.

But the identified schizophrenic may engage in attack as well as defense. He may attempt to turn the tables upon the parent, either by responding as though the parent's initial message were of some sort different from what the parent intended, or he may seek to impose upon the parent those prohibitions which surround the double bind—the prohibition on commenting upon incongruity or the prohibition on withdrawing from the field—or he may attempt to insist upon response.

All of this, both attack and defense, is sane behavior in the sense of being understandable under the circumstances as defined—by the schizophrenic subject. The boundary of sanity is, however, crossed when the subject uses these tricks of communication in situations which the common man—one hesitates to say the "normal"—would not perceive as the schizophrenic seems to perceive them.

This discussion is not meant to digress into an elaborate discussion of learning theory (Bateson, 1942; Harlow, 1949; Ruesch and Bateson, 1951). It is limited to asserting that recurrent experience of reinforcing contexts, which, though they may vary in content have again and again the same formal pattern, will result in a learning to expect this formal pattern. The individual with such experience will expect the repetition of such patterns and will even act as though such patterns surrounded him. And he will do this even when the indications for the existence of these patterns are minimal or would be subliminal for other persons with a different history. For example, the whole theory of transference in Freudian psychoanalysis depends upon this or some similar assumption. The patient is seen as responding to the analyst as though the latter were behaving in ways in which the patient perhaps unconsciously believes that his parent behaved. In other words, he responds in the presence of the analyst as if the latter's communication provided patterned contexts similar to those in which he learned his eating, walking, sphincter control, and the like.

In terms of this premise from learning theory, it becomes expectable that the individual subjected to repeated double-bind traumata will act as though this traumatic context continually surrounds him, even at times when more normal individuals would regard such behavior as "crazy."

So much for the identified overtly schizophrenic member of the family whom I have pictured as vis-à-vis a "parent." Actually, he must in general deal with two parents, and I shall now describe the family system from their points of view.

One of the patients with whom we have worked extensively sent to his mother on Mother's Day a commercially printed card which said "For someone who has been like a mother to me." In so doing, he was of course putting her in a double bind. From her point of view, any future spontaneous maternal behavior on her part was threatened with being relabeled and perhaps mislabeled as some sort of theatrical display and hypocrisy not coming from the heart. However much the son's jibe may have been deserved, it was still a threat to the mother's "self." She immediately came to the hospital with the card in her hand "to know what he meant." With extreme courage the son managed to say that he had meant "to sting her a little," but this reply she could not accept; she had to force him to complete confusion and a verbal agreement that it was "all a mistake."[3]

This incident illustrates one of the most destructive forms of double bind, namely the attack upon spontaneity or sincerity. This is overtly used by the parent when the identified patient does something which might seem to be generous or kind. "You only did it to please me. You didn't really *mean* it" or even "you only did it because I asked you to." And conversely, every therapist who has dealt with the overtly psychotic person is familiar with the patient's suspicious attack (often covert) upon his therapist's motives and spontaneity. Characteristically this species of double bind sets the inner process of the mind or heart against the outward overt behavior, and the victim is placed in precisely the position which I envisaged for the New Guinea culture: either the inner man must be sacrificed or the outer behavior will court destruction.

In fact, the double-binding interaction is a sort of battle around the question of whose self shall be destroyed. And a basic characteristic of the family, which is shared by all the relevant members, is the premise that the self is destroyed or can be destroyed in this battle—and *therefore* the fight must go on.[4] "Tweedledum and Tweedledee *agreed* to have a battle."

But in the families which we have studied we find almost universally implicit agreement on the part of the parents to deny that any such bat-

---

3. Compare Jay D. Haley, "The Family of the Schizophrenic: A Model System." *Am. J. Nerv. Ment. Dis.* 129 (1959): 357–74.

4. For a mathematical analysis of the conditions for homeostatic balance in armaments races, see, for example, L. F. Richardson, "Generalized Foreign Politics," *British Journal of Psychology Monograph Supplement*, no. 23 (1939).

tle exists. And the identified patient, though he may know about the battle, dares not remark upon it. The family, after all, is not an isolated entity. It is a part of the larger community and has all sorts of contacts outside, and the "sane" members of the family are always anxious about these. One patient neatly expressed the matter when I asked him what he thought his mother was most afraid of. He replied "the aperiential securities," neatly telescoping into a single neologism both her fear of outward loss of prestige vis-à-vis the neighbors should she cease to maintain physiologic control, and her inner fear of what her bowels might do if she should succeed in controlling them.

The role of the father seems in general to be less heroic than that of either the patient or the mother. And indeed one's first impulse when confronted with such a family is to try to give the father a shot in the arm which will enable him to stand up and challenge the basic hypocrisy and cruelty with which he is surrounded. Perhaps this impulse is appropriate. I do not know as yet.

Be that as it may, the father, as he is, acts as another factor in maintaining the family homeostasis within its restricted range. His behavior vis-à-vis the identified patient may range from giving his passive consent to the operations of the mother—which operations she commonly practices also upon him—to an active participation in constructing traumatic contexts for the patient. He may join in the insistence that the patient shall not escape from the field and in the insistence that the patient respond. He may actively tease the patient, thereby further reducing the latter's self-confidence; and it is probable (though here our data are poor) that the father may contribute to the double binds by remarks which are contrapuntal to the messages of the mother, so that the identified patient is sometimes sandwiched not between two utterances of the mother, but between an utterance of hers and another coming from the father.

In one instance, the mother scolded her sixteen-year-old psychotic son for calling his three-year-old younger sister a "boy." The father joined her in forbidding this, and she turned on him and told him to shut up—*she* would handle it. If the boy obeyed his father even when the father was only repeating what the mother had said, he would be going against his mother's wishes.

As regards the related matter of conflict between mother and father, the findings are clear: *covert* conflict tends to increase the psychotic symptoms of the identified patient, whereas the change from covert to overt conflict tends to diminish these symptoms. And the same generalization seems to apply to authority figures *in loco parentis*, such as the doctor and the nurse (Stanton and Schwartz, 1954).

No doubt the concealment of the conflict constitutes a message to the identified patient: probably a command that he shall not comment upon the disagreement. This may be sufficient to evoke from him that behavior which he has learned to exhibit in those double-bind contexts. But the matter is not clear and the concealment of the parental conflict might equally be, to that offspring, a destructive demand for self-control. Interestingly enough in the Balinese ritual drama, trance behavior is evoked in the young men by *overt* conflict between Witch and Dragon, the parental protagonists (Bateson and Mead, 1942).

## The Cultural Problems

The following summary of the clinical picture of the family is an effort to bring out some of the questions which anthropologists might answer. What has here been sketched is unfortunately not a theory of schizophrenia, nor even a theory of the communicational aspects of that pathology. Rather, it is a *family* of such theories. From what has been said, one could construct a vast range of different communicational models, any one of which would be possibly schizophrenogenic. I have not attempted to select one of these alternatives, nor have I even attempted any classification within the family of possible explanatory models. For example, too great a focus on the mother in the pathogenic family has been avoided because there is no a priori reason within the theory which would lead us to expect this relative to have special significance. It is true, of course, that she has special functions in the prenatal and infantile period of life. But this circumstance is, in a sense, irrelevant or accidental to the formal cybernetic model. The entities or individuals composing such a model are not human, and schizophrenogenic models could therefore be set up in which the role assigned to the mother could be assigned to any other member of the intimate unit, or—and this is the more interesting case—this role could be unlocalized. The family unit as a whole could behave *as if* it contained a member whose role would be that assigned here to the pathogenic mother; but it conceivably might contain no such member. The pathogenic nature of the family unit might result only from its characteristics as an organizational network. If we see an engine behaving as if it contained a governor, we are not entitled from this external characteristic of the engine to say that in fact there is a *localized* governor inside the system. The self-corrective characteristic of the system may result from the total network structure.

To summarize, then, what can be said about the family of theories offered here, what are the common characteristics of all members of this family of theories?

(1)   The theories assume three levels or systems of gestalten: A, B, and C, so related that A is a part of B, and B is a part of C.

(2)   In this system of wheels within wheels, the A's are entities capable of internal homeostasis, complex learning, and complex external communication with each other. They are the analogues of human individuals.

(3)   The gestalt called B is composed of several A's. It is the analogue of the family. This unit also is characterized by internal homeostasis and probably certain sorts of primitive learning.

(4)   The largest gestalt, C, is the analogue of the community. It is composed of many B's. This, too, is a homeostatic unit, complexly organized, and susceptible of changes which are the sociological analogues of learning.

(5)   The theories of pathogenic process suggest that these three homeostatic gestalten may be interrelated in the following way: The A's, or individuals, contain processes of the "positive feedback" or "regenerative" type, i.e., processes which, if uncontrolled, would lead to unlimited directional change and therefore to the destruction of the A system as such. These regenerative processes are, however, limited by superposed homeostatic controls. (It will be noted that these statements about the internal functioning of the individuals are beyond the scope of psychological or anthropological investigation. We can only see and hear the external communication of the individual. Inside the "black box" is physiology.)

(6)   The unit B is so constructed that its stability depends upon some process in a direction which precludes or is precluded by the homeostatic processes within the individuals. The family can be stable only if the individual relaxes that internal control upon which his personal stability depends.

(7)   Similarly, the stability of B within the larger community unit C depends upon homeostatic processes which preclude those upon which the stability of B depends.

Our prediction amounts to this: in any such total system, the units at the B level, the families, will have the characteristics which we have called *schizophrenogenic*. That is, the identity of the component individuals will be blurred in their communications with each other, and every component individual will be under some pressure pushing him or her toward that *reductio ad absurdum* of the blurring of identity which we call *schizophrenia*.

Lastly, the stability of the family unit will be enhanced if one member of the family takes this path toward the *reductio ad absurdum*.

With this generalized picture, let me now turn to my colleagues in anthropology and present them with some questions:

(1) Anthropology has devoted a great deal of work since the publication of Ruth Benedict's *Patterns of Culture* to showing how character formation operates in different cultures. In the main, they have shown that the patterns of child raising and the family configuration within which the child is a member are congruent with the patterns of adult life in the various areas of religion, mythology, warfare, technology, art, etc. But the accent has been put upon answering always the positive question: "How are the babies in the given culture made into characteristic members of that culture?" Now here is the converse question: "How are the babies prevented from becoming exaggerated versions—caricatures—of the cultural norm?" We know that in some cultures such exaggerations of particular cultural patterns occur sporadically from time to time. What failures of what preventive process lead to these sporadic exaggerations? And how is their more frequent occurrence prevented?

(2) The first question is really the paradigm for the others. What we need in order to construct a generalized theory of the family (within which the pathogenic family will be a special case) is a mapping of the homeostatic mechanisms which determine family organizations. How are the three homeostatic systems listed above—the individual, the family, and the community— interrelated so as to avoid the conflicts of homeostasis which are here proposed as pathogenic? The anthropologists have given one-half of an answer to questions about homeostasis. They collect the data which will demonstrate that learning, or character formation, or organizational differentiation proceed in some given direction. But they do not also ask the converse question: "What are the upper limits of process in this direction?" Is the process limited by some corrective feedback? And what variables activate this feedback? What "symptoms" in individual behavior or subgroup characteristics serve to evoke the corrective process?

(3) And apart from these general questions about homeostasis in human communities, what has been said about schizophrenia poses a number of more specific questions. It is not much use

to ask the anthropologist to bring us statistics about the incidence of schizophrenia in different cultures, until the disease has been defined in some way which will be cross-culturally acceptable. We can, however, ask questions about the sorts of family pathology that occur in the particular cultures which anthropologists study. I have mentioned earlier the very conspicuous differences in family subculture which occur among the middle-class families in urban northern California.[5] We need similar studies of family subcultures in the supposedly more homogenous preliterate communities. Work of this kind is a necessary preliminary to a study of the pathologies of family homeostasis in different cultural settings. Only after this can we meaningfully ask about the specific roles of father, mother, spouse, grandparents, and so forth, in the pathogenic families in the particular culture.

To conclude on a more positive note, what has been said here has exposed vast areas about which we know almost nothing. But it is a great advance that we can now ask questions of the sort which I have tried to raise. We have in our hands the conceptual tools which enable us to pose the questions, and we have had these tools for less than twenty years. We are only just beginning the exciting task of exploring their potentialities.

## References

Bateson, Gregory. 1936. *Naven*. London: Cambridge University Press.

—. 1942. "Social Planning and the Concept of 'Deutero-Learning.'" *Conference on Science, Philosophy, and Religion; Second Symposium*. New York: Harper & Brothers. [Also in *Steps to an Ecology of Mind*.]

—. 1958. "Epilogue 1958." In *Naven*, 2nd ed. Stanford: Stanford University Press.

Bateson, G., and M. Mead. 1942. *Balinese Character: A Photographic Analysis*. New York: New York Academy of Sciences.

Bavelas, Alex. 1959. In *Group Processes; Transactions of the Fourth Conference*. New York: Josiah Macy, Jr. Foundation.

Harlow, H. F. 1949. "The Formation of Learning Sets." *Psychol. Rev.* 56:51–65.

Jackson, Donald D. 1957. "The Question of Family Homeostasis." *Psychoanal. Quart.*, Supplement, 31:79–90.

Redl, Fritz. 1959. In *Group Processes; Transactions of the Fourth Conference*. New York: Josiah Macy, Jr. Foundation. (The regenerative characteristics of groups of chil-

---

5. [*Editor's Note:* See footnote 2.]

dren are here discussed in detail, and analogous examples are drawn from the field of animal behavior, including organizations of ants and bees.)

Romney, Kim. 1956. "Structural Analysis of Cross-cousin Marriage." Ph.D. dissertation, Harvard University.

Ruesch, J., and G. Bateson. 1951. *Communication: The Social Matrix of Psychiatry*. New York: W. W. Norton & Company, Inc.

Stanton, A. H., and M. S. Schwartz. 1954. *The Mental Hospital*. New York: Basic Books, Inc.

Von Neumann, J., and O. Morgenstern. 1955. *Theory of Games and Economic Behavior*. Rev. ed. Princeton, N.J.: Princeton University Press.

Waddington, C. H. 1957. *Strategy of the Genes*. London: George Allen & Unwin, Ltd.

# 10

## *A Social Scientist Views the Emotions*<sup>*</sup>

The central point which I want to make is that we have at the present time two scientific languages for the discussion of affect and, further, that these two languages are mutually translatable. The first is the beginnings of a scientific language for describing the psychology of an individual. The second is the beginnings of a language for describing relationships between individuals.

Dr. Pribram has used the term "signals of state" and this I believe is a perfectly appropriate term in discussion of individual psychology, but when we begin to talk about relationship between individuals the event which Pribram calls a signal of state takes on a different aspect. The wag of the dog's tail which for individual psychology signifies an inner state of the dog becomes something more than this when we ask about the functions of this signal in the relationship between the dog and his master. I want to suggest to you that it becomes an affirmation or a proposal about what shall be the contingencies in that relationship. I think it was Warren McCulloch who pointed out that every message has a report aspect and a command aspect. The firing of neuron B in the chain A B C is, on the one hand, a report that A fired immediately previously and, on the other hand, it is a command that C shall fire immediately after. Matters become more complex when we deal with circular relationships between learning organisms instead of relationships between neurons, but what I am trying to say is related to this paradigm of McCulloch's.

Let me explain what I mean by the contingencies of relationship. Any context of learning can be defined in formal terms according to the contingencies which govern (or make predictable) reinforcement. In a Pavlovian experiment the occurrence of the so-called unconditioned

*This paper was prepared for the Symposium on Expression of the Emotions in Man, held at the meeting of the American Association for the Advancement of Science, December 29–30, 1960, in New York. Reprinted from *Expression of the Emotions in Man,* edited by Peter H. Knapp, by permission of International Universities Press, Inc. Copyright © 1963 by The International Universities Press, Inc.

stimulus—the meat powder—is contingent upon the conditioned stimulus, and upon the lapse of time. It is not contingent upon the subject's behavior. In other types of learning context the reinforcement may be variously contingent upon time, probability, the subject's behavior, peculiar combinations and characteristics of the stimulus, and so on. It is in this sense that I use the word "contingency."

Let us suppose that the relationship between organisms A and B can be represented by . . . *abababababa* . . . where the lower-case letters stand for behaviors or signals emitted by A and B. In such a sequence we can see every lower-case letter as having not two aspects as McCulloch proposed but three. In any triad of signals, *aba* or *bab,* the first item is a stimulus, the second is a response, and the third is a reinforcement. But every single item of the total sequence is a member of three such triads. In one it is the stimulus, in another it is the response, and in a third it is the reinforcement.[1]

If I do not respond as you expect to the stimulus which you give me, I am punishing or frustrating you either for that behavior which you thought would stimulate me in a certain way, or for your incorrect assessment of the rules of contingency in our relationship.

Now we should notice that in any such sequence the signals of state stand out conspicuously as having preponderantly the reinforcing function. Of course these signals are also stimuli for the other person and responses to the other person, but they are outstandingly either reinforcements of what the other has just done or are statements about how future behavior of the other will be received with reward or punishment.

Signals of state in the language of psychology thus become either reinforcements or signals about the contingencies of reinforcement in the language which would describe relationship.

Notice that the occurrence of an expected punishment may be a positive reinforcement of the subject's view of the contingencies of the situation and, conversely, an unexpected reward may be painfully confusing.

Next, I think I should underline the fact which is familiar to all of us: these signals of state which function to define the contingencies of rela-

---

1. I have here focused attention upon the triad partly in order to simplify presentation and partly because this unit of interchange has figured so conspicuously in experimental studies of learning. A more complete formal presentation would indicate that any item in the sequence of interchange may be a "response" or "reinforcement" for *any* earlier item and that it may be "stimulus" for any later item. It is also possible for any group of items to function as a unit of this sort. The problem of describing such series becomes methodologically similar to the problem of describing orders of redundancy in such stochastic series as codes and ciphers.

tionship are usually nonverbal, often unconsciously emitted, and often unconsciously received. We do not stop to analyze the structure and grammar of our relationships while we are participating in them. Indeed, to do so would be to change this grammar. Instead, we trust to the fact that we are all members of a culture and have therefore been trained in expectations regarding the contingencies of relationships. This training, of course, involves a more abstract order of learning—learning of a higher logical type—than that which I was talking about in discussing the triads of stimulus, response, and reinforcement. I call it a "higher" type of learning because the gestalten with which it deals are larger, but this learning about the contingencies of relationship is in general more archaic and more unconscious than the learning of the single adaptive act.

Here again we encounter an important parallel between the "signals of state" and the signals which define the contingencies of relationship. It is not too much to say that the language of nonhuman mammals is limited to signals of this higher order. It is a commonplace to say that cats and dogs cannot talk about things or ideas, they can only express emotions. Clearly, however, they manage to get across, even to human beings, a number of ideas and even to communicate demands for things. What is interesting in the present connection is that these relatively concrete communications are achieved by signals which have a relatively high order of abstraction. These are the signals which a psychologist would call signals of state, but which I am here calling definitions of the contingencies of relationship. When I open the refrigerator door, the cat comes and rubs against my leg stating some variant of the proposition "meow." To say that she is asking for milk may be correct, but it is not a literal translation from her language into ours. I suggest that more literally we should translate her message as "be mamma." She is trying to define the contingencies of relationship. She is inviting me to accept those contingencies and to act in accordance with them. She may step down somewhat from this high abstract level by indicating urgency—"be mamma now"; or she may achieve a certain concreteness by ostensive communication—"be mamma now in regard to that jug"; but, in its primary structure, her communication is archaic and highly abstract in the sense that its prime subject matter is always relationship.

In passing, it is interesting to note that the metaphoric language of dreams is intermediate between the relational language of the cat and the objective language which human beings think they would be able to use if only it were possible to stop dreaming. In dream, we define relationships with an utter disregard for the relata. I perceive the contingencies of relationship between myself and my mother as being comparable to the contingencies which would obtain between a little man in a desert and a spring on top of a granite mountain. The mountain appears in a dream and the "interpretation" of the dream becomes possible when we see that the mountain is the analogue of one of the relata in the original perception.

Let me now discuss very briefly what happens when communicational pathology is introduced at the level of those signals which define the contingencies of relationship. As you might suppose, it is precisely at this level that "feelings" get hurt.

Notice first of all that in the language describing relationship many words which are commonly used to describe individuals now become technical terms for systems of contingency in the interchange. Such words as *dependency, hostility, trust,* and even the names of feelings or emotions such as *fear* and *anger,* can be translated by the formal characteristics of the sequences in which they occur.

It follows necessarily that misunderstandings and inconsistencies (either deliberate or accidental) regarding the contingencies of interchange are likely to be profoundly traumatic. These misunderstandings have been the subject of the research into the experiential base of schizophrenia which we have been conducting at Palo Alto for the past eight years. What has come to be called a "double bind" is in fact a sequence in which A and B punish each other for discrepancies in how each sees and acts upon the contingencies of the interchange. This also has been the subject of extensive experimentation with mammalian subjects.

In the classical experiments, the animal is educated by the experimenter to believe that reinforcement is contingent upon his (the subject's) discriminating between two stimuli, e.g., an ellipse and a circle. When this premise of the relationship between subject and experimenter has been intensely communicated, the experimenter starts to fatten the ellipse and flatten the circle without warning the animal that this process will result in a formal change in the contingencies of the relationship. When finally the stimuli become indistinguishable, the animal gets punished or finds himself put in the wrong when he acts according to the contingency pattern which the experimenter had taught him. This is grossly unfair and the animal starts to exhibit symptoms of profound disturbance. These phenomena are conventionally called experimental neuroses, but since the procedures which induce these symptoms are formally comparable with the sequences which seem to induce schizophrenic behavior in man, the term *psychosis* would perhaps be more appropriate.

At the human level, let me very briefly illustrate what happens by an extract from a work of fiction by Travers (1934). Mary Poppins, the English nanny, has taken the two Banks children to get gingerbread. In the little old gingerbread shop, there are two large sad young women, Miss Annie and Miss Fannie. Mrs. Corry, a tremulous, whispy little old lady, the mother of Annie and Fannie, comes out from the back of the shop:

> "I suppose you've all come for some gingerbread?"
>
> "That's right, Mrs. Corry," said Mary Poppins politely.
>
> "Good. Have Fannie and Annie given you any?" She looked at Jane and Michael as she said this.
>
> Jane shook her head. Two hushed voices came from behind the counter.
>
> "No, Mother," said Miss Fannie meekly.
>
> "We were just going to, Mother—" began Miss Annie in a frightened whisper.
>
> At that Mrs. Corry drew herself up to her full height and regarded her gigantic daughters furiously. Then she said in a soft, fierce, terrifying voice:
>
> "Just going to? Oh, *indeed!* That is *very* interesting. And who, may I ask, Annie, gave you permission to give away *my* ginger-bread—?"
>
> "Nobody, Mother. And I didn't give it away. I only thought—"
>
> "You only thought! That is *very* kind of you. But I will thank you not to think. *I* can do all the thinking that is necessary here!" said Mrs. Corry in her soft, terrible voice. Then she burst into a harsh cackle of laughter.
>
> "Look at her! Just look at her! Cowardy-custard! Cry-baby!" she shrieked, pointing her knotty finger at her daughter.
>
> Jane and Michael turned and saw a large tear coursing down Miss Annie's huge, sad face, but they did not like to say anything, for, in spite of her tininess, Mrs. Corry made them feel rather small and frightened.

In this sequence Mrs. Corry sets up the rules of contingency in such a way that Annie and Fannie would naturally suppose that this is a context in which to have given gingerbread would be approved. The two young women have been caught in similar traps before, but even so they get caught again.

Annie is even further penalized for the pain which she feels.

# 11

## The Message of Reinforcement*

*Nature has no Outline, but Imagination has. Nature has no Tune, but Imagination has. Nature has no Supernatural, & dissolves: Imagination is Eternity.*
—W. Blake, *The Ghost of Abel, 1822.*

### 1. Information, Messages, and Redundancy

In this essay, these words will be used as follows: If from any PART of a sequence of events an ideal receiver can make better than random guesses at other parts of the sequence, I shall say that the part contains "INFORMATION" or a message about the remainder, and that the sequence as a whole contains REDUNDANCY.

If A says to B "it is raining," this verbal event PLUS the raindrops outside the window together constitute a redundant sequence for B. If B looks outside, he will get less information from the falling drops than he would have got, had he not heard A's message. He could have guessed with better than random success that he would see rain.

The case of the receiver who is not "ideal"—i.e., who does not already know about all the redundancy patterns of the observed system—is more complicated. Under certain circumstances he may acquire information about sorts of redundancy of which he was previously unaware. I shall say that such information about patterns of redundancy is of higher order or higher logical type than that which the ideal observer can acquire. The latter, like the hypothetical player of a Von Neumannian game, is by definition incapable of such learning.

*This essay was written in 1966, and is reprinted, by permission of Mouton de Gruyter, from *Language Behavior: A Book of Readings in Communication,* edited by Johnnye Akin, Alvin Goldberg, Gail Myers, and Joseph Stewart, 1970. This essay was prepared under N.I.H. Career Award No. HEW 7K3-MH-21,931-02 and U.S. Naval Ordnance Test Station Contract No. N.123-(60530)53792A.

## 2. Definition of Learning

Let us define LEARNING as the receipt of INFORMATION by an organism, a computer, or any other data-processing entity. This definition is intended to include all sorts and orders of information, ranging from the single bit which we suppose to be received in the single firing of a single neural end organ to the building up of complex chunks of information—i.e., constellations of neural structures and events—about relationship, philosophy, religion, mechanical systems, etc. The definition also will include internal learning—the building up of information regarding the changing states and characteristics of the learning entity itself. After all, there are many parts of any learning entity which are themselves concerned with the processing of information, so that what I am calling "internal learning" is, in fact, the receiving of information by such parts.

The purpose of this definition will be to provide some clue to the structure of contexts of "learning" (in the more conventional sense), and in particular to consider what sorts of information are provided by those events or experiences which are called REINFORCEMENT.

It is important to note that this definition says nothing about consciousness. If a man speaks correctly in a given language, we shall say that he "contains" information about the grammar of that language. If he KNOWS that he has that information, we shall say that he contains information of a higher logical type.

## 3. Classification of Information

From this definition, the next step is to consider how information shall be classified, remembering that the purpose of the classification is to understand the phenomena of "learning" as above defined.

Two alternative methods present themselves: (a) classification based upon Russell's Logical Types; and (b) classification based upon the location and status of the information in the program and circuitry of the organism or computer.

Other sorts of classification could, of course, be examined. It would be orthodox, for example, to classify information according to its relevance and usefulness for the various "needs" of the organism. The result would be a system of categories resembling "instinct" theory. A large amount of speculation and pseudoexplanation is already associated with this way of thinking in economics, "functional" anthropology, and animal ethology. Masses of data have been dissected into this procrustean bed but it still seems to me that the explanatory principles, i.e., "instincts," invoked in these studies resemble the "dormitive principle" proposed by Molière's learned doctors to explain the physiological effects of opium.

In this essay I shall therefore confine myself to the more tangible types of explanation—the logical types of Russell and the status of information in programs. The first, it will be noted, is a set of characterizations inherent in the actual items of information, while the second is descriptive of methods of storage and use of that information. Neither of these classifications can be pushed very far in the present state of our knowledge, but it is instructive to examine the resemblance and contrast between the two systems.

In regard to the logical types, it is sufficient here to call attention to the fact that contrasts of logical typing, derived from the abstract world of logic, have implications for the real world of learning and organization. But the logical model must be used with caution because there are also important differences between the real world and that of logic.

In the world of logic, the statement of a grammatical rule for a given language tells the logician nothing about what a speaker of that language is saying at a given moment, but in the real world, knowledge of the grammar may help a man to decipher a text in that language. Moreover, in the real world, there may be some sort of conflict between items of information of contrasting type. Teachers of language believe today that the study of grammar actually interferes with learning to speak a foreign language and do their best to prevent the would-be learner from using his own language as a model when he attempts to speak the new language; and yet nobody doubts that some (perhaps unconscious) knowledge of grammar is useful to a writer or that a knowledge of Italian is useful to the learner of French. Above all, it is evident that the (almost undescribable) experience of having learned one foreign language will enable a man to learn another more quickly and easily.

These considerations suggest that in the natural history of learning the functional relationship between, e.g., grammar and speech is not merely a matter of formal logic and the theory of types but is also shaped or colored by some other factor. It appears that information about grammar (i.e., information of higher type) is under certain circumstances most useful when least "conscious." This suggests that not only the logical typing of a piece of information but also its location and status in the circuitry of the organism may affect its usefulness in learning.

This problem of natural history is not precisely the same as any that the logician encounters. For him, there are strict and definable limits to what propositions can be arrived at by induction or deduction from a given set of propositions of given types. For an organism, the limits are perhaps less sharply defined and, above all, are of a different kind. The organism does not ask, "What conclusions are logically supported by this given set of premises?" He asks, rather: "What in the light of these premises is worth trying?" He operates by TRIAL AND ERROR, and the information provided by past experience or by the genome determines the SET of alternatives among which he will make random trial. In many cases, the organism will appear to be more rigid than the logician: The set of alternatives available to the organism may seemingly contain only one member, where the logician would have seen many. On the other hand, sometimes the organism will arrive by trial and error at discoveries which the ideal logician, who may not guess, could never have allowed himself to make. "Life," it has been said, "is the art of drawing sufficient conclusions from insufficient evidence."

In addition, the task of classifying messages and meaningful actions of the real world in terms of the theory of logical types is complicated by another matter which, ideally, should not concern the logician. At least in theory, a logician, after spending many years examining the ramifications of a given tautology (say Euclidian geometry) based upon a given set of axioms and definitions, should be able without perseveration to turn around and start to build another tautology based upon another set of premises. An organism cannot do this, and of course, insofar as logicians are themselves organisms, they cannot achieve freedom from this perseveration. The most abstract premises—and especially those of which the logician is least conscious—are likely to remain unchanged even when he thinks he is making a new start.

In all real entities capable of processing information, some sorts of information are necessarily more deeply and irreversibly built into the computing system than are others. In the language of the computer engineer, some parts of the program are "hard" while others are "soft." "Soft" items can easily be changed when the program is to be adapted for some other related use, but to change the "hard" items may involve an almost total restructuring of the program.

The writer of a computer program has some choice as to how he builds his program. He can, within limits, decide which items he will permit to be "hard" and which he will keep "soft." He will be guided in this choice by his expectations regarding future applications of the program. If he foresees that certain components of the program will have to be altered in future applications he will be wise to represent these components in ways that can easily be changed. Other, expectably constant, components he will permit to be "hard."

Inevitably and ideally, there will be a correlation between degree of generality on the one hand and constancy on the other. General propositions and propositions about form will rarely need to be changed, but propositions regarding specific details or content will expectably vary from one occasion of use to the next. From this it follows that there will be a tendency for the programmer, guided only by pragmatic considerations, to classify his instructions and items of information AS IF he were guided by the theory of logical types. Items of higher, more abstract and general type are likely to be programmed "hard"; while items of lower and more specific type are likely to be programmed "soft."

An analogous phenomenon is recognizable in the learning organism. Indeed, the very human logician, mentioned above, who had difficulty in changing his most basic premises, is an example. He permitted those premises which had been true for him for a long time to become hard. He then could not change his program without pain.

Another example is provided by the phenomenon of "transference" in psychoanalysis. The patient attempts to structure his relationship to the analyst on the model of early relationships which he has experienced with parents or other character-forming persons, i.e., the patient will bring to the new situation abstract premises about RELATIONSHIP derived from his past. These premises have commonly the characteristic that they are self-validating (Ruesch and Bateson, 1951). In most transactions the holder of the premise can act in such a way as to make the premise appear true. It follows from this characteristic that the premise will have SEEMED true to the patient throughout a long sequence of experiences, so that when he finally comes to analysis, the premise will be already programmed "hard." In the picturesque language of Wilhelm Reich the premise will be "armored," i.e., it will now have, connected with it, a whole network of interdependent premises from which, if the primary premise were somehow excised, it could easily be regenerated.

The learning organism, however, differs from the system composed of programmer PLUS computer in that while the programmer is influenced by his expectations, the organism is a product of its past. Habit formation has sorted out the constant from the changeful so that that which for a long time has seemed recurrently true has become deeply embedded in the circuitry of the organism while the changeful remains under flexible control.

What mechanisms may lie behind habit formation we do not know, but certainly this continual sorting and sifting of sorts of propositions within the learning organism has many parallels in other evolving stochastic systems. In the learning organism an essential function of this sorting process is economic: the more flexible circuits must be reserved for dealing with the more changeable phenomena (cf. Bateson, 1962). The decisions of the programmer are economic in the same sense.

All in all, it appears that, if we are to classify information in a way that shall be appropriate in a study of learning processes, we must be guided by the following considerations:

(a)   that it is desirable to discriminate those items of information which are "hard" programmed in the organism from those which are "soft";

(b)   that in the ongoing life of the organism there is a process of sorting, which in some of its forms is called "habit formation." In this process, certain items, which have been learned at "soft" levels, gradually become "hard";

(c)   that this process must in general be guided by the constancy of the apparent truth of the items to be learned—the more constant being, in general, selected for hard programming;

(d)   that constancy is likely to correlate with generality, so that information about forms is more likely to be hard programmed than information about their contents. (In general, items of higher logical type are likely to become hard programmed.);

(e)   that the converse of "habit formation," i.e., the disruption of hard programmed items, is a form of learning which is always likely to be difficult and painful and which, when it fails, may be pathogenic (cf. Bateson et al., 1956).

## 4. The Distribution of Information

It is evident that information is "unevenly" distributed in the perceptual universe of any organism. This unevenness of distribution is exemplified by the subjective experience of an English speaker who must learn a language like German or Latin, in which the verbs are commonly placed at the ends of the sentences. He must learn to wait for the information contained in the verb which, when the sentence finally reaches its end, will tell him not only what the action was but how the other items of the sentence are interrelated. Certain sorts of information are aggregated in the verb, and the learner of German is conscious of lacking this information which he had expected to receive earlier. The verb when it is finally reached seems to illuminate (i.e., contains special information about) the earlier parts of the sentence. (Native speakers of German are perhaps not conscious of this phenomenon.)

A more formal illustration of unevenness in the distribution of information is provided by Attneave's elegant experiments (Attneave, 1959) on the outlines of visible forms. A picture in three colors is created by coloring the squares of a grid. Such a picture will have areas of, say red, white, and blue, each area containing many squares of the grid. A similar but blank grid is given to a human subject who is asked to guess the color of each square in turn. If he guesses wrong, he must guess again, so that he finally knows the color of each square and can mark it appropriately with a crayon on his blank grid. Rather rapidly the subject discovers that the distribution of the colors contains redundancy—the communication theorist's word for regularity or pattern. Thereafter his errors occur most frequently at the boundaries of the colored areas. A map of these errors becomes, in fact, an outline drawing of the colored picture. This experiment illustrates two important (if tautological) platitudes: that information about shape is aggregated at boundaries, and that the inside of an homogeneous set contains no information except for the repeated affirmation of homogeneity.

## 5. The Distribution of Classes of Information

We now ask: Does the unevenness of distribution of information in the experiential universe contain any regularities which might relate to that classification of information whose outlines we considered above? Specifically: If we classify what is to be learned according to either its constancy or its logical typing, shall we find that the resulting classes of information are differently located in the experiential universe? Is information about form distributed in the universe in a way which is different from the distribution of information about content?

But, these questions are already partly answered by the examples of uneven distribution given above. In Attneave's experiments a certain SORT of information was shown to be concentrated at those boundaries or outlines which delimited areas of uniformity; and this information at the boundaries is clearly more formal and more general than the information to be got from single colored squares within the uniform patches.

But these boundaries have, in a sense, no real existence, being made up only of squares of color exactly like the other squares which they surround. As Blake puts it, "Nature has no Outline." In other words, among aggregates or sets of similar items, those particular items which happen to be on a boundary come to transcend their individuality as members of the set and carry information about the set as a whole. In natural history, certain members of a class, differing from their fellow members only in being located in a "boundary," come to stand as labels or names for their class. (This contradiction of Russell's rule—that no member of a class can be the name of that class—is apparent rather than real. In communication theory and in the theory of logical types, there are, of course, no things: only MESSAGES carried by these objects or events. A single object can carry many messages and these may be of various types. Russell's rule insists only that a name or message of a given type shall not be classified as a name or message of a different type. The map is not the territory, even when the physical territory is the only embodiment of the map.)

The same phenomena can be considered in terms of constancy of informational content. While the perception of each item of an aggregate of red squares carries or proposes the fact of that square's redness, the marginal squares when encountered by the experimental subject propose a new constancy or "rule": that now the subject will be well advised to guess "red" for each succeeding square until he again encounters a change at a new boundary.

It is at the point or moment of CHANGE that new constancies are proposed.

## 6. Patterns of Search

But all this is accessible and useful to the experimental subject ONLY if he can acquire information of a still higher order, namely the information that the total system of colored squares contains redundancy, such that squares of similar color tend to be aggregated in patches. (At the start of the experiment he is given no reason to believe this. For all he knows, the colors could be randomly distributed or their distribution might be governed by any kind of simple or complex patterning.)

We must ask then about the location of this still higher order of information, though no complete answer can be given.

If, however, we consider the Attneave experiments more precisely, a part of the answer will emerge. The subject was asked to guess the color of each square and arrived at information about the rules for distribution of these colors. But clearly how soon he arrives at this abstract information will depend upon the ORDER in which his sample of data is collected. In the actual experiments, he is asked to guess the color of successive squares in order, following their ranking in the grid. If, on the other hand, he had been asked to guess squares in a random order, he certainly would not have achieved his inductive step so soon. He would have had to scatter errors randomly over the grid until the acquired information rather clearly showed that similar squares were aggregated in patches. In the final completed map of his errors, the boundaries of the patches of squares of uniform color would be less clearly marked.

In sum, the ability of an organism to acquire information about patterning and redundancy in the world must always depend upon certain characteristics of habits of the organism itself. In the total system, organism PLUS environment, there is a necessary interplay between the patterns of redundancy in the environment and the SEARCH PATTERNS of the organism. Certain sorts and orders of redundancy will be more accessible to certain search patterns but more inaccessible to others. Indeed, this generalization follows as a truism from the unevenness of distribution of information in the phenomenal world. The organism must, IF IT CAN, learn to look in the right places, in the right order, for the right sorts of information. Consequently, it is caught in a limited view of the universe by its search patterns, insofar as these are rigidly defined and unchanging. No pattern of the universe which cannot be discovered by these patterns can exist for that organism.

We noted above, however, that it is precisely the self-validating premises that are likely to become hard programmed, and it is clear that search patterns because they cannot commonly be disturbed by that which they cannot discover are likely to become hard programmed.

In spite of the tendency to become hard programmed, search patterns can certainly be learned and possibly unlearned, and this phenomenon has been variously named "set learning" (Harlow), deutero-learning (Bateson), or more generally, "learning to learn." The precise synonymy of these terms is still obscure but certainly the learning of patterns of search is an acquisition of information of a rather high abstract order. This information is both subtly related to that information which is to be acquired by the search and subtly related to the structuring and redundancy patterns of the universe in which the search is to be conducted. The universe may contain many sorts of patterning other than those sorts which interest the organism. These irrelevant patterns may, however, complicate or restrict the process of search.

It may well be that any particular pattern (or redundancy) in the method of search will necessarily blind the searcher to certain possible patterns in the universe; and that only RANDOM search can ultimately catch all possible regularities. This ideal will be achieved, however, only by a searcher with infinite time and in a universe which makes available infinite series of data.

Real organisms in real environments will necessarily have to resort to particular patterns of search, and this restriction of search will be accompanied by a corresponding restriction in the patterns which can be discovered.

## 7. The Triad of Learning

We are now ready to think about the curious circumstance that the study of "learning" in the psychological laboratory is usually structured around a triad of events: Stimulus–Response–Reinforcement. In the past, I have often suspected that this triad is only an artifact of the laboratory, useful because it provides a vocabulary for talking with psychologists, but harmful insofar as it restricts discourse to what can be said in this vocabulary. But the matter is not so simple.

After all, to say that the triad is an artifact of the laboratory, would mean that it is derivative from the SEARCH PATTERNS of the psychologists. Now it is probably true that every search pattern restricts what can be found and what can be discussed in terms derivative from that pattern. But it is also true that certain obscure, but coercive, regularities must govern the learning or evolution of such patterns. The psychological experimenters are, themselves, organisms. They possess "Imagination" in Blake's sense and, therefore, they too seek for and recognize "Outlines." Their search patterns, BECAUSE they are self-validating, must be somehow related to the structures of the data field.

I have implied above that all learning, above the very simplest level (at which, for example, the colored square proposes only the fact of its own color), is in truth acquisition of information about "outlines."

The question of the "reality" of the stimulus-response-reinforcement triad thus becomes a question about outlines of the second order or meta-outlines. The psychologist seeks to discover outlines among the phenomena of animal learning—but this learning is itself the discovery by the animal of outlines in its experience.

## 8. The Sliding Triad

The triadic pattern CAN be imposed upon any three events in a human interchange. If, for example, A and B interact to give the sequence . . . a b a b a b a b . . . , where a and b stand for interactive behaviors of A and B respectively, then any . . . a b a . . . or . . . b a b . . . CAN be regarded as such a triad. There are no primary outlines which would tell us whether a given . . . a . . . is "stimulus," "response," or "reinforcement." But, at least in occidental cultures, the individuals concerned do seem to have opinions which would classify interactive behaviors as parts of such triads. Lacking primary outlines, they are often in disagreement about how the sequence should be punctuated. A will assert that a given . . . a . . . was only a response to some previous . . . b . . . ; but B will say that . . . a . . . was an example of A's initiative and spontaneous aggressivity. And so on.

These disagreements clearly support the idea that the triadic structure of the learning sequence can be "real" for organisms other than psychologists. It would seem, however, that while some need or process of logic may compel the organisms to perceive their interaction as structured in triadic sequences, there is no similar compulsion which will determine precisely how this sequential structure is to be imposed on the series of interactive behaviors.

The program is "hard" and, as we might expect, it determines form but not content.

## 9. The Triad as a "Context"

The fact that the triadic pattern does not require particular content is, however, not a sufficient explanation of the curious floating or sliding characteristic of the triad. It is characteristic of all patterns that they define form but not content. This particular pattern is unusual in being both (presumably) valuable to the organism and indeterminate as to its beginning and end. The wider notion of "context" has, however, this same sliding characteristic. A "context" can be imagined around ANY event by grouping neighboring or "related" events along with it within an imaginary temporal boundary. And indeed the triad which we are discussing would seem to be a special case of "context."

The notion of "context" is primary and fundamental for all communication. No message or message element—no event or object—has meaning or significance of any kind when totally and inconceivably stripped of context. Without context, an event or object is not even "random."

When the notion of context is admitted it becomes evident that every context has its metacontext, and so on ad infinitum. Insofar then as every event carries information about its context, we must grant that every event is relevant, i.e., carries information about every step of that infinite series which is the hierarchy of contexts. In this sense, every event becomes INFORMATIONALLY relevant to the whole universe (which is not the same as causally relevant). Here we shall limit discussion to those orders of information which occur within the learning triad and within the interactional sequences which immediately surround that triad.

In the simple case of the Attneave experiments, the boundary squares carry two sorts of information. Not only does each boundary square propose its own color, it also proposes (when appropriately encountered) a CONTEXT within which the subject gathers that he will do well to guess that succeeding squares are of that same color. The "set" for which the boundary square is a "label" is not just an aggregate or list of items; it is partially structured or ordered (relative to the search pattern) in such a way that the boundary squares become "context markers," i.e., signals which give information about sameness or change, i.e., RELATIONSHIP among other signals.

## 10. The Messages of Reinforcement

In the more complex case of the triadic context of "learning," we ask therefore which components carry meaning or information about which others.

In terms of the conceptual framework which I have built up it is clear that the event which is called the "reinforcement" carries information of at least five sorts:

(a)   The event called reinforcement proposes the fact of its own occurrence. It is perceptible.

(b)   It proposes certain characteristics ("rightness" or "wrongness") in the sequential relation between "stimulus" and "response." And, if reinforcement is metacommunicative to the relationship between the other two components of the triad, it follows that "learning" will usually depend upon at least a triad of events. Three events are necessary if one is to be a message about a relationship between others. We may say that the triad is REAL, in the sense that it is, for certain sorts of information transmission, a minimum.

(c)   It proposes that a certain contingency pattern among the three components in sequence is or shall be characteristic of the ongoing interchange.

(d)   It proposes the even more abstract notion that the ongoing flow of interactive behavior is, in general, divisible into segments having some sort of contingency pattern.

(e)  It proposes that the SEARCH PATTERN of the learning subject is "right" in the sense that this search pattern will discover this particular triadic patterning.

Any event carrying these five types of information can, appropriately, be called a reinforcement.

But the matter does not end there. The normative information (<b> above) about "rightness" and "wrongness" is such as would explain the enhancement or extinction of the given "response" in presence of the given stimulus, but the information (<c> and <d>) which proposes the patterns of contingency is more profound and more necessary. WITHOUT IT, the enhancement or extinction of response could not be expected. For "learning" (as the word is ordinarily used in psychological laboratories) to occur at all, the organism must, either by experience or phylogeny, have become capable of receiving information (<c> and <d> above) of rather abstract types.

It is also important to note that both the information which reinforcement carries in regard to the contingency pattern within the triad, and the information (<e>) about the search patterns of the learner are non-normative. At these levels, even "negative" reinforcement may become desirable and may be SOUGHT by the learning organism. If the organism is unsure about what contingency patterns are expectable in a given interaction, he may be reassured when he encounters punishment.

As a schizophrenic patient once put the matter: "If it's not the way I want it, I'll prove it."

# References

Attneave, F. 1959. *Applications of Information Theory to Psychology*. New York: Henry Holt and Co.

Bateson, G. 1962. "The Role of Somatic Change in Evolution." *Evolution* 17: 529–39. [Also in *Steps to an Ecology of Mind*.]

Bateson, G., D. Jackson, J. Haley, and J. Weakland. 1956. "Toward a Theory of Schizophrenia." *Behavioral Science* 1, no. 4: 251–64. [Also in *Steps to an Ecology of Mind*.]

Ruesch, J., and G. Bateson. 1951. *Communication: The Social Matrix of Psychiatry*. New York: Norton and Norton.

**Order ID: 105-5911601-3701048**

Thank you for buying from booksaremyfriends on Amazon Marketplace.

| | | |
|---|---|---|
| **Shipping Address:**<br>Peter D. Glickenhaus, Jr.<br>1000 N DUKE ST APT 16<br>DURHAM, NC 27701-1850 | Order Date:<br>Shipping Service:<br>Buyer Name:<br>Seller Name: | Feb 4, 2009<br>Standard<br>Peter Glickenhaus<br>booksaremyfriends |

| Quantity | Product Details | Price | Total |
|---|---|---|---|
| 1 | **Sacred Unity : Further Steps to an Ecology of Mind**<br><br>**Merchant SKU:** Bookshelf10C108(4.98)<br>**ASIN:** 0062501003<br>**Order-item ID:** 06035359254290<br>**Condition:** Used - Very Good<br>**Comments:** Fast shipping from Connecticut. Secure bubble mailer packaging. | $4.85 | |

| | |
|---|---|
| Subtotal: | $4.85 |
| Shipping: | $3.99 |
| Total: | $8.84 |

**ORDER TOTAL: $8.84**

**Thanks for buying on Amazon Marketplace**. To provide feedback for the seller please visit www.amazon.com/feedback. To contact the seller, please visit Amazon.com and click on "Your Account" at the top of any page. In Your Account, go to the "Where's My Stuff" section and click on the link "Leave seller feedback". Select the order or click on the "View Order" button. Click on the "seller profile" under the appropriate product. On the lower right side of the page under "Seller Help", click on "Contact this seller".

# 12

## *The Double-Bind Theory—Misunderstood?**

As I read Dr. Stevens's letter (*Psychiatric News,* Nov. 18, 1977), I am forced to agree that double-bind "theory" has contributed its share to the sufferings of those who are called (and sometimes call themselves) "schizophrenics." But suffering is the inevitable product of action combined with ignorance. Metrazol, insulin, lobotomy, EST, and the inhumanity of gross contempt have contributed to the mass of human suffering which radiates from "schizophrenia"; and the modern solution—chronic intoxication by chemotherapy—is not the last word. The matter is simple! We are all deeply ignorant and there can be no competition in ignorance.

However, there are a few small insights which I believe are available to those who are willing to look into the ideas which we generated about twenty-two years ago:

(1) If the word "schizophrenia" is to be used at all—and I would still use it—it should be used to refer to a recognizable and definable aggregate of formal characteristics of personal interaction.

(2) The definition of these sequences will require concepts derived from *Principia, Laws of Form,* and double-bind theory.

(3) The etiology of these sequences is expectably diverse. The structure of all recursive systems is such that from the examination of the "symptoms" only poor guesses at the roots or history of the "pathology" can be offered. Try to etiologize trouble in the cooling system of an automobile and you will discover that the initial "push" might have come from any point in the circuit of causes and effects.

---

*This article was written ca. December 1977, and is reprinted from *Psychiatric News* 13 (1978), by permission of *Psychiatric News.*

(4)   It follows that the schizophrenic phenomena (i.e., appearances) could—and probably do—have etiologic roots of very various kinds. Double-bind theory certainly does not exclude the possibility of schizophrenic appearances being favored and even determined by genes, by invading organisms, by dietary deficiency or excess, by autointoxication, by gross traumatic experience, by family process, by psychotherapy, and even by spite or despair. The latest explanatory trick is the notion—tenable so far as double-bind theory is concerned—that these appearances may have roots in some characteristics of mutual function or dysfunction in the relations between right and left hemispheres. No combination of these etiologies can be excluded.

(5)   But, in addition to this expectable diversity of etiology, it is still true that many characteristics of biological and human interaction are progressive and self-validating. Human error, folly, and spite may have primary deep roots in genetic combinations or in diet or in intoxication, but still error, folly, and the like become by progressive self-validation a part of their own etiology. If double bind enters into the *definition* of schizophrenia, it will expectably become part of the self-promoting dance which contributes to maintaining and perhaps originating that condition.

(6)   There is no primary assumption in double-bind theory that the appearances of schizophrenia are *bad*. The theory is not normative, still less "pragmatic." It is not even a *medical* theory (if there can be such a thing).

(7)   The theory concerns the role of logical typing and related matters such as cybernetics and Laws of Form in the description of human behavior. And by the word "role" I suggest that these formal notions have explanatory value, i.e., that description of the appearances can be mapped onto relations which obtain among the formal concepts.

(8)   The appearances to which double-bind theory is certainly relevant include, besides schizophrenia, humor, poetry and art, religion, hypnosis, altered consciousness, and dream. Among these, the phenomena of schizophrenia are not in any sense central. Historically, it happens that the pathway of early formulation led through cultural anthropology to learning theory, and thence to animal play. I was struck by the fact of metacom-

munication at the prehuman level, and I received the first grant from Chester Barnard's office in the Rockefeller Foundation to "investigate the role of logical typing in human and animal communication." Among our various insights in this period was the discovery of the necessarily close overlap between metaphor and metacommunication—a metacommunicative signal is often absent in schizophrenic utterance. Up to this point our contribution was simply to begin to place "schizophrenia" in relation to other aggregates of phenomena of related logical type (humor, religion, play, etc.).

(9)   It was possible to map the schizophrenic phenomena onto a classification of learning which I had proposed some fifteen years previously. That theory had natural links with logical typing theory and so fitted naturally with my formal classification of the modes of human interaction (humor, etc.).

(10)   Dr. Stevens asserts that today "the entire mental health profession including most (of psychoanalysis) has come to recognize what Freud and Kraepelin long ago predicted, i.e., that schizophrenia is a disease of the brain, not the family." She also implies that this conclusion is supported by "controlled research." Was it not Dr. Johnson who asserted, "The Law, sir, is an ass"?[1] But I will agree with the entire profession and the great names thus far: that the appearances of schizophrenia may be produced by parasitic invasion and/or by experience; by genes and/or by training. I will even concede that schizophrenia is *as much* a "disease" of the "brain" as it is a "disease" of the "family," if Dr. Stevens will concede that humor and religion, art and poetry, are likewise "diseases" of the brain or of the family or of both. I would only warn Dr. Stevens that the words "*as much*" italicized in the previous sentence should not be taken too literally. Comparisons between epistemologic positions are, of course, nonquantitative. What I will not agree to is the maltreatment of language which would separate psychosis from the remainder of the vast spectrum of human antics—both greatness and misery. Nor will I agree to that monstrous premise of medieval epistemology which would separate "mind" from "body."

---

1. [*Editor's Note:* Alas, it was not. See Charles Dickens, *Oliver Twist*, Chapter 51.]

In regard to the usefulness of double-bind theory in the psychotherapy of "schizophrenia," not much can be said:

(1) It may be true that understanding of the theory is helpful to
some patients.

(2) It may be true that some therapists are helped by some intellectual understanding of double-bind theory. But, in this business
the understanding "heart" (perhaps the right hemisphere?)
can do more to heal than can the intellect. The intellect is
naive and, too often, vulgar.

(3) *There is no hurry.* Medical practitioners are, of course, in a hurry to apply the newest gadget, drug, or trick. Hurry is the
corollary in action of an empirical philosophy; and empiricism
is, by definition, lack of theory. There is nothing naughty in all
that. It's how things are. Hurry is, at that level, necessary, and
whatever is done to control charlatanism, patients will still suffer. Their suffering will be part of the price of "progress."

(4) But the introduction of *theory* into this scene is something else
again. No doubt theory has a part of its roots in experience
but—to embroider the metaphor—the root system of theory is
very different from the root system of empiricism. I do not
need schizophrenic patients or unhappy families to give my
thinking empirical roots. I can use art, poetry, or porpoises, or
the cultures of New Guinea and Manhattan, or my own
dreams, or the comparative anatomy of flowering plants. After
all, I am not limited to inductive processes of argument. I can
use deduction and, especially, abduction. It is abduction which
enables me to draw my instances of a given regularity from a
vast range of different universes of experience. If I were better
trained as a mathematician, I would have additional powers of
judgment, power to choose between sense and nonsense.

(5) So today something new is happening—and not only in the
field of mental health. Theory is becoming available to action-
oriented people, whose first impulse is that which is primarily
in empiricism. "Take it on the wards and try it. Don't waste
years trying to understand the theory. Just use whatever hunch-
es seem to follow from it." Such people are likely to be frustrated and their patients hurt.

(6) Theory is not just another gadget which can be used without
understanding.

# 13

## *The Growth of Paradigms for Psychiatry**

Let me try to place historically where we were back in 1948, when I joined Jurgen Ruesch at what was then called the Langley Porter Clinic. The circumstances of my leaving Harvard to go West aptly characterize the times. I had a difference with the faculty at Harvard. I was a visiting professor, and they and I felt I would be reappointed. Just before the committee that, presumably, was going to reappoint me was to meet, a graduate student said he wanted to ask a question. About halfway through lunch, he finally screwed up his courage to say, "Mr. Bateson, do you think anthropologists ought to be analyzed?"

Well, the answer to that was complex. I could say, "Please, not all of them," or "It doesn't matter," or "If you're going to work on family structure, it might be useful." I gave the third answer. The boy was interested in querns (blocks made of stones and used to grind grain); he specialized in what is called "material culture." He dashed to his preferred professor, Carl Coon, and said, "Bateson says anthropologists ought to be analyzed." And, because the preferred professor happened to be chairman of the committee that was to reappoint me, that was the end of my connection with Harvard.

However, like many divorces, this obviously was mutual, for (though I had not said what was reported) if they wanted to kick me out for that opinion, I did not belong there anyway. I was an anachronism in that epoch.

Meanwhile, I had been sharing an office with Alfred Kroeber of the University of California, and he knew what had happened. He instantly telegraphed to somebody, and within a week I was a member of the team of Jurgen Ruesch, in the new Department of Psychiatry at the University of California in San Francisco. We had not yet met each other.

*This article is based on an address delivered November 17, 1976, to the Langley Porter Clinic, San Francisco, and is reprinted, by permission of Grune & Stratton, Inc., from *Communication and Social Interaction: Clinical and Therapeutic Aspects of Human Behavior,* edited by Peter F. Ostwald, 1977.

That places it in time, in the days when psychoanalysis was a battle-front of a rather special kind. Today, I would say the other two answers would be much more relevant: "Please don't psychoanalyze all anthro-pologists because they will share too much of epistemology," and "Perhaps it doesn't matter."

So I came out to California, where I worked with Jurgen Ruesch full-time for two years, and then started to work part-time at Langley Porter and part-time with the Veterans Administration in Palo Alto. In those two years, my beginnings as well as the premises of *Steps to an Ecology of Mind* were established.

To place this in the long, unfinished history of serious psychiatry (by which I mean the growth of a formal underpinning of all the behavioral sciences) is more difficult. Such underpinning is not yet completed. We are still working on it, trying to do what, say, Newton did for physics.

J. Von Neumann (1944) tried it with the theory of games, and in the beginning of his book he hopes wistfully that somebody would provide a fiction for the behavioral sciences that should serve as their Newtonian particle—that elegant fiction upon which physics was built. Later, scien-tists corrected the Newtonian particle in all sorts of ways, but that first, essential step had been made.

I think the history of formal behavioral science begins with Fechner and Weber in Leipzig, about 1840. Weber had made the discovery that ratio is what makes a difference, and Fechner saw that this was impor-tant. So Fechner gets the credit, though the first step was Weber's. That discovery, of course, puts the whole of the hard sciences out of the realm of what we are interested in. In the hard sciences it has always been assumed that causes have real dimensions of Length, Mass, Time, or some combination of these; e.g., Energy has dimension, $ML^2/T^2$ (Mass x Velocity squared). But the Weber-Fechner generalization implied that stimulus as a "cause" of sensation or behavior was of zero dimensions—a ratio between similar dimensions (or a difference between dimensionally incomparable complexes or gestalten). This made the whole methodolo-gy of the hard sciences irrelevant to any consideration of behavior or psy-chic science—a clean sweep! After that there was no point in fussing with quantitative experiments. Altogether, an extraordinary feat.

I do not know whether Fechner knew quite how important his law was, but he did know that the discovery about ratios—which was an empirical and (surprisingly) an experimental discovery—was outstanding-ly important. He went a little insane with it, I think, and wrote a very curi-ous book about life after death (Fechner, 1836/1943). He realized, of course, that difference is not located in either space or time. Where is the difference between this paper and that desk top? Obviously not in the paper; obviously not in the wood. It certainly is not in the space between them, and it is a little hard to say that it is in your senses *and* my senses.

In fact, difference is dimensionless because it tends to be a ratio between two similars of some kind; and ratios between similars have no dimensions because the dimensional aspect "cancels out." The difference between these things is still the difference between these things after I mail this thing to Alaska or to any other place. We deal with something that is not localized and that is, in a certain sense, not physical. On the other hand, it can trigger a sense organ.

What you do as a perceiver, always, is to compare. If you do not have an external event to trigger you, you make an event by a scanning process so that the yellow of the paper against the brown of the table can be perceived by micronystagmus. The difference becomes an event in time.

Perception of states is always very poor, or zero (I am never quite sure which, but certainly very poor). It must be clear that you would not know when to respond, if you did not have an event structure. A state gives you no "when." Put a frog in a saucepan of cold water and have him settle down comfortably; then very slowly raise the temperature. It is said that if you raise the temperature slowly enough, the frog will not jump, and ends up boiled; there is no "when" for him to perceive. Always, perception depends on change or gradient[1] (a statement that follows from Fechner's contribution).

The next great contribution probably was that of Alfred Wallace, who went to collect butterflies in the rain forests of Ternate, in Indonesia. Following an attack of malaria, he had a psychedelic (or delirious) trip, in which he discovered natural selection. He wrote a long letter to Darwin about it—not the best person to have written the letter to—and in that letter stated, "The action of this principle" (which he called the "struggle for existence") "is exactly like that of the centrifugal governor of the steam engine, which checks and corrects any irregularities almost before they become evident; and in like manner no unbalanced deficiency in the animal kingdom can ever reach any conspicuous magnitude, because it would make itself felt at the very first step, by rendering existence difficult, and extinction almost sure to follow" (Wallace, 1858).

---

1. It is probably not correct to say that perception depends upon "gradient," which has always real dimensions. Rather, it must depend upon difference so set in time or space as to be perceptible.

It is notable that he saw natural selection as chiefly a stabilizing device rather than an evolutionary process. It is, of course, both. Wallace created the first cybernetic model, but since he did not know that he had done anything of importance he gets little credit.

Wallace's model is cybernetic inasmuch as he recognized the recursive nature of its self-corrective mechanism. He failed, however, to recognize that both the steam engine and the evolutionary process depend upon information. If he ever read Fechner (which is improbable), he failed to see that perception as conceived by Fechner provided another model—difference being "causal" in all three cases: evolution, perception, and the engine with a governor.

Wallace spoke as if only the scientist were controlled by information. No deficiency can reach "conspicuous" magnitude, and the machine corrects irregularities "almost before they become evident"; and the words "conspicuous" and "evident" refer only to senses of some human observer. Wallace did not say—perhaps did not dare to say—that the engine and the ecology have lower thresholds for perception of change or irregularity than human observers can have.

Next came Whitehead and Russell with *Principia* (1910) and the discovery of those hierarchies of message material called "logical types," the discovery of the "meta" relation, as we roughly call it. Again, the discoverers only half knew the monstrous power, the wide significance, of their discovery. It sometimes seems as if every great breakthrough in science is only the discovery of the wider relevance of something said many years before. Whitehead and Russell seem to have seen their work concerning the foundations of mathematics as an abstruse and abstract matter, not as something fundamental to all human interaction and all evolutionary process.

The credit for discovering the importance of *Principia* in engineering and in human natural history goes, surely, to Norbert Wiener (1948) and Warren McCulloch. I learned this discovery from them and brought this powerful insight with me to the Langley Porter Institute. Jurgen Ruesch and I were indeed "standing on the shoulders of giants."

So, in 1948 the problem was clear: The problem as set by context (whether or not one knew that this is what one was doing), was to build the underpinnings for the behavioral sciences—their Newtonian particle. How to start?

We did all sorts of odd things. For me, the turning point was a conversation with Jurgen one morning, not in his little office but over on my side. We were groping for what are called "definitions" of communication: What is a message? What do we mean when we say that those actions are a message? Can there be "private" actions? Ruesch started the conversation with: "Suppose a man is peeing in the woods and he thinks nobody is looking at him, or maybe, in fact nobody *is* looking at him. Is his act of peeing against a tree all by himself a message? Shall we call it a message?" And we pushed that one around. Either he or I then moved on to the next question: "If there is in fact somebody watching, but the man who is peeing does not know there is somebody there, is he sending a message? If the man who is peeing does know the watcher is there, it definitely becomes a two-way exchange. It is a one-way message for the watcher, even if the first man does not know that the watcher is there. But it definitely becomes a two-way message if, unbeknownst to the watcher, the first man knows that the watcher is there. The action might be purposive, to give certain indications to the watcher. One can imagine all sorts of indications he might want to give—for example, that he is not in a hurry, that he has time to stop, and so on. Finally, there is the case in which they could both know; then it would be a statement of intimacy, or all sorts of things. Does each know that the other knows?

Out of that conversation grew another question. We had been reading Lorenz's *King Solomon's Ring* (1952) at the time, and about the jackdaws that say "kiaw" before they fly for home. Does the jackdaw who says "kiaw" and then flies for home know that his saying "kiaw" is, in fact, a message to another jackdaw, which will make the second jackdaw fly for home and say "kiaw"? (This, of course, is not a question you can answer by looking inside the jackdaw.)

On the other hand, with a little care in defining the question, you can start an answer. The question became: Does jackdaw number one have use of the information, "My saying 'kiaw' will affect jackdaw number two"? Actually, there are various symptoms or indications that can occur only if jackdaw number one does have that piece of information. This is, as you see, not a question about consciousness[2]; it is a question about what information you can use.

Does jackdaw number one know? Do jackdaws know that their messages are messages? This was a question heavy enough with theoretical load to shake the San Andreas Fault. Though we did not know it, we were asking about the epistemology of jackdaws, and the word "epistemology" had suddenly jumped out of philosophy to become a cross-cultural word. You have an epistemology and I have one, but they are not

---

2. We never touched the field of consciousness and I don't intend to now, in spite of being told by my publisher on the back of my own book that this is "A document of inner space." I hate metaphoric space almost as much as I hate metaphoric energy.

necessarily the same. Indeed, a study of the difference between them moves up another level to the science of metaepistemology.

If jackdaw number one knows that his message is a message, then it should be possible to find him correcting his messages if he gets them wrong. It might be possible to find him saying "kiaw" louder if the other jackdaw is farther from him. It might be possible to find that he is able to deceive the other jackdaw. All these things become possible only with the next logical typing: One can deceive *only* if he knows his messages are indeed messages.

So, Weldon Kees and I went to the Fleishhacker Zoo and there ran into a seldom-remembered fact: Animals engage in something called "play." To engage in play, they must have at least two logical types in their interaction. From there we went on to study the word "play" and the interaction of the otters in the zoo. We photographed them and began to get a set of concepts involving logical types. The occurrence of play meant that there are actions that label other actions.

What constitutes an "action"? An action is a piece cut out from the flow of behavior, by the observer, a piece of the behavior of one "individual" cut out from the flow of interaction of two or more individuals.

Where the cut is made is obscure; why there, and not elsewhere? Do jackdaws see the flow as divided up into "actions"?

Where does an action begin? When I came into this room I sat in this chair; where did that action begin? Is there an action of getting into a chair that is separate from getting out of a chair? It would seem that labels get stuck on chunks of behavior, but how do you delimit the chunks for the words to stick on? Do the jackdaws and the otters do this? These questions, which appear to be very simple, were the beginnings of a profound change in the paradigms of psychiatric theory. Indeed, the whole of our thinking—our ideas of how to think—about problems of behavioral science has changed.

From now on the focus of theory in these sciences will inevitably be upon form rather than content, and our perception of form that starts from the forms defined in *Principia* will evolve along with (but lagging behind) future advances in the foundations of mathematics.

We were not alone in this change of focus from content and narrative to form. Warren McCulloch[3] was with us, and a few others. But we at Langley Porter had the thrill of being in the front line. Thus, do we now

---

3. See, for example, McCulloch's collected essays, *Embodiments of Mind* (Cambridge, Mass.: M.I.T. Press, 1965).

have central paradigms for psychiatry and behavioral science? Do we have any fictions that will do for psychiatry what the Newtonian particle did for physics?

It is too soon to answer that question, but parts of an answer can be offered. First, it is now clear that the medieval view of mind/body relations as a sort of demonic possession is obsolete. Second, although the realm of ideas, information, mind—call it what you will—is immanent in, and inseparable from, the realm of physical appearances, it must be approached with its own special preconceptions and premises. The physical analogies will not do, and the analogies of method taken from the hard sciences will not do.

The new science will form around profoundly nonphysical ideas: the nature of the relation between name and that which is named, the nature of recursive systems, and the nature of difference.

## References

Fechner, G. T. 1943. *Büchlein vom Leben nach dem Tode* (1836). Translated into English with an Introduction by William James. New York: Pantheon. (Originally published, 1904.)

Lorenz, K. Z. 1952. *King Solomon's Ring*. New York: Crowell.

Von Neumann, J., and O. Morgenstern. 1944. *Theory of Games and Economic Behavior*. Princeton, N.J.: Princeton University Press.

Wallace, A. R. "On the Tendency of Varieties to Depart Indefinitely from the Original Type." In P. Appleman, ed., *Darwin: A Norton Critical Edition*. (Reprinted from *Journal of the Linnean Society, Zoology* 3 (1858):45–62.

Whitehead, A. N., and B. Russell. 1910. *Principia Mathematica*. Cambridge: Cambridge University Press.

Wiener, N. 1948. *Cybernetics, or Control and Communication in the Animal and the Machine*. New York: Wiley.

# PART III

## Epistemology and Ecology

# 14

## *Mind/Environment**

I suppose the question is, at any given moment in human life, and especially for people who are engaged in applied behavioral science in some
form or other, the helping trades—the question is: "What's happening?"
Well, you have certain data. But suppose you are from Mars and you're
looking into this room. You saw Harley [Shands] make a little talk at the
beginning; and then you saw that probably the oldest, or nearly the oldest, man in the room got up. You may have seen that a chair was put
here, sort of ready for him, to make it informal. You will observe, of
course, first of all, that everybody is sitting on the floor, that is, that
they're under gravity determination, and that there are a number of
other physicochemical determinants of what's happening. And all of
this is part of the answer to the question "What's happening?"

And so you are concerned with acting upon human behavior in
some way, in terms of your knowledge of what's going on. And this can
only be done with safety or wisdom if you have a pretty wide scope of
knowledge of all the possible factors and dimensions necessary to
understand what's going on. One of these will be gravity, impact, the
ordinary physicochemical stuff, and I'm not going to talk about that
because I'm not that sort of a scientist, and if I were engaged in manipu-
lations of human behavior, I wouldn't worry much about gravity—I'd
sort of take it as a given. Perhaps incorrectly.

So, all right, we've separated off one whole category of
determinants—those due to physical force and impact. Now, this leaves
a second world of explanation with again many subdivisions in it. This is
the world of explanation in which a "cause"—I use the word in quotes—
is, in general, a difference. A simple sort of case is an amoeba. If you
don't give him any dinner he starts to get active. He starts to locomote

*This lecture was delivered to the Department of Psychiatry Grand Rounds, Roosevelt
Hospital, New York, in 1969, and is reprinted, with editorial changes, from *Social Change*, no. 1
(1973), by permission of Gordon and Breach Science Publishers, Inc.

more than he would have. That is, you get a situation which contrasts very deeply with the matter of forces and impacts, in that the energy expenditure of the amoeba is, over a considerable range of circumstance, an inverse function of the energy input. If you don't give him dinner, he starts to locomote. And if you look around the world, you'll find that there are a great many cases in which things go backwards in this sort of way. In plants, growth is an inverse function of photosynthesis. So that if you've got a stem of a plant, a soft stem that is not too woody—and the light is falling on one side—it will grow more rapidly along the other side, away from the light, and this will bend the whole thing over toward the light. It grows faster on the side away—the plant's equivalent of the amoeba's movement—again depending on an inverse function.

In such a world, difference makes a difference, difference being quite a different thing from force or impact. We are out of the world of the hard sciences into the world in which difference becomes determinative. Now difference is very interesting, because—if I ask you to locate a difference, you will find that you cannot do so, because obviously it is not *in* this, it is not *in* that, it is not in the space between, and it's not in the time between. Differences can be spread over time, of course.

A difference is an elementary idea. It is of the stuff of which minds are made. It's *not* something in the realm of the hard sciences. And the moment you set up your hard science circuits in such a way as that difference will make a difference, then the thing you have created—it may be out of hardware, it may be out of God knows what—the thing which you have created begins to show characteristics of mind. It operates with ideas.

So, in addition to the world of the hard sciences, we have the world of mind. There are all sorts of more complicated things, you know. There is the world of mind which tries to deny the reality of mind. A large part of our scientific culture tries to do this. And when you want to try to understand why scientists do what they do, especially biologists, one of the things you have to allow for is that they are trying to deny the reality of mind in a world which has mind. And this leads to certain maladaptations in their functioning.

We've now defined a world of mind. There are various directions in which we can go from that point. One of the rather interesting directions is the point of overlap between these two sorts of explanation. Among the interesting ones is one they call *synaptic summation* (Fig. 1), where typically you have neurons A and B, and they both impact upon neuron C. The firing of A is insufficient to trigger C, B is insufficient to trigger C; the firing

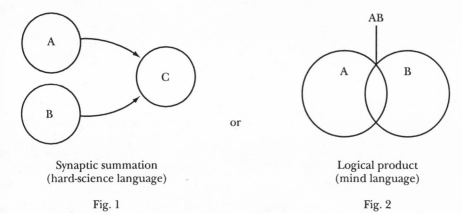

Synaptic summation
(hard-science language)

Logical product
(mind language)

or

Fig. 1                                                    Fig. 2

of A and B combined, if within a sufficiently small number of microseconds, triggers C. And this, interestingly enough, is called "summation" by the hard sciences. And if you're talking hard science, perhaps that's the right word for it. But if we are talking the language of mind, then we are *not* dealing with a case of *summation,* we are dealing with a case of a *logical product.* Imagine a diagram (Fig. 2) in which we have all the possible firings of A, and all the possible firings of B. In this group, we have the case where both A and B fired and in fact the functions of the firings of A are to break the functions of B into two classes—those firings of B which are accompanied by A and those firings of B which are not accompanied by A, and vice versa for the other way around. We are dealing here with a question of a logical product, not something in the hard sciences. It's something in the world of logic, in the world of mind. When you're talking about synaptic summation, you are in fact talking about a classical instance in which on the one hand it is possible to use hard-science language and say summation, and on the other it's possible to use mentalist language and say logical product. And there are various other sorts of classical meeting points where you can think one way or the other.

But which way you want to think matters. One of the main pathologies of psychological and psychiatric thinking is that these two ways of explanation are continually being crisscrossed, mixed up, and confused. We then get a whole economics of psychic energy in Freudian psychology and a whole mess of nonsense recurring over and over again in psychology, because people will think that the hard-science world should somehow be a part of the mental world, in which there are nothing but mental phenomena. There are no things, coconut palms, bits of chalk, or what have you in these circuits, you know. There are only complex

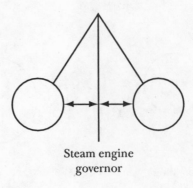

Steam engine
governor

Fig. 3

transforms of differences which we pick out of the things or the coconut palms or whatever.

All right. I don't want to spend too much time on that one. But it has to be said and it has to be said over and over again, because if people don't hear that, then they don't hear anything else.

Remember I mentioned that if you are going to operate by difference, it becomes exceedingly easy to use the difference in *either* direction. All you have to do is to use the *fact* of difference to trigger an energy generation, and which way the difference triggers the trigger is largely an arbitrary matter. It therefore becomes quite easy to make the energy expenditure the recipient of the difference, which is your input. You can make a positive input inhibitory or excitatory. The steam engine with a governor (Fig. 3) can be so connected that the closer the balls fall to the shaft, which is rotating, the greater the fuel supply, in which case you'll get a self-corrective system; or you can have it the other way around—the closer the balls fall, the less the fuel supply, and conversely the further they fly apart, the greater the fuel supply. Your system will then have a middle point, and if it's on the upper side of that middle point, it will run away in the direction of greater and greater activity, or below that middle point it will subside toward less and less and become stationary.

Now, this means that what we're talking about is not merely difference, but difference in circuit, the energy provision for the next step in the circuit always being provided by that next step. The difference itself does not *provide* the energy, it only *triggers* the expenditure of the energy. We talk then about differences and *transforms of difference*. Obviously a neural impulse is a very different sort of a thing from a difference in light or a difference in temperature, which is what triggers the end organ. When such differences are transformed in successive ways through the system, mind becomes a very complex network of pathways, some of them neural, some of them hormonal, some of them of other kinds, along which difference can be propagated and transformed.

When you've said that, you can then start asking, "Well, if you couldn't locate a difference, can you locate a mind?" This becomes a rather peculiar operation, because if you are going to understand things and build explanatory systems, especially mental explanatory systems, you will want to have within the system you're talking about pathways that are relevant to that system. That is, if you want to account for the route followed by a blind man, you will need to include the blind man's stick as a part of the determinant of his locomotion. So, if mind is a system of pathways along which transforms of difference can be transmitted, mind obviously does not stop with the skin. It is also all the pathways outside the skin relevant to the phenomenon that you want to account for.

Nor does the mind stop with those pathways whose events are somehow reported in consciousness, whatever that means. You must also include the underpinnings of the conscious mind, the "unconscious," down to the hormones as part of the network of pathways along which transforms of difference can be transmitted.

And clearly, action must be included in this, too. If you consider a man felling a tree with an ax, from one stroke of the ax to the next, the behavior of the ax, looked at by our Martian, is self-corrective in regard to the cut face of the tree trunk. The actual channels, which you would have to map out to understand a man cutting down a tree with an ax (it doesn't matter where you start—it can start with the face of the tree), would include differences in the cut face of the tree, differences in light waves reaching the eye, differences in the behavior of the end organ and showers of impulse in the optic nerve, differences transmitted over very complex networks, going out to differences transmitted to muscles, to differences in the movement of the ax, to differences in the next cut in the face of the tree. The "mental" system involved in cutting a tree is not a mind *in* a man who cuts a tree but a mind which includes differences in other characteristics in the tree, the behavior of the ax, and so on, all around a circuit which in essence is a completed circuit.

Now notice that most of the way we usually talk is quite out of step with the way I have just been talking. We say, "I cut down the tree." What that means is quite obscure in terms of the way I have been talking, in which the tree was part of the mind which cut it down. Not quite— because as already mentioned, at the beginning, we distinguished between hard-science talk and communicational talk. The world of information and the world of hard science are different worlds, and as Kant pointed out a very long time ago, the "thing in itself," the tree, the ax, can never enter into the communicational world of explanation. All that can enter are differences in tree face, differences in ax behavior, etc.

There are, of course, an infinite number of differences contained in this very generous piece of chalk here. If you want to make a total description of this piece of chalk, you would have to mention an infinite number of circumstances, map it onto three dimensions under a microscope or what have you. At a certain point you'll break down. Only *selected* differences of this piece of chalk become what we call information, and enter into the circuit under transformation, because the differences between the chalk faces are not differences between chalk faces when they get through my retinal end organ or tactile information—they have become differences in neural showers, etc., etc. The thing-in-itself never enters—only selected differences within the system that we're talking about do.

Now, not only do differences exist in circuits, they also exist in contexts, for, in the whole communicational world, nothing means anything except in the presence of other things. That is, a given phoneme, the sound of the letter "p," is totally meaningless except as part of, say, the word "perhaps"; but the word "perhaps" is totally meaningless except as part of a sentence, such as, "Perhaps it's a piece of soap." But the sentence, "Perhaps it's a piece of soap," is totally meaningless unless one knows the general setting in which it's said. In fact, it might be said on a stage and would mean something totally different from when it's said in a bathroom; and it was here said, I may say, as an example of a sentence which certainly meant nothing about soap. Perhaps. Its context was framed in such a way that you were not led to take a literal meaning out of the sentence, "Perhaps it's a piece of soap."

Now this is exceedingly important, because the ability to do that, to pull chunks of communicational material out of context into a frame of play, imagination, example, illustration, what have you, is an incredibly important part of human mental activity. It is the world of play, fantasy, etc. And the ability to not quite know, or to pretend you don't quite know when you've done this is, of course, one of the things we call schizophrenia.

Now, context is a hierarchically structured business. That is, the phoneme "p" is in the context of the word "perhaps," "perhaps" is in the context of the sentence, the sentence is in the context of the bathroom or the lecture podium or something, and so on.

We are endlessly dealing with this sort of a business. We have two persons. In order for B to understand A and for A to understand B, it's almost continuously necessary for them to put frames on this context. Take this behavorial chunk here (see Fig. 4)—A will almost inevitably see

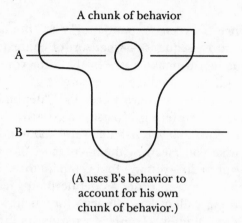

A chunk of behavior

(A uses B's behavior to
account for his own
chunk of behavior.)

Fig. 4

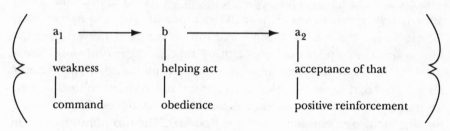

Fig. 5

his behavior as something happening in a chunk like that. And he will say that he did this because B did this, or that he did this in order to make B do that, and so forth.

We frame up our behavior into various sorts of sequential chunks. And we give various sorts of names to these chunks, usually giving the names sort of crooked. That is, we may say that A is very "dependent." What we mean by saying "A is dependent" is simply that there are chunks of interchange between A and B which have a certain formal characteristic (see Fig. 5). A is dependent on B—where $a_1$ is an indication of "weakness," b is a "helping act," and $a_2$ is an "acceptance" of that. And if A is able to see this ongoing stream as rather often containing patterns of that kind, he will think he is dependent on B. B may not think so at all, because it's up to the individual, after all—and culture, conventions, etc., various sorts of overdetermination—to see things his way. So B may very well say that $a_1$ was really a command, b was an act of obedience, and $a_2$ was a positive reinforcement. And B may very well say that A is "dominant," where A has been thinking that he was "dependent."

So the difference between "dependency" and "dominance" is how you read structure into a sequence—what sort of contextual frames you slide over the sequences to make sense of them for yourself. What the observer may think will be something else again.

Now I want you to notice these words like "dependency," "dominance," "spectatorship," "suffering," "passive-aggressive"—and a number of other descriptive terms that you habitually use about individuals. If you really want to say what you mean by them—which I think most psychiatrists don't really want to do—you will find you have to spell out *contexts of interchange* between persons in order to define their meaning. That is, there is not something called dependency which is inside people and which makes them dependent. There is a regularity in their external behavior vis-à-vis other persons, involving the behavior of other persons— because if other persons don't play, it doesn't work out right. This is actually what we mean by these "psychological words." For example, we say, "What do you mean by 'fatalism'?" Now the easy way to answer that question is to say, "I mean the sort of thing that an organism would learn, would acquire, if he were subjected to learning contexts of a certain kind." That is, if he were subjected, let us say, to Pavlovian contexts, where we have a conditioned stimulus, a response, and an unconditioned stimulus—i.e., a buzzer, salivation, and meat powder. The two stimuli are firmly connected by a time, which is usually fixed in the experiments.

Now if you learn that your universe is made up of strings of that kind, so to speak, you would then become a Pavlovian dog, and you would expect the universe to be made up of strings of that kind; and that universe is one in which you can't do anything to make things happen, but you can reasonably look at the stars in order to predict what's going to be happening so that you can be ready with your saliva when it happens. Now, astrology would be a perfectly good science in such a universe. But you might avoid engineering, and you might avoid the whole philosophy of manipulation. In a certain sense, you would be a fatalist. (There are other sorts of fatalism, of course.) This gives you a way of making a fairly precise form of words for what you mean by something like "fatalism"; equally, "dependency," "dominance," "suffering," etc.

Now the very interesting thing is—and here we come to the question about the unconscious—if you are subjected to contexts of learning (and we are all continually subjected to contexts of learning because all contexts are contexts of learning, more or less), you will tend *not* to resolve those aspects of a problem which have been solved once already. This means that in any problem that you encounter in the world, there are going to be some items which are more or less unique: in this lecture hall, the podium is so much above the audience and so far from them, and that's unique to this lecture hall, but in other lecture halls it's a little different. On the other hand, there are a great many things in common between this lecture room and other lecture rooms which I don't have to make special allowance for when I lecture in this room as opposed to the others.

What is unique from context to context is going to have to be dealt with; what is general from context to context can be handed over to what for a moment we will call "habit." Now it so happens that it is the more abstract features of the situation which tend to be more generally true; the more finely detailed things vary from instance to instance. We then get the rather curious phenomenon that the reasonably lazy mind will economize by sinking the more abstract characteristics of situations to essentially lower levels which are in general less conscious. So that when your patient comes into the therapy room with a more or less ready-built transference, he repeats what he has in fact done in childhood. He has sunk a number of rules for handling personal relationships which he learned in dealing with his parents and siblings, and when he comes into your consulting room, he operates in terms of that sunken material. This is more abstract than whether the person he is addressing has a beard or hasn't got a beard; he adjusts to all the fine detail, and acts in an overall pattern derived from childhood. And what we get is a complex system of rather highly abstract generality, which it is exceedingly difficult for us to alter.

The difficulty in altering these generalizations arises because it isn't at all easy to test them. The Pavlovian dog believes that the universe is made of sequences, and that the conditioned stimulus and the unconditioned stimulus are fixed by a time interval. The only way of testing that, you see, is to act as though he could influence the events. But this is precisely what he's learned not to do. And if he doesn't interfere, then he will in fact perceive a universe in which these regularities are reasonably true, and the whole thing becomes a self-fulfilling proposition.

This goes for almost all generalizations at the level that we're talking about—generalizations about dependency and other more abstract patterns of human relationships. And in a sense, the art of being a psychoanalyst is to construct situations, which you could not do in the outside world, in which the patient will in fact discover that his generalizations about relationship are *not* true. The outside world in general does not provide him with such situations, which are crucial tests of his generalizations. He sees a world which looks as if it verified the way he "unconsciously" believes it to be.

At the moment, I'm specifically interested in social systems that have these characteristics, and how these conceivably can be corrected. The moment you have these habit-forming characteristics, which are not confined to individual organisms—ecosystems do it, cities do it—you have what the computer people call "hard programming": a certain characteristic of the behavior of the system is so deeply built into the system that it affects almost everything the system does, and nothing short of very violent change will change that deep programming. This is the problem of psychotherapy, after all—how are you going to change the deeply programmed material. This is one of the things I'm very interested in at present.

I am also very much interested in the problem of how an entity of this general kind can recognize another entity of this general kind. And I strongly suspect that this is where aesthetics is going to link up with systems theory. When you see a primrose on the river's brim, what do you actually see? The quote is, "A primrose by a river's brim, a yellow primrose was to him, and it was nothing more." On the other hand, if you see a primrose and it *is* something more, aesthetically, then I suspect that the primrose contains formal characteristics of symmetry, imperfect symmetry, complex interwoven patterning, and so forth, which indicate that the primrose itself is a mentally governed piece of morphogenesis, and that the aesthetic thing is a recognition of that, for better or worse, for beauty or ugliness. This is one of the matters I'm now rather interested in.

*Question:* It seems that you are applying science to psychoanalysis rather than applying psychoanalysis to science. . . .

*Bateson:* In a sense, I'm seeking to apply systems theory to the known body of knowledge of which, for example, psychoanalysis is a piece, in order to get a platform on which science can be built. I mean, we've got an awful lot of pieces, you see, and very little core knowledge.

There are also questions of method. One of the characteristic methods which you have been taught is that science consists in collecting some facts, whatever they are, making a hypothesis, making then a prediction from the hypothesis, and taking that prediction back to the facts. I would maintain that this is mostly nonsense. And it is nonsense of a particular kind, namely that kind which Molière has stigmatized as the creation of *dormitive principles.*

Let's say the problem is a Ph.D. examination in which the learned doctors ask the candidate, "Why does opium put people to sleep?" And the candidate, in dreadful Latin, replies, "Because, learned doctors, it contains a dormitive principle," whereupon they all cheer and say, "How right he is." Now about three-quarters of all the hypotheses in the behavioral sciences are fundamentally dormitive principles. "Anxiety" is a dormitive principle. "Emotion" is a dormitive word. It's just like "anxiety."

We were talking about the "sinking" of generalizations about relationships to rather lower levels of consciousness, and somewhere down there meeting with genotypic determinations of propositions about relationships. The computing of such matters—"Do you love me?," "Am I dependent on you?," and so forth—is in general an unconscious business, or partly unconscious in the sense that when you are working in accord with your computations and everything is working out nicely, you have certain somatic, visceral "feelings" about it. And when frustrated in these unconscious computations, you have other visceral feelings about it. Now these visceral feelings are, I think, what people mean by emotions. It's fairly clear, as I've said, that most of psychiatry—interview psychiatry anyway—is concerned with straightening people out at these levels, which is only another way of saying straightening them out at the level of their emotional computations, their computations about relations, not about what *I* do, but about what I do *in a relationship*.

Of course it's very difficult to talk about this stuff in a civilization which is, oh, at least seventy percent insane in its major premises about the nature of man and the nature of relationships. One of the interesting insanities is the notion which really came to a head in the nineteenth century during the Industrial Revolution, which was helped along by Darwin and other persons, namely that the unit of survival is either an individual or family line or a species or subspecies or something of the kind. Now, in terms of that premise, we have been building machines and fighting the environment. We have now achieved, I hope, empirical proof that that premise won't do any longer; in fact, the unit of survival is *organism in environment*, and not organism *versus* environment.

The question of whether it's you versus me, or you and me *as part of* something which includes us both, is, of course, right at the base of why you might think I was out to do you in, and why you might be right, because, after all, I am a member of this culture.

*Question:* How "dormitive" is the term "schizophrenia"?

*Bateson:* Well, a great many people use that term dormitively. That is, they talk as though there were something inside my skin which made me talk funny, you know. On the other hand, talking about schizophrenia in this way has sort of focused attention on some *behavioral* characteristics which I've paid a good deal of attention to—*not* supposing that there is a *something* called schizophrenia inside these patients which makes them do this. In fact, my main question has been, how is schizophrenia related to such things as humor, religion, poetry—obviously something bigger, a genus or family of behaviors which are all somehow related formally. This seems to me a nondormitive way of approaching it. Does that answer your question? I mean, obviously the word "schizophrenia," as used in law courts and such places, is being used mainly in a dormitive sense. And then you get the use of the term by the geneticists, who believe that the solution to all problems is to find a gene which will serve as a dormitive principle. Now geneticists are beginning to discover that genetics isn't quite like that. . . .

*Question:* Could you compare your use of the word "unconscious" with other abstractions you've talked about?

*Bateson:* Let us suppose I am under hypnosis, and a suggestion has been given, of which I may or may not be aware, that my hand is to rise. My hand starts to rise and I am not conscious of the complete context in which that hand is rising because I didn't catch the stimulus (the suggestion) when it was given to me. And I'm not conscious of "raising my hand." From where I sit, *it* is rising. But I'm fully conscious of the hand rising. I can see that, and the hypnotist knows it. I know it and he knows it. We can agree on that. Now, in my terms, I'm "unconscious" of those pieces of information which I cannot put my finger on, so to speak.

I cannot give any reasonable report of what Harley looks like to me. The amount of material in the visual images is so much greater and in general not of a kind which translates easily into words. I cannot report this, but I am pretty conscious of what he looks like to me. What he *really* looks like—that may be different. Of course, I'm totally unconscious of the process by which I make the image of Harley. That image is there and I can "look at it," but how I made it and the whole business of putting perspective into it—all that is a mental process to which I have no access whatsoever, as far as I know, and no amount of talking on a couch backwards is going to help me to say how I make these perspective images.

*Question:* No matter how complicated is the process of arriving at an image of me, you're quite clear that it's not the image of somebody else.

*Bateson:* Oh yes. That's a very long way from being able to verbalize the image of you. I have been talking about using a word like "unconscious," which has nothing to do with the two-person system, at least as it was being used psychologically. Of course, originally the word is con-scious, meaning knowledge which is shared. But I accepted the invitation to use the word "unconscious" in a more or less Freudian sense as precisely that knowledge which is not shared by the self. And I have been talking at the level of diagrams of interpersonal relations. I've tried, I think, never to talk about arcs of circuits which are incomplete. Now, in general, if you want to talk about arcs of circuits which *are* complete, the best place to look for them is in two-person systems, where you may look to see what happens between the two persons. But there aren't many arcs which are complete within the individual.

*Question:* The whole conception of unconscious, or unconscious mind, has relevance only in the social context of people who accept that notion.

*Bateson:* I'm not content there, though. The problem isn't where it was in, say, 1880, when the problem was the existence of unconscious mental processes. In 1969, the problem is, what in heck is consciousness, since unconscious mental process presents no new mystery as such. We don't know much about it, but that it should be unconscious is not mysterious. The mystery is what we call conscious.

# 15

## *The Thing of It Is*\*

The thing of it is that these are very difficult things to talk about because there are three aspects of the matter which people think are different problems, different concerns, which in fact boil down to being all one matter. I put these three up on the board. One of them is *evolutionary theory*, and that is a matter, you know, which is dealt with in one sort of book. Another is *mind/body problems,* and that is dealt with in another sort of book. And the third is *epistemology*, and that is dealt with again in another sort of book.

I want to get across to you that these three apparently different matters are in fact all one subject of discourse and that you cannot handle one without simultaneously handling the others. If we are going to talk about "consciousness," I would like to aim that word specifically at an awareness of these three things and their interrelations.

Let us start from where we were last night. We had a lot of Cartesian diagrams in which time was horizontal and responsibility or narcissism or something or other was the vertical coordinate. These diagrams were on the model of what Descartes thought was the way to think—a model which has been extraordinarily profitable in thinking about a lot of things like planets and temperatures and even perhaps populations. (I'm not too sure about populations.) The model is, at any rate, fashionable still among those who study populations.

Now, it's not an accident that the man who designed those graphs was the man who also formalized the dualism between mind and matter. And it's very curious that this should be so. I want to get across to you that when you do this—when you start arranging your words and explanations on that sort of a tautology, that set of basic notions about how things are related—you will of necessity end up with the sort of split

\*This talk was delivered to a Summer 1975 Lindisfarne Conference, and is reprinted from *Earth's Answer: Explorations of Planetary Culture at the Lindisfarne Conferences,* edited by Michael Katz, William P. Marsh, and Gail Gordon Thompson, 1977, by permission of Lindisfarne Press.

between mind and body that Descartes ended up with. That split, you know, has been the battleground of science, especially of biology, for a very long time. And the problem is how to get away from it.

You see, the moment you go to the extreme materialistic end, which has these dimensions and quantities in it, and the nice curves and all the rest of it, the moment you specialize on that side, the thing bubbles up on the mental side with all sorts of mental-spiritual notions which you excluded from your materialism. You squeezed them out from one context and they bubbled up in another. The moment you do that, you're split wide open.

Now, it may be that there are total splits in the universe. I prefer to believe that it is rather one universe than two, but the only real argument for that, you know, is Occam's razor; it's less trouble to believe in one universe than to believe in two. It's miraculous enough that there be one. Believe me.

There is also, you see, a consciousness of how it is to think, how it is to engage in trial and error and so on, and that consciousness, as far as I can make out, is roughly called *prajna* in Tibetan Buddhism. It's a useful word if that's what it means. (It's always difficult to be sure with Sanskrit.) So what do we do?

There's a very curious theorem called Euler's theorem. You remember at school you were taught you should not add apples and miles. And that was a very useful thing to learn. It's very useful in reading equations to sort out the syntax of the dimensions. If you have $E = mc^2$, you have to remember that m is of the dimension of mass (not matter but mass); c is of the dimension of length divided by time—it's a velocity. So $c^2$ is length squared divided by time squared. E therefore is of the dimension of mass times the square of a length divided by the square of a time, and that's all E is, you know. A *quantity*, of those dimensions.

Now, Euler's theorem in topology says that in any polyhedron—that's a solid, three-dimensional figure with edges and faces and apices where the edges meet—that the number of faces plus the number of apices equals the number of edges plus two. Let me do that on the blackboard.

$$\text{Faces} + \text{apices} = \text{edges} + 2$$

There's a horrid question, you see: What is the dimension of the number "2"? We have been grossly adding surfaces to meeting points and then equating them with edges, and then there's this "2." We appear to have mixed our dimensions hopelessly. What is the solution to this difficulty?

The theorem stands. It is probably the "fundamental" theorem of topology. How then is it right that these quantities should be added in this funny way? And what is the dimension of "2"? I made a crack on the side last night, asking Jonas [Salk] whether he was sure that the subject matter we are dealing with is a subject matter within which the concept of dimensions, and therefore quantities and graphs and all the rest, is appropriate. Is this an appropriate language for talking about such matters at all? I sort of let that pass as a wisecrack last night, but now we have to face it more seriously.

You see, a fellow in a speedboat thinks he is going at a "speed." He thinks he can measure the speed with a speedometer. But that's really not true in psychology. The truth is that he's having fun. And the relationship of the fun to the speed is very obscure. Perhaps what he's having fun with is (his opinion about) the probability of disaster. Probabilities, you know, are of zero dimensions. I don't know the dimensions of "opinion."

You see, we've been pulling these analogies and metaphors out of physics and then trying to map human behavior, love, hate, beauty, ugliness onto those metaphors.

God, language is a lousy invention, isn't it?

*Question:* Are you sure it's a dimension?

*Bateson:* Language? I'm sure that it is not a dimension. I am sure that the epistemology for forms and patterns is different from the implicit epistemology of hard science. We have *names* of faces, *names* of edges, *names* of apices, and that's what we're playing with. Not *faces, edges,* and *apices.* And because the whole thing is removed to a higher level of abstraction, in a curious way it becomes legitimate to add them together and subtract them and all the rest of it. Euler's theorem is in the Platonic universe, in the universe of ideas, and not in the universe of dimensions. In this Platonic universe, the analogues of dimensions are names and classes and logical types. We are dealing not with "real" dimensions but with descriptions of dimensions, and the big enlightenment comes when you suddenly realize that all this stuff is *description.* And when you realize that, then you realize that it's possible to be wrong in how you organize your descriptions, and it's possible to be wrong for this reason: the creatures we talk about—people, sea urchins, starfish, beetles, plants, cabbages, whatnot—all these creatures themselves contain description. The DNA are descriptive prescriptions, injunctions, for how to make a bird or a man or whatever. And these injunctions, therefore, themselves contain epistemology. They contain an implicit theory of the nature of description. You can never get away from theories of the nature of description whenever, wherever you have descriptions. All descriptions are based on theories of how to make descriptions. You cannot claim to have no epistemology. Those who so claim have nothing but a bad epistemology. And every description is based upon, and contains implicitly, a theory of how to describe. The Cartesian coordinates contain a theory of how to describe, and for many purposes, I believe, it is an inappropriate and dangerous theory—one which in the end leads to various sorts of quantification of "things" which probably should be regarded as patterns, not quantities. It also leads to conceptual separation of mind from matter. You see, you can be wrong in describing the anatomy of a human being when you say he has five bananalike objects on the end of each limb, because, you see, he might not have "five fingers" on the end of each limb, but "four angles between fingers." The question is, what is there in the genetic injunctions, the prescriptive descriptions, for how to make a hand? Is there a number at all? "Five," or "four," or whatever? Is there conceivably a rule of symmetry there? Is each limb itself primarily bilaterally symmetrical, like a feather? We have here an almost total gap in our genetic knowledge.

There are a few little spots in genetics where there are indications of what the epistemology, what the theory of prescription, might be. Let me give you a couple of cases because I want now to start thinking in terms of biological systems or universes which are organized by information, i.e., by significant *differences* rather than by forces or impacts.

Vertebrates and chordates are, on the whole, bilaterally symmetrical in their ectoderm and mesoderm. The endoderm is always profoundly asymmetrical. There are a few cases of asymmetry—and fairly superficial asymmetry—in ectoderm and mesoderm (in owls and cetaceans). Why the endoderm is more asymmetrical than the rest, Lord alone knows. So we ask, where does the bilateral symmetry come from? Not the genes. Oh no. It's doubtful whether the DNA and genes could ever be able to tell the embryo how to orient itself. An unfertilized frog's egg (and this has been known since the 1920s and presumably this goes for all vertebrates) is, so far as we know, radially symmetrical. It has a differentiated north pole and a south pole but is the same all around the equator. It's pigmented down to rather below the equator. This top ("animal") end is fairly clear of fat, while the other ("vegetal") end is heavily fat. The egg is sort of yellow down here and nearly black on the top. But it's the same all the way around, so far as we know. The nucleus is located somewhere near the top. Now, how will the egg decide on the line of bilateral symmetry, the plane of bilateral symmetry?

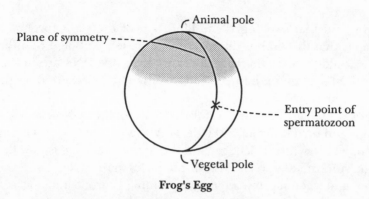

**Frog's Egg**

The answer is that a spermatozoon will enter somewhere below the equator. That defines three points—two poles and the point of entry—and that line of longitude, that meridian, will be the middle line of the embryo. You don't have to have a spermatozoon; you can do it with a fiber of a camel's-hair brush. Just prick it and the egg will develop and will make a complete frog which will be haploid. It will only have half the number of chromosomes it should have and will be sterile, but it will catch flies and hop like any proper frog. All the information for catching flies and hopping is there.

This experiment tells us something of what the genetic code looks like. The genetic code—the unfertilized egg—has sufficient information to pose a question. It can set the egg to a readiness to receive a piece of information. But the genetic code does not contain the answer to that question. It must wait for something outside the egg, a spermatozoon or a camel's-hair fiber, to fix it. This, you see, sets a whole stage for asking, *what is the unit of embryology?* And the unit is not just that egg; the unit is the egg *plus* the answer. And without the egg plus the answer, you cannot go on to the next phase. And so on.

Let me now give you another piece of experimental data about the nature of this whole business. We take a newt embryo, and I will draw it in profile, facing to the right. At a certain point a low mountain starts to

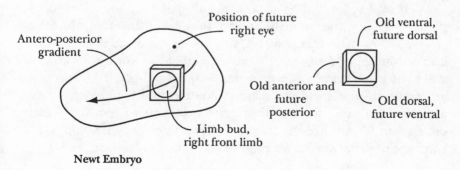

**Newt Embryo**

swell up, and that swelling is the limb bud of the right forelimb. And remember that this limb is different from the left limb and that that difference couldn't be in the DNA, because the same DNA are in the cells on the right side that are in the cells on the left. So where does the difference come from?

Anyway, that is the limb bud for the right forelimb. Now we cut it out and lift it and turn it through 180 degrees and put it back in. The former front edge is now the back edge, and the old ventral edge is now the dorsal edge. And the old posterior now points forward. It'll grow in the new position, and when it grows what do you think? It grows into a *left* leg!

Why?

It grows into a left leg because it knows. It has received the information or injunction and is governed by the information. I'm not talking about consciousness, I'm talking about being determined by information. I do not know whether it's conscious. I'm not a limb bud of an amphibian.

It seems that the body of the embryo has a fore and aft gradient which was determined before it even developed a bulge which was the bud. Such gradients are informational gradients. Lord knows what they depend on—it could be clockwork for all I know. It doesn't matter, you see. Any difference could serve as information. It could be electrical, chemical, what have you.

That fixes the fore and aft differentiation in the bud. But the dorsal-ventral information comes much later. We did our operation before the bud knew the dorsal-ventral answers, which later it gets from its neighborhood. So now this edge is told to be a "dorsal" by the neighboring tissues; and the old dorsal edge is told to be a "ventral" by the neighbors. The ground plan for the limb is complete. It must come out this way. The proximal-distal dimension is unchanged, so the ground plan is that of a *left* leg. We have inverted one dimension (the dorsal-ventral) but not the other. If you invert one dimension of a three-dimensional object, as in a mirror, you get the inverted mirror image.

This world of morphogenesis obeys a topological logic. One-dimensional inversion gives you the mirror image, two inverted dimensions give you the ortho image again, and three dimensions give you the inverted image again. What I'm saying is that the world into which we are moving, the world in whose terms we have to think, is a world of patterns, and in that world there are tautologies and logics which we can use for explaining, for building accurate language and for creating some rigor. It's not like the langage of quantities and such things. It's a language of patterns and, for most of us, an unfamiliar business.

We have a major problem in front of us to create the language in which we can talk about evolution, about morphogenesis, about epistemology, and about mind/body.

We are going to deal with trial and error in these matters, and the old lineal and transitive logic that we were brought up with was devoid of time. There were some nice patterns in Euclid and elsewhere, but timeless: "If straight lines are defined in this way and points are defined in that way and triangles are defined so and so, and if two triangles have three sides of the one equal to three sides of the other, then the two triangles are equal, each to each." That's the way I learned it. But look at the word "then." There's no time in that "then." There is nothing but logic in it. Now, consider the sequence: "If a frog's egg receives a spermatozoon on a given meridian, then that meridian will define the plane of bilateral symmetry." That "then" has time in it. Sequential time. An effect follows always with a delay.

If Epimenides was right in saying that Cretans always lie, and he was a Cretan, was he a liar or not a liar? If he was a liar, then he was not a liar. If he was not a liar, then it was untrue that Cretans are always liars, and so on. Now, look at the "then" in that paradox. If yes, then no. If no, then yes. If the "then" is logical, there is paradox, but if the "then" is causal and temporal, the contradiction disappears. The sequence is like that of the electric bell on the front door. If the circuit is complete, then a magnet is activated which will break the circuit. If the circuit is broken, then the magnet will not be activated, and the circuit will be restored. If the circuit is restored, then the magnet will be activated, and the circuit will be broken, and so on. So we get an oscillation, and the paradox "if yes then no; if no then yes" contains a real *temporal* "then."

Such oscillating systems are operated by thresholds—not by states but by *differences* and changes and even differences between changes. There is information not only in our words but also in the processes which we describe. It's nice to have the explanation in step with the system of ideas within the process which you are explaining.

This is what I keep saying. If we are going to say that the thing has "five fingers," we may be wrong because really it has four gaps between fingers—four relationships between fingers—because growth is governed by relationships, not by the absolutes.

Now, if you are going to face oscillating systems, you meet a very curious circumstance—that a certain degree of *reality* is imparted to the "system," the chunk of living matter. There is a justification of some sort in drawing a line around it, perhaps giving it a name. That justification is based on the fact of autonomy, of literal "autonomy," in that the system names itself. The injunctions which govern the system necessarily are messages which *stand for* or name the system. The system is auto-self-nomic, self-naming or self-ruling. And that is the only autonomy there is, as far as I know. It's recursiveness, and recursiveness is crucial to any system containing *if-then* links, where the "then" is not a logical but a temporal "then."

I'm now starting to build up, you see, slowly, to where we can begin to think. By introducing time into the if-then relations, we have made classical logic obsolete. But that doesn't mean, you know, that it is now impossible to think. It means that classical logic is a poor simulation of cause. We used to ask, "Can computers simulate logic?" But computers work on if-then relations that are causal: *"If* this transistor tickles that transistor, *then* such-and-such." That's a causal "if-then," with time in it.

The truth of the matter is that logic is a very poor simulation of computers and other causal systems. But this does not mean that there are not regularities, patterns, and epistemologies; there are other ways of describing which are better representations of how to think. I keep coming back to the assertion that what we deal with are descriptions, second order *representations* of how it is. How it primarily is, we don't know. We can't get there. The *Ding an sich* is always and inevitably out of reach. You have sense organs specially designed to keep the world out. It is like the lining of your gut, which is specially designed to keep out foreign proteins, to break down the foreign protein before it enters the bloodstream. The protein must be broken down to amino acids. Only the amino acids are allowed through. Your sense organs similarly break down the information or "news" to the firing of end organs, which is another piece of this whole business. The mystery of epistemology is still how anything knows anything, how it is that an egg can be organized; and you're only eggs, and I'm only eggs, you know. We're the phenotypic tryout of eggs. The hen is the egg's way of finding out whether it was a good egg. If the hen's no good, the egg was lousy. It had the wrong genes or something. The system is all trial and error. That's not quite what Samuel Butler said, but pretty near it. He said the hen was the egg's way of making another egg. It's really the egg's way of finding out if it was any good in evolutionary terms.

So we face two levels of trial and error. There is the evolutionary testing of the phenotype, but also there is the thinking which happens inside the phenotype—another stochastic process with a shorter time span. The same sort of thinking has got to be used to analyze evolution as the thinking you use to analyze thought. Not that they're the same process. I do not believe that what you think can alter your ova or spermatozoa; I'm not preaching a Lamarckian message at all. Indeed, quite the contrary. I am saying that there is a nonquantitative and nonlineal way of thinking about things which is common to the evolutionary process and the process of thought. And therefore, epistemology and evolution go hand in hand. The problems of mind/body obviously are the same sort of business. And what you think about evolution is going to be the reflection of what you think about mind/body relations and what you think about thought. It's all going to move along together.

But thought processes and evolutionary processes are of different logical type. Never the twain shall meet. Let us examine for a moment the nature of purpose in individuals and in adaptive changes in phylogeny. Pragmatism. Wonderful.

But let us suppose that in biological evolution there were a direct communicational bond between individual experience which will induce somatic change, as it's called, and the DNA injunctions to be passed on to the next generation. Let us imagine for the moment a Lamarckian universe, in which, if I tan myself in the sun, this will in some degree be passed on as increased brownness of the skin of my offspring. In such a system, my offspring will have lost a flexibility. They will no longer have my freedom. By hypothesis, I am flexible. I go brown in the sun, or I bleach with no sun. But Lamarckian theory would presume a rigidity in my offspring, a reduction of their ability to bleach with no sun. Obviously a Lamarckian theory will in the end enforce an increasing rigidity, a loss of the ability to adapt, and that won't do. Things are going to get too tight. Our description of the body is made up of a very large number of variables, which interlock in all sorts of rings and loops, so that if you start tightening on any one of them, you will ipso facto tighten others, ending up with no tolerance or flexibility anywhere. This happens with disease or even with a cold in the head. We put people in bed and keep them warm when they have a cold because they've lost a lot of flexibility by being stressed up to the maximum or minimum somewhere in their organization. We therefore protect them during that period.

Evidently Lamarckian inheritance would present severe problems for biological evolution, and the barrier between somatic change and genetic change seems to be quite important. I said earlier that this barrier or contrast is really a contrast in logical typing, and this is important. The trouble is that I don't want my offspring to be more brown than I. I want them to be more able to turn brown. This will pay evolutionary dividends. But this is a change of different logical type from what Lamarckians envisage. In social evolution there is no barrier corresponding to that between phenotype and genotype. Consider the invention of carbon paper. This prevented the slavery depicted in Dickens's lawyers' offices where miserable people are copying documents. That was made largely obsolete by the invention of carbon paper. Fine, but within a few years of the invention of carbon paper, we started to use it for personal letters, even for love letters, because, after all, posthumously we'd like our biographers to have access to our most romantic thoughts. Today our filing cabinets are overfull. The adoption of any invention becomes irreversible very quickly. It becomes built deeply, irreversibly, into the physiology of our society within very few years of invention. There is no barrier between immediate adaptation and pickling the change into society.

For this reason, more than for any other, I distrust consciousness as a gimmick added to the evolutionary scene. Conscious cerebration is much too fast. It doesn't give any time for growth into the new state of affairs. There is no trial and error or tentative assimilation which would slowly flow, hesitate and flow, hesitate and flow, into new patterns.

If I were to try to *apply* my theories to the changing social scene, I think that that is where my pragmatic remarks would focus—not on the question of immediate adaptations, but on long term changes. I would want some sort of meta trial and error which would deal with the question, "Is the adaptation one which we can really stand?" This would give us some chance of adapting not just to the immediate problem of who dies of what or the traffic accidents or the minor discomforts of the suburbs. We might have time to ask: "If we make this adaptation in law, in technology, in whatever, to disease, to discomforts, to traffic accidents, what will be the implications of that adaptation to the rest of the system, which is all interlinked?" In the end, it is the meta-adaptation, the adaptation of the total adaptive system, that is going to kill us or let us live.

# 16

## A *Formal Approach to* Explicit, Implicit, *and* Embodied *Ideas and to Their Forms of Interaction**

The differentiation of a new paradigm in biological thought does not happen suddenly or at an identifiable moment. It is, therefore, difficult to describe. It is even difficult to say that any given part of the unfolding of the new vision was due to one rather than another of the workers in the field.

Both the beginning and the end of the process of growth of the new paradigm are obscure. I can say today that in 1865 Mendel showed the 3:1 ratio and the phenomena of "dominance" and "recessivity" in biological heredity; and I can say that of course it was immediately evident that the determinants of animal and vegetable form must be memories or injunctions or *mental* "causes" very different from the physical "causes" (impacts, forces, etc.) which at that time were fashionable in scientific explanation. Of course, any Pythagorean or even Lewis Carroll would have seen this at once. But Lewis Carroll never saw Mendel's papers, and to my knowledge no Pythagorean commented upon them. Nobody saw that Mendelian dominance fell under the rubric of the Bellman's inverted joke about messages: "If I say it three times it is true."

So when I grew up in a household devoted to genetics—indeed, my father coined that word in 1908—it was still necessary to call the elements of Mendelian heredity "factors." Nobody could then see or would risk the notion that these must be *ideas* or chunks of *information* or *command.*

Retrospectively we can say that the course which biological theory could follow was already set in 1865, but this was not evident to anybody at that time, not even to Gregor Mendel.

---

*This essay was written in 1976, and is reprinted, by permission of Grune & Stratton, Inc., from *Double Bind: The Foundation of the Communicational Approach to the Family,* edited by Carlos E. Sluzki and Donald C. Ransom, 1976.

Similarly, I can say today that what we were doing in 1955–1960 was the beginning of a formal science which would study the forms of interaction among explicit, implicit, and embodied ideas. But at that time our work was called—seemed to us to be—the study of "family organization" and of "double binds."

It was from psychiatry that we got our money, and we let ourselves be strongly and disastrously influenced by the need to apply our science in that field. However well-intentioned the urge to cure, the very idea of "curing" must always propose the idea of power. And we were influenced also by the older, realistic or thingish epistemology from which we were diverging. ("Real" is from Latin *res*, a thing.)

We were inevitably stupid—bound, like the protagonists in a Greek tragedy, to the forms and shapes of processes which others, especially our colleagues, thought they saw. And our successors will be bound by the shapes of our thought.

This monstrous lag in scientific and philosophic thought is due precisely to that circumstance which we were so slow to recognize. Namely, the circumstance that the process of our studying the formal shapes of ideas is itself a thought process, pedestrian and tied by the leg to a massive ball of habit.

Perhaps the most convincing evidence that evolution is a mental process is in its slowness, its fits and starts, its errors and stupidity. In a word, its conservatism. In a universe conceived by physics, there could be no stupidity, no conservatism, no tragedy, and no humor.

Twenty years have gone by since we deduced[1] the necessity of pathologies of logical typing and recognized that these could be something like schizophrenia.

These twenty years have, for me, been rich. I withdrew from the study of hospital psychiatry into wider fields of animal behavior, learning theory, evolution, and ecology. This change of focus was, in part, dictated by the state of the art. It seemed to me that the view of the world, the epistemology, which lay behind double-bind theory needed *abductive* support. ("Abduction" was Peirce's word for that part of the process of inquiry which proposes that a given set of phenomena is a case under some previously proposed rule.)

The very circumstance that the concept of "double bind" was a product of deduction, the resolution of a reductio ad absurdum in conven-

---

1. See Haley's article on the history of the ideas [in *Double Bind*, edited by Carlos E. Sluzki and Donald C. Ransom (New York: Grune & Stratton, 1976)] for the evidence that the turning point in the discovery of the new paradigm was a deduction.

tional epistemology, indicated that the new epistemology must be supported by extension into many other fields. Other bodies of phenomena must be brought into the domain of the new tautology.

I must also confess that I was bored and disgusted by the Augean muddle of conventional psychiatric thinking, by my colleagues' obsession with power, by the dumb cruelty of the families which (as we used to say) "contained" schizophrenia, and appalled by the richness of the available data. "Mussen wir *alles* ansehen?" "Must we look at *everything?*" said the German girl as she climbed the steps to enter the British Museum.

Formal recognition of *mind* as the central concept of all biology could be stated in many ways, forgetting often enough that "formal recognition" is itself a mental process and that "mind" is the generator of all form, but returning, again and again, to these two pervasive truths: In the nonmental world—for example, in the epistemology of nineteenth-century physics—there are no classes and no distinctions. Atoms have no ideas, though, of course, "atoms" are the ideas of men. The mental world, i.e., the epistemology which could contain such concepts as "double bind," has its roots in the twin facts of *distinction* and *classification*.

In other words, what we had done in our research project was to transplant epistemological concepts from the shop of the philosophers—Whitehead, Russell, and the others—into the hurlyburly world of natural history.

The transition was the more difficult because in the 1950s there were two mutually contradictory forms of conventional epistemology, derived from the ancient superstitious division between mind and body.

According to one view, the ecology of mind was that system of relations between ideas which had been identified by scholars as "logic" plus pathologies of logic where the rules of argument had been "broken."

According to the other view, all that stuff about "ideas" was nonsense and all relationships between events—whether the falling of stones or the writing of poetry—should be explained under the rubric of causality.

Tangled growths of scholarship surrounded both of these epistemologies. The behaviorists and the idealists had both created vast imaginary domains of explanation. On one side there were the edifices of intellect where the *implicit* had been elegantly unfolded from "self-evident" premises and postulates to build such great tautologies as arithmetic and Euclidean geometry. But none of these could ever serve as the explanatory frame for learning and adaptation because conventional logic could never admit the oscillations and contradictions of recursive systems. The "if . . . then . . . " of logic was timeless.

On the materialist and "behaviorist" side, "causality" had the advantage of assuming temporal sequence. The "if . . . then . . . " of causality provided a unidirectional flow. But the explanations were so reductionistic that the (to me) evident phenomenon of classification was excluded. There could be no classes in a world of pure causality.

If "play" was a "class" of animal actions, if the animals themselves had a classification of behavior, then crude "behaviorism" was a failure.

A class can never be a thing and can never have that peculiar "reality" of things that can be counted or weighed. You cannot count the number of double binds in a sample of behavior, just as you could not count the number of jokes in a comedian's spiel or the number of bats in an inkblot. There are no bats, but only "bats."

But in the 1950s it was not possible to say much of what I have written above. Most of it was, for me, only dimly apprehended. The disqualification of logic was already clear, but the categorical bankruptcy of behaviorism was then a matter of taste or smell rather than cogent argument. The behaviorists were even more obviously power hungry than the curers. One of them put the matter clearly: I had asked him why he, an organism whose actions were supposedly to be explained by the invocation of causes, was performing learning experiments on fishes. He said, "Because I want to *control* a goldfish."

So neither logic nor behaviorism would do.

For me the break came by luck. I was asked to give the Korzybski Memorial Lecture in 1970, and in preparing what I would say I was led by the courtesies of the occasion to try to link my epistemological problems to what Korzybski had fought for. I asked a crucial question: What gets from the territory onto the map?

The answer to this question was obvious. *News of difference* is what gets across, and *nothing* else.

This very simple generalization resolves (at least for some time to come) the ancient problems of mind and matter. Mind always operates at one remove away from matter, always at one *derivative* (dx/dt) away from the "external" world. The primary data of experience are *differences*. From these data we construct our hypothetical (always hypothetical) ideas and pictures of that "external" world.

"Wise men see outlines and therefore they draw them," as William Blake said long ago, and, except for chiaroscuro—which, too, is compound of differences—there is nothing inside the outlines except sameness, which differs from difference.

A *report of difference* is the most elementary idea—the indivisible atom of thought. Those differences which are somehow not reported are not ideas. Bishop Berkeley would have been pleased.

And the Weber-Fechner Law emerges as the cornerstone or fundamental theorem of psychology. It seems that Weber made the factual discoveries and that it was Fechner who saw the vast philosophic importance of what had been discovered. For him, in the 1840s, the law was heavily encrusted with mystical ideas about immortality, but he was surely right in believing that the relation between percept and external circumstance was the same as the relation between *difference* and *state*.

Finally, let me relate back all this epistemology to that set of special cases of epistemological error called "schizophrenia."

It is not that these cases are more important or more fundamental than other varieties of creativity which spring from the tangles of epistemological contradiction. Humor, art, poetry, religion, hypnosis, and so on are equally rich, equally informative, and equally alien to the epistemologies of both logic and direct causality.

He who would discover for himself what ideas are made of and how ideas combine to make a mind must wander in one or more of these transcontextual mazes.

This book [*Double Bind*] happens to deal in part with schizophrenia, so I will take that maze as our example.

Twinges of "schizophrenia" can be experienced in many ways, but too often the inducing experience conceals the epistemological nature of the induction. Indeed, the practitioners of such induction—priests, artists, hypnotists, demagogues, showmen—commonly take care to conceal the nature of their operations.

Let us then embark upon the experience with all the cards face up (and note, in passing (and note also in passing that the words "in passing" communicate precisely what the demagogue would wish to communicate; he wants you to not linger in critical analysis of the epistemological twists which he is offering you), the hypnotist's and demagogue's trick of saying "us" when he means "you," and the trick of the same rascal who exposes his trick for your distraction).

Consider a difference between two objects, say, a sheet of paper and a desk top. One is white and the other is brown; one is thin and the other is thick; one is flexible and the other is rigid; and so on.

But these "characteristics" are not really *in* the paper and the desk top. They are *embodied* in interactions between paper and desk top *and* in interactions between desk or paper and your sense organs.

Consider now these embodiments of differences. Rub the paper on the desk top; try to cut the wood with the edge of the paper, and so on. Get a "feel" of the aggregate of differences between the paper and the wood. Call this feeling "news" of the difference A/B (where A was paper and B was wood).

Now take two quite different objects, say plate and butter, and go through the same drill to get a feeling of the difference C/D (where C was plate and D was butter).

Now meditate to get a feeling of the difference between A/B and C/D.

Finally return to the conventional world of "things" by touching and naming each object.

Conventional epistemology, which we call "sanity," boggles at the realization that "properties" are only differences and exist only in context, only in relationship. We abstract from relationship and from the experiences of interaction to create "objects" and to endow them with characteristics. We likewise boggle at the proposition that our own character is only real in relationship. We abstract from the experiences of interaction and difference to create a "self," which shall continue (shall be "real" or thingish) even without relationship.

An epistemological crisis is provoked by enforcing the idea that even *things* have character only by their differences and interactions.

If these feelings (which for me are like fear of loss of balance or support) are indeed related to the schizophrenias, then it appears that schizophrenia should be thought of as a response to epistemological transition, or to threat of transition.

Whether the transition itself would be for better or for worse is another question.

# 17

## *The Birth of a Matrix, or Double Bind and Epistemology\**

The title of this presentation is, metaphorically, upside-down. A matrix, to judge from its etymology, is supposed to give birth, not receive it. And yet what I want to talk about is very definitely the birth of a matrix, the story of how a quite complicated network of ideas grew together in the course of my life.

This network of ideas or matrix has been fertile, not in the sense that it has given birth to ideas separate from itself but in the sense that it has given birth to more parts of itself, that the matrix has been a growing thing, getting more and more complex, wider and wider in its scope, and, I believe, more and more fertile as time has gone on. Double-bind theory has been and is part of this general epistemology, not an induction or deduction from it.

It's difficult to say where the story begins. The matrix, after all, is an epistemology, and, specifically, it is a recursive epistemology; at the same time, it is an epistemology of recursiveness, an epistemology of how things look, how we are to understand them if they are recursive, returning all the time to bite their own tails and control their own beginnings. The old worm Ouroboros is an odd worm—as Cleopatra said of her worm—and that which is odd about him is that he conceals not only his recursive nature but also all the implications of recursiveness. I am not sure that he is inherently shy or self-concealing, but I am sure that if you grew up in a world where thought was preponderantly lineal in structure (and we all did) you would find it extraordinarily hard to see the clingings of Ouroboros.

*This address was delivered to a conference entitled "Beyond the Double Bind," held March 3–4, 1977, in New York. Reprinted from *Beyond the Double Bind: Communication and Family Systems, Theories, and Techniques with Schizophrenics,* edited by Milton M. Berger, 1978, by permission of the Estate of Gregory Bateson.

There are certain things which are necessary to the method of science in a world in which thinking is preponderantly lineal: if A then B; if B then C; and so on, never returning to its starting point to say, for example, if D then A. The ordinary processes of scientific advance in a lineal world, a world of lineal thought, are, after all, experiment, quantification, and, if you are anywhere within the realm of medicine, you will be expected to take a "clinical posture." And I want to suggest to you right at the beginning of this conference that experiment is sometimes a method of torturing nature to give an answer in terms of *your* epistemology, not in terms of some epistemology already immanent in nature which the Ouroboros might conceal. Quantification will always be a device for avoiding the perception of pattern. And clinical posture will always be a means of avoiding that openness of mind or perception which would bring before you the totality of the circumstances surrounding that which you are interested in.

Of course, clinical people are interested in etiology and the causes of how their patients got to be the way they are. But I'm interested in something much wider than that. I'm interested in what is an *idea*? And what ideas, what *pattern of ideas* was fed in to make the patients go as they have gone and be as they now are? About most of that, you see, I cannot clinically do anything at all.

As regards psychotherapy, all I would claim as a contribution from double-bind theory is greater insight; and I do not mean insight for the patient, which some practitioners think useless or harmful. I mean that the theory gives the therapist who works with schizophrenics or with families more insight into his patients and perhaps more insight into his own actions—if that be desirable.

"Beyond the Double Bind"! I am not sure what that means, but it seems to me that there are two components of the story which might be "beyond."[1]

The first of these is the general epistemology and the second is the extension of theory to illuminate the phenomena of adaptation, addiction, and the positive aspect of culture change. (We have plenty of theory and experience of how cultures go downhill and decay—nothing on how either cultures or persons can ever climb to richer organization of life.)

Let me deal first with the epistemology and how it grew.

---

1. I do not in general approve of the use of spatial and physical metaphors in the scientific discussion of communicational and mental matters. These metaphors always promote false epistemology.

## Part I: The Background

I plan to give you a rather long list of the various insights and circumstances of my life which have brought me to where I am. And notice, in passing, that I am not in the field of psychiatry anymore. That was a trip I took for ten years; I am still investigating the same problems that I was investigating then, but the psychiatric data are no longer at the core of my questing.

The story starts almost in my childhood. My father was a sort of geneticist even before the rediscovery of Mendel's papers. He was a geneticist of—what shall I say—of morphogenesis. He was especially interested in the phenomena of symmetry, which is a segmentation of an organism into two parts, one the mirror image of the other, as well as in segmentation of all kinds, whether it might be radial in the starfish or linear in the earthworm, the lobster, and ourselves. Because we, after all, are also segmented animals: our ribs repeat, our vertebrae repeat, and so on.

This strange, very rigorous zoological father was deeply skeptical of much that Darwin had said. He knew, incidentally, that Samuel Butler's Lamarckism was nonsense. Even so, Butler seemed to him a very important critic of Darwinian thinking, and, of course, a much more amusing character. The carriers of an orthodoxy can rarely afford to laugh.

Looking back and trying to see the scientific world through the eyes of childhood at the breakfast table, I see old Darwin as a rather tyrannical and rather foolish old bore, a sort of King Lear, while Lamarck was a much more feminine, much more charming figure, naughty perhaps. Nobody told me that he spent the last twenty years of his life impoverished, laughed at, and blind. It was not for nothing that Lamarck had the name "le Chevalier." Every child, you know, prefers the cavaliers to the roundheads, and it was onto such an unending polarity that I saw the ideas of Lamarck and Darwin dissected. Of course, Lamarck was "wrong" and Darwin was "right." But it was always nice to find weaknesses in the Darwinian position.

So I was named for Gregor Mendel. But by the time I was big enough to know what any of it was about, there was already a good deal of latent disappointment in our house that Mendelism had not turned out to be, not quite, the basis of evolution.

And still with it all, there was the pre-Darwinian discovery of homology, of formal comparability between parts, or rather between the *relations* of parts; this was the outstanding characteristic of the evolutionary picture. But even though today I know that all immanent biological formalisms are, in some sort, *ideas,* Darwinian theory prevented me from even the beginnings of such a heresy. (Had I seen this clearly, I would never have left zoology for anthropology.)

My first real research was a study of some mutant partridges of the genus *Alectoris*.[2] Of course I scarcely knew what I was doing, but I did happen on something which I already then knew was interesting: namely, that a mutation, or whatever, could carry the striping from one part of the body to another. Evidently the striping of the scapular feathers was due to the same circumstances, or causes, as the striping of the belly feathers. It followed that, from the point of view of the message, "Be striped," the feathers of the back could, under certain circumstances (what circumstances?) receive that message. There must, therefore, be a comparability between the feathers of the back and the feathers of the belly. I put the matter to you in very crude, groping terms.

I want you, if possible, to see it as I saw it then. Obviously this proposes a sort of "comparability" different, perhaps, from the comparability proposed by homology. Could we perhaps say that under the circumstances of genetic organization there was a comparability between the dorsal feathers, the scapular feathers, and those of the belly? But, then, where did this sort of comparability begin and end?

A similar question which fascinated me for some time fell between the tail and the lateral fins of a fish.[3] The question was this: Does the gene, or whatever causes the double tail of a double-tailed goldfish, extend its action to the lateral fins? Are they modified in a corresponding direction to that of the double tail? Doubling, perhaps, one could hardly expect, since each lateral fin is already a component of a doublet, the right fin plus the left fin; and what the gene did to the doubling of the tail was to make a right half of the tail separate from the left half of the tail. But then there is the question of the drooping of the tail fins. Does the same gene make the lateral fins droop? I believe that the answer to these questions is "No." The gene which affects the tail is limited by the obvious formal nonhomology between tail and lateral fins. The tail, after all, is a median organ, and the fins are bilateral; it's a very long step, in the world of ideas, from one to the other.

So, I was already carrying a lot of questions in my head about the problems which morphogenesis had to solve, and even then the solution to those problems was trending away from a traditional zoological language (or epistemology) in which the determinants would be referred to

2. See W. Bateson and G. Bateson, "On Certain Aberrations of the Red-Legged Partridges *Alectoris rufa* and *saxatilis*," *Journal of Genetics* 16 (1926).

3. See "Experiments in Thinking About Observed Ethnological Material," reprinted in *Steps to an Ecology of Mind.*

as "factors" or "forces," etc., to a very different way of talking in which the forms would seem to be achieved by some use of ideas or injunctions.

The outstanding problem was, of course, how these ideas or injunctions could be related to the interacting matter of which the body is made. What of Descartes?

Even then, I think that for me the fact of communication and the fact of regularity, symmetry, etc., in anatomy, were going hand in hand. But it wasn't till twenty years later when I was working at the Langley Porter Clinic that I managed to say that Goethe's regularity in the anatomy of flowering plants was comparable to the regularity which linguists find in language. I had always regarded the teachers of grammar and the teachers of comparative anatomy as pedantic old bores, but I was utterly fascinated, and still am, with the discovery that when you use language rightly to describe a flowering plant you will say that a leaf is a lateral organ on a stem which is characterized by having a bud, namely a baby stem, in its axil. So the definitions became: a stem is that which bears leaves, and a leaf is that which has a stem in its angle; that which is in the angle of a leaf is a baby stem; and so on. Each component of the anatomy is defined by its relation to the others. The old grammatical definitions—that a noun is the name of a person, place, or thing; a verb is the name of an action, and so on—are simply wrong. A noun is a word having a certain relation to an object or predicate; a predicate is that which has a certain relation to nouns and verbs and so forth; and each part is defined by its relations.

So there is a formal resemblance between that anatomical base of homology which Goethe discovered in the flowering plants and the grammar which pedants have long known in linguistics. Again, I saw formal mentalism underlying physical phenomena. But I still had not been able to say to myself, you see, what it was, about the partridge feathers and about the double-tailed goldfish, that made me sure that those points were a major breakthrough. A breakthrough into what? That's always the question. If somebody had told me that I was building a new epistemology, I would have said, "Yes, of course." But by myself I wasn't able to say, for example, that the credibility or even necessity of believing the new epistemology is enormously increased when the ideas *in the phenomena*—not the ideas in my head but the ideas in the organized phenomena—occur in layers. Today it's impossible for me to see feathers or a crab's claw without realizing that there are not only ideas in form, but ideas about ideas, and even ideas about ideas about ideas. I didn't know that I was looking for Russellian types.

I am trying to build up for you, in your "minds," as we say, ideas about how I built up in *my* "mind" a system of ideas, an epistemology, about how ideas work in the outside world, in the world of fish and New Guinea cultures. And notice that the accent is on the word "*how.*"

The next burst of ideas came—really took shape—in the writing of *Naven,* a book about my New Guinea fieldwork. The beginning of this burst of ideas I owed to Margaret Mead and, through her, to Ruth Benedict. It was Ruth's little book *Patterns of Culture* which started that whole school of anthropology called "culture and personality." It began as a typology of cultures. Margaret set up a classification of three New Guinea cultures with which she had worked. She published that in a book called *Sex and Temperament,* and I had been in on the preliminary thinking which lay behind the classification in *Sex and Temperament.*

In *Naven* you'll find that there is again a typology. I used Kretschmer's typology of cyclothyme/schizothyme mentalities, as a tool, to describe the difference between the sexes in Iatmul society. But this was not very satisfactory. The way to phrase scientific questions is with the word "how" and not with the word "why." But typologies, you know, do not answer either "how" questions or "why" questions. Therefore, a typology is only a way station. It may be a necessary way station, but always the next step is toward "how." I searched in *Naven* for a set of process answers to the typological phenomena.

These process answers centered around the notion "schismogenesis." And this concept is precisely halfway from Descartes and away from simple materialism to the new epistemology which could contain the double-bind theory.

Schismogenesis is a process of interaction whereby directional change occurs in a learning system. If the steps of evolution and/or stochastic learning are random, as has been maintained, why should they sometimes, over long series, occur, recurrently, in the same direction? The answer of course is always in terms of interaction, but in those days we knew approximately nothing of ecology.

I have talked in other places about the directional evolution of the horse and how it is necessary, if we are to understand this directional process, to talk not about the horse alone but about the relation between horse and grass in which the two interacting organisms must change and fit and fit and change in a process which is dialectic and relational.

Billiard balls do not respond to each other's responses, which is the essential component of schismogenesis, armaments races,[4] the creation of tyrants and willing slaves, performers and spectators, and so on.

---

4. See L. F. Richardson, "Generalized Foreign Politics," *British Journal of Psychology,* monograph no. 23 (1939).

So from a static classification of types I was pushed by (my) analysis of New Guinea data to hypotheses of process. Competition, spectatorship, domination, and the like, were primarily words for potentially progressive patterns in relationship—not unipolar psychological words for "roles." (Schizophrenia too is a word for one end of a relationship!) But from process the next step was obvious and was already built into *Naven*. Of course, the next step is the typology or classification of process.

From classification to process to classification to process. That is how the hierarchy of logical types got into the theory. First, there was the classification of persons (or cultures); then I looked for the processes of interaction which generated and maintained the differences between persons; then, I classified those processes (into "symmetrical" and "complementary"); last came the questions about processes of interaction between symmetrical and complementary processes.

The methodology of theory has another name: "epistemology," and those who enjoy such matters may find pleasure in adding one more step to the above ladder of alternations between studies of typology and studies of process. I have discussed another such alternating ladder.[5] This was the hierarchic alternation of "calibration" and "feedback" in biological and social systems. The typology-process ladder and the calibration-feedback ladder are by abduction, surely, cases under the same rule. Comparing the two ladders should lead to stating the rule.

The classification of schismogenic patterns of interrelating into "symmetrical" and "complementary" was another giant stride toward double-bind theory because it set the base for "learning-to-learn" (or "Learning II," as I later called it) and led to recognition by me of *context,* i.e., recognition that the terms of schismogenic theory are also terms for contextual structure; and that "learning-to-learn" is, indeed, for the learner a learning of context.

Descriptions of "role" and character of individuals became simply spin-offs from descriptions of particular learning-to-learn resulting from identifiable contexts.

If you want to state the meaning of a description of character—courageous, passive–aggressive, dominant, sly, *enfant terrible,* dependent, bullying, impatient, etc., etc.—the correct way to do this is to describe a formal context of learning (i.e., of Learning I) in which that particular component of character would be learned (in Learning II).

---

5. See "Formal Research in Family Structure," published in *Exploring the Base for Family Therapy,* M. Robert Gomberg Memorial Conference, edited by Nathan Ackerman et al. (New York: Family Service Association, 1961).

That was all clear in 1942[6] but it took fourteen years to ask the contrary question:

*What happens when learning-to-learn (Learning II) is disrupted?*

The answer to that question, of course, would have been "double-bind theory." So, already in 1942, the epistemology was ready to receive or generate the double-bind concept. But I knew so little at that time:

I did not know that I had a new epistemology on my hands.

I had never heard of Russell's logical types.

I did not see that this was all a new approach to and a partial evolution of the body/mind problem.

I knew nothing of cybernetics beyond the positive feedbacks of schismogenesis. Negative feedback, information theory, and all that were to me unknown.

I had never looked at "play" or considered the logical typing of this context-defining concept.

I had never knowingly met a schizophrenic.

But, as I said above, the epistemology (still unlabeled as such) was ready for the "double bind." And from my point of view the double bind and the data on schizophrenics and their families came, when they came, as a very exciting addition to and validation of a complex network of theoretical thought.

Neither billiard balls nor disembodied spirits, I suppose, can get themselves into the extraordinary traps and anguish that are generated in a schizophrenogenic family.

You will excuse me if I digress to conclude this part of the story with an excerpt from the writing of a notable schizophrenic. His biography is almost an ideal source book for data on double binds:

> I would not always overcome my exasperation. But even then I was frequently influenced by a spirit of bravado and defiance of the doctors, to whom I knew my letters were subjected for inspection; I was determined, if they declared that my anger at being confined, and at my treatment, was a proof of my madness, that they should have evidence enough of it. . . . Even a deeper motive lay hid under all this violence of expression; and this may perhaps by many be deemed an insane motive: I knew that, of all the torments to which the mind is subject, there is none so shocking, so horrid to be endured as that of remorse for having injured or neglected those who deserved our esteem and consid-

---

6. G. Bateson, "Social Planning and the Concept of Deutero-Learning," reprinted in *Steps to an Ecology of Mind.*

eration. I felt for my sisters, my brothers, and my mother: I knew they could not endure to look upon what they had done towards me, to whom they were once so attached, if they rightly understood it; that they could know no relief from the agony of that repentance which comes too late, gnawing the very vitals, but in believing me partly unworthy of their affection; and therefore I often gave the reins to my pen, that they might hereafter be able to justify themselves, saying he has forfeited our respect, he has thrown aside the regard due to his parentage and to his kindred—he has deserved our contempt, and merited our abandonment of him.[7]

## Part II: The Epistemology

As it took shape, this epistemology came to have five principal components.

(1) It is suitable to use the words "mind" and "mental process" for what happens in systems which contain multiple parts, and what I shall call "mental processes" are in fact events in the organization and relationship among those parts.

This means that notions which would attribute mentality to single atomies or parts of atomies—protons, electrons, and such—are, so far as I am concerned, unnecessary and irrelevant. This rubs out most of the theology of Teilhard de Chardin and of Samuel Butler from whom I have learned a great deal.

(2) It is characteristic of mind and mental process that, in many of the steps which make up the circuitry of the mind, events are triggered not by force or impact, but by *difference*.

A difference is a phenomenon about which most people have thought little. It is strange that we should be so unaware of the simplest processes in which we participate that it is necessary to talk about the nature of such a pervasive notion as difference! I became aware of this matter under lucky circumstances.

I had the good fortune to be asked to give the Korzybski Memorial Lecture some years ago.[8] In preparing that lecture, I wanted to say

---

7. From: John Perceval's *Narrative of the Treatment Experienced by a Gentleman. . .*, 1840. Republished as *Perceval's Narrative*, edited by G. Bateson (Palo Alto: Stanford University Press, 1961): 211–12.

8. G. Bateson, "Form, Substance, and Difference," Ninth Annual Korzybski Memorial Lecture, reprinted in *Steps to an Ecology of Mind*.

something generous about Korzybski and re-examined his old aphorism, "The map is not the territory." Coming back to that familiar phrase after years of thinking about other aspects of epistemology and now knowing that epistemology is a branch of natural history, I realized that what gets from the territory to the map—i.e., from the outside world to the brain—is *news of difference*. If there is no difference in the territory, there will be nothing to say on the map, which will remain blank. And, further, I saw that any given map has rules about what differences in the territory shall be reported on the map.

What gets to the map is news of difference and what remains there are differences which, by stylized coding, become reports of that news.

These traits happen to apply to sense organs—a fact which was discovered in the 1830s and labeled the Weber-Fechner Law. It seems that Weber observed the facts and Fechner saw their enormous importance, so epoch-making at that time that nobody understood what he was saying and he himself went a little insane.

That "law" says more about "difference" than I have said above. It asserts, on the whole correctly, that the particular differences upon which perception depends are not subtractive or additive differences, but ratios. Another way of saying this was that the "sensation" is proportional to the logarithm of the intensity of the "stimulus" or input. To get twice the sensation, e.g., weight, you must encounter four times the smaller weight.

To this "law" Norbert Wiener added a second part which I think he never published fully, though I consider it to be the most important item in "psychology" after the original Weber-Fechner Law. Wiener was working on the formal structure of that cybernetic oscillation of muscle called clonus and found that the tension of an isometric muscle is proportional to the logarithm of the frequency of neural impulses reaching the muscle. A most elegant finding, which shows that (expectably, though it took one hundred years to get there) the efferent side of the brain works by the same epistemological limits as the afferent. Or, we might say that the muscle vis-à-vis the efferent nerve which serves it is precisely comparable to a sense vis-à-vis differences arriving from outside.[9]

Notice that difference of the sort I am concerned with is *dimensionless*. It is a ratio between two things—temperatures, weights, brightness, etc.—which have real dimensions in mass, length, and time, or combinations of these. But the ratio between any pair is a measure from which

---

9. This discovery is mentioned in the Introduction to Wiener's *Cybernetics: Or Control and Communication in the Animal and the Machine* (New York: John Wiley & Sons, 1949).

the dimensionality is, so to speak, cancelled out to make a nondimensional concept. The physicists call it "zero dimensions."

Since it has zero dimensions, difference, of course, carries no energy. It is of the realm of entropy and negentropy.

It is also true that difference is not located in space. I have here a piece of yellow paper and a piece of white paper, but the difference "between" them is not in the yellow paper, nor is it in the white paper, nor is it in the space between them. It is, we might say, in the *time* between them. But that time is not a time belonging to the pieces of paper. It is our time—the time which we need to scan from one piece of paper to the other.

In general, sense organs, especially the retina, accommodate to states and achieve their reports by *scanning* static differences. If I make a thick dot with chalk upon the blackboard, I cannot feel it if I merely place my fingertip vertically down upon it. But if I scan it by sense of touch, moving my finger across it, I feel it at once and can even judge its thickness. The retina similarly scans the visual field with micronystagmus. Without nystagmus it "sees" nothing.

(3) Along with the fact of a dimensionless variable being triggered by difference goes the fact that systems which achieve mental process must be so constructed that energy is available ahead of the stimulus event at all those steps in the mental process where difference is the trigger.

The muscle must have energy from its metabolism if it is to respond to the neural impulse; the nerve must have energy available from metabolism if it is to respond to the previous nerve or the end organ; and the end organ must have available metabolic energy if it is to respond to, say, a *decrease* in brightness.

In general, apart from extremes of physical starvation or physico-chemical conditions which might prevent the degradation of potential energy in the cell, there is *enough* stored energy in the cell for it to do its thing. We deal not with an energy budget but with budgets of entropy, negentropy, available pathways and patterns.

The fact of available energy makes possible the perception of nonexistent events and phenomena, where these differ from possible realities. We can be aware of *not* receiving a letter, and the amoeba can become more active and go hunting when it is starving.

At the same time, the isolation of the mind from "real" impacts and forces and its confinement in the more abstract, derivative world of difference is, no doubt, one of the circumstances which lead men to imagine a separation between mind and body.

Difference is *immanent* in matter and in events.

(4) The systems which are minds are characteristically circuits of cause and effect. They may be regenerative, i.e., subject to runaway, or they may be self-correcting, or they may oscillate. In all cases, we are concerned with cybernetic systems!

But note that the word "cybernetics" has become seriously corrupted since it was put into circulation by Norbert Wiener. And Wiener himself is partly to blame for this corruption of the conception in that he associated "cybernetics" with "control." I prefer to use the term "cybernetic" to describe complete circuiting systems. For me, the system is man-and-environment; to introduce the notion of "control" would draw a boundary between these two, to give a picture of man versus environment.

We used to argue about whether a computer can think. The answer is, "No." What thinks is a total circuit, including perhaps a computer, a man, and an environment. Similarly, we may ask whether a brain can think, and again the answer will be, "No." What thinks is a brain inside a man who is part of a system which includes an environment. To draw a boundary line between a part which does most of the computation for a larger system and the larger system of which it is a part is to create a mythological component, commonly called a "self." In my epistemology, the concept of self, along with all arbitrary boundaries which delimit systems or parts of systems, is to be regarded as a trait of the local culture—not indeed to be disregarded, since such little epistemological monsters are always liable to become foci of pathology. The arbitrary boundaries which were useful in the process of analyzing the data become all too easily battlefronts, across which we try to kill an enemy or exploit an environment.

(5) Systems which achieve mental process are commonly, when sufficiently complex, characterized by the hierarchies of logical types, which have been discussed above to some extent.

In the formal construction of circuits, we shall expect that information (i.e., news of difference) *about* events in one circuit may be "fed back" to change some parameter within that circuit. It is the use of information about information that is characteristic of multiple-step hierarchies.

In a more lineal paradigm, the hierarchies of naming and classification are similar. The ladders—name, name of the name, name of the name of the name; and item, class, class of classes, etc.—are familiar.

Less familiar are the errors which people continually and disastrously make in failing to recognize the logical typing of their own ideas. The concept "exploration" provides a typical paradigm. Psychologists are surprised that "exploration" in rats is not extinguished if the rat encounters danger or pain inside boxes which he explores. But "exploration" is not a name of an action. It is the name of a *context* of action, or perhaps of a class of actions which class is to be defined by the animal's perception of the context in which he is acting. The "*purpose*" of exploration is to find out which boxes (for example) are safe, where "purpose" is a partial synonym for "name of context." Now if the rat finds an electric shock in the box, his exploration has been a success. He now knows that that box is unsafe. He obviously will not give up exploring after that success.

Similarly "play" and "crime" are words of approximately the same logical type as "exploration." These are not names of particular actions but for *classes* of actions, to be classified together in accordance with the organism's vision of the context in which he/she is acting. In the case of "play," the players will not easily understand that punishment or prohibition of the actions of play should extinguish "play." Often children will respond by trying to throw the category of "play" around the forbidding action of the adult, either inviting the adult into some game or mocking him as he stands there outside the game.

The case of crime is more disastrous. "Crime" is not a name of an action. Like "play," it is a name for an aggregate of actions classified together under the aegis of similar view of context in which the actions are to be performed. In the case of crime, the actions are indeed partly directed *at* the authorities who would forbid the crime.

Of course, the punishment of the particular actions which the policeman catches will not extinguish the perception of context which characterizes the criminal's class of actions. You cannot stop a man from being a *criminal* (whatever that is) by punishing something which he does. We still go on trying to do this, but five thousand years of trying show that it doesn't work.

The techniques of Delancey Street in San Francisco will perhaps be more successful.[10]

In sum, all behavioral science and all analysis of mental process are liable to fall on their face when logical typing is ignored. The matter is, of course, specially important in regard to schizophrenia and the double bind.

Finally there are two points which must be added to the above outline of an epistemology. These do not rate as necessary specifications of the proposed epistemology, but the reader may find that these points clear the way for an understanding of the system proposed.

10. C. Hampden-Turner, *Sane Asylum* (San Francisco: San Francisco Book Company, Inc., 1976).

First, *logic is a very poor model of the world of mental process.* We used to ask whether computers could simulate all conceivable steps of logic, but it turns out that this was precisely a wrong question. The truth of the matter is that logic cannot simulate all the steps of causal systems operating in time.

Logic breaks down when confronted with the paradoxes of abstraction—the Cretan liar or Russell's more sophisticated version of this, the question whether the class of classes which are not members of themselves is a member of itself. Logicians have been boggling at these paradoxes for three thousand years, but if such a paradox is proposed to a computer, it will answer: "Yes, no, yes, no, yes, no . . . " till it breaks or runs out of ink.

The computer operates by cause and effect; it follows that when events inside the computer are used to simulate the "if . . . then . . ." of logic, the "then" becomes temporal. "If I close this switch, then (almost immediately) the light will light."

But the "if . . . then . . . " of logic contains no time. "If three sides of this triangle are equal to three sides of that triangle, *then* the triangles are equal." There is no time in that "then."

So, when simulated in the world of causality, the Russellian paradoxes come to work like this:

"If at $time_1$ the Cretan's statement is true; then at $time_2$, it is untrue; if it is untrue at $time_2$; then it is true at $time_3$; and so on. . . . " There is no contradiction, and the old "if . . . then . . . " of logic is obsolete.

A second point which may help the reader to put this all together is the fact that a great deal of personal epistemology is concealed from consciousness. It is, so far as I know, inaccessible to consciousness, buried under the very process of conscious perception. When we say that we see, feel, taste, hear some external phenomenon or even some internal event—a pain or a muscular tension—our ordinary syntax for saying this is epistemologically confusing.

What I see when I look at you is, in fact, my image of you; or you see your image of me. These images are, seemingly to us, projected out into the external world, but they are very far from being that about which we say "We see it." To quote Korzybski again: "The map is not the territory," and what I see is my map of a (partly hypothetical) territory out there: your face, your green shirt, etc.

Very few people seem to realize the enormous theoretical "power" of this distinction between what I "see" and what is out there. Most assume that, in fact, they see what they look at and they assume this *because* there is total unconsciousness of the processes of perception.

I may be conscious of turning my eyes in a given direction, and I may be conscious of an image of things out in that direction. But between those two moments or items of consciousness, I am conscious of nothing.

My mental machinery provides me not with news of its processes, but with news of its products. Indeed, there is a certain common sense in a world so constructed that organisms shall not be bothered with news of processes and they shall be given the product only. But, in fact, the processes of *making* images are of very great complexity, and can be experimentally investigated. A pioneer in this field was Adelbert Ames, Jr., from whose experiments I received a most salutary series of epistemological shocks.

Let me describe one of these experiments briefly so that you know what I am talking about. You will then realize that a disruption (by double bind) of the premises underlying perception could become a very serious matter. I hope that you will extrapolate from the sensory and gestalt experiments of Ames to imagine the deeper pathologies which are disturbances of premises of former sureness of belief.

Ames had me stand at the end of a table about five feet long. Halfway down the length of the table was a package of cigarettes, supported away from the surface of the table on a spike and stand. At the far end of the table there was a paper book of matches similarly supported.

Ames said, "What do you see? Where and how big?" And, of course, the objects were where they appeared to be and had their familiar size. In all Ames's experiments you were made to state the objective "truth" before being subjected to illusion.

Ames then said, "Look. Standing up from the edge of the table at your end there is a plank of wood with a hole in it. Look through that hole and tell me what you see."

So I stooped down and looked through the hole down the length of the table. Again the objects were as I knew them to be, in spite of the fact that I now had only monocular vision through the hole.

Ames said, "You can slide the plank sideways to get parallax. Do that."

And as I moved the plank, Hey, Presto! the scene (my image) changed. The Lucky Strike package was at the far end and seemed to have doubled its length and breadth. The book of matches had moved up to halfway down the length of the table to the former position of the package of cigarettes and was now only half its proper size. It looked like a book of matches from a doll's house.

What had happened?

When I slid the plank sideways, I operated levers of whose existence under the table top I was unaware. These levers moved the two objects to *reverse* the effects of parallax. Normally, objects close to a moving observer seem to get left behind fast while distant objects seem to travel with you—for example, in a railroad train. In this case, the distant object, the matches, was made to appear to get left behind.

My unconscious and inaccessible image-making processes accepted these data of pseudoparallax and made the image accordingly. But, of course, the objects still subtended the same angle at my eye. So I saw what looked like a double-sized pack of cigarettes at five feet away. The premises of seeming parallax were stronger than my knowledge of the true size and position of the objects.

In other words, my processes of perception did a complex piece of mathematics to ascribe to the objects that position which they would have had if the artificial parallax had been real parallax. "I" had no conscious control or awareness of this complex *intellectual* feat; my perceptive processes used premises which occidental man was not able to put into words until the laws of perspective were studied by Renaissance artists.

The unconscious epistemology—the *how* of using our senses—is a deeply concealed body of knowledge; and the concealment of that knowledge comes between the conscious understanding and the external world to make us sure of the reality of "self," so that when unconscious premises of epistemology are disrupted by double-bind experience, we feel that our safe illusions about "self" are shaken.

How *right* the insight of the schizophrenic who writes the first person pronoun with a lower case "i."

## Part III: Beyond the Double Bind

Already in 1956, in the paper which first, rather prematurely, announced double-bind theory[11] we knew that double binds were powerful, not only in a destructive or painful sense, but also in a "therapeutic" sense. We used to talk at that time of the "therapeutic double bind," and in that paper, an instance of this was described, from a narrative of Frieda Fromm-Reichmann's therapy.

Fairly soon after that it was noted, I think by Haley, that the strate-

---

11. [*Editor's Note:* G. Bateson, D. D. Jackson, J. Haley, J. Weakland, "Toward a Theory of Schizophrenia," reprinted in *Steps to an Ecology of Mind*.]

gies of Milton Erickson's hypnotic induction and hypnotic therapy were forms of double bind in which the hypnotist put the subject "in" a bind.

Indeed, without any theoretical knowledge of what I was doing, I had been using double binds during World War II as a device in propagandizing the enemy. We had a small radio station in Chittagong which broadcast to the Japanese-occupied territories of Southeast Asia. We professed to be a Japanese official station and our policy was very simply to read the enemy propaganda every day and to rebroadcast it with thirty percent exaggeration.

It is around the concept of "therapeutic double bind" that a lot of thinking needs to be done; this thinking will, I hope, lead to a considerable advance in human and ethical understanding of adaptation and addiction—viewing the whole contemporary pathology of man's international, intranational, and ecological crisis as a network of neurotic adaptation, i.e., a network of addictions.

At the same time, I believe that these studies should lead to some understanding of cultural advance. We know and see so much of cultural decadence and decay that our ignorance of cultural advance becomes conspicuous.

Let me begin by giving you the story of a double bind which we inflicted upon a dolphin at the Oceanic Institute in Hawaii.[12]

> Consider a very simple paradigm: a female porpoise (*Steno bredanensis*) is trained to accept the sound of the trainer's whistle as a "secondary reinforcement." The whistle is expectably followed by food, and if she later repeats what she was doing when the whistle blew, she will expectably again hear the whistle and receive food.
>
> This porpoise is now used by the trainers to demonstrate "operant conditioning" to the public. When she enters the exhibition tank, she raises her head above surface, hears the whistle and is fed. She then raises her head again and is again reinforced. Three repetitions of this sequence is enough for the demonstration and the porpoise is then sent offstage to wait for the next performance two hours later. She has learned some simple rules which relate her actions, the whistle, the exhibition tank, and the trainer into a pattern—a contextual structure, a set of rules for how to put the information together.

---

12. From "Double Bind, 1969," in *Steps to an Ecology of Mind* by Gregory Bateson. Copyright © 1972, 1987 by Jason Aronson Inc. Reprinted with permission of the publisher.

But this pattern is fitted only for a single episode in the exhibition tank. She must break that pattern to deal with the *class* of such episodes. There is a larger *context of contexts* which will put her in the wrong.

At the next performance, the trainer again wants to demonstrate "operant conditioning," but to do this the trainer must pick on a different piece of conspicuous behavior.

When the porpoise comes on stage, she again raises her head. But she gets no whistle. The trainer waits for the next piece of conspicuous behavior—likely a tail flap, which is a common expression of annoyance. This behavior is then reinforced and repeated.

But the tail flap was, of course, not rewarded in the third performance.

Finally the porpoise learned to deal with the context of contexts—by offering a different or *new* piece of conspicuous behavior whenever she came on stage.

All this had happened in the free natural history of the relationship between porpoise and trainer and audience. The sequence was then repeated experimentally with a new porpoise and carefully recorded.*

Two points from this experimental repeat of the sequence must be added:

First, that it was necessary (in the trainer's judgment) to break the rules of the experiment many times. The experience of being in the wrong was so disturbing to the porpoise that in order to preserve the relationship between porpoise and trainer (i.e., the context of context of context) it was necessary to give many reinforcements to which the porpoise was not entitled.

Second, that each of the first fourteen sessions was characterized by many futile repetitions of whatever behavior had been reinforced in the immediately previous session. Seemingly only by "accident" did the animal provide a piece of different behavior. In the time-out between the fourteenth and fifteenth sessions, the porpoise appeared to be much excited, and when she came on stage for the fifteenth session she put on an elaborate performance including eight conspicuous pieces of behavior of

---

*K. Pryor, R. Haag, and J. O'Rielly, "Deutero-Learning in a Roughtooth Porpoise (*Steno bredanensis*)," U.S. Naval Ordnance Test Station, China Lake, NOTS TP 4270.

which four were entirely new—never before observed in this species of animal.

The story illustrates, I believe, two aspects of the genesis of a transcontextual syndrome:

First, that severe pain and maladjustment can be induced by putting a mammal in the wrong regarding its rules for making sense of an important relationship with another mammal.

And second, that if this pathology can be warded off or resisted, the total experience may promote *creativity*.

It was necessary to give the dolphin unearned fish (of course, without whistle) in order to maintain the relationship between trainer and porpoise. That is, we had to tell the animal that in spite of her failure to solve the problem, she was still "loved."

Consider this as a special case, and ask whether there could be other cases which would differ from this in that the learning organism—be it dolphin, be it human—would not need the reassurance of "unearned fish."

If such cases could be found and if, indeed, it appeared that such cases were common in human or animal life, then we would have before us a type of sequence which would explain "progress" in spite of the simultaneous and familiar processes of decay and degradation of mental and cultural life.

Under what circumstances will an organism put itself into a position of painful double bind, gratuitously? Could such a creature be urged on by some dim conception that at the far end of such a disciplinary adventure—such a sequence of deutero-learning sequences—there might be some "spiritual" or even "hedonic" reward?

The question becomes more profound and even urgent when we consider the whole nature of adaptation in the wide context of biological evolution. (Note that the vast network of processes called "biological evolution" constitutes a "mind" and achieves mental process as defined above in my outline of an epistemology.)

In biological evolution, adaptive changes occur during the lifetime of an individual, adjusting him or her to various forms of stress, effort, demands placed upon skill, and the like. (These somatic, "acquired" changes are, of course, not passed on by Lamarckian heredity.) They are achieved, however, at a certain cost. What is consumed is entropy, i.e., uncommitted possibilities for change in many different physiological and neural variables and parameters. The uncommitted alternatives (entropy) are lost, eaten up by commitment and by becoming unchangeable parts of patterns (negentropy). Adaptive changes limit the possibilities for future adaptation in other directions.

For example, the man who is sick has set many of his physiological variables at special and even extreme (maximal and minimal) values in order to resist the effect of his illness. As a result he is under "stress." We shall be wise to keep him indoors and warm so as not to subject him to further "stress." The logic of thus protecting him depends upon the idea that there is a finite amount of *potential* change which the body is capable of achieving, and that when it is achieving some one adaptive change its ability to achieve any other change is thereby reduced. Its flexibility is reduced.

There is, if you please, an economics of flexibility.[13]

What will happen if another stress is added is that at some point in the total physiology there will be contradictory demands upon some variable. This contradiction—the demand that the variable be increased to meet stress A and simultaneously decreased so that stress B may be met—will constitute a deep-seated double bind.

Such double binds will characteristically be met by responses at a higher logical type level. If, for example, the body is stressed by high altitude, it will first ward off death by emergency measures such as panting and speeding up of the pulse. If the organism stays at these high altitudes, there will be *acclimation*, i.e., physiological changes will occur to make the panting and tachycardia unnecessary. The organism will "climb" to a higher logical type of adaptation which will provide an economy—a saving—of flexibility. The panting and racing of the heart will now be saved and be available for some further stress. Without acclimation, this new stress could not be met, except perhaps by death.

There is, however, a gimmick in the story: While acclimation is an economy of flexibility as long as the animal remains at high altitude, should he come down to sea level his acclimation will now be a disadvantage. He will find that the acclimation has now become a source of stress.

Emergency measures like panting or tachycardia could be relaxed immediately on leaving the situation of stress, but he will not be able to relax his acclimation for days or weeks.

In a word, our organism has become *addicted* to the high altitude by the deep adaptations which he has achieved under that stress.

It appears then, that adaptation and addiction are *very* closely related phenomena. In passing, we will note that in this postwar period every nation that individually adapted itself to war is still addicted to the adap-

---

13. G. Bateson, "The Role of Somatic Change in Evolution," reprinted in *Steps to an Ecology of Mind.*

tive responses which it then achieved, and that that higher entity, the international system, is still addicted in the same way.

How many nations are doing research on the formal aspects of addiction? It should be worth a few billions, quite apart from applications to the drug field and the phenomena of ecological pollution, etc., etc.

Be all that as it may, we still have time to consider a fictitious animal which has long fascinated me and is relevant to this whole business of adaptation, addiction, and double binds as a possible source of positive advance. I refer to Lewis Carroll's Bread-and-butter-fly.

> "Crawling at your feet," said the Gnat (Alice drew her feet back in some alarm), "you may observe a Bread-and-butter-fly. Its wings are thin slices of bread-and-butter, its body is a crust, and its head is a lump of sugar."
> "And what does *it* live on?"
> "Weak tea with cream in it."
> A new difficulty came into Alice's head. "Supposing it couldn't find any?" she suggested.
> "Then it would die, of course."
> "But that must happen very often," Alice remarked thoughtfully.
> "It always happens," said the Gnat.
> After this, Alice was silent for a minute or two, pondering.[14]

If we ask of what did the Bread-and-butter-fly die, we have to answer that he died of a double bind. Not of the peculiar traumata of a head dissolved in weak tea, nor yet of simple starvation, but of an impossibility of contradictory adaptation.

The dinosaurs probably got caught in some evolutionary cul-de-sac of similar form. And we ourselves are all too likely to perish of an impossibility of adaptation to peace and a frugal technology.

Let me now consider another organism similarly beset with contradictory demands of environment. I am still searching for contexts in which organisms will make adaptations of high logical type, transcending their double binds without "unearned fish." The organism which I ask you to observe is a mountain climber.

He starts at dawn—unrewarded and unbribed in any simple way—and he starts to climb. After a few hours, his legs start to hurt; his lungs start to hurt; his head starts to hurt; his backpack begins to get subjectively heavy; and his blisters grow. He is in a progressively miserable state.

---

14. Lewis Carroll, *Through the Looking-Glass,* Chapter 3.

At this point, the commonsense thing for him to do is to sit down, thus relieving his legs; eat the lunch in his pack, thus reducing its weight; and, after lunch, he should start downhill, for home.

Similarly, the drug addict, suffering the first pangs of withdrawal, will, commonsensically, give himself another fix.

The nation addicted to warfare similarly will speed up its end of the armaments race and then step firmly on the toes of any available rival nation.

But our mountain climber has no common sense. He goes on climbing, and that with no unearned fish except such reinforcement as he can *reflexively generate* for himself. He goes on, into more pain and more suffering, until he reaches the top of the mountain. At this point, he has *as he sees it* completed a sequence. He then can turn around or perhaps he may eat his lunch there at the mountaintop. After that he can go downhill toward home.

Why do mountain climbers do this? It should be impossible. But drug addicts sometimes also unaided break their addiction "cold turkey." Could an addict ever become addicted to "cold turkey"?

About nations, I do not know. (The Germans have a cry "*Sieg zum Todt,*" "Conquer unto death," which ironically describes the time structure of their wars, winning all the preliminary battles and losing the war, but this is no answer to the present problem.)

I have known two great mountain climbers, George Leigh Mallory, whose bones are somewhere on Everest, and Geoffrey Young, who was the first one-legged man to climb the North Face of the Matterhorn. Mallory did not answer our question. He is said to have said that he climbed Everest "because it is there." He died on his second attempt.

Young used to talk of the *discipline* of not listening to the body when it screams for relief.

What is *discipline*?

We talk of "taking pains," and the French, more aware than we of recursive and reflexive trains of phenomena, say, " . . . *se donner la peine de* . . . ," " . . . to give oneself the pain or trouble to . . . ."

Why does the Zen monk sit through hours of agony in the lotus position, his legs getting more and more paralyzed and his head getting more and more addled? And while he does this, why does he contemplate or wrestle with a *koan,* a traditional paradox, a sort of conceptual double bind?

In this region there are answers which are certainly "beyond the double bind," and yet equally certainly the answers will be related to double-bind theory. We can only speculate about components of these answers:

(1)  They will surely include reference to ideas of *completion* of tasks.

(2)  They will include reference to "self"—that half mythological entity whose apparent subjective reality somehow increases in situations of reflexive awareness.

(3)  We shall be talking about addictions to the feat of "cold turkey" defeat of all addictions of lower logical type.

(4)  We shall face some sort of positive addiction to the pains of facing double binds and conquering them.

(5)  We shall need a formal definition of *practice*. What is the musical performer doing between his public appearances? He, too, is engaging in behavior which (even if rewarded in the concert hall) is fundamentally related to double binds. It is a part of the long grind from quick superficial adaptation through automatism to the final skillful control of automatism.

At the present time, all this is speculation. But there are already some guidelines and the matter is not trivial.

# 18

## *This Normative Natural History Called Epistemology**

Let me tell you where I stand today and what, for me, came out of all that work in New Guinea and Bali and, later, with schizophrenics and dolphins.

As you know, the difficulty was always to get people to approach the formal analysis of mind with a similar or even an open epistemology. Many people claim to have no epistemology and must just overcome this optimism. Only then can they approach the particular epistemology here proposed. In other words, *two* jumps are required of the reader, and of these the first is the more difficult. We all cling fast to the illusion that we are capable of direct perception, uncoded and not mediated by epistemology. The double-bind hypothesis—i.e., the *mental* description of schizophrenia—was itself a contribution to epistemology, and to evaluate it was an exercise, if you please, in a sort of metaepistemology. Epistemology itself is becoming a recursive subject, a recursive study of recursiveness. So that anybody encountering the double-bind hypothesis has the problem that epistemology was already changed by the double-bind hypothesis, and the hypothesis itself therefore has to be approached with the modified way of thinking which the hypothesis had proposed.

I am sure that none of us in the 1950s realized how difficult this was. Indeed, we still did not realize that, if our hypothesis was even partly correct, it must also be important as a contribution to what I have sometimes called the "fundamentals"—our stock of "necessary" truths.

So what I have to do now is to tell you how, for me, an epistemology grew out of ethnographic observation and cybernetic theory, and how

*"Afterword" by Gregory Bateson, copyright © 1977 by Gregory Bateson, from *About Bateson: Essays on Gregory Bateson,* edited by John Brockman. Used by permission of the publisher, Dutton, an imprint of New American Library, a division of Penguin Books USA Inc. Written in 1977, this article is here reprinted, edited, and has been given a new title taken from the body of the text.

this epistemology determines not only double-bind theory and all the thinking that has followed in the field of psychiatry but also affects evolutionary thinking and the whole body/mind problem.

I have to present here a description of an epistemology, and then I have to fit the double-bind hypothesis and thoughts about evolution into that epistemology. In a word, I have to invite the reader to come in *backward* upon the whole business.

From time to time I get complaints that my writing is dense and hard to understand. It may comfort those who find the matter hard to understand if I tell them that I have driven myself, over the years, into a "place" where conventional dualistic statements of mind/body relations—the conventional dualisms of Darwinism, psychoanalysis, and theology—are absolutely unintelligible to me. It is becoming as difficult for me to understand dualists as it is for them to understand me. And I fear that it's not going to become easier, except by those others being slowly exercised in the art of thinking along those pathways that seem to me to be "straight." My friends in New Guinea, the Iatmul, whose language and culture I studied, used to say, "But our language is so easy. We just talk."

So let me start by trying to characterize my epistemology as it has grown under my hands, with some notable influence from other people.

First, it is a branch of natural history. It was McCulloch who, for me, pulled epistemology down out of the realms of abstract philosophy into the much more simple realm of natural history. This was dramatically done in the paper by McCulloch and his friends entitled "What the Frog's Eye Tells the Frog's Brain." In that paper he showed that any answer to the question "How can a frog know anything?" would be delimited by the sensory machinery of the frog, and that the sensory machinery of the frog could, indeed, be investigated by experimental and other means. It turned out that the frog could only receive news of such moving objects as subtended less than ten degrees at the eye. All else was invisible and produced no impulses on the optic nerve. From this paper it followed that, to understand human beings, even at a very elementary level, you had to know the limitations of their sensory input.

And that matter became part of my experience when I went through the experiments of Adelbert Ames, Jr. I discovered that when I see something, or hear a sound, or taste, it is my brain, or perhaps I should better say "mind"—it is I who create an image in the modality of the appropriate sense organ. My image is my aggregation and organization of information about the perceived object, aggregated and integrated by me according to rules of which I am totally unconscious. I can, thanks to

Ames, know *about* these rules; but I cannot be conscious of the process of their working.

Ames showed me that I (and you), looking through our eyes, *create*, out of showers of impulses on the optic nerve, images of the perceived that appear to be three-dimensional images. I "see" an image *in depth*. But the way in which that image is given depth depends upon essentially Euclidian arguments within the brain and of which the perceiver is unconscious. It is as if the perceiver knew the premises of parallax and created his image in accordance with those rules, never letting himself know at any conscious level that he has applied the rules of parallax to the shower of impulses. Indeed, the whole process, including the shower of impulses itself, is a totally unconscious business.

It seems to be a universal feature of human perception, a feature of the underpinning of human epistemology, that the perceiver shall perceive only the product of his perceiving act. He shall not perceive the means by which that product was created. The product itself is a sort of work of art.

But along with this detached natural history, in which I, as an epistemology, describe the frog or myself—along with that natural history goes a curious and unexpected addition. Now that we have pulled epistemology down from philosophy and made it a branch of natural history, it becomes necessarily a *normative* branch of natural history. This study is normative in the sense that it will chide us when we ignore its strictures and regularities. One had not expected that natural history could be normative, but indeed, the epistemology which I am building for you is normative in two almost synonymous ways. It can be wrong, or I can be wrong about it. And either of those two sorts of error becomes itself part of any epistemology in which it occurs. Any error will propose pathology. (But I *am* the epistemology.)

Take the statement in a previous paragraph: The organism builds images in depth out of the shower of impulses brought to the brain by the optic nerve. It is possible that this statement is incorrect, that future scientific study of the act of perception may show that this is not so, or that its syntax is inappropriate. That is what I mean by being in error in the first way. And the second way of possible error would be to believe that the images that I see are in fact that which I am looking at, that my mental map *is* the external territory. (But we wander off into philosophy if we ask, "Is there *really* a territory?")

And then there is the fact that the epistemology I am building is *monistic*. Applying Occam's razor, I decline to pay attention to notions— which others assert to be subjectively supported—that mind or soul is somehow separable from body and from matter. On the other hand, it is absolutely necessary, of course, that my epistemology shall allow for the natural history fact that, indeed, many human beings of many different cultures have the belief that the mind is indeed separable from the body. Their epistemology is either dualistic or pluralistic. In other words, in this normative natural history called epistemology there must be a study of errors, and evidently certain sorts of error are predictably common. If you look over the whole span of my work, starting with the notion of schismogenesis, or starting even with the patterns in partridge feathers, and going from that to schismogenesis in New Guinea, to end linkage in national character, to the double bind, and to the material we got from the porpoises, you will see that up to a certain date my language of report is *dualistic*.

The double-bind work was for me a documentation of the idea that mind is a necessary explanatory principle. Simple nineteenth-century materialism will not accept any hierarchy of ideas or differences. The world of mindlessness, the Pleroma, contains no *names*, no *classes*.

It is here that I have always in my thinking followed Samuel Butler in his criticisms of Darwinian evolution. It always seems to me that the Darwinian phrasings were an effort to exclude mind. And indeed that materialism in general was an effort to exclude mind. And therefore, since materialism is rather barren, it was hardly surprising to me as an epistemological naturalist to note that physicists, from William Crookes onward, have been prone to go to mediums and other tricksters. They needed solace in their materialism.

But the matter was always difficult. I could not tolerate the dualism seriously, and yet I knew that the narrow materialistic statement was a gross oversimplification of the biological world. The solution came when I was preparing the Korzybski Lecture, when I suddenly realized that of course the bridge between map and territory is *difference*. It is only *news of difference* that can get from the territory to the map, and this fact is the basic epistemological statement about the relationship between all reality out there and all perception in here: that the bridge must always be in the form of difference. Difference, out there, precipitates coded or corresponding difference in the aggregate of differentiation which we call the organism's mind. And that mind is immanent in matter, which is partly inside the body—but also partly "outside," e.g., in the form of records, traces, and perceptibles.

Difference, you see, is just sufficiently away from the grossly materialistic and quantitative world so that mind, dealing in difference, will always be intangible, will always deal in intangibles, and will always have certain limitations because it can never encounter what Immanuel Kant called the *Ding an sich,* the thing in itself. It can only encounter news of boundaries—news of the contexts of difference.

It is worthwhile to list several points about "difference" here.

(1) A difference is not material and cannot be localized. If this apple is different from that egg, the difference does not lie in the apple or in the egg, or in the space between them. To locate difference, i.e., to delimit the context or interface, would be to posit a world incapable of change. Zeno's famous arrow could never move from a position "here" in this context to a position "there" in the next context.

(2) Difference cannot be placed in time. The egg can be sent to Alaska or can be destroyed, and still the difference remains. Or is it only the news of the difference that remains? Or is the difference ever anything but news? With a million differences between the egg and the apple, only those become information that make a difference.

(3) Difference is not a quantity. It is dimensionless and, for sense organs, digital. It is delimited by threshold.

(4) Those differences, or news of differences, which are information, must not be confused with "energy." The latter is a quantity with physical dimensions (Mass x the square of a Velocity). It is perfectly clear that information does not have dimensions of this kind,[1] and that information travels, usually, where energy already is. That is, the recipient, the organism receiving information—or the end organ or the neuron—is already energized from its metabolism, so that, for example, the impulse can travel along the nerve, not driven by the energy, but finding energy ready to undergo degradation at every point of the travel. The energy is there in advance of the information or the response. This distinction between information and energy becomes conspicuous whenever that which does not happen triggers response in an organism. I commonly tell my classes that if they don't fill in their income tax forms the Internal Revenue people will respond to the difference between the forms which they don't fill in and the forms which they might have filled in. Or your aunt, if you don't write her

---

1. But, of course, a *difference* in energy (not itself of the dimensions of energy) can generate news of difference.

a letter, will respond to the difference between the letter you do not write and the letter you might have written. A tick on the twig of a tree waits for the smell of butyric acid that would mean "mammal in the neighborhood." When he smells the butyric acid, he will fall from the tree. But if he stays long enough on the tree and there is no butyric acid, he will fall from the tree anyway and go to climb up another one. He can respond to the "fact" that something does not happen.

(5) Last, in regard to information and the identity between information and news of difference, I want to give a sort of special honor to Gustav Fechner, who in the 1840s got a whiff of this enormously powerful idea. It drove him almost mad, but he is still remembered and his name is still carried in the Weber-Fechner Law. He must have been an extraordinarily gifted man, and a very strange one.

To continue my sketch of the epistemology that grew out of my work, the next point is recursiveness. Here there seem to be two species of recursiveness, of somewhat different nature, of which the first goes back to Norbert Wiener and is well known: the "feedback" that is perhaps the best-known feature of the whole cybernetic syndrome. The point is that self-corrective and quasi-purposive systems necessarily and always have the characteristic that causal trains within the system are themselves circular. Such causal trains, when independently energized, are either self-corrective or runaway systems. In the wider epistemology, it seems that, necessarily, a causal train either in some sense dies out as it spreads through the universe, or returns to the point from which it started. In the first case there is no question of its survival. In the second case, by returning to the place from which it started, a subsystem is established which, for greater or less length of time, will necessarily survive.

The second type of recursiveness has been proposed by Varela and Maturana. These theoreticians discuss the case in which some property of a *whole* is fed back into the system, producing a somewhat different type of recursiveness, for which Varela has worked out the formalisms. We live in a universe in which causal trains endure, survive through time, only if they are recursive. They "survive"—i.e., literally *live upon themselves*—and some survive longer than others.

If our explanations or our understanding of the universe is in some sense to match that universe, or model it, and if the universe is recursive, then our explanations and our logics must also be fundamentally recursive.

And finally there is the somewhat disputed area of "levels." For me the double bind, among other things, as a phenomenon of natural history, is strong evidence that, at least in the natural history aspects of epistemology, we encounter phenomena that are generated by organisms whose epistemology is, for better or for worse, structured in hierarchic form. It seems to me very clear and even expectable that end organs can receive only news of difference. Each receives difference and creates news of difference; and, of course, this proposes the possibility of differences between differences, and differences that are differently effective or differently meaningful according to the network within which they exist. This is the path toward an epistemology of gestalt psychology, and this clumping of news of difference becomes especially true of the mind when it, in its characteristic natural history, evolves language and faces the circumstance that the name is not the thing named, and the name of the name is not the name. This is the area in which I've worked very considerably in constructing a hypothetical hierarchy of species of learning.

These four components, then, give you the beginnings of a sketch of an epistemology:

(1) That message events are activated by difference.

(2) That information travels in pathways and systems that are collaterally energized (with a few exceptions where the energy itself in some form, perhaps a light, a temperature, or a motion, *is* the traveling information). The separation of energy is made clear in a very large number of cases in which the difference is fundamentally a difference between zero and one. In such cases, "zero-not-one" can be the message, which differs from "one-not-zero."

(3) That a special sort of holism is generated by feedback and recursiveness.

(4) That mind operates with hierarchies and networks of difference to create gestalten.

I want to make clear that there are a number of very important statements that are not made in this sketch of an epistemology and whose absence is an important characteristic. I said above that, as I see it and believe it, the universe and any description of it is monistic; and this would imply a certain continuity of the entire world of information. But there is a very strong tendency in Western thinking (perhaps in all human thinking) to think and talk as if the world were made up of separable parts.

All peoples of the world, I believe, certainly all existing peoples, have something like language, and, so far as I can understand the talk of linguists, it seems that all languages depend upon a particulate representation of the universe. All languages have something like nouns and verbs, isolating objects, entities, events, and abstractions. In whatever way you phrase it, "difference" will always propose delimitations and boundaries. If our means of *describing* the world arises out of notions of difference (or what G. Spencer Brown's *Laws of Form* calls "distinction" and "indication"), then our picture of the universe will necessarily be particulate. It becomes an act of faith to distrust language and to believe in monism. Of necessity we shall still split our descriptions when we talk about the universe. But there may be better and worse ways of doing this splitting of the universe into nameable parts.

Finally, let me try to give you an idea of what it felt like, or what sort of difference it made, for me to view the world in terms of the epistemology that I have described to you, instead of viewing it as I used to and as I believe most people always do.

First of all, let me stress what happens when one becomes aware that there is much that is our own contribution to our own perception. Of course I am no more aware of the processes of my own perception than anybody else is. But I am aware that there are such processes, and this awareness means that when I look out through my eyes and see the redwoods or the yellow flowering acacia of California roadsides, I know that I am doing all sorts of things to my percept in order to make sense of that percept. Of course I always did this, and everybody does it. We work hard to make sense, according to our epistemology, of the world which we think we see.

Whoever creates an image of an object does so in depth, using various cues for that creation, as I have already said in discussing the Ames experiments. But most people are not aware that they do this, and as you become aware that you are doing it, you become in a curious way much closer to the world around you. The word "objective" becomes, of course, quite quietly obsolete; and at the same time the word "subjective," which normally confines "you" within your skin, disappears as well. It is, I think, the debunking of the objective that is the important change. The world is no longer "out there" in quite the same way that it used to seem to be. Without being fully conscious or thinking about it all the time, I still know all the time that my images—especially the visual, but also auditory, gustatory, pain, and fatigue—I know the images are "mine" and that I am responsible for these images in a quite peculiar way. It is as if they are all in some degree hallucinated, as indeed they partly are. The shower of impulses coming in over the optic nerve surely contains no picture. The picture is to be developed, to be created, by the intertwining of all these neural messages. And the brain that can do this must be pretty smart. It's my brain. But everybody's brain—any mammalian brain—can do it, I guess.

I have the use of the information that that which I see, the images, or that which I feel as pain, the prick of a pin, or the ache of a tired muscle—for these, too, are images created in their respective modes—that all this is neither objective truth nor is it all hallucination. There is a combining or marriage between an objectivity that is *passive* to the outside world and a creative subjectivity, neither pure solipsism nor its opposite.

Consider for a moment the phrase, *the opposite of solipsism.* In solipsism, you are ultimately isolated and alone, isolated by the premise "I make it all up." But at the other extreme, the opposite of solipsism, you would cease to exist, becoming nothing but a metaphoric feather blown by the winds of external "reality." (But in that region there are no metaphors!) Somewhere between these two is a region where you are partly blown by the winds of reality and partly an artist creating a composite out of the inner and outer events.

A smoke ring is, literally and etymologically, introverted. It is endlessly turning upon itself, a torus, a doughnut, spinning on the axis of the circular cylinder that is the doughnut. And this turning upon its own in-turned axis is what gives separable existence to the smoke ring. It is, after all, made of nothing but air marked with a little smoke. It is of the same substance as its "environment." But it has duration and location and a certain degree of separation by virtue of its inturned motion. In a sense, the smoke ring stands as a very primitive, oversimplified paradigm for all recursive systems that contain the beginnings of self-reference, or, shall we say, selfhood.

But if you ask me, "Do you feel like a smoke ring all the time?" of course my answer is no. Only at very brief moments, in flashes of awareness, am I that realistic. Most of the time I still see the world, feel it, the way I always did. Only at certain moments am I aware of my own introversion. But these are enlightening moments that demonstrate the irrelevance of intervening states.

And as I try to tell you about this, lines from Robert Browning's "Grammarian's Funeral" keep coming to mind.

> Yea, this in him was the peculiar grace . . .
> That before living he'd learn how to live. . . .

Or again,

> He settled *Hoti's* business—let it be!—
> Properly based *Oun*—
> Gave us the doctrine of the enclitic *De*,
> Dead from the waist down.

And again, there is the misquotation that is going the rounds today,

> A man's reach should exceed his grasp,
> Or what's a meta for?

I'm afraid this American generation has mostly forgotten "A Grammarian's Funeral" with its strange combination of awe and contempt.

Imagine, for a moment, that the grammarian was neither an adventurous explorer, breaking through into realms previously unexplored, nor an intellectual, withdrawn from warm humanity into a cold but safe realm. Imagine that he was neither of these, but merely a human being rediscovering what every other human being and perhaps every dog—always instinctively and unconsciously—knew: that the dualisms of mind and body, of mind and matter, and of God and world are all somehow faked up. He would be terribly alone. He might invent something like the epistemology I have been trying to describe, emerging from the repressed state, which Freud called "latency," into a more-or-less distorted rediscovery of that which had been hidden. Perhaps all exploration of the world of ideas is only a searching for a rediscovery, and perhaps it is such rediscovery of the latent that defines us as "human," "conscious," and "twice born." But if this be so, then we all must sometimes hear St. Paul's "voice" echoing down the ages: "It is hard for thee to kick against the pricks."

I am suggesting to you that all the multiple insults, the double binds and invasions that we all experience in life, the impact (to use an inappropriate physical word) whereby experience corrupts our epistemology, challenging the core of our existence, and thereby seducing us into a false cult of the ego—what I am suggesting is that the process whereby double binds and other traumas teach us a false epistemology is already well advanced in most occidentals and perhaps most orientals, and that those whom we call "schizophrenics" are those in whom the endless kicking against the pricks has become intolerable.

# 19

## *Our Own Metaphor: Nine Years After**

Dear [Cap],

I said I would reread "Metaphor" and tell you how that conference looks as I look back on it, nine years after.

First of all, it looks like it did at the time, and this is a great tribute to your achievement as a reporter. Rereading, I again experienced the passionate frustration and murk of the middle days of the conference. Again I paced around the castle like a zombie between the sessions, and again I was the battleground on which Tolly and Gordon and Barry[1] and the rest deployed their intellectual gambits—and their passion.

I get a very different sense of Warren McCulloch's part in all of it. Of course he was our leader and it was his life's work which, acting through me, had brought us together. But he was, like Moses, a leader who could and did bring us to the edge of the promised land, where he himself could never enter.

His last speech makes a special sort of sense if you read it as spoken in that context. . . .

So what of the "promised land"? Did any of us enter it? And were the grapes any bigger?

Are we any nearer to diverting the human species away from its compulsive hobby of raping the environment? And each other.

Are there ever any new ideas? And can they be "right"—or even a little less wrong?

---

*This letter to daughter Mary Catherine Bateson was written June 26, 1977, as a potential afterword for a new edition of her *Our Own Metaphor: A Personal Account of a Conference on the Effects of Conscious Purpose on Human Adaptation* (New York: Knopf, 1972), the report of the Wenner-Gren Conference on the Effects of Conscious Purpose on Human Adaptation, held July 17–24, 1968, at Burg Wartenstein, Austria, and chaired by Gregory Bateson. This letter is previously unpublished.

1. [*Editor's Note:* Anatol W. Holt, Gordon Pask, and Barry Commoner.]

Following the rereading—three or four days later—I begin to see the whole drama in what is, for me, a new way.

I found that I had to face a dividing of the ways, and surely the same decision point must have been faced by many before I ever got there. Plato, surely. T. S. Eliot, perhaps. McCulloch?

Anyhow. It was clear to me, coming out of the re-experienced agony, that either we know *nothing*, or most strangely we know it all.

If epistemology must always come between me and my organic perception of the world, and similarly must always come between me and any understanding of myself; if my epistemology is the organizing principle of all my understanding; then I can never know anything. My machinery and processes of knowing simply constitute one enormous blind spot. A spot through which I cannot even see that it is blind. Not even any darkness.

By epistemology I mean the processes of knowing and (if we know anything) it is pretty clear that these processes shape and limit what can get from the "outside" through our sense organs to inclusion in image or understanding.

The visual epistemology of the frog will only permit him to perceive objects which move and subtend less than ten degrees at his eye. And our visual epistemology will only let us receive news of those differences which either already exist as events in time (i.e., what we call "changes") or which we can convert into events by moving our retina in micronystagmus.

There is no "direct experience"; and Kant's "*Ding an sich*" is always *necessarily* filtered out by the very nature of our processes of knowing. And, it appears, the "*Ding*" must be filtered out by *all* processes of knowing whatsoever.

I used to teach a class of young would-be psychiatrists and always devoted one session to the question: If there be organisms with high intelligence (high enough to make flying saucers) on some other planet, what can we surely predict about their nature? One of my predictions was that those organisms must surely be subject to the pathologies and paradoxes of logical typing. Either schizophrenia must be there or it must be somehow prevented. In the same sense, I would predict that those spacemen can have only indirect experience.

So—all experience is subjective? And since the subject is *systematically* fallible we can be sure of nothing. That's one pathway.

The other path is more interesting and perhaps does even more than malt can—"To justify God's ways to man."

There is the interesting possibility that we might attach meaning to

the word "systematically." If the "self" as a perceiver were *randomly* fallible, then there would be no hope of any knowledge or understanding.
But I am (personally) sure that neither perception nor even dream or
hallucination contains more than a very small random element—and
that random component always only indeterminate within a limited sub-
set of alternative possibilities.

What if:

(A) What we can perceive of self is our own metaphor; and

(B) We are our epistemology; and

(C) Our inner world *is* that epistemology, our microcosm; and

(D) Our microcosm is an appropriate metaphor of the macro-
cosm?

What if "Truth" in some very large and, for us, overriding sense is
information not about *what* we perceive (the green leaves, the stones,
that voice, that face) but about the *process* of perception?

I am always mumbling about what I call "natural history" and that
without natural history all knowledge is dead or dull or pious. And
now, it begins to look as if the natural history of that oak tree is the natural history of *me* (and you). Or at least as if there is a macrocosmic
natural history with which all the little natural histories are so con-
formable that understanding a little one gives a hint for understanding
the big one.

We could then imagine a theory alternative to Darwin's "natural selection" or "survival of the fittest." Our theory would move Darwin's old
notion over into the realm of epistemological reality. We would say that
death—i.e., loss of internal organization—is the end of all microcosms
which become nonconformable with larger macrocosms. (My old
friend, the Bread-and-butter-fly died of a double bind, a disharmony.
Alice says, "That must happen very often," and the Gnat can only say, "It
always happens.")

These thoughts will carry us back into a sort of totemism. We begin
to see ourselves as metaphors for the oak and the beetle, and our
thought processes (which are necessarily interaction) become the
metaphor for evolution.

So man (and the beetles and spiders and oaks and protozoa) evolved
in the image of their own evolution? Because evolution is a mental process, with the therefore necessary *limitations* of all epistemology.

And the ancient religious form called "totemism" is indeed the
crude forerunner of the only monism.

(Am I right, that there *can* be only one monism?)

And the "eternal verities" of McCulloch and St. Augustine ("7 + 5 = 12") are indeed facets of the very nature of the twin processes of "thought" and "evolution."

So what about "conscious purpose"?

I think that the idea of conscious purpose is a sort of a fake, an artifact or epiphenomenon, a biproduct of a disastrous process in the history of occidental thought.

The Christian church in the eighteenth century was already afraid that its dualisms (God/his creatures; soul/body; Church/congregation; etc.) would collapse under scientific insight. So, fifty years before Lamarck and one hundred years before *The Origin of Species,* William Paley was *defending* the dualism of Genesis from the expected attack.

How did he know the attack was coming? From the encyclopedists? Possibly.

Anyhow, his defense of the dualism was in terms of "purpose." He argues that if you look at your watch, you will see that it is *designed* to tell time. His explanation of this is that it was designed by a human designer. Similarly, the claw of a crab or the hand of a man is evidently designed to hold things. His explanation—and the *only* explanation—of this is that the crab and the man were designed by a heavenly Designer.

Paley thus fell into setting the stage of scientific thought in such a context that the scientists felt constrained to explain "design" in nature.

Perhaps we should not entirely blame Paley and his "Evidences." After all, not only Darwin but the whole Industrial Revolution was the climax of occidental man's increasing obsession with design.

I suppose "design" to be the physical realization, first on the drawing board and then in metal, of conscious purpose.

I think we can go a little further. When we recognize that there is *no* design in "Nature," this perception will set us free from the old controversy, so that we can go on to recognize that indeed the phenomena called "adaptation," "acclimation," "addiction," and so on are always brought about by the *dualism of interactive process.* It takes two or more organisms and an environment, all interacting, to generate and regulate *any* evolutionary process. And the resulting process may be beneficial (to whom?) or stabilizing or lethal.

Of course, the lethal processes are the least visible because they don't last long, but they are probably the most frequent. So—a fig for "design."

So we come back to the figment of conscious purpose.

Samuel Butler in Festing Jones's version of the "Notebooks" speculates about the lady who was in search of "The Lost Chord." He says,

Her family had always been unsympathetic about her music. They said it was like a loose bundle of fire-wood which you never can get across the room without dropping sticks; they said she would have been so much better employed doing anything else.

Fancy being in the room with her while she was strumming about and hunting after her chord! Fancy being in heaven with her when she had found it!

Fancy being on earth with the human species while it strums about hunting its conscious purposes.

With love,

Gregory

# 20

## *The Science of Knowing**

If you want to know—to understand—what's the matter with contemporary education, established medicine, holistic medicine, parent-child relations, conservatism, radicalism, government, religion, and the international scene, you will do well to study biology, and especially that branch of biology which is called *epistemology.*

Even this scientific discipline will not help you much because all the sciences together contain rather little knowledge of education and the rest, but it will help a little.

Epistemology is that science whose subject matter is itself. It is the name of a species of scientific study and talk. We set out to study the nature of study itself, the process of the aquisition of information and its storage.

The conventional definitions of epistemology would place it in philosophy and regard it as beyond empirical research—the discussion only of how we can know anything.

· But how we acquire knowledge or information is a matter of observation and even experiment: How do the monarch butterflies find their way to the butterfly tree in the Esalen canyon? Not one of them has ever been here before.

The study of physics and how physics is done and the study of the language of physics in which the resulting knowledge is ordered and stored—all that can be a matter of empirical knowledge. It is a science as much as it is a branch of philosophy. It is not physics; it is a realm of knowledge where mathematics and logic and linguistics should meet to work on a common mass of data.

The study of art and poetry and of how these things are done and how history is done—all these are epistemology, *along with the study of how epistemology is done.*

_____

*This essay, written in 1979, is reprinted from *The Esalen Catalog* 17, no. 2 (1979), by permission of Esalen Programs. Some repetitious material has been deleted.

It follows that epistemology is the great bridge between all branches of the world of experience—intellectual, emotional, observational, theoretical, verbal, and wordless. Knowledge, wisdom, art, religion, sport, and science are bridged from the stance of epistemology. We stand off from all these disciplines to study them and yet stand in the very center of each.

Epistemology is inductive and experimental and, like any true science, it is deductive and, above all, *abductive*, seeking to put side by side similar chunks of phenomena. It notes that the structure of the mammalian face with a so-called "nose" between two so-called "eyes" is formally to be compared with the structure of a sentence whose so-called "subject" has a certain positional relation to so-called "verb" and so-called "object." We know that the thing in the middle of an elephant's face is its "nose" because it is located between two eyes.

Of course, there are no *things* for the science of epistemology to study—we study only ideas—only the ideas of things. No *noses* but only "noses."

When the elephant was still a fetus, long before its nose was useful for smelling or for lifting heavy logs, that incipient organ was somehow a "nose"—a relational, positional nose—in the organizational system of information upon which the embryology hinges.

"What the Frog's Eye Tells the Frog's Brain" and "What Is a Number, that a Man May Know It, and a Man, that He May Know a Number?" These are titles of essays from Warren McCulloch's wonderful book *Embodiments of Mind*. These are essays fundamental to epistemology as a science. In the living of the frog, the only input that can reach the frog's mind (its total organization) through the frog's eye is input about *moving* objects. It cannot see the stationary. The experiments are simple at least in principle. When an electrode attached to a galvanometer is placed on the frog's optic nerve, it becomes at once evident that *motion* in front of the eye is necessary in order to create an impulse in the nerve.

By the same token, our human machinery for perceiving—our sense organs—can receive news only of difference. And within the wide category of difference, we can perceive only those differences which are either already events in time or which can be converted into events in time. We can do a little better than the frog. She sees only the moving fly, but we can see the fly which is not moving. We do this by converting the external static difference between fly and background into an event on our retina. The eye vibrates in its socket to create a scanning. The image of the fly moves relative to the rods and cones and thereby triggers their action.

So, epistemology insists that the stuff of knowledge is always made of the news of difference. But what's wrong with contemporary education? And the international scene? And all that?

Well, the next step from news of single differences is to the building up of *patterns* or configurations. Quite a step! And one which cannot be filled in here. Suffice it to say that notions like "aggression," "crime," "wealth"—and even "god"—are highly abstract patterns which continually provide the tramlines upon which our thought travels forward to decisions of all kinds.

If we have wrong ideas of how our abstractions are built—if, in a word, we have poor epistemological habits—we shall be in trouble—and we are.

# 21

## Men Are Grass: Metaphor and the World of Mental Process*

This is a tape of a lecture intended to be given at the Lindisfarne Fellows' Meeting at Green Gulch in June 1980. I wish I were there with you, but when it appeared that I very likely would not be able to get to Green Gulch for this meeting, I talked to Bill Thompson and suggested that I dictate a tape to be played if he should so desire—failing which, I am sure that somebody else in this room is very capable of taking the first pitch in talking to you at this meeting. Bill advised me that I should talk about what has most been exercising my mind in the last two or three months, and offer that to you as a basis for your discussions. I have had two things on my mind. One is very general, perhaps too general, and the other rather specific. If I were there among you, I would prefer to speak mostly on the specific matter, hoping for discussion which I could use, but since that is apparently not to be, let me offer you the general matter, which, in effect, becomes a survey of almost everything I've done in my life. A survey of a direction in which I have tried always to be moving, though that direction, of course, gets redefined and redefined from project to project.

I grew up in the middle of Mendelian genetics. And the vocabulary that we used then was a curious one. We used to speak of Mendelian factors. Now the word "factor" was a word coined to avoid saying "cause," and at the same time to avoid saying "idea" or "command." You will remember that in the nineteenth century there had been deep and bloodthirsty battles around the Lamarckian concept of the inheritance of acquired characteristics. And this concept was tabooed because it was believed, I think incorrectly, that it necessarily introduced a supernatural

*This address was delivered by tape recording to the annual meeting of the Lindisfarne Fellows, June 9, 1980. Edited by Mary Catherine Bateson, it is reprinted from *Lindisfarne Letter*, no. 11 (1980), by permission of Lindisfarne Press.

component into biological explanation. This component was variously called "memory," "mind," and so forth, but I don't believe it was a supernatural component. It would seem to me to fit with very little modification into the general scene of biological explanation, though its fitting would indeed alter the basis of biology from the very ground up and would alter our ideas about our relationship to mind, our relationship to each other, our relationship to free will, and so on. In a word, our complete epistemology. Here in what I have just said you will notice the assumption that epistemology and theories of mind and theories of evolution are very close to being the same thing, and epistemology is a somewhat more general term which will cover both the theories of evolution and the theories of mind.

The battles over this battleground had been fierce and bloody, and, with a few exceptions, nobody wanted to go through those battles again. So we are still going through them. In any case, it seemed safer at that time to refer to the causal agencies, or the explanatory components of genetics, as factors rather than commands or memories. Darwin, as you may know, had funked the issue of mind and matter in the last pages of *The Origin of Species*. There he suggests that while his evolutionary theory accounted for what had happened to living things once biological evolution had started on the face of the earth, it is possible that that vast inheritance did not start on earth, but reached earth in the form of bacteria, perhaps riding on light waves or whatever, a theory which I've always felt was a little childish. I've been told by a member of the Darwin family that it was probably put in because he was afraid of his wife, who was an ardent Christian. Be all that as it may, the mind/body problem or the mind/matter problem was avoided in those early days of the twentieth century. It is still largely avoided in zoological schools, and the terms "Mendelian factor," "allele," etc., were all rather convenient euphemisms to avoid acknowledging that the field of inquiry was split wide open.

My father, in the 1890s, had set out to do approximately (and this is really very strange) what I have been trying to do in the last few months. Namely, to ask, if we separate off, for the sake of inquiry, the world of mental process from the world of cause and matter, what will that world of mental process look like? And he would have called it, I think, the laws of biological variation, and I would be willing to accept that title for what I am doing, including, perhaps, both biological and mental variation, lest we ever forget that thinking is mental variation.

And, of course, I walk into this field with a lot of tools that my father never had. It perhaps is worth listing these quickly: there's the whole of cybernetics, there's the whole of information theory, and that related field which I suppose we might call communication theory, though as you will see I don't much like the word. Organization theory would be a little better, resonance theory perhaps a little better still. In addition, and very importantly, I have a rather different attitude toward Lamarck, and toward the supernatural, and toward "God." A hundred years ago these things were dangerous to think about, and there was a feeling that how one classified them could be wrong. Personally, I feel that how one classifies the inheritance of acquired characteristics (is it a case of ESP?) is largely a matter of taste, but has tied into its tail, like all matters of taste, the threat that there are many ways of performing this classification which will in fact lead to disaster. If you want to call these ways of classifying wrong, it's all right by me, but personally I want to know more about the total mental web we're talking about, so that the word "wrong" or the words "bad taste" or whatever shall take on a natural history meaning. And that's what I'm really trying to do, to discover, to explore. And I start from a position which is a little more free to take an overall view than was the position of the previous generation.

Then too, I start from the position in which I have some idea of the nature of what I want to call "information." Namely, that this "stuff" is precisely not that, a thing, and that the entire language of materialism, good as it may be for the description of relations between material things, reflecting back upon the things, is lousy as a way of describing the relations between things to reflect forward upon their organization. In other words, the entire materialistic or mechanistic language is inappropriate for my use, and I simply have to have the courage to discard it. This means, of course, that in my mental world or universe I acknowledge no things, and, obviously, of course, there are no things in thought. The neurons may be channels for something, but they are not themselves things within the domain of thought, unless you think about them, which is another thing again. In thought what we have are ideas. There are no pigs, no coconut palms, no people, no books, no pins, no . . . you know? Nothing. There are only ideas of pigs and coconut palms and people and whatever. Only ideas, names, and things like that. This lands you in a world which is totally strange. I find myself running screaming from its contemplation, and essentially running back to a world of materialism, which seems to be what everybody else does, limited only by the amount of their discipline. What I feel driven to ask is, give me a pound, a little mass, a little time, a little length, some combination of these called energy. Give me power, give me all the rest of it. Give me location, for in the mental world there is no location. There is only yes and no, only ideas of ideas, only news of messages; and the news is news, essentially, of differences, or difference between differences, and so on. What is perpetually happening in the works of the most learned philosophers, as well as of people like myself, is a quick dash back into the idioms and styles and concepts of mechanical materialism to escape from the incredible bareness—at first appearance—of the mental world.

Now, notice that in this throwing out of our favorite devices for explanation, a lot of very familiar stuff upon which we are deeply dependent has gone out with the bathwater, and I think good riddance. Notably the separation between God and His creation: that sort of thing doesn't exist anymore. Notably the separation between mind and matter: we won't be bothered by that anymore except to look at it with curiosity as a monstrous idea that nearly killed us. And so on.

I think it is time that I provided my mental world with a little furniture. So far all you've had is the idea that it is full of ideas and messages and news, and that the intangible filter which is between the material and mechanical world and the world of mental process is simply this filter of difference. That while ten pounds of oats is in the sense of materialism real, the ratio (and I repeat the word ratio: I don't mean the subtractive difference—the contrast, if you like, yes) between five pounds and ten pounds is not a part of the material world. It does not have mass, it does not have any other physical characteristics—it is an idea. And there is always this shift to a first derivative between the mechanical world and the world of mental process. I derived this point in about 1970 from Alfred Korzybski. Those of you who are here may remember the Lindisfarne meeting where A. M. Young and I had a confrontation, I think a rather unfortunate one perhaps. He was saying very much the same thing as this and extending it in certain ways which meant that he was going to, as I saw it, forget the rule of dimensions, and indeed the whole of logical typing, in his understanding of mental life. I thought that was a very severe mistake; I don't know who was right. In any case, that's the first positive characteristic that I have given you about the mental world.

Let me now bring in another: a whole family of descriptive propositions, descriptive of epistemology, about which it's not quite clear whether they belong on the mechanical side or on the side of mental process. I favor the latter, but let's consider it. These are the propositions which St. Augustine, a very long time ago, called Eternal Verities, of which Warren McCulloch, a dear friend of mine, was always fond, if you can be fond of anything quite so impersonal. The Eternal Verities of

St. Augustine were such propositions as "three and seven are ten." And he averred that they had always been ten and always would be ten. He was not interested, of course, in this division between the mental and the mechanical or physical that I am talking about, so he didn't touch that as far as I know. But we are interested in that. My feeling is that there is a contrast between what I call quantity and what I call pattern, and in this contrast I see number, at least in its simplest forms, smaller forms, as inevitably of the category and nature of pattern rather than of the nature of quantity. So number is perhaps the simplest of all patterns. In any case, St. Augustine was a mathematician, and in particular an arithmetician, and he seems to have had a feeling that the numbers were very special things, a feeling, of course, which is not unfamiliar to most of you who have thought a little about Pythagorean numerology and other related things. Then, after all, the contrasts between numbers are very much more complex than the mere ratios. We could say, I suppose, that the contrasts—pattern differences—between numbers fall off as the numbers get bigger and bigger, but I'm not sure the numerologists will permit us to say that. What seems to be clear is that at least in smaller numbers the pattern differences, between say three and five, are drastic indeed, and form in fact major taxonomic criteria in biological fields. I am after all interested in this realm of pattern or number or mental process as a biological realm, and the biological creatures, plants and animals, certainly seem to think that their concern is much more with number than with quantity, though above a certain quantitative level, a certain size of number, as I pointed out in *Mind and Nature*, numbers become quantities, so that a rose has five sepals, five petals, many stamens, and then a gynoecium of a pistil system based on five. The contrast between four sides of a square and three sides of a triangle is not four minus three, being one; it is not even the ratio between four and three. It is very elaborate differences of pattern and symmetry which obtain between the two numbers as patterns.

So it would seem that this pattern aspect of numbers at least belongs in the mental world of organisms. Now I want to introduce into that world another component, which I confess is rather surprising. It's been clear for a long time that logic was a most elegant tool for the description of lineal systems of causation—if A, then B, or if A and B, then C, and so on. That logic could be used for the description of biological pattern and biological event has never been at all clear. Indeed, it is rather sharply clear that it is unsuitable, at least in the description of such circular causal systems and recursive systems as will generate the paradoxes. Now, for those you can muddle along, maybe completely, I don't know, with a correction of the lineal system by appeal to time. You can conclude your Epimenides paradox with the statement: yes at time A, and if yes at time A, then no at time B; if no at time B, then yes at time C; and so on. But I do not believe that this is really how it's done in nature. I mean you can do it on any page of your book, but it's another thing to say that these are the logical causal trains, or whatever, which in fact occur in organisms and their relationships and their tautologies of embryology and so on. You will see that this is a very unlikely solution.

On the other hand there is another solution which I would like to present to you. Would somebody please place on the blackboard these two syllogisms side by side. The first is a syllogism in the mood traditionally called Barbara:

> Men die.
> Socrates is a man.
> Socrates will die.

And the other syllogism has, I believe, a rather disreputable name, which I will discuss in a minute, and it goes like this:

> Grass dies.
> Men die.
> Men are grass.

Thank you. Now, these two syllogisms coexist in an uncomfortable world, and a reviewer the other day in England pointed out to me that most of my thinking takes the form of the second kind of sequence and that this would be all very well if I were a poet, but is inelegant in a biologist. Now, it is true that the schoolmen or somebody took a look at various sorts of syllogisms, whose names are now, thank God, forgotten, and they pointed to the "syllogism in grass," as I will call this mood, and said, "That's bad, that does not hold water. It's not sound for use in proofs. It isn't sound logic." And my reviewer said that this is the way that Gregory Bateson likes to think and we are unconvinced. Well, I had to agree that this is the way I think, and I wasn't quite sure what he meant by the word "convinced." That, perhaps, is a characteristic of logic, but not of all forms of thought. So I took a very good look at this second type of syllogism, which is called, incidentally, "Affirming the Consequent." And it seemed to me that indeed this was the way I did much of my thinking, and it also seemed to me to be the way the poets did their thinking. It also seemed to me to have another name, and its name was metaphor. Meta-phor. And it seemed that perhaps, while not always logically sound, it might be a very useful contribution to the principles of life. Life, perhaps, doesn't always ask what is logically sound. I'd be very surprised if it did.

Now, with these questions in mind, I began to just sort of look around. Let me say that the syllogism in grass has a quite interesting history. It was really picked up by a man named E. von Domarus, a Dutch psychiatrist in the first half of this century who wrote an essay in a very interesting little book, which has more or less disappeared, called *Language and Thought in Schizophrenia.*[1] And what he pointed out was that schizophrenics tend, indeed, to talk, perhaps also to think, in syllogisms having the general structure of the syllogism in grass. And he took a good look at the structure of this syllogism, and he found that it differs from the Socrates syllogism, in that the Socrates syllogism identifies Socrates as a member of a class, and neatly places him in the class of those who will die, whereas the grass syllogism is not really concerned with classification in the same way. The grass syllogism is concerned with the equation of predicates, not of classes and subjects of sentences, but with the identification of predicates. Dies—dies, that which dies is equal to that other thing which dies. And von Domarus, being a nice, you know, honest man, said this is very bad, and it is the way poets think, it's the way schizophrenics think, and we should avoid it. Perhaps.

You see, if it be so that the grass syllogism does not require subjects as the stuff of its building, and if it be so that the Barbara syllogism (the Socrates syllogism) does require subjects, then it will also be so that the Barbara syllogism could never be much use in a biological world until the invention of language and the separation of subjects from predicates. In other words, it looks as though until 100,000 years ago, perhaps at most one million years ago, there were no Barbara syllogisms in the world, and there were only Bateson's kind, and still the organisms got along all right. They managed to organize themselves in their embryology to have two eyes, one on each side of a nose. They managed to organize themselves in their evolution. So there were shared predicates between the horse and the man, which zoologists today call homology. And it became evident that metaphor was not just pretty poetry, it was not either good or bad logic, but was in fact the logic upon which the biological world had been built, the main characteristic and organizing glue of this world of mental process which I have been trying to sketch for you in some way or another.

---

1. E. von Domarus. "The Specific Laws of Logic in Schizophrenia," in *Language and Thought in Schizophrenia*, ed. Jacob Kasanin (Los Angeles and Berkeley: University of California Press, 1944).

Well, I hope that may have given you some entertainment, something to think about, and I hope it may have done something to set you free from thinking in material and logical terms, in the syntax and terminology of mechanics, when you are in fact trying to think about living things.

That's all.

# PART IV

## Health, Ethics, Aesthetics, and the Sacred

# 22

## *Language and Psychotherapy—Frieda Fromm-Reichmann's Last Project**

In the fields of psychiatry and psychoanalysis—and even anthropology—one thing more than any other makes progress difficult. It is this: that to embark upon a new area of investigation is not merely to begin looking at a new part of the universe external to the self. The universe of humanity does not have that objective character which has been a source of reassurance to the natural scientists since the days of Locke and Newton. Rather, for those who study human behavior and human mentality, the world takes on a Berkeleyan character. The trees in our wood are in some sense functions of our perception. The old Berkeleyan motto, *esse est percipi*—to be is to be perceived—leads on the one hand to such philosophical toys as the question: Is the tree there in the wood when I am not there to see it? But on the other hand it leads to a very profound and irresistible discovery that the laws and processes of our perception are a bridge which joins us inseparably to that which we perceive—a bridge which unites subject and object.

This means that, for everybody who would work in the sciences of man, every new discovery and every new advance is an exploration of the self. When the investigator starts to probe unknown areas of the universe, the back end of the probe is always driven into his own vital parts.

Of course this is really no less true of the natural sciences and mathematics. Indeed, the great changes which have occurred in physics and mathematics in the last thirty years have had this character—especially the discovery of relativity and the discovery that even Euclidean geometry deals not with the objective natural history of external space, but

*This is the text of the Frieda Fromm-Reichmann Memorial Lecture, read by Gregory Bateson at the Veterans Administration Hospital, Palo Alto, California, June 3, 1957. It is reprinted, with several minor editorial changes, from *Psychiatry* 21, no. 1 (1958), by permission of *Psychiatry* and the William Alanson White Psychiatric Foundation.

with what I may call "space" in quotation marks. I mean space not as it exists, but as it is defined by the perceiver—or the imaginer.

Be that as it may, the retreat into a perhaps spurious objectivity has been a reassurance and a defense for natural scientists for nearly two hundred years, and this defense has really never been available to the students of man. Here and there in certain branches of psychology, sociology, and economics, the attempt has been made to create or ape this spurious objectivity, but I believe that the results have always been sterile. The imitative attempt is obviously out of place in any science concerned with men's mental processes or communicative behavior. Here, to increase awareness of one's scientific universe is to face unpredictable increases in one's awareness of the self. And I wish to stress the fact that such increases are always in the very nature of the case unpredictable in nature.

It was, however, to this double task that Frieda Fromm-Reichmann dedicated her life, and I should like to relate an adventure in exploration upon which she embarked in her last year. In one sense, to embark upon such an adventure at the age of sixty-seven took extraordinary courage, but in another sense you can say, if you will, that she was dedicated to this species of double task and therefore could not not embark upon it.

When Frieda came to the Center for Advanced Study in the Behavioral Sciences, she came with the definite intention of adding to the tools of her insight. She hoped to synthesize into her psychoanalytic background whatever skills and insights she might be able to glean from semantics, linguistics, and the theories of communication—no small ambition. She already had extraordinary sensitivity to the overtones and nuances of human behavior, but she said that she felt insufficiently conscious of the actual nonverbal cues from which she arrived at her conclusions. It was her hope to achieve a greater consciousness in this sphere for herself. She was also concerned for psychiatrists in general, and especially for psychiatric students. She hoped that if it were possible to transcribe and point to the nonverbal transactions, this would provide an enormously valuable tool for the teaching of psychiatry.

The first barrier she encountered was that the experts in these other fields knew less about psychiatry than she did about semantics and linguistics. Her first task was therefore to get them to analyze some psychiatric data in terms of their special techniques. The result was that one of the linguists at the Center laid aside the dictionary of an American Indian language upon which he was working, and started to transcribe, with the finest phonetic discriminations then available, a psychiatric

interview of which a tape recording had been especially prepared at
Chestnut Lodge. This work by Norman McQuown was published in
*Psychiatry.*[1]

As usually happens when one science meets another, inadequacies
of existing knowledge were disclosed. Linguistics had carefully turned
its back upon what were loosely called paralinguistic phenomena—the
overbreathings, grunts, sighs, laughter, sobbing, and the like, which
form an important part of everyone's comment upon what is transpir-
ing between himself and the other. As the focus upon transcribing the
psychiatric interview became more intense, it became obvious that what
was required was a more nearly total study of these paralinguistic phenomena.

Next it appeared that there was no satisfactory line to be drawn
between the paralinguistic phenomena which could be recorded on a
tape and the vastly greater range of phenomena which were perceptible
only to the eye. I mean the stream of significant movement, posture,
gesture, and the like. The concept *language* was enlarged to include all
communicational events originating in a human body.

It was therefore necessary for Frieda Fromm-Reichmann to add
another skill to her project. She not only had to push the linguists into
an area which they had postponed investigating, but also to add a kinesi-
cist to the team. She therefore prevailed upon the authorities to invite
Ray Birdwhistell to the Center for three days, and having verified the
richness of the kinesic field, arranged that he be at the Center during
the remaining months of her stay there.

So her team now consisted of five persons. Somewhere along the
line she had added another psychiatrist, Henry Brosin, and another linguist, Charles Hockett. At this point, I began to be lucky. The team
needed films of psychiatric material upon which they could immediately
start work. I was present at their planning session on the first day of
Birdwhistell's time at the Center, and found them dismayed at the
prospect of losing precious weeks while appropriate film was prepared. I
was able to say that I had such film ready for their examination. This was
film of family interaction in several households in which psychiatric
problems were known to exist, in the sense that one or more of the
members of each of these families was in psychotherapy. And I suggested that while they were doing a kinesic and linguistic analysis of the
interaction within one of these families, it would certainly be possible to

1. Norman A. McQuown, "Linguistic Transcription and Specification of Psychiatric
Interview Materials," *Psychiatry* 20 (1957): 79–86.

secure film of the therapist at work with whatever members of the family might be receiving psychiatric aid. This was afterwards done.

But a very important change was introduced into the project by the circumstance that the family films were available *before* the film of therapeutic process. This accident shifted the project from a study of linguistics and kinesics in psychotherapy to a study of the natural history of these phenomena in the family constellation.

Let me talk for a minute about the part which Frieda played in the coordination of this team. Anthropologists and linguists and such are by way of being a basket of crabs. Some of us are rigid, some of us want to be prima donnas, some of us rigidly want to be prima donnas. For most of us it was a new experience to deal with material so intimate that we were deeply affected through our empathy and identification with the mothers and fathers and children on the screen. You may imagine that such a group, stimulated by such material, would present something of a problem in group therapy if the project was to succeed.

Frieda, I need hardly say, was a great therapist and a great lady, and I think that one of her great contributions to this team was that we fought very little about matters which were not worth fighting about. One did not in Frieda's presence say things which one could recognize as second-rate. Perhaps even one's power to recognize the second-rate was in some way enhanced when she was around. It was not that she behaved didactically, but rather that her very presence insisted upon simplicity. I cannot tell you what paralinguistic or kinesic cues she emitted which had this effect; I can only say that it was not done by verbal or lexical signals.

Indeed, recalling the sessions when she worked with us, first at the Center and later in the Department of Anthropology and Linguistics at Buffalo, I don't think she said very much at all. She was enthusiastic, she was critical, and she was a touchstone. We would offer her our interpretation of this or that group of data, and she would comment, usually adding her interpretation to ours rather than pushing ours aside.

One episode is interesting. Those of you who have ever worked in the field of systematic botany will know that the experts who look after the vast collections of dried and pressed plants in herbaria commonly have a difficulty in identifying a living growing plant. If you bring it to the herbarium for identification they will say, "Let us press it for a couple of days and we will be able to tell you what it is." Frieda had a converse difficulty in looking at the sound films of human behavior—as also did Henry Brosin.

I had the feeling from the films and from the experience of participating in the making of the film that one of the families upon which we were working showed signs of grave distortion of communication but, while it was possible to discuss these signs, they did not seem so serious to the two psychiatrists. Later, they went together and visited the family and saw its members not flattened on the movie screen, but in the flesh. They then very quickly perceived that there was something seriously wrong, and both agreed about this.

I think the point is not merely that they now saw the living people, but that they had direct experience of how it felt to interact with these people. They had seen them on the screen, interacting with each other and with me, but from this it was not possible to be sure how it would feel to interact in person with them.

So far as I can see, this difficulty is real and inevitable, and the dream that it might be possible to train psychiatric students in diagnosis and perception by the use of film material must always face this limitation, that human diagnosis depends upon human interaction, not as observed through a one-way screen or the lens of a camera, but as felt in the actual participating experience. It is only possible to tell what sort of person the other is from a combination of observation of his communicative habits and an introspective observation of what sort of person one is oneself when dealing with him. The general point which I made earlier about discoveries in the science of man—that every discovery concerning human behavior in the external universe is also a discovery about the self, and often an unwelcome discovery in that inner field—applies also in the field of observation and diagnosis. It may well be that diagnosis cannot really be based upon purely objective data such as films and tape recordings, but must always have the additional data of personal experience.

I am not, of course, deprecating the near miracles which can be achieved by highly trained and perceptive people, looking at a Rorschach protocol or a specimen of handwriting. All I am saying is that this is something different, and that the final judgment regarding the *gravity* of psychiatric signs can perhaps be made only from living experience.

The film material has, however, one special advantage which I think is worth mentioning, and which has colored my personal experience in working with the project which I am trying to describe: The film contains an objective external representation of the interviewer. It does not, of course, satisfy the dream of Robert Burns, who wished that some power would give us humans the gift to see ourselves as others see us, because as I have said, what the others see is amplified by their subjective experience of interacting with us. However, the interviewer does get an external view of his own behavior—a sort of data not otherwise accessible at all. And if the interviewer works on the film material, as I did, with other members of a team, he will discover that their perception of his behavior is often quite different from what he himself had hoped or consciously intended.

In a word, there were for me moments of considerable pain when the others were interpreting my actions, and I was forced to see those actions on the screen. At such times, Frieda extended a basic wide friendliness which made it easier for me to evaluate what was being said without those feelings of rejection which would otherwise make the comments unacceptable. It was not that she reassured by diminishing the force of the critical comment. What she did was to lend that strength which enabled one to receive the comment.

Similarly, in dealing with data on family interaction, there was always a tendency among members of the project to identify with that member of the family who was suffering trauma at a given moment, and to express this identification in the form of either kinesic or linguistic mimicking—caricature—of the person who unwittingly inflicted the trauma. Frieda was always conscious—or perhaps I should say deeply aware and governed by her awareness—that both the hurt person and the person who inflicted the hurt were equally parts of a larger disordered process which neither could understand or control.

There seems to be a sort of progress in awareness, through the stages of which every man—and especially every psychiatrist and every patient—must move, some persons progressing further through these stages than others. One starts by blaming the identified patient for his idiosyncrasies and symptoms. Then one discovers that these symptoms are a response to—or an effect of—what others have done; and the blame shifts from the identified patient to the etiological figure. Then, one discovers perhaps that these figures feel a guilt for the pain which they have caused, and one realizes that when they claim this guilt they are identifying themselves with God. After all, they did not, in general, know what they were doing, and to claim guilt for their acts would be to claim omniscience. At this point one reaches a more general anger, that what happens to people should not happen to dogs, and that what people do to each other the lower animals could never devise. Beyond this, there is, I think, a stage which I can only dimly envisage, where pessimism and anger are replaced by something else—perhaps humility. And from this stage onward to whatever other stages there may be, there is loneliness.

That is as far as I can go in recounting the stages through which man progresses toward an image of God. What I am trying to express is the idea that Frieda Fromm-Reichmann was a stage or two ahead of the rest of us in this progress. And naturally I do not have the power to express that which is beyond me.

No one knows the end of that progress which starts from uniting the perceiver and the perceived—the subject and the object—into a single universe.

## Reference

McQuown, Norman A., ed. *The Natural History of an Interview.* University of Chicago Library Microfilm Collection of Manuscripts in Cultural Anthropology, series 15, nos. 95–8.

# 23

## *The Moral and Aesthetic Structure of Human Adaptation**

By the word "moral" and the words "human adaptation," I intend to indicate that this conference is a continuation of last year's conference on the "Effects of Conscious Purpose on Human Adaptation." At that meeting we reached consensus that certain sorts of shortsightedness which ignore the systemic characteristics of man, human society, and the surrounding ecosystems are *bad* when implemented by a powerful technology. The word "immoral" was not used for these deluded attempts to achieve human purposes but, at least where the shortsightedness is almost willful, I see no reason to avoid the word.

It also became clear at the last conference that these immoralities form a *class* of cases such that practice in analyzing one case will facilitate the understanding of others. It is not just a matter of learning to analyze all the relevant relationships and variables whenever we set out to tamper with organisms: we can learn something about the characteristic interlocking of these relationships—whether we describe the interlocking in cybernetic terms or by means of occurrence graphs.

In fact, hand in hand with the repetitiveness of relations in the undisturbed systems, there is a repetitiveness of the sorts of immorality whereby these systems become corrupted and pathological. There is a general *structure* of immorality, and, similarly, a general structure of those mental processes which would avoid such shortsightedness.

Our first conference dealt at considerable length with these matters but we said very little about what adaptive actions can be undertaken by man and still be *moral*, in the sense of not deteriorating the larger systems of which man is a part.

*Written November 5, 1968, this essay was the invitational paper for the Wenner-Gren Symposium on the Moral and Aesthetic Structure of Human Adaptation, held July 19–28, 1969, at Burg Wartenstein, Austria, chaired by Gregory Bateson. This essay is previously unpublished. Some closing material has been deleted.

I hope that in the coming conference we may work toward a consensus regarding the structure of such moral planning and action, including also some planning toward the correction of those popular false premises which lead to harmful action.

What is lacking is a *Theory of Action* within large complex systems, where the active agent is himself a part of and a product of the system. Kant's "Categorical Imperative" might provide a first step in this direction. It seems also that great teachers and therapists avoid all direct attempts to influence the action of others and, instead, try to provide the settings or contexts in which some (usually imperfectly specified) change may occur.

I think, however, that we are not yet surely ready to tackle this gigantic problem of planned intervention.

At the first conference I held the group back from problems of action for several reasons:

I believed that we had what the Bible calls "beams" in our own eyes—distortions of perception so gross that to attempt to remove "motes" from the eyes of our fellow men would be both presumptuous and dangerous. After all, we, too, are creatures of a civilization which certainly since the Renaissance and possibly for a much longer time has cherished such irrational principles as reductionism, the conceptual division between mind and body, and the belief that ends justify means. It was therefore probable that any plan of action which we might devise would itself be based upon these erroneous premises.

Indeed, the very errors that we would set out to correct, e.g., the cultural errors of reductionism and mind/body separation, are themselves buttressed by homoestatic mechanisms. We were in agreement that to try to alter any variable in a homoestatic system without awareness of the supporting homoestasis must always be shortsighted and perhaps immoral; and yet, we would boldly go out to attack epistemological errors which are deeply rooted in our culture and supported by complex vested interest in all branches of that culture—in art, education, religion, commerce, science, and even in sport and international relations.

Moreover, there may be a whole order of explanation and determinism that is still unexplored. It is surely not an accident that the alpha animal of the group is commonly the most beautiful, even to human eyes, and that it is this animal that is the most decorated with hair and feathers and—among humans—with fancy costumes. To what extent is the "dominance" of the alpha animal determined and/or supported by aesthetic determinants? For lack of a better term I am calling this *aesthetic* determinism.

It seems to me that, quite without an exhaustive analysis of the relevant cybernetic factors, some people are guided away from the courses of action which would generate ugliness—that there are people who have "green thumbs" in their dealing with other living systems. I am inclined to associate this phenomenon with some sort of aesthetic judgment, an awareness of criteria of elegance and of the combinations of process that will lead to elegance rather than ugliness.

In our previous conference we were concerned with the moral aspect more than with the aesthetic. It may be that the latter is a totally separate order of explanation, but I suspect that the two are closely related and that the difference between them is only a difference of logical type. As I see it, moral judgment is concerned with discriminating and identifying *classes* of cases; and this is especially true when the moral system is condensed into a legal code. The aesthetic, on the other hand, seems to be more intimately concerned with the relationships which obtain within each particular case. In spite of many attempts, the rules of aesthetic judgment have never been satisfactorily condensed.

It may be, however, that the dichotomy between moral and aesthetic is a by-product of the premise of mind/body division or of the similar division between consciousness and the remainder of mind. Certainly occidental people expect to be more aware of and more articulate about moral judgments than about aesthetic. We say, "*de gustibus non disputandum*" as though the aesthetic were no suitable subject for doubt or scientific analysis. And yet we agree that some people, more skilled in these matters than others, are able to contrive objects or sounds which those others can agree are beautiful.

We know little of what makes some teachers, some political leaders, some gardeners, some psychotherapists, some animal trainers, and some aquarium keepers great. We say vaguely that these skills depend upon *art* rather than science. Perhaps there is scientific truth behind this metaphor.

We know virtually nothing about the processes whereby a baseball pitcher computes his action or whereby a cat estimates her jump to catch a mouse. But it is certain that these computations are *not* done the way an engineer would do them: the cat and the pitcher do not use the differential calculus.

Even, it would seem from Gertrude Hendrix's paper last year that there is some sort of *opposition* between verbal understanding and that more total and nonverbal understanding which is necessary for transfer of learning.

We also touched briefly last year on the notion that the conference group was, in some sense, its own "central metaphor." That in our deliberations we were using the group itself as a sort of analogic computer from which insights into systemic process could be derived.

These considerations suggest that the cat and the baseball pitcher might achieve their miracles of precision by some similar procedure—using themselves as "central metaphors." (What happens when the cat and the pitcher *practice* their skill?)

In sum, what is here suggested is that systemic shortsightedness, reductionism, the grosser forms of body/mind dichotomy, etc., may be mitigated or avoided by mental processes in which the total organism (or much of it) is used as a metaphor. Such mental processes will not probably follow the long and tedious path of computing all the relations between relevant variables but will use various sorts of short cuts and best guesses. But they will still reckon with the fact that the ecosystem or society is *alive*.

As I remarked last year, the ancients who endowed forests and lakes with personality were not without wisdom. Such mythology surely made it easier for men to use themselves as analogues in the attempt to understand nature.

We face perhaps what Sir Geoffrey Vickers has called an "ecology of ideas."[1]

If it be true that certain people are specially gifted in the art of acting upon complex systems with homoestatic or ecological characteristics, and that these people do not operate by spelling out the interaction of all relevant variables, then these people must use some inner ecology of ideas as an analogic model. (By "ideas" I mean thoughts, premises, affects, perceptions of self, etc.)

But if this skill is, in some sense, really an "art," then it is possible that the inner "ecology of ideas" is a close synonym of what might also be called *aesthetic sensibility*.

These notions suggest, finally, that there may be another approach to the problems of a Theory of Action.

As I write this, on November 5, 1968, the nation is voting to choose a President and the voters are faced by alternative candidates—none of whom even claims to have either aesthetic or biological insight into the affairs of a large nation.

Be that as it may, I suggest that before we proceed to a consideration of theories of action, we should devote some time to the question of aesthetic determinism for the following reasons:

---

1. See Vickers, *Value Systems and Social Process* (Tavistock Publications, 1968).

(a)  It is conceivable that there is a whole other order of determinative factors, to ignore which would be as fatal as to ignore the homoeostatic aspect of biological systems.

(b)  It is possible that the aesthetic approach, with its special emphasis upon patterns and the modulation of patterns, may be a natural development out of mem-theory and o-graphs.

(c)  It is possible that the aesthetic is in some way closely related to or derivative from the cybernetic.

(d)  It is possible that the aesthetic approach may provide short cuts to the evaluation and criticism of plans for action.

(e)  It is possible that aesthetic perception may be characteristic of human beings, so that action plans which ignore this characteristic of human perception are unlikely to be adopted, and even unlikely to be practicable.

(f)  It is possible that aesthetic computation and aesthetic creativity are subject to pathological disturbance. Certainly creative and artistic processes are in part determined by epoch and cultural milieu. It is likely therefore that pathologies of culture will produce pathologies of aesthetic perception and monsters of aesthetic creation.

(g)  But, conversely, if the aesthetically monstrous be symptomatic of cultural pathology, then we have to remember that in all such cases, the symptom is the system's attempt to cure itself. The creation of the appropriate monstrosities might therefore be a component in corrective action. It is possible that some contemporary artists are actually doing things which we in our conference hope to plan to do.

For these and related reasons, I think that we should take a good look at the problems of aesthetics *before* we go on to the problems of action.

# 24

## *A Systems Approach**

The increase in family therapy over the last twenty years denotes more than the introduction of a new method and more than a mere shift in the size of the social unit with which the therapist feels that he must deal. Indeed, the very change in the size of the unit brings with it a new epistemology and ontology, i.e., a new way of thinking about what a *mind* is and a new concept of man's place in the world.

In the early days of family therapy, those of us who dealt with institutionalized schizophrenics felt driven to do family therapy because it made no sense to send the remitted patient home from the hospital into a home setting which would promote the symptoms which the patient had only recently given up. Family therapy in those early days therefore took the shape of defending the patient against what the family might do to him. In early phrasings of double-bind theory the patient was labeled as the "victim" of parental binding, and the "schizophrenogenic" mother was a target of psychiatric attack. We thought in terms of patient versus family, and the key word was "versus."

But rather soon, it became clear that all members of a family containing schizophrenia were equally victims and that the family as a whole—including the patient—required to be changed. The word "versus" was no longer appropriate in describing relationships within the family, and the key word became "part of." It was necessary to see each individual as part of a system which as a whole was functioning badly.

## Systems Theory

This emphasis upon the whole system denoted a change from the conventional concepts of individual psychology to some form of systems theory or cybernetics.

*Written in 1971 as an evaluation of "Family Therapy," by Jay Haley, this essay is reprinted from the *International Journal of Psychiatry* 9 (1971), by permission of Jason Aronson, Inc. Some introductory material has been deleted.

But, what is a system?

A system, after all, is any unit containing feedback structure and therefore competent to process information. There are ecological systems, social systems, and the individual organism *plus* the environment with which it interacts is itself a system in this technical sense. The circumstance that the family as a unit came to be thought of as a system must lead back inevitably, I believe, to considering the individual as a system.

It follows that the ways of thinking evolved by psychiatrists in order to understand the family as a system will come to be applied in understanding the individual as a system. This will be a fundamental change within the home territory of psychology, i.e., in the study of the individual, and a corresponding change in the philosophy and practice of individual psychotherapy. The polarization of opinion then will not be simply between practitioners of individual therapy and practitioners of family therapy but between those who think in terms of systems and those who think in terms of lineal sequences of cause and effect.

## Individual Psychology and Systems Theory

This is not the place, and the time is not ripe, for detailed prediction about what will happen to individual psychology and the techniques of treating the individual when systems theory becomes assimilated into this field. It is worth noting, however, that many parts of conventional individual psychology have long been ready for framing within systems theory, notably the Freudian concept of psychological conflict where the contrasting poles of thought or motivation are conventionally assumed to be interactive, each promoting the other.

In other areas the assimilation will not be so easy. Many of the common concepts of individual psychology, which are handled as nouns in the language of psychologists and even to some extent reified, will, no doubt, be translated into a language of process. Such concepts as ego, anxiety, hostility, psychic energy, need, etc., will have a new appearance and a very different status in the total system of explanation. These changes will be difficult to assimilate.

Perhaps even more difficult will be the shift in the boundaries of the individual mind. The basic rule of systems theory is that, if you want to understand some phenomenon or appearance, you must consider that phenomenon within the context of all *completed* circuits which are relevant to it. The emphasis is on the concept of the completed communicational circuit and implicit in the theory is the expectation that all units containing completed circuits will show mental characteristics. The mind, in other words, is immanent in the circuitry. We are accustomed to thinking of the mind as somehow contained within the skin of an organism, but the circuitry is *not* contained within the skin.

Consider the case of a man felling a tree with an ax. Each stroke of the ax must be corrected for the state of the cut face of the tree after each chip flies. In other words, the system which shows mental characteristics is the whole circuit from the tree to the man's sense organs, through his brain to his muscles and the ax, and back to the tree. This is not the unit which psychologists are accustomed to considering but it is the unit which systems theory will force them to consider.

Very little thought will show that this change in relevance from thinking of man versus tree to thinking of man as part of a circuit which includes the tree will change our ideas of the nature of self, the nature of power, responsibility, and so on.

It might even lead the human race to a sort of wisdom that would preclude the wanton destruction of our biological environment and preclude some of the very peculiar attitudes we exhibit toward patients, foreigners, minorities, our spouses, and our children—and even each other.

# 25

## *The Creature and Its Creations**

In the present chapter we shall follow Paley's argument backwards: we shall accept Paley's premise that the symptoms and evidences of mental creation are always to be found in the products of that creating. Moreover, I have already asserted that the evolutionary process is in a formal sense analogous to (or simply a special case of) mental creativity, and this assertion is attested by the characteristics of its created products, the living creatures.

Now, taking another step down the ladder whose each step is the relation between a creator and a creature, we shall see that the created products, the poems and the works of art, produced by those living creatures are in turn marked by the evidences of that mental creativity.

The "Criteria of Mind" discussed in [Chapter 4 of *Mind and Nature*] are now to be searched for among the products of mind.

Finally I shall argue that the very nature and purpose of art and poetry is to exemplify the creativity of mind and that this is the appropriate fundamental theorem for a science of aesthetics. In creativity, mind is brought together, and this integration is a close synonym of "beauty."

Wordsworth mocks that, to "Peter Bell,"

> A primrose by a river's brim
> A yellow primrose was to him,
> And it was nothing more.

To the poet, the primrose can be something more. I suggest that this something more is, in fact, a self-reflexive recognition. The primrose resembles a poem and both poem and primrose resemble the poet.

---

*Written ca. 1974 as a chapter opening for *The Evolutionary Idea* (which eventually became *Mind and Nature*), this essay has been re-edited with the aid of a later manuscript version. It is reprinted by permission of the Point Foundation from *CoEvolution Quarterly*, no. 4 (1974).

He learns about himself as a creator when he looks at the primrose. His pride is enhanced to see himself as a contributor to the vast processes which the primrose exemplifies.

And his humility is exercised and made valid by recognizing himself as a tiny product of those processes. Even within his own living, his conscious self is little more than a middleman, a publisher and retailer of the poems.

Be all that as it may, we return to consider data. For this purpose, "Mary had a little lamb" would perhaps serve as well as "To be or not to be . . . ," but for the sake of keeping overt the reflexive mode, I shall begin with the easier task of examining an overtly reflexive poem: Wallace Stevens's "The Man with the Blue Guitar."

Here the poet baldly asserts two-thirds of the way through the longish poem:

> Poetry is the subject of the poem,
> From this the poem issues and
>
> To this returns. . . .

So let us take him at his word and consider first this poem as an overt statement of the poet's view of his own creativity and consider this statement as a source of evidences of mind at work.

The poet sees himself as divided from "Things as they are." Indeed, there is a matter about which the organism (the poet, in this case) can say nothing, and this matter is, in this poem, called "Things as they are." Perhaps it—this ineffable matter—is only a fiction. But "they" (the world of audiences—of people "as they are") criticize the singer (the poet):

> They said, "You have a blue guitar,
> You do not play things as they are."

But this, after all, is the circumstance for all organisms. Between us and "Things as they are" there is always a creative filter. Our organs of sense will admit no thing and report only what makes sense. "We," like the general of a modern army, read only intelligence reports already doctored by agents who partly know what we want to read. And our outputs are similarly doctored—the outputs must, forsooth, be harmonious. The "Blue Guitar," the creative filter between us and the world, is always and inevitably there. This it is to be both creature and creator. This the poet knows much better than the biologist.

# 26

## *Ecology of Mind: The Sacred**

In the last few days, people have asked me, "What do you mean, ecology of mind?" Approximately what I mean is the various kinds of stuff that goes on in one's head and in one's behavior and in dealing with other people, and walking up and down mountains, and getting sick, and getting well. All that stuff interlocks, and, in fact, constitutes a network which, in the local language, is called *mandala*. I'm more comfortable with the word "ecology," but they're very closely overlapping ideas. At the root, it is the notion that ideas are interdependent, interacting, that ideas live and die. The ideas that die do so because they don't fit with the others. You've got the sort of complicated, living, struggling, cooperating tangle like what you'll find on any mountainside with the trees, various plants and animals that live there—in fact, an ecology. Within that ecology, there are all sorts of main themes that one can dissect out and think about separately. There is always, of course, violence to the whole system if you think about the parts separately; but we're going to do that if we want to think at all, because it's too difficult to think about everything at once. So I thought I would try to unravel for you some of the ecology, something of the position and nature of the *sacred* in the ecological system.

It's very difficult, as you probably know, to talk about those living systems that are healthy and doing well; it's much easier to talk about living matters when they are sick, when they're disturbed, when things are going wrong. Pathology is a relatively easy thing to discuss, health is very difficult. This, of course, is one of the reasons why there is such a thing as the sacred, and why the sacred is difficult to talk about, because the

*This lecture was delivered at Naropa Institute, Boulder, Colorado, in the summer of 1974. Excerpt from *Loka: A Journal from Naropa Institute,* edited by Rick Fields. Copyright © 1975 by Nalanda Foundation/Naropa Institute. Reprinted by permission of Doubleday, a division of Bantam Doubleday Dell Publishing Group, Inc.

sacred is peculiarly related to the healthy. One does not like to disturb the sacred, for in general, to talk about something changes it, and perhaps will turn it into a pathology. So rather than talking about the healthy ecology of the sacred, let me try to get over to you what I am talking about with a couple of examples where the ecology seems to have gone off the tracks.

In the fifteenth century in Europe, many Catholics and Protestants were burning each other at the stake, or were willing to be burned at the stake, rather than compromise about questions of the nature of the bread and the wine used in the Mass. The traditional position, which at the time was the Roman Catholic, was that the bread is the body of Christ and the wine is the blood. What does that mean? The Protestants said, we know what that means—the bread *stands for* the body, and the wine *stands for* the blood. The proposition for which they were burning each other was, on one hand, "the bread *is* the body," and on the other, "the bread *stands for* the body." I do not want to suggest to you that one of these sides is perhaps better than the other, but I do intend that this whole argument is one of fundamental importance when related to the whole of the nature of the sacred and to human nature.

The point is this—that in the various layerings of your mind, or at least in the computer part of your mind (the part in your head), there are various layers of operation. There is ordinary "prose" consciousness—present indicative–type consciousness. That is what you perceive to be true in the sense that you perceive it, i.e., the cat *is* on the mat if you see the cat on the mat. That's the sort of normal waking state that most of us have. In that normal waking state, you are quite able to say that this thing that you perceive can also be a symbol—for example, a stop sign does not actually stop an automobile, but it is a symbol or message that tells people to stop the automobile. You can draw all sorts of distinctions in that normal everyday "prose" space in your mind.

On the other hand, in that part of your mind that dreams, you cannot draw these distinctions. The dream comes to you with no label which says that it's a symbol, a metaphor, a parable. It is an experience that you really have as you dream it; and except in those funny marginal half-asleep states, it's not even something labeled as a dream. That sort of a label is not something which that part of the mind can deal with, or accept.

So now if we go back to the proposition about the bread and wine, we find that to the left hemisphere of the brain, it is perfectly sensible to say that the bread "stands for" the body or is a symbol for the body. To the right hemisphere, the side that dreams, this means nothing at all. To the right hemisphere, the bread *is* the body, or it's irrelevant. In the right side of the brain, there are no "as if's," metaphors are not labeled "metaphors." They're not turned into similes. This is a good part of the problem with schizophrenic people, with whom I dealt for a long time. They are more Catholic than the Catholics, so to speak. They feel rather strongly that the metaphoric is the absolute. All right, so there was a religious war—a struggle—between these two sides in the fifteenth century, about the interrelationship of ideas.

Now, it is my suspicion that the richest use of the word "sacred" is that use which will say that what matters is the *combination* of the two, getting the two together. And that any fracturing of the two is, shall we say, anti-sacred. In which case, the Roman Catholics and the Protestants of the fifteenth century were equally anti-sacred in their battles. The bread both *is* and *stands for* the body.

Now, one of the very curious things about the sacred is that it usually does not make sense to the left-hemisphere, prose type of thinking. This then can be disastrously exploited in two different ways. It's a double exploitation problem. Because it doesn't make any prose sense, the material of dream and poetry has to be more or less secret from the prose part of the mind. It's this secrecy, this obscuration, that the Protestant thinks is wrong, and a psychoanalyst, I suppose, wouldn't approve of it either. But that secrecy, you see, is a protecting of parts of the whole process or mechanism, to see that the parts don't neutralize each other. But because there is this partial screen between the two parts—the prose, and the poetical or dream—because there is this barrier, it is possible to use one side to play with people's emotions, to influence them—for political purposes, for commercial purposes, and so on.

What are you going to do about the *use* of the sacred? There is a very strong tendency in occidental cultures, and increasingly in oriental cultures, to misuse the sacred. You see, you've got something nice, central to your civilization, which bonds together all sorts of values connected with love, hate, pain, joy, and the rest, a fantastic bridging synthesis, a way to make life make a certain sort of sense. And the next thing is that people use that sacred bridge in order to sell things. Now at the simplest level this is funny, but at another level, it begins to be a very serious sort of business. We can be influenced, it seems, by any confidence trickster, who by his appeals makes cheap that which should not be made cheap.

And there's this other strange business with the sacred, and that is that it's always a coin with two sides. The original Latin word "*sacer*," from which we get our word, means both "so holy and pure" as to be sacred, and "so unholy and impure" as to be sacred. It's as if there's a scale—on the extreme pure end we have sacredness, then it swings down in the middle to the secular, the normal, the everyday, and then at the other end we again find the word "*sacer*" applied to the most impure, the most horrible. So you get a notion of *magical power* implied at either end of the scale, while the middle is prose, the normal, the uninteresting, and the secular. Now there is the question of what happens in social processes, in human relations, in internal psychology, in getting it all together in one's mind. What happens when the pure end is violated by sacrilege? Of course at once you get various sorts of disaster, so that the pure end confers not only blessing, but also, when it is violated, becomes a curse. As all the Polynesian cultures know very well—every promise carries a curse on its tail. So in a sense the double-endedness of the sacred is logically expectable.

There's a whole lot which is not understood about this whole species of damage that goes with attack on the sacred. And still less is known about how to repair such damage. This is roughly what we were working on back in the 1950s and 1960s with schizophrenia—the notion of the relation between the right side, the more abstract, more unconscious parts of the mind, and the left side, the more prose parts of the mind. We found that the *relation* was the vulnerable spot. And that the relation, when damaged, required insight into the nature of the damage on the part of the therapist. So if the therapist is trying to take a patient, give him exercises, play various propagandas on him, try to make him come over to our world for the wrong reasons, to manipulate him— then there arises a problem, a temptation to confuse the idea of manipulation with the idea of a cure. Now, I can't tell you the right answers—in fact, I'm not sure I would if I could, because you see, to tell you the real answers, to know the real answers, is always to switch them over to that left brain, to the manipulative side. And once they're switched over, no matter how right they were poetically and aesthetically, they go dead, and become manipulative techniques.

This is, I think, really what all these disciplines of meditation are about. They're about the problem of how to get there without getting there by the manipulative path, because the manipulative path can never get there. So, in a way one can never know quite what one is doing.

Now this is a very Taoist sort of statement that I've been giving you all the way through. That is, while it may be fairly easy to recognize moments at which everything goes wrong, it is a great deal more difficult to recognize the magic of the moments that come right; and to contrive those moments is always more or less impossible. You can contrive a situation in which the moment *might* happen, or rig the situation so that it *cannot* happen. You can see to it that the telephone won't interrupt, or that human relations *won't* prosper—but to *make* human relations prosper is exceedingly difficult.

There are typological questions here, both in Jungian typology, and in Buddhist typology. There are people for whom a Taoist view of the world is more congenial, others for whom an action-oriented view of the world is more congenial. And perhaps the action-oriented people can do a little more toward contriving what is to happen to others. I don't know. I always find that if I try to contrive it, it always goes wrong.

There are things, you know, that give people like me the shivers. Some people will put potted plants on the radiator—and this is just bad biology. And I guess that, in the end, bad biology is bad Buddhism, bad Zen, and an assault on the sacred. What we are trying to do is to defend the sacred from being put on the radiator, misused in this sort of way. I think this can be done without violence. For example, I remember as a small boy of eight or nine in England the first occasion I had to tie a bow tie. For some reason I couldn't get any help, and so I tied a bow, and it stood up vertically. I don't know how many of you have ever tried to *tie* a bow tie. I tried again, and it stood up on end. I then did a piece of thinking which I still think of as one of the great intellectual feats of my life. I decided to put this little twist in it in the first bow, so it would not stand up vertical, but would stand up horizontal—and I did it, and it did! I've never quite been able to think it through since, but I can still produce the little monstrosity when I have to wear one! Now, what have I learned? I learned how to tie a bow tie, yes, but I also learned that it is possible to think through such problems as how to tie a tie, make a pretzel, and other such things. Also, I learned that, having discovered how to do it, I can now do it without all the rigmarole in my head—I've got a trick for doing it. But spiritually, aesthetically, it will never be the same again as that first time, when my whole mind and soul was in the business of thinking how to do it. There was a moment of integration when I achieved it.

All these different sorts of learning, these multiple mandalas, are what we are talking about. It's a matter of how to keep those different levels, rings, whatever, *not* separate, because they can never be separate, and *not* confused, because if they get confused, then you begin to take the metaphoric as absolute, as the schizophrenic does. For example, say I'm learning something less solitary than how to tie a bow tie, say I'm learning to act as a host or a guest, in an interpersonal relationship. Now, the host-guest relationship is more or less sacred all over the world. And, of course, one of the reasons why, to go back to where we started, is that bread and wine *are* sacred objects. Now bread and wine are sacred, not because they represent the body and blood of Christ, but because they are the staff of life, the staff of hospitality, so we *secondarily* relate them with Christ, with sacrifice, and the rest of it. The sacredness is real, whatever the mythology. The mythology is only the poetical way of asserting the sacredness, and a very good way, maybe, but bread is sacred, whether or not you accept the Christian myth. And so is wine. These levels, these modes of learning, and their going along together, are the keys to certain sorts of mental health, and joy.

And before I close, I should say a word about being a scientist. You see, I've been talking to you, not as a priest, or a member of the congregation, but as an anthropologist. And we anthropologists have our values rather differently constructed from those of nonscientists. If you're seriously dedicated to anything, be it art, science, or whatever, that which you are dedicated to is going to be a pretty big component in what is sacred to you. But we scientists are, or should be, pretty humble about what we know. We don't think we really know any of the answers. And this has some very curious effects. On the whole, most people feel that a great deal is known, and what is not immediately knowable they throw into the supernatural, into guesswork, or into folklore. But the scientist won't allow himself to do that. We really believe that someday we shall know what these things are all about, and that they *can* be known. This is our sacred. We are all sort of Don Quixote characters who are willing to believe that it is worthwhile to go out and tilt at the windmills of the nature of beauty, and the nature of the sacred, and all the rest of it. We are arrogant about what we might know tomorrow, but humble because we know so little *today*.

# 27

## *Intelligence, Experience, and Evolution*\*

What I want to say, quite simply, is that what goes on inside is much the same as what goes on outside. And I say this not from anything like a Buddhist position, but just from the position of an ordinary working stiff engaged in occidental sciences.

Norbert Wiener, the inventor of the word cybernetics and many other things, had a habit, when he was puzzled about some theoretical problem, of sitting in front of a curtain on which the wind was blowing, so that there were movements in the curtain which would fill his eye, so to speak. This would keep his brain in a similar sort of movement, and on top of that movement he liked to do his thinking. His feeling was that if the brain was in itself still, the mere addition of problems and data and so forth to it wasn't much use. What was useful was to pour data, ideas, problems, etc., onto a brain which was already, in some sense, in motion. And I would like to make this a sort of central keynote for the things I want to say, both about what's in here and what's out there.

Job had a rather similar problem. But he got stuck; that's what went wrong with Job. William Blake looked at the Job story and did a definitive series of illustrations for what happened. In the first illustration you see Job and his family sitting under a tree, and all the musical instruments are hanging on the tree; and they all look all right, except they are reading books, and in front of them are all the sheep—because he was a great owner of sheep, a wealthy man. And there is a dog looking after the sheep, except that the sheep are all asleep, and the dog is asleep with his head on the sheep. All the musical instruments, as I say, are hung up in the tree, and everybody is being *very virtuous.*

\*This essay is adapted from a lecture delivered March 24, 1975, at Naropa Institute, Boulder, Colorado. Copyright © 1976 by Naropa Institute. All rights reserved. Appearing originally in *Re-Vision* 1, no. 2 (1978), this article has, with the permission of *Re-Vision Journal,* been readapted from the tape recording of the original lecture.

Satan, you remember, then goes to God, and God says, "Look at my servant, Job." (God, in the illustrations, looks exactly like Job and is in fact his self-portrait, so to speak, his mirror image.) And God says, "What a virtuous man Job is." And Satan says, "Ha! Let me get at him." And Satan performs a very useful function (which I gather that gurus and teachers perform in Buddhism) of just giving hell to the person who thinks he knows the answers. And Satan kills all the crops, and he kills all the children, and he destroys all the property. Yet Job continues to be proud of his piety.

And later, Satan, after going up and down on the face of the earth and walking to and fro in it, again sees God, and God says, "Well how is it?" And Satan says, "Let me touch *him*, his skin." And he throws sore boils on Job.

And then there are about twenty-five chapters of very tedious discussion of the nature of suffering, and why it exists in the universe, and whether it is connected with sin or not, and so on and so on, until finally the solution to the problem of piety is provided: "Then the Lord answered Job out of the whirlwind, and said, Who is this that darkeneth counsel by words without knowledge? Gird up now thy loins like a man; for I will demand of thee, and answer thou me. Where wast thou when I laid the foundations of the earth? Declare, if thou hast understanding." And so on. This goes on for three chapters and is, fundamentally, a lesson in natural history: "Knowest thou the time when the wild goats of the rock bring forth? Or canst thou mark when the hinds do calve? Canst thou number the months that they fulfill? Or knowest thou the time when they bring forth?" And so on.

Now, the question is: Why is a lesson in natural history—ranging through meteorology, astronomy and the Pleiades, the nature of the ocean and why it stops at the place it does, the various animals, etc.— somehow a remedy for a certain sort of piety from which Job suffered? That is, what is it in what's out there which is somehow a reflection of what's in here, such that if you get stuck on what's in here, you can in some degree correct it by dedicating yourself to looking at what's out there—among the animals and the plants and the stars and the weather? You see, there are other remedies besides meditating, and one of them is to look at the living world—a thing which very few people do. And when they do do it, they have very few words to say why they did it. There are a lot of people who find that a walk in the woods is somehow good for their livers or their spiritual livers—and don't quite know why, I suppose.

And that's the problem I want to suggest to you is worth thinking about, and to suggest to you that thinking about it is related to thinking about why Norbert Wiener was able to think better about theoretical problems when looking at curtains which were being blown in the wind.

## Worlds of Interaction

Roughly, it looks as though we live in three interlocking, interwoven worlds. One of those isn't of very much use to us but needs to be defined for purposes of being clear. It is the world which the Gnostics and Jung called the *Pleroma,* which we might think of approximately as the world of billiard-ball physics. This is a world in which things are not alive. They're billiard balls, they're stones, they're astronomical objects, and so forth, and they respond to forces and energy exercised upon them. One billiard ball hits another, and the second one responds with energy derived from the first. Or they live in fields of "force" and move subject to gravity and such things. That's why it's a world. And if you want to know what happens, you examine the quantity of how hard a ball is pushed or hit, and its response is a simple function of how hard it was hit or pulled or pushed.

But the world of living things is different. Living things respond to the *fact* of being hit. There are facts as distinct from forces. There are ideas. And these facts are essentially nonphysical. What you respond to, what you can see, is difference. You can see that this is different from that. We say the difference is that one is black and the other is white. We might ask where the difference lies. It obviously does not lie in the white. It does not lie in the black. It does not lie in the space between them. It possibly lies in the time between them, because really the way you see this is by rubbing the whole thing with your retina and detecting a bump, a difference—the difference becoming a bump, and a bump being an event in time. By converting differences which may be static into a bump in time, you know there's a difference. Or you do this by their being already moving out there, which is what a frog sees, or a lizard sees. The little lizards in Hawaii sit on the mosquito screens at night, and when the moth comes, whoop!, the lizard focuses on the moth which has landed there. He now stands still. He can't see the moth anymore because the moth is not moving; he can only receive information about movement. He can't do what you and I would do— move his eye to scan (your eye is vibrating all the time, you know)—because he doesn't have the corrective mechanisms to discount the movement of his eye and know that the thing he sees isn't moving when it appears to be moving. So he's got to stay still and wait. Then the moth makes one more move and, whack!, he gets him.

This is the other side of the same story from which we started. Just as Norbert Wiener liked to have his mind stirred by a curtain in order that he could think about something, so the lizard and the moth are in an impossible static freeze until the system starts to move. It's the same business. And this general statement is true for the two other worlds that I want to talk about.

Let's put aside for the moment the first world, the world of physical forces, and deal with the other two worlds: one, the world of thought and learning, and the other, the world of evolution. And the first thing to say about these two is that they are very much alike. They are so alike that people keep wanting to play the one on the other. Even before Darwin, Paley was defending the world from the theory of evolution by saying: Look at your watch. If you look at your watch you will see at once that it was made to tell the time. It has some sort of "purpose" built into its nature, into its structure. And you know how that happened. A watchmaker, being a thinking creature, built the purpose into it. So now look at the dragonflies, coconut palms, and what have you, around in nature. Observe that they, too, have purpose. And if watchmakers made watches to have purpose, and if pigs and coconut palms have purpose built into them, then there must be an external supernatural that built purpose into the pigs and coconut palms. This was the argument. And notice that this argument is an argument from one world of mental activity—the human thing "up here" (well, more than just up here, because it's in here, too, and it's out there where I can see you, and so on). The outside things, the horses and the goats and the hinds on the hillside, are, as I say, in their relations very much a reflection of the way this thing up here works.

For example, Scott's expedition to the Antarctic was set up like a watch with a whole set of purposes, and a whole set of technology to meet the purposes. Scott had some rather fancy notions, that it was wrong to use dogs to pull sleds and that you shouldn't eat the dogs after they'd pulled the sleds. So he used ponies instead, which worked very poorly, because they were not really fitted for Antarctic life. A series of things went wrong. Not *one* thing, you see. It wasn't just that the ponies didn't do it quite right. It was a hundred small things—till the expedition got behind schedule; the weather went on, on schedule; winter tightened up; winds increased; they got further off schedule. They did actually reach the Pole, found Amundsen's mark there, realized they'd lost the race, and this wasn't good for their morale. And not only did they now of course not have any ponies, they were pulling their sleds by manpower. One of them broke a leg—Oates—and walked out into the snow because he decided he was a nuisance. Heroic—but didn't save the other men's lives. They all froze.

Now, they didn't freeze because of *one* thing; they froze because of a whole massive adaptation, on probably twenty different fronts, that went wrong. This is important.

We tend, in our technology, to limit as closely as we can the adaptation of our machines to the world and of ourselves to the machines; and we sort of focus in like mongooses on single-purpose activity and think, quite wrongly, that that is what it is to be alive—to be able to pursue a single identified purpose. Oh no. What it is to be alive is to be able to handle highly multiple purposes and to be able to handle them by virtue of highly complex movement in the receiving end, in the head maybe, or wherever it is. In order to solve complex problems of mathematics or engineering, Wiener fed himself with waves on a curtain, or movement in water, or various things—to keep his brain unspecified, unspecialized, into which new information could come and evoke previously unknown answers.

Now this whole business outside—the evolutionary business—is a business of trial and error, just like any other part of life, really. And in that trial and error you've got not just horses, pigs, goats, hinds, insects, beetles, trees, etc., but the interrelations between those outside things as well.

## Evolution: The Interlocking of Species

For example, we know quite a lot in biology now about the "evolution of the horse." And the American Museum of Natural History has hundreds of fossil horse skeletons to show the path by which evolution went from Eohippus, a five-fingered, five-toed, presumably soft-footed creature about as big as a medium-sized dog, up to the present horse with one toe on each foot, four toes gone, one left, with a great big toe nail on the end which is the hoof. The teeth very highly changed, with a gap in the middle so you can put your pen into a horse's mouth and he can't bite you in the middle. He's got the cutting teeth in front and grinding teeth behind and nothing in the middle, and an elongated face—like a horse. So, we know quite a bit about what he looks like, and the steps by which he got there, judging from the skeletons of all the horses.

Now the truth of the matter is that this is not, you know, the story of the evolution of the horse; and the horse isn't the thing that evolved.

What evolved actually was a *relationship* between horse and grass. This is ecology. If you want a lawn, which is the equivalent in the suburbs of a grassy plain, there are certain steps you have to take. First of all you go and buy a lawn mower. This is the equivalent of those front teeth of the horse. And you have to have this in order to prevent the grass from going to seed. If the grass goes to seed, it dies. It's done its thing, it thinks, and it dies. So you keep it from going to seed with a mower. Secondly, if you want to make a tight turf, you have to squash it down, so you buy a roller—at best one of those rollers with sort of fists on it all over that'll knock it down. This is a substitute for horses' hoofs. And finally, if you really want to have a good lawn, you go and buy a sack of manure and substitute for the back end of the horse. So that one way or another you are in fact pretending to be a horse in order to deceive the grass into doing ecologically what it would do if it had hoofed animals living on it.

Thus the unit of what's called evolution out there, is really not this species or that species. It is an entire interlocking business of species. And curiously enough the whole progress, so-called, of evolution is stimulated by the need to stay put. The grass changes and the horse changes, and the grass changes and the horse changes, and they change in such a way that the relationship between them may stay constant. And evolution essentially is a vast operation of interlocking changes, every particular change being an effort to make change unnecessary, to keep something constant. One of the big mistakes made in mid–nineteenth-century biology was the notion that natural selection is a force for change. It's not. Natural selection is a force for staying put, for going on with the same dance that you were in before, not for inventing *new* dances. Not for staying *still*, you know; nobody can do that. If you want to stay still, you get caught like Job, as you may say with your pants down, and everything goes wrong. What you've got to do is to change in such a way that the system of changing has a certain steadiness, a certain balance, equilibrium . . . maybe a very complicated one. There is no reason why a dance should be limited. It can be enormously complex.

And that's the dance outside.

The dance inside is very much the same. The dance inside has another characteristic which is interesting. First of all, it's not a dance of pigs and coconut palms. You don't have any pigs and coconut palms inside your heads. Or machines or money or whatever it is you are interested in. All those are not in your heads. There are only ideas of those things in your heads. And ideas, as we already noted, are fundamentally of the nature of difference and are mythical. They are not located in space or time. Immanuel Kant got that one straight. Ideas are not like sticks and stones. They have a curious relationship to each other. You can have ideas about ideas. You cannot have stones about stones. In fact the word "about" has no meaning at all in the physical universe. "About" is a word which only can mean something in the world of ideas. It's a relationship that doesn't exist in the *Pleroma*, in the physical universe. And because you have ideas about ideas in your head, you can get into an awful mess. I think this is one of the reasons why people meditate, is somehow to let settle or let unravel the incredible tangles which arise out of the fact that you can have ideas about ideas.

You see, it's all nonsense. There are no pigs and coconut palms "in here." The only pigs and coconut palms that you have any contact with are ideas in your head about pigs and coconut palms. You "invent" the pigs and coconut palms. Well, this isn't quite true. The problem really, you see, is if you can detect difference, then you can, of course, see or receive news of outlines. And really, conceptually and philosophically speaking, you live in a world of outline drawings, and you create the corporeal world, as Blake called it, to fill in between the outlines. You can detect difference. I see that here's a man with blue pants. No, no, wait a minute; I don't see a man with blue pants. You see, I invented the fact he is a man. But he will support me in that. I see his blue against the red-orange of the mat under him. I see he's got a striped shirt. And I *think* the pants are blue all over. I'm not really very good at seeing the blue in the middle of the area that's covered by pants. I see the outline, the information of blue. If there were a break in the blue, that would make another outline. So I feel pretty safe really in saying that the blue pants are blue all over. But I'm not very good at seeing that. You see, I've got the same problem, really, that the lizard had on the screens at night trying to get the moth. Where he could only see movement, I'm almost totally restricted to seeing outline. It is similar with hearing, although with hearing I do a little better. But a steady tone will taper off, and in about half a minute I won't hear it unless it's pretty loud, or unless there are some sort of changes in me which enable me to hear it. One, as they say, accommodates. All right. So with all this, we receive news of differences, we build up partly by filling in the outlines, partly by differences between differences, and we build up this great complex of thinking about an organized universe out there with the aid of a rather similar thing in here, inside.

The business of thinking, the business of learning, becomes very much like the business of evolution when you realize that it is all the time partly experimental—feeling, grasping, exploring (exploring is perhaps the word). It's called trial and error (it should be called success and error, shouldn't it?) among which you then find your way. What is difficult is for you to stand where I am, and for me to stand where you are, and to look at Gregory Bateson here, Gregory Bateson vis-à-vis a lot of organisms out there listening, feeling their way by trial and error in the things that I'm saying, while I'm feeling my way by trial and error in the saying of those things. Looking at it from this crow's-eye perspective, I can now see a dance, so to speak, of ideas progressing, feeling their way, weaving, involving both you people and me in a sort of ongoing process comparable, if you like, with the problem of the horse and the grass, in which both horse and grass are evolving along together to make a constancy, to make a sort of a balance, a sort of a steady state (the technical term) in which we can operate.

Now, with that much picture available in your minds at the moment, I want to look at another aspect. If I have a surface of water in a basin, and I apply a tuning fork or vibrator of some kind to the basin, I will get a set of what are called "stationary waves" on the surface of that water. These appear to be stationary, but their stationariness, of course, is partly a fiction because every wave only has its existence because of forces (I use the word physically) between it and the next wave, etc., etc. The whole thing is a dynamic structure, not a static structure. Now let me put into that surface an external object, let me poke it with a pin or a rod. Now that whole phantom on that surface is going to be changed by the presence of that rod invading it. Say that around backwards and you've got the statement that all over the pattern of that surface is information about the invading rod. There is a change everywhere in that surface which could conceivably be used as information about the invader. It appears on the whole—this is what the neurophysiologists are now getting—that the way information is stored in the brain is very much like that. It's not like a photographic negative with everything spot for spot in the negative corresponding to spot for spot out in the world. The information on what is called the hologram is spread, and it is spread in that wave surface.

Now I want you to think back to Scott and his Antarctic expedition where adaptation is not particular adaptation: adaptation is the adaptation of *all* the relations between *all* his characteristics and *all* the other characteristics. And when it starts to go wrong, it goes wrong here, it goes wrong there, it goes wrong there. And when the pathologies meet, so to speak, you've got real trouble and people get killed. Now if that is the way it works, then we've got to be awfully careful about how we play at being mongooses, saying, "*This* is important, *that* is important," breaking things down into particulars. And really what's been happening in science is an enormous buildup of a philosophy which is throwing away the outlines and retaining the relationships, so that if A has an effect on B, the words "has an effect on" are represented as something between them, and the things themselves we don't think about anymore. We think only about what happens *between* them, and about the relations between the relations.

## World as Dilemma

This, you know, leads us into a world which begins to be quite odd. We ask why did the dinosaurs become extinct? It's a lousy question. Now the probable reason why the dinosaurs became extinct, if you want to spell this out, is worked out in *Through the Looking-Glass*. Alice is shown the insects of Through-the-Looking-Glass-Land, and there is the Bread-and-butter-fly. We on this side have butterflies; they have Bread-and-butter-flies. The Bread-and-butter-fly has wings made of thin slices of bread and butter. It's an English Bread-and-butter-fly, you see. And its head is made of a lump of sugar. And Alice says, "What does it live on?" And the Gnat who is acting as guide says, "Weak tea with cream in it." At this point Alice saw a difficulty in the Darwinian adaptation of this animal. You see, Lewis Carroll never loved Darwinian evolution, I'm sure. So Alice says (because Alice is always optimistic—she wants the animals to live), "Supposing it couldn't find any?" (Because obviously if it did find any, its head would dissolve in its food.) The Gnat says, "Then it would die, of course." Alice says, "But that must happen very often." The Gnat says, "It always happens."

Now, all right, let us say we are now paleontologists and we are studying fossil Bread-and-butter-flies and we wonder why they became extinct. The answer is not that they became extinct because their heads were made of sugar. The answer is not that they became extinct because they couldn't find their food. The answer is that they became extinct because they were caught in a dilemma; and the world is made that way, and is not made the linear single-purpose way. And so on, ad infinitum.

This is a funny business, because the whole of language, as we are accustomed to using it, assumes that you can talk about "this," and the uses of "this," and the single purposes, and given the effect of "this," and so forth and so forth. And right at the center of saying things of that kind is our use of the first-person pronoun, "I." If the Bread-and-butter-fly used the word "I," what would it mean? It would mean a walking dilemma, due to my sugar on my head and my stupid habit of drinking tea with cream in it. When you use the word "I," what really do you mean in terms of a language which would be acceptable, not so much to Buddhism, but just to ordinary natural science? What is this entity, "I," "you," "me"? Well, we mean one end of an interaction, yes? One end of a lot of interactions. "I," at the moment, "am." If you make a diagram of the room, I'm that which you can't see inside of, and this differentiates me. In a sense, my existence is demonstrated by my opacity.

If you could see what is happening in all my nerve fibers and all my inputs and all my outputs, then it wouldn't be very sensible to draw a line around me and say he is limited there. There is a mass of pathways for messages and information to travel on in this room. If you want to make a diagram of the room, that's what it would look like. And here's a chip of it: this piece is Gregory Bateson. And the pathways cross something which is my skin maybe, but the skin is not itself a pathway. They go through the skin. The skin is a pickup affair. It's not the blind man's stick. It's the end of the blind man's stick, not the stick. The stick is the pathway it goes along. Where does the blind man begin? Can we cut him off halfway up the stick? But you're cutting the line of communication when you cut there. The rule for any sort of systems theory is to draw around the lines of communication, so far as you can. Of course, there aren't any isolated systems, really.

So that we arrive, as we push this, at a world which is very unlike the world represented by ordinary language, at a world which is essentially double in its structure. There is something called learning, at a rather small level of organization. (I don't say simple, but small.) There is something called evolution, at a much larger gestalt level. There is a funny sort of imperfect coupling between these two levels. We are mainly at the small learning level, but still creatures of the much larger level. This is a curious sort of paradoxical world to live in, in which we do our best. It's sometimes, you know, a joke—because jokes essentially are between two gestalt levels, two levels of configuration, and when they twist on each other we laugh, or cry, or make art or religion, or go schizophrenic. Now what are we going to do? There isn't, of course, a question of doing, really.

There are sorts of movement, I suppose, and one of the most interesting sorts is that movement which you achieve through the discovery that you are torn between these two levels of worlds. This is grotesquely confusing, grotesquely unfair. (I think the sensation is of unfairness.) And out of that unfairness comes, I believe, some sort of a wisdom on the other side. This is the thing that R. D. Laing has been saying. I've said it from time to time. And various sorts of people in various religions have said it. That through that double, twisted . . . what we called a double bind some years ago, there is (if you can keep the things confronting each other somehow, without backing out or getting caught by the state mental hospital system) another stage of wisdom (I don't know about a final one—that would be another question) on the other side. I can't talk about that because I don't know about it. But I think that there is now beginning to be, in fairly hard-science terms, a base for beginning to think about some of those problems.

And that's about what I wanted to try and say to you.

# 28

## *Orders of Change**

Anybody who tries to talk about change is in trouble from the word go. So, before we begin, I'm going to complain a little about the nature of that trouble.

The monstrous thing about language is that it contains words like "it." The difficulty with change is that you never know what *it* is. You remember Alice going through the woods and finding a mushroom, I suppose an amanita. On top of the mushroom is a caterpillar, who is sort of a prototype of all psychiatrists. The caterpillar, when he finally notices Alice (like a good guru, he pretends not to notice), turns to her and says, "Who are you?" Alice says, "I don't know because you see I've been changing so much." The caterpillar says, "Explain yourself." And Alice says, "I cannot explain myself." That is *it* for Alice, but the *that* which has been changing is not something that you can point to. Is Alice, at the moment when she's talking to the caterpillar, the same Alice with a difference, or is she a totally different Alice? Now that difficulty of being unable to identify the *it* runs through all discussions of change.

Alternatively, if you avoid talking about some substantive, some *it* which undergoes the change, and use the word *it* to describe the change, to refer to the change itself, "it's" what I am studying, then you have condensed into that single word a whole mass of sentences, and everything is as ambiguous as before. So it occurred to me that one should take a good look at a word like "stable." Surely one should be able to use the word "stable" without getting into these troubles.

I wanted a way of dissecting the word "stable" with regard to what I was trying to describe, and suddenly I saw that what I was engaged in

*This lecture was delivered August 10, 1975, at Naropa Institute, Boulder, Colorado. Excerpt from *Loka II: A Journal from Naropa Institute,* edited by Rick Fields. Copyright © 1976 by Nalanda Foundation/Naropa Institute. Used by permission of Doubleday, a division of Bantam, Doubleday, Dell Publishing Group, Inc.

was a false natural history of my own procedure. The truth of the matter is that the word "stable" is not applicable to any part of the cat, or the chair. It is applicable only to propositions in my description. *The cat is black* is a proposition which is stable. I discovered that I wasn't talking about *the cat,* but that I was talking about my *description* of the cat, and that that was all I ever had to talk about anyway. You know, inside my head I have no direct experience of a cat. I only have the reports from my eyes, my fingers, my ears, my sense of smell, and with all that I can build up quite a good picture of a cat, but all I've got is a picture of a cat. Maybe it's endowed with smell, feel, weight, movement, sound, but it's still only a picture of a cat, so when I say something is stable, the word *stability* refers to a component in that picture, that description of the cat. This realization was such a relief. But carried along with that, there is a problem: that a description of a complicated animal or a person or a human relationship or a ritual in New Guinea or whatever, contains items of very different degrees of particularity, of concreteness. For instance, I say a cat has claws. If I begin distributing the claws among the toes, this begins to get complicated. A one-toed cat would still have a claw on each toe; a five-toed cat has five claws. I obviously don't have to enumerate the number of toes in order to say it has claws. The statement about the claws is independent of the number of toes and vice versa. Yet in the organization of the cat, those things must somehow be connected. All these connections inside a description are difficult to deal with, and they have to be unraveled if you talk about stability or if you talk about change.

So you see, it's an awful mess. When you have this sort of a mess, which obviously is an artifact to some degree of your use of language, what are you going to do? You cannot throw away language, which happens to be the most beautiful and elegant tool that we are provided with. So, let's see what you can do to make some *order* out of language without trusting all the habits that you had before. Throw them away. Just be naked in front of a lot of descriptive chips and bits of information. Are you going to find enough order not to have to handle all the little bits separately?

Let's look at change. By change I mean a ceasing to be true of some little chip or big chunk of descriptive material. When I look at something, the lens in my eye throws an image on my retina. That's a real image, just as real or unreal, as samsaric or unsamsaric, as the image in a photographic camera. If I move my eye, this rather static image is translated into events in time, into changes. I can only pick up change, news of static differences which I, one way or another, have converted into changes, states one to states two.

I started to study change on the assumption that there was something called "not change," and I arrived in a world in which the only thing that is ever reported to me is change, which either goes on independent of me or is created by my movement—change in relationship to me. Either it moves or I move. Whichever way, the relationship has got to change and this is all that I can get data on. So the static physical world is at best a guess.

How are we going to start classifying changes to introduce order? One of the best classifications, I think, is in terms of reversibility. If I go out in the sun, I'll go brown, and if I stay indoors at my desk I go pale again. When I go out again, I'll go brown. Now it takes a little while, obviously. It may take some days before I reach a new equilibrium. The amount of my brownness shall probably be a fairly simple mathematical function of the amount of sunshine. Now that goes both ways. Reduce the sun, the brownness is reduced; increase the sun, the brownness is increased. So I can make statements about the changes in brownness, and now I can also make another statement lying behind that about the relationship of brownness to sun.

In addition, I can ask a more abstract question. If I'm interested in, say, evolution or learning, one of the things I will ask is the old, old question: can I pass on the brownness to my offspring? You'll notice that that question is already bankrupt as a result of what we've been saying. That question should be phrased, "Can I throw away the self-correctiveness and fix the brownness on one end of the scale?" The Lamarckian theory always assumes that you're going to throw away your flexibility in favor of rigidity in the next generation. But it's not whether I'm passing on the brownness, it's whether I'm passing on the fixedness of the brownness—a fixedness which I never had and therefore wasn't in a position to pass on.

In order to maintain that freedom of whether to turn brown, or of whether to increase my blood pressure when I get excited, whether to remind myself that I need food when I get hungry, my entire self-corrective mechanisms need all sorts of much deeper background stuff. If you really think about this, you'll find that you've now got another layer of ways to classify change. First we said that change is either reversible, part of a self-corrective circuitry, like tanning, or it's not self-corrective—if I cut off my little finger, it doesn't grow again. The question is: Is the change reversible and self-corrective, and is it fast or slow? If I don't have the power to go brown in the sun, the power to change my blood pressure to fit my excitement, the power to know when to put more food in me to replace low blood sugar, the power to warm myself when my body temperature falls and cool it when it rises, I'm in for trouble.

The deeper things in us get disturbed to the point, possibly, of death. A major descriptive proposition—*Gregory is alive*—may be disturbed in its truth by an inability to control my temperature when I get a bit of malaria. So that the top balancing changes are in fact the safeguard for much deeper things which preferably should not change. I mean, I prefer to be alive.

We now have deep changes, or deep propositions, whose change when it occurs becomes very serious. It's like an acrobat. He's walking on a high wire, and he's got a balancing stick. Now whenever he feels himself fall over that way, he tilts his balancing stick, pushing this side down, raising this side, and thereby gets a little bit of torsion in his own body to balance himself, to not go over that side. If he overdoes it, he'll have to do the reverse to not go over that side. He may wobble, he may oscillate like any other self-corrective system with a governor. What he's essentially doing is using the changeability of his relationship to the balancing pole to preserve a basic proposition: *I am on the high wire*. When you're riding a bicycle, you've got the same thing, or you steer with the front wheel in order to maintain your approximate verticality. If the front wheel is clamped, you will fall off.

Now what I've done is to begin to place us in a rather strange world which doesn't contain anything except news, reports of difference, reports of change, preferences for change, preferences for stability, etc. There is really no high wire, no balancing pole, only states of a balancing pole, states of you on a high wire. From the moment I saw that the word "stable" refers only to states, not to the cat, not to me, and not to the object—from the moment when I discovered that "it" was an error, I was living in a world of ideas, very important ideas and elegant ideas. To live in a world of ideas is to be alive. I don't really think a water jug lives in a world of ideas; it doesn't have the necessary circuits. It doesn't have experience, it doesn't have information.

So here we are floating in a world which consists of nothing but change, even though we talk as if there was a static element in the world, as though it was possible to say this shirt is green, that one striped or blue. But all I can really say, as I explore the world in front of me by rubbing my retina against it, is that all I get is reports on where things feel different. And so we live. And within that we say that things are beautiful, things are ugly, we have pain, some food tastes better than others, we're tired, we're bored, we get angry—all sorts of shenanigans. And I think probably the next thing to suggest to you is that that world of news can in a very curious way either destroy or enrich you.

The difference between *this* and *that* is not, of course, in this, it's not in that, it's not in the space between them. I can't pinch it. Where is it?

We can say the jug is on the table. Now that is to say that there is an aggregate, a tangle of differences which I call a jug: this is narrow, that's fatter, that's open, that's closed and that's brown and this is yellow. But the tangle seems to be here and the table there, and I cannot locate any of the details of this tangle where the carriers of those details live, so to speak. You only deal with the relationship between the thing and some other thing, or between the thing and you, or part of you, never the thing itself. You live in a world that's only made of relationships. When you say that the table is hard, all you're saying is that in a conflict, in a confrontation between the table and your hand, your hand had to stop moving at a certain point. The table won. If the table had been soft, your hand would have won. You're talking about something between the two things.

If you didn't have all the disadvantages of being human, especially the disadvantage of language, you would not communicate except in terms of relationship. There is no reason to believe, as far as I know, that any characteristic like hardness is attributed to something by prelinguistic mammals. It's pretty obvious that porpoises with their sonar can tell the difference between one sort of ping and another sort of ping, and I think they probably refer the ping to the object that they're sending out their sonar beam against. It takes a beam and an object to make a ping, and the ping is really only a statement of relationship. As far as I know, all prelinguistic animals only know about relationships. That is, when they talk, the cat's meow when you come home from work is not "I'm hungry." It is "Mama." It's a statement of the relationship between cats and you. The sound which the cat makes is in general a filial sound—the sound of a child to a parent. It identifies the relationship between you and the cat, and upon the identification of that relationship, you are supposed to go to the icebox and get out whatever you generally get for your child, the cat. And this goes for almost all of animal communication. It's noises or gestures or bodily movement which suggests a certain sort of relationship, and upon that suggestion of the relationship, the other organism is supposed to act.

Now you are not so very far from the cats and dogs. You are near enough to them so you care more about your relationships than about any other single thing in the world. You may have put various sorts of shields and protection on them. We all do. But still under all that protection that's where you live, that's where love and hate and self-respect and pride and shame and a thousand things of that nature all are—in what is between you and other people, and your clues to all this all the time are the sort of thing I'm talking about.

So I'm interviewing a thirty-five-year-old mother of a "problem" child, a little boy of five. I should say that I'm on one end of the couch, average length, and the mother is sitting on the other end, and the little five-year-old is on the floor. Across the room twenty feet away is a young man with a movie camera recording it all. (It's wonderful what people will do to each other.) The mother starts to say, "Mr. Bateson, you know, bedtime in this household, in this house, it's awful. It's hell. We say to him fifty times 'go to bed, stay there,' but he always gets up, he won't stay, and then he goes, he gets this little puppet. He calls it Tucky." Tucky is a little finger puppet, you know, little dog-shaped finger puppet. "Can't think why he calls it Tucky. I've looked in all the children's books, there's nothing, no little dogs called Tucky." I say, "Yes, he gets the puppet." "Yes," she says, "he gets that puppet and then he comes and he says, 'Mummy, Mummy, Tucky wants to kiss you.' Gee! He knows all the tricks for getting through, doesn't he?"

Now what is the sequence? The sigh in the mother's voice between the quote "Tucky wants to kiss you," and "Gee, he knows all the tricks for getting through"—in the middle of that pause there is a sigh which is clearly audible on the tape, a deep, almost heartbroken sigh. That is, Mama knew that "Tucky wants to kiss you" is a heartbreak statement, and that already the child is substituting Tucky for self because it's safer. But in substituting Tucky for self, the child has made a comment on this thing between himself and Mama, and he is now to be put in the wrong about this thing between himself and Mama with the statement, "Gee, he knows all the tricks for getting through." It's near enough to being a true statement, so she can make it and not see exactly what she's doing, but at the same time, what at one level was a statement of tragedy becomes at the next level a statement of wicked manipulation, worldly tricks. "He knows all the tricks for getting through." And, you see, he mustn't hear that sigh. Or he mustn't signal that he heard it. So, what we have is a buildup. You can build up this tangle to a point of no exit, and this is what, on the whole, my patients always do. When I say they build it up, of course, this is only one-half of the truth; the other half of the truth is that their parents, the authorities around them, their siblings, and I too, help them do it.

Now we get to the next question of change: When you build up by a succession of changes which are in the end all changes about propositions about where you are, and which are mostly unconscious ones, what are the moments by which such tangles get dissolved? I can give you one example: I'm filming a six-year-old boy in his own home, with Mama and a stuffed animal. He's on a couch, the stuffed animal is on the coffee table in front of the couch, the camera is over on the other side of the coffee table. Mama goes and sits with him on the couch; he picks up

the stuffed animal, and the battle starts between him and Mama. He hits
Mommy over the head with the stuffed animal. Now she freezes because
she is in front of the camera too, so she gets out from in front of it as
quickly as possible. I go over and sit on the couch, and ask young Mark
what the name of the stuffed animal is. Mark says, "He does not have a
name, nobody has a name." You know, one of the terrible things about
psychosis is that the psychotic is accurate on the nature of the self, the
nature of names, the nature of all the things that I started talking to you
about at the beginning of this talk. I say, "I thought there was a little boy
here named Mark." Mark says, "Stop talking. Shut your mouth." And I
say, "I can't talk with my mouth shut." Mark says, "Don't be funny." He
then picks up the stuffed animal and hits me over the head with it. Now
we have a battle with a stuffed animal which I quite enjoy, and at the
end of the battle he looks at the stuffed animal and the silk scarf around
its neck has come undone. "It's come undone." Tears. And I say, "Don't
you know how to tie it?" "I can't tie it." "I'll show you. You put this piece
of the silk across that piece, like that. You do that. Right, now give it to
me. Now you put this one under. You do that." And in about three minutes he has made a bow around the animal's neck, and he then says,
"And his name is Bimbo."

Let me conclude by coming back to the change which I referred to
earlier when I said that the first piece that came loose was the word "stable." When the word "stable" came loose, this was a great opening up
for me of a whole realm of thinking and re-examination of other aspects
and ways of weaving life together. I think these moments are the things
they call satori, mindless satori of one kind or another, the moment of
resolution of a koan, that sort of thing. And I think that the place to put
these moments, as a sort of final level to our classification of change, is
on top of the ladder of the whole scale of changes, the whole structure
of organization into which one puts one's ideas, sense data and all the
rest of it—one's experiences of dealing with one's friends, as well as
what the sunsets look like in the trees. There is a possibility of change in
the system of all these built-up structures. This is not something we
know much about, but the existence of a place like Naropa Institute is
obviously somehow related to those possibilities.

# 29

## *The Case Against the Case for Mind/Body Dualism**

My first response to Charles Tart's defense of Mind/Body Dualism was, "O God, do we have to go back, again, to the late Paleolithic?"

And then: "But, after all, the cave paintings are still among the world's great works of art, and the empathic totemism which surely accompanied them must have been one of the world's most loving and most ennobling religions."

But was that religion a bunch of dualisms of Mind/Body, God/Man, and the rest?

And obviously, the cloven hoof was already there. Think of the "Sorcerer" of the Trois Freres cave. If ever religion graphically proposed dualism, it was by the sanctification of masked figures. It is a slippery sequence of dualisms from "man inside mask" to "possessing demon inside lunatic" to "mind inside body" to "Out of Body Experience" and the doctrine of "Trans-Substantiation."

Who can claim to be quite free from that schizophrenia—that habit of false concreteness—which identifies the metaphor with its referent?

But we make progress. We are still far from identifying the logical types and modes of the message material generated in the right and left hemispheres respectively, but it seems that, with exceptions of various kinds, the right hemisphere is the source of what used to be called "primary process" thinking—sequences other than the indicative, the logical, and the "true-or-false." The left brain material can be qualified by "perhaps," "it's as if. . . ," "I guess," "I wish," "I see," "I heard that," and

*This article is a reply to "The Case FOR Mind/Body Dualism," by Charles T. Tart, in *CoEvolution Quarterly*, no. 11 (1976). Reprinted from *CoEvolution Quarterly*, no. 12 (1976), by permission of the Point Foundation. (Excerpt from "Burnt Norton" and "The Dry Salvages" in *Four Quartets*, copyright 1943 by T. S. Eliot and renewed 1971 by Esme Valerie Eliot, reprinted by permission of Harcourt Brace Jovanovich, Inc., and Faber and Faber Ltd.)

so on. And such qualification saves the material from the false concreteness which indicative messages will always propose, and which the undisciplined left hemisphere commonly prefers. "It's six o'clock" seems less ambiguous than "Time and the bell have buried the day." But do not be deceived into thinking that T. S. Eliot's line means "the pubs are now opening."

The *metaphors* of the right brain are not and cannot be qualified—do not need qualification. Try it: "It is as if the day were buried by time and the bell," or "I guess time and the bell somehow together buried the day," or "Which day did they bury?"

Try doing this sort of thing to the whole passage.

> Time and the bell have buried the day,
> The black cloud carries the sun away.
> Will the sunflower turn to us, will the clematis
> Stray down, bend to us; tendril and spray
> Clutch and cling?
>
>   Chill
> Fingers of yew be curled
> Down on us? After the kingfisher's wing
> Has answered light to light, and is silent, the light is still
> At the still point of the turning world.
> —T. S. Eliot, in "Burnt Norton,"
>     from *Four Quartets*

*But what does it mean?*

That, you see, is the thaumaturgist's question, which invites the vulgarity of the fundamentalist. If you spell the question out, it means: "How shall we say *the same thing* in the language of the left brain?" And the correct answer is simply, "Don't try. It cannot be done." The left brain cannot achieve that particular qualification of its own utterance which is inherent, and therefore not further needed, in all right-brain productions. It is the folly of the deaf linguist to believe that translation is commonly possible.

And when attempted, translation from the right to the left is teratogenic, a creating of monsters. My anthropological colleagues have done their share of this. They assert, against all aesthetic sense, that the paleolithic frescoes were magical devices to enable the hunters to kill the beasts.

Perhaps the people who leave their bodies could stay with their bodies if they once could grasp the fundamental truth that religion is unifying and ancient, where magic is divisive, degenerate, and late. Rituals first affirmed man's unity with weather, landscape, beast and fellow man. Only later did the rituals come to mean appetitive control of this and that. The Body/Mind dualism is appetitive.

Were those beautiful reindeer and bison—so alive, so precise in posture and movement—were they perhaps some atonement (at-ONE-ment) for the killing?

Be all that as it may, it is still so that to be fully present in the present, here and now, and of the Body, is strangely difficult. Sometimes, I am told, a *koan* will help us in this "occupation for the saint."

> To explore the womb, or tomb, or dreams; all these are
>       usual
> Pastimes and drugs, and features of the press:
> And always will be, some of them especially
> When there is distress of nations and perplexity
> Whether on the shores of Asia, or in the Edgware Road.
> Men's curiosity searches past and future
> And clings to that dimension. But to apprehend
> The point of intersection of the timeless
> With time, is an occupation for the saint—
> No occupation either, but something given
> And taken, in a lifetime's death in love,
> Ardour and selflessness and self-surrender.
> For most of us, there is only the unattended
> Moment, the moment in and out of time,
> The distraction fit, lost in a shaft of sunlight,
> The wild thyme unseen, or the winter lightning
> Or the waterfall, or music heard so deeply
> That it is not heard at all, but you are the music
> While the music lasts. These are only hints and guesses,
> Hints followed by guesses; and the rest
> Is prayer, observance, discipline, thought and action.

—T. S. Eliot, in "The Dry Salvages,"
  from *Four Quartets*

# 30

## *Symptoms, Syndromes, and Systems**

There is a proverb that those who live in glass houses—and especially those who share glass houses—should hesitate to throw stones at each other; and I think it is appropriate to remind every occidental reader of this essay that he lives in the same glass house with the medical profession, along with the Christian religion, the Industrial Revolution, and the educational system of which the others are products.

In other words, we all share in a tangle of presuppositions many of which have ancient origins. As I see it, our troubles have their roots in this tangle of presuppositions many of which are nonsense. Rather than point the finger of blame at one or another of the parts of our whole system—the wicked doctors, the wicked industrialists, the wicked professors—we should take a look at the foundations and nature of the system itself.

It makes but little sense to accuse the doctors of not using holistic spectacles when they look at their patients, if we shirk the holistic vision at the very moment of our accusation.

Under the holistic lens, our criticism of the doctors becomes clearly an ignoring of the total system within which we and the doctors have our existence, and that system includes the whole of our contemporary civilization. It would not be "holistic" to concentrate all our attention upon the *symptoms* of something wrong and, at the same time, to accuse the doctors of seeing only symptoms.

I ask then what is it—what sort of habit of mind is it—that leads to paying too much attention to symptoms and too little to system? And I ask this question knowing surely that I have two places in which to look for an answer. One of these is in the natural history of medical institutions, doctors and patients, and the other is in the remainder of the

*This article was written May 30, 1978, and is reprinted from *The Esalen Catalog* 16, no. 4 (1978), by permission of Esalen Programs.

civilization. Can we recognize "*symptomophobia*" in our universities, our churches, our economic institutions, and our family relations?

Let me examine first a social symptom where we can see what's happening. After that we can look at a physiological symptom where what is happening is hidden inside the body. Think of traffic. There are too many cars on the roads and too many restless people; and too much pollution of the atmosphere by the cars. Altogether that makes up what the doctors call a "syndrome," a nest of symptoms.

Of course this syndrome really has its roots in overpopulation and unwisely applied engineering skill, and in medical victories over epidemics. Public health, just like individual medicine, is symptom-activated. We all share in the pathology which we would blame on the doctors.

At the social level, what happens is simple: *Somebody gets paid to make the pathological trend more comfortable.* We treat the symptoms—we make more roads for the more cars, and we make more and faster cars for the restless people; and when people (very properly) die of overeating or pollution, we try to strengthen their stomachs or their lungs. (Insurance companies hate death.) For overpopulation, we build more houses. And so on.

That is the paradigm: Treat the symptom to make the world safe for the pathology. But, it's a little worse than that: We even look into the future and try to see the symptoms and discomforts coming. We predict the jamming of traffic on the highways and invite bids for government contracts to enlarge the roads for cars that do not yet exist. In this way, millions of dollars get committed to the hypotheses of future increase in pathology.

So, the doctor who concentrates upon the symptoms runs the risk of protecting or fostering the pathology of which the symptoms are parts.

So—what about pain? There are several answers to the problem of pain, several strategies for dealing with it: (1) Get a local anaesthetic and get rid of it; or, more radically, cut the sensory nerve serving the painful part. But these methods of symptomatic treatment make sense— if at all—only if the *message* of the pain is being heard and attended to. (2) Grin and bear it. Again, this course only makes sense after the message has been assimilated. (3) Attend to—and perhaps *treat*—the systemic context in which the pain was generated, i.e., act upon the *message* of the pain.

I have often wondered why pain is so persistent—why does it go on after its existence has been noted? I think the answer is that the message of pain changes as the pain persists. A new pain simply calls attention to the part which hurts, and if this were the only message of pain, the owner of the pain would simply be influenced by the pain in the direction of curing only the symptom. But pain can go on and on—and then the message changes. The owner is forced (or should be forced) to examine and perhaps treat larger areas of relevance. He should be driven from symptom consciousness to attend to the larger system.

But the problem is still how to jump from thinking about the part to thinking about the whole.

In biology there are no values which have the characteristic that if something is good, then more of that something will be better. Economists seem to think that this is true of money but, if they are right, money is thereby shown to be certainly unbiological and perhaps antibiological. For the rest, good things come in optima, not maxima. For every desirable substance or experience there is an optimum amount such that more than the optimum is toxic. This is obviously true of such good things as oxygen, calcium, food, entertainment, clothes, psychotherapy, rage, and perhaps even love. All become toxic when consumed in excessive quantities.

Any part of any biological whole must stay in proportionate size; if it becomes bigger, the part must always become a threat or a danger to the whole. So it begins to look as if the difficulty may be related to the almost unimaginable change of sign.

It is easy to see that if there are too many automobiles, a lot more roads will make matters worse. It is not so easy to see that *more automobiles* might make people see the larger gestalt more clearly.

During World War II, I was able to do one interesting thing—I was able to establish in Chittagong a small radio station aimed at the enemy-occupied areas of Burma, Thailand, and Malaya. The station was planned to neutralize enemy propaganda. So the propagandic policy was simple: We listened to the enemy's nonsense and we professed to be a Japanese official station. Every day we simply *exaggerated* what the enemy was telling people. We argued that the enemy would probably tell lies as big as he dared and therefore that it would be a good idea (from our point of view) to have him appear to tell still bigger lies. Exaggerating the symptom . . . .

I always suspect that patients in psychotherapy exaggerate their traumatic histories and their symptoms by a factor of about three—and that this is good for them.

And then there is the very interesting theory which lies behind homeopathic medicine. If you suffer from a syndrome of symptoms—x, y, and z—you should find a poison which would in normal doses cause the same set of symptoms. This drug you should take in microscopic doses to get a reversed effect.

I am suggesting, you see, that we and the doctors are not merely hooked on the habit of overattention to symptoms, we are also hooked on the habit of thinking in material terms. We all think that pharmacology and the science of traffic limitation are *quantitative* sciences; that if much is bad, then a little more will be worse. But, in truth, this is often not so. We live, rather, in a world of pattern and communication, a world of ideas, and in that world all theories of dosage are partly upside-down. In the purely material world there could be no irony, and a monstrous lack of humor of all kinds. But in the world of patterns and ideas, irony is everywhere; and by irony you may (perhaps) reach that small enlightenment which is a moment of seeing the larger gestalt.

# 31

## *Seek the Sacred: Dartington Seminar**

*Question:* What is aesthetic? What is the sacred? What is consciousness? What is the relationship between them? You seem to suggest that consciousness is very important but at the same time rather treacherous because it undermines our better attempts at the aesthetic and the sacred.

*Gregory Bateson:* You just quoted me as saying that consciousness becomes destructive. I certainly didn't say that. What I did say is that conscious-purpose very rapidly becomes destructive. "Purpose" is a very dangerous concept. Consciousness, I don't know. I have been very careful to say as little as possible about consciousness. The trouble with consciousness is that in the nature of the case it focuses in. There is something that they call the "screen of consciousness," and this to me is almost a mechanical analogy. We receive the products of our mental activities, the images, but the creation of those images is beyond us. It is an extraordinary and miraculous process. It is a beautiful process. But what in the end I am conscious of is a subtraction from the totality and the totality cannot be reported to consciousness. The more you have to report to consciousness the more machinery it requires to operate the whole thing, and soon the head gets bigger than the body and then the head has the problem of reporting on itself and it has to get bigger than itself. Consciousness is always going to be selective. When you get the other two, the sacred and the aesthetic, which are very closely related, you are partly standing off to see a whole. Consciousness is tending to focus in, whereas notions like the sacred and the beautiful tend to be always looking for the larger, the whole. That is why I distrust consciousness as a prime guide.

---

*The following is an extract from a discussion with Henryk Skolimowski and others at Dartington Hall, England, in October 1979. Reprinted, edited, from *Resurgence* 10, no. 6 (1980), by permission of *Resurgence.*

*Q:* What is this something that the aesthetic embraces and the consciousness cannot?

*GB:* Let us start with the very elemental. If you say, "How do you know that an elephant's trunk is its nose?," the answer is that it is between two eyes and north of a mouth. And a thing that sticks out and is between two eyes and north of a mouth is a nose. How do you know this is a leaf? What is a leaf? A leaf is a thing which grows on a stem. What is a stem? A stem is a thing which has leaves and little stems in the angles of the leaves.

If you want to define the parts, you define them by relations, as you define the nose of the elephant.

When you went to school you defined a sentence, analyzing a sentence, to put it more correctly. "A noun is the name of a person, place or thing." In more modern linguistics, we gave that up and we think of a noun as a word which can be a subject of a sentence. What is a sentence? It is that which has a noun for a subject. The parts of speech get defined in all their relations, just as you define the parts of the elephant's face or you define the parts of a plant. The comparative anatomy of the parts of a sentence all depends upon the same sort of mental function in you the analyst. As that came into focus in your head and I gave you that bridge, a little "spark" flew, and that spark is something very close to what we are talking about. That is an elementary example of something which is at the roots of beauty and something which is at the roots of the sacred. It is at the roots of how the world tends to be a unified world and not a dualistic world.

*Q:* Would it be correct to suggest that the aesthetic is this unifying glimpse that makes us aware of the unity of things which is not consciousness?

*GB:* That is right; that is what I am getting at. That flash which appears in consciousness as a disturbance of consciousness is the thing that I am talking about.

*Q:* What is the function of the aesthetic in human life and does it function in the lives of animals?

*GB:* In the lives of animals, yes, it is fairly evident. I was very much struck in the Chicago zoo where they have a pack of wolves. There was a pack of eleven wolves living on three or four acres of open land, fenced in, but the wolves had that much freedom anyway. They have dug a hole in the middle where they have their babies, their den. They are doing quite nicely there. They have a pack organization with a lead animal and it is perfectly obvious. It is also very evident that the alpha animal is much the most beautiful animal in the pack, in terms of sheer physique, in terms of condition, in terms of how he handles himself and how he looks out at the world. It would seem that his status as alpha animal is somehow related to that, and I think you find a good deal of that in other animals.

We should look at those animals which are able to play and consider whether there isn't aesthetic in the play-courtship combination. I don't think you are going to find it in creatures like oysters, whose sense organs are rather limited and whose sexual activities are conducted by ova and spermatazoa free swimming in the water. They don't get together. But I think you will find there is a fairly large span of creatures that use something like an aesthetic to get the sexes together.

*Q:* What is the sacred?

*GB:* We live in a very peculiar Protestant universe. I myself am a fifth-generation unbaptized atheist. We are sort of ultra-Protestant. We protested against even protest. Therefore the thing to do is obviously to go back to the fourteenth or fifteenth century when they were burning each other at the stake for what today looks a quite crazy sort of proposition.

The Catholics were saying that the bread *is* the body and the wine *is* the blood, and the Protestants wanted to say, the bread *stands for* the body and the wine *stands for* the blood. This difference seemed to them one for which it was reasonable to burn people and reasonable to be burned. What on earth is this point? The point is this. That, to a part of the mind there is no distinction between the two. "Stands for" and "is" are the same thing. But the Protestant, logical, straightforward part of the brain cannot accept this. The part of the brain that dreams, which on the whole is the part that the artist uses most, is perfectly willing to accept the statement that "the bread is the body," and that of course is the part of the mind that really belongs in church. What Protestantism did, in a sense, was to exclude from the church the very part of the mind which belongs in the church, in favor of a commonsense logic and a passionate desire that everything should make logical sense.

*Q:* Are you telling us that in making everything clear, logical, and connected in a linear way we have lost a part of our being which is the sacramental?

*GB:* Not quite. We have lost a wholeness of being which would include "that" and the "other" side together. I don't want to say that the fantasy brain, the primary process brain, is the sacramental. I think the sacramental is being damaged all the time.

The damage is the taking apart. The sacredness is the coming together.

The sacred is the hook up, the total hook up and not the product of the split.

*Q:* You said that in the Chicago wolf pack it was the most beautiful wolf physically that seemed to be the natural leader. That does not seem to be true with our own society. Do you think that when we overcome some of the wrongness and when we have come back to "unity," if we ever do, that someone more physically beautiful will be our leader?

*GB:* Well, one thinks of various images of Christ, of Jehovah, and so forth. One thinks, for example, of the whole body cult in California, looking for beautiful people and making people as beautiful as possible with exercises, going along with a psychic cult to try to make them live fuller lives.

You become a head man in a Balinese village by a very specific process, which involves marriage, having at least one child of each sex, not having lost any body part, and so on. They are extraordinarily interested in large wholes of which the village is one, and of which the human family is one, so that the unit has to be complete. Completeness is one of their points of beauty. Their aim is toward a very abstract sort of completeness which is not far from an aesthetic point.

*Q:* Would you like to reflect on the capacity to symbolize?

*GB:* I never use that word. I don't like using it because the word tends to cut things up and then people talk of symbols as if they were parts of a dictionary and you could have a dictionary of flowers, like Ophelia: a rue means this and a rose means something else. Dictionaries of symbolism always seem to me to be cheap representations of what really happens. I don't like dictionaries of words. I think they mostly tell lies. Words are not really like that. Do not think as you have been taught to think especially by language, in terms of those items which are related, but always think in terms of the relationship between them. Language always says, "The lemon is yellow," and obscures the relationship between the yellow and the lemon, or it says you have "five fingers." The correct answer to "How many fingers do you have?" is not "Five." The correct answer is that what I have is four relationships between fingers. I think that it is clear enough to be able to bet a thousand to one that "I have five fingers on this hand" is a wrong statement. What the right statement is, I don't know. If you begin to look at your hand, or indeed any organic object, in terms of its relations and not in terms of its things, you will suddenly find that that object is about four times as beautiful as you thought it was.

Take your hand home and take a good look at it sometime.

This is sort of a noisy place to do that. It is always surprising when you want to do a little meditating to discover the difference between thinking of the things and thinking of the relationship between the things. This has to do with the sacred very much.

*Q:* When you describe the "spark," you are talking about more than the state of the relationships between relationships.

*GB:* It is like trying to track an afterimage. You stare at the light and you look away and you see an afterimage and you follow it and it keeps running away from you and you try to catch it. I experience something— for lack of a word, I call it a spark. There is a whole series of things which will give you a flash. We could do a comparative study of a dozen differ- ent sorts of flash to make a language for describing flashes, which would be a very useful language. There are a lot of them.

I don't know what sort of a child I was. Now I am in my seventies and a lot of things in the last five or ten years have been happening— not changes but sudden discoveries.

You know, one went off into the hills to find a donkey and at the age of seventy one discovered one had been riding on one for sixty years.

I think what one did was in some way to give oneself permission to discover that one is riding on the donkey. That giving oneself permis- sion is very close to the sort of things we are talking about. That things like art and things like poetry and rhythmic prayer or whatever are not in a way discoveries, or rather, they are discoveries in the literal etymo- logical sense of the word. They are uncoveries of that which one knew before. Then sacredness has something to do with this covering and un- covering deeper components.

*Q:* Could you answer the meaning of the sacred and the meaning of consciousness in terms of the function of the sacred and the func- tion of consciousness?

*GB:* I have avoided the word "function" three times this evening very carefully. I have no idea what the word means. Do you mean usefulness? The function of a hand is to fit on the end of an arm. Is that a correct use of the word "function"? No. I thought it wasn't. There is a miserable thing here, that keeps coming up, that a phrase like "the purpose of," "the function of," is inherent in the next substantive that you mention after the words "function of." The function of the aesthetic, the function of the hand, etc. Whereas function is inherent in relations and not in things. An ax does not have a use. The use of an ax is related to its position between a person and a tree. Now if you want to ask about the function of aesthetics I will say, well, between what and what, within what whole are you attributing function to what parts? "Function" is a part word and not a whole word. Aesthetics and sacred tend to be whole words, words about wholes, and you can't talk about the function of a whole. It is no good saying, "What is the meaning of the universe?"

*Q:* But why not?

*GB:* Because to say, "What is the meaning of the universe?" assumes there is another entity for whom the universe has meaning. Meaning is not internal. It is between parts.

*Q:* You do not have to assume that there is something beyond in order to ask the question, "What is the meaning of the universe?"

*GB:* To whom?

*Q:* To you or me.

*GB:* You are part of the universe.

*Q:* What will you say about the mechanistic view?

*GB:* There are several things which are called mechanistic points of view. The thing which is preponderantly called a mechanistic point of view is a point of view derived from the science which grew out of Newton and Locke and became the Industrial Revolution and became *the* science. Essentially, how to get across those arcs and how to ignore the circuit structure. In a sense, in introducing the circuit structure in the bottom half of that iceberg, I am blowing all hell out of the Newtonian and Lockean materialistic point of view. The Newton-Locke mechanism is related, in fact, to the separation of mind and body, mind and matter.

*Q:* How do you think we can become more in tune?

*GB:* Take your hand home and take a good look at it as an aggregate of relationships and not as an aggregate of objects. On the whole, an artist or many artists doing a representational job on a landscape, say, see that landscape partly not as a tree, a house, a hill, but as this shape with that shape. And the shapes are to be related and the artist forgets while he is drawing the picture that he is drawing a hill, a house, a tree.

This is the same thing that I am talking about when I say you might look at your hand and see that it is a bunch of relationships. It has a very curious sort of effect on one to meditate oneself into that view.

*Q:* I have been getting very lost in a lot of the words that have been going around. To me almost it seemed we were losing what we were talking about.

*GB:* You have to talk about it with a good deal of care. I am sure you can lose everything by talking about it badly. To talk about things well is not easy. We have on the whole been taught to talk very badly. The schooling which we all come out of is quite monstrous. It goes back in fact to Locke and Newton and to Descartes and dualism. It is not an accident and it is a very curious juxtaposition that this same man around 1700, Descartes, created three of the major tools of our contemporary thinking. One: the split between mind and matter. Two: the Cartesian coordinates, the graph—you put time on the bottom and you make a variable. And, three: the *cogito*—"I think, therefore I am." Those three things go together and have simply torn the concept of the universe in which we live into rags.

# 32

## *"Last Lecture"**

*Returning to the place from which I started, and knowing the place for the first time.*

*T. S. Eliot gives the recipe for a last lecture.*

*I started in the biology taught in Cambridge in the 1920s, corrected somewhat by boyish collecting of various invertebrates: lepidoptera, coleoptera, mollusca, odonata, etc.*

*Looking at all that with eyes changed by anthropology and dolphins and schizophrenia, I see that I never traveled far from where I started.*

*What is form, pattern, purpose, organization, and so on . . . ?*

*Those were my questions when I started and are still my questions.*

*There have been advances: Cybernetics has helped, and Whitehead-Russell have helped, and "Laws of Form" and Information Theory and Ross Ashby.*

*But mysteries remain.*

*The world looks more elegant than it did. . . .*

In T. S. Eliot's words, "The end of all our exploring will be to arrive where we started and know the place for the first time." So, here I am in Britain where I started and from which I have been away almost continuously since 1927 when I was twenty-three. It was then that I started to go to New Guinea. I returned in 1929 from a study of head-hunting people to the high table of St. John's College, Cambridge, and found myself very unhappy there. It seemed to me that the undoubtedly elegant exchange of intellectual embroidery which occurred at the high table was somehow emotionally dishonest, so I fled down into Somerset, where I wrote up my New Guinea material, submitted it for a Fellowship, got my Fellowship, and returned to New Guinea.

---

*Asked to deliver what he would be willing to call his "last lecture," Bateson responded with this draft, written September 29, 1979, for distribution to the press, of a lecture delivered October 28, 1979, at the Institute of Contemporary Arts, London. Previously unpublished.

On my second trip I learned a good deal about how New Guinea etiquette works, how beautifully it dovetails together. And when I returned again—returning again to the place from which I started—to the high table of St. John's College, Cambridge, I was fascinated and enchanted by the elegance of that system where again parts function together, fitting together with every detail "at home taking its place to support the others." And so on. "The easy commerce of the old and new." And so on. I turned to my neighbor at high table and remarked on this beauty of functioning—and it was, I assure you, not a critical but a loving comment, a delighted comment. He turned immediately to his neighbor on the other side and started a conversation about the weather.

That was one of the details, one of the small experiences which contributed to my actually leaving the country and going to America. My trade and my bent was to be conscious of the social system of which I was part, and in England it was almost a premise of the British social system that you shall not be too conscious of how it works.

But I am speaking of thirty-five years ago, and since then some heavy years have gone by—World War II and the vast disruptions that followed World War II. Today we are in an epoch in which the very deep things of which we were happily unconscious are now rumbling with change. I think it is time for you Britons, and for my friends in America—for the whole Western world and perhaps for the Oriental world—to pay attention to that rumbling. We have to become conscious of those things of which we were previously happily and *for our own good* unconscious.

So I return today to the place from which I started with a determination to know the place for the first time or to help you know it. Especially I want to offer you the thinking which I've done since 1927.

There are two pieces of this thinking which I want to offer you. Both of them have to do with the problems of education in the wider sense of that word. So it's appropriate that this lecture has been sponsored by Dartington Hall, where advanced thinking on the subject of education has been done over the last fifty years.

The first concerns the relation between what used to be called a "body" and what used to be called a "mind." These words still persist, but I will use them both as if they were already obsolete, where I hope they will arrive fairly soon. For the formal separation we could perhaps blame Descartes in the seventeenth century, but of course we can glance back to the Paleolithic and, alas, a contemporary look will reveal all sorts of modern cults and semilunacies where it is believed that mind and body are separate. (I understand that there is quite a cult of O.B.E. these days—Out-of-Body Experience—the notion that a something which is not a something may hop out of your body and sit on the windowsill, look back at the body for a minute, and then go wandering and return with a narrative of its adventures.) I regard all that as lunatic extrapolation from a Cartesian position in which I simply do not believe.

It seems to me important for our notions of responsibility and our notions of what a human being is, that we accept very firmly that body and mind are one. The bridge which makes these two one was, I believe, discovered about 130 years ago by Gustav Fechner. Psychologists will recall that in Leipzig in 1834 Weber discovered that perception was related to ratios of intensity in the "stimulus." Weber himself doesn't seem to have made much of this, but he was the actual discoverer. He discovered, for example, that the ability to perceive the difference between two weights is based on the ratio between them and not upon the subtractive difference. So if you can discriminate between two ounces and three ounces, you will also discriminate six ounces from four, and indeed three pounds from two pounds. Now that discovery, that the first and most fundamental step of mental life—the receipt of news from the outside—depends upon difference, and that the differences are in fact ratios, is basic for epistemology, the science of how it is that we can know anything. Fechner contributed to the natural history of how it is that we can know anything. We can only know by virtue of difference. This means that our entire mental life is one degree more abstract than the physical world around us. We deal in what mathematicians call derivatives, and not in quantities—in ratios between quantities but not in quantities. This, you see, is a bridge between mind and body, or between mind and matter, but, at the same time, it differentiates mind from matter. Incidentally, Fechner's contribution supports Immanuel Kant, who already in the eighteenth century saw that there are a million facts (*Tatsache*) in a piece of chalk, but a very few of these become effective. Most of them do not make a difference. In the more modern language of information theory, we may say that information is *difference which makes a difference* and that of the infinite number of differences immanent in this chalk very few become information. There is the fact that this chalk is here in London and differs therefore from some other piece of chalk in New York. But that is not an effective difference that makes a difference. It doesn't enter into an information processing system. This is basic to our notion of what is life, our notion of what is death. It is basic for religion.

I want to put a second point before you now, another epistemological point. First of all I assert that, if you are going to talk about living things, not only as an academic biologist but as yourself a living thing among living things, it would be nice if you could talk a language which would be somehow isomorphic with—would be in step with—the language in terms of which living things themselves are organized. For example, you have two eyes, one on each side of your nose, and you can point to that and use everyday language to say so. But everyday language hides the truth that the development of those eyes in that location—or that nose located between them—is a relational matter. It is brought about by internal exchange of news about the organization as it develops and news of the *relations* between the parts of that organization. That's how you come to get two eyes, one on each side of your nose. We don't know how to say that. We know very little about the real underlying organization of the shapes and forms of living things. We do not know how the zebra makes his stripes or the tabby cat or the tiger. We do not know how the repetitious series of ribs is formed. We know a little bit about those processes and there is some experimental work on such things. But we don't know much.

Let me put it this way. If I ask you how many fingers you have, you will probably answer, "Five." That I believe to be an incorrect answer. The correct answer, I believe, is, "Gregory you are asking a question wrongly." In the processes of human growth, there is surely no word which means finger, and no word which means five. There might be a word for "branching," a command of some sort identifying the contingencies of branching. If that is so, then the right question would be: How many relations between pairs of fingers do you have? And the correct answer, of course, is four. The relation between one and two, the relation between two and three, between three and four, four and five. (It is unlikely, I think, that the relation between number four and five acted back upon the relation between one and two—but conceivable.)

You should be counting not the things which are related, but the relationships; not the relata, but the relationships. How many branchings did it take to make a hand? Not how many fingers were a result of those branchings.

Look at your hand now. I don't know whether you can do it in such a public place as this, in such an unquiet place as this. I recommend you take your hand home and take a look at it when you get there—very quietly, almost as part of meditation. And try to catch the difference between seeing it as a base for five parts and seeing it as constructed of a tangle of relationships. Not a tangle, a pattern of the interlocking of relationships which were the determinants of its growth. And if you can really manage to see the hand in terms of the epistemology that I am offering you, I think you will find that your hand is suddenly much more recognizably beautiful as a product of relationship than as a composition of countable parts. In other words, I am suggesting to you, first, that language is very deceiving, and, second, that if you begin even without much knowledge to adventure into what it would be like to look at the world with a biological epistemology, you will come into contact with concepts which the biologists don't look at at all. You will meet with *beauty* and *ugliness*. These may be real components in the world that you as a living creature live in.

It's not a new idea that living things have immanent beauty, but it is revolutionary to assert, *as a scientist,* that matters of beauty are really highly formal, very real, and crucial to the entire political and ethical system in which we live.

Very well. I have offered you two central points in what I might call biological epistemology. First, that all mental life is related to the physical body as difference or contrast is related to the static and the uniform. And second, I have offered you the idea that the viewing of the world in terms of *things* is a distortion supported by language, and that the correct view of the world is in terms of the dynamic relations which are the governors of growth.

In passing, note that the whole of possessiveness would come out very differently if we viewed our possessiveness not numerically in terms of pounds or dollars but relationally. What is it to possess five fingers *versus* what is it to possess four relationships between fingers? Is the word "possession" applicable at all to relations?

Perhaps that will suffice to show that what I am saying, if taken seriously—and I say it in all seriousness—would make an almost total change in the way we live, the way we think about our lives, and about each other and ourselves.

Perhaps a curriculum is like a hand in that every piece and component of what they would call a curriculum is really related ideally to the other components as fingers are related to each other and to the whole hand. In other words, it is nonsense except as sort of a Faustian shortcut to learn large quantities of listed material unless the learning of those lists can be developed into some sort of organic whole. I am not against the learning of lists. I am against the failure to assimilate the components of lists together into a total vision, a total hearing, a total kinesics, perhaps, of the wholes with which we deal. We are all familiar with the difficulties that Anglo-Saxons face when they learn languages. Englishmen and Americans are notoriously stupid and awkward when they come to a foreign country and try to talk the native language. This is a sharp and clear example of exactly the point that I am trying to make, that we Anglo-Saxons do not learn to live in a language because we believe that it is made of separate parts. We call these "words" and we make them into dictionaries. But that is not how the natives of the place learn to speak as children nor how they speak today. It is not even how we speak our own English—a language notorious for the number of poets it has produced. We have lost by the time we are twelve the idea of language as a living organized pattern.

So what is a living organized pattern and how is it carried and transmitted in an educating system? Let us look at that aspect of psychology which on the whole psychologists most hate to consider. We put an organism—a rat or a dog, or a graduate student—in a context of learning, and in that context he learns certain linkages between outside "stimulus" and "response" and "reinforcement." But that is not the end of the story. In my family, we had for a long time a female Keeshond dog. She became finally the mother of some pups, and I was privileged to watch the weaning of one of these pups. It was done, as weaning is done in all Canidae, by pressing the puppy down. The mother presses the puppy down with her mouth open on the back of his neck. If after that the puppy again asks for milk, he is again pressed down. So far the story is quite simply a story of operant conditioning with negative reinforcement. And it would fit any textbook of psychology. But the next step was a quasi-battle which became an affectionate play between mother and puppy. The puppy attacked mother's mouth with his mouth, and she and puppy then had a mutual mouthing game. In other words, the learning context is woven into a total relationship and does not stand out as a single incident. It's not just "learn not to ask for tit" but a much more complicated business in a total woven fabric of relationship and love.

And if dogs achieve that order of complexity, you may be pretty sure that human beings could and should achieve two or three orders of greater complexity.

The matter becomes a little more complex already among the wolves. In the Chicago zoo they have a pack of wolves living on three or four acres of rough ground. They have a den in the center which they dug and where they have their pups. They live a fairly civilized life. Every now and then, an ambulance goes down the road outside the zoo, its siren screaming. When the wolves hear the sound they all howl in a most beautiful sound and after they have howled they all come together and—what do you think—everybody mouths everybody else's mouth. They go into what the anthropologist would call an aggregation rite (*rite d'aggregation*) which has its roots way back in the weaning procedure which I described.

And now, perhaps because you are Anglo-Saxons and I am an Anglo-Saxon, you will want to ask me, "But how are we to achieve such a holistic education?" And that question is already a confession that we are in general not doing it. The question springs from an already dissected universe and not from an organized universe, and therefore asks for an answer which cannot be the answer. It asks for an answer in terms of a dissected universe, and that answer I will not give you. It would not be an answer.

We face a paradox in that I cannot tell you how to educate the young, or yourselves, in terms of the epistemology which I have offered you except you first embrace that epistemology. The answers must already be in your head and in your rules of perception. You must know the answer to your question before I can give it to you. I wish that every teacher, schoolmaster, parent, and older sibling could hear the thunderous voice out of the whirlwind: "Who is this that darkeneth counsel by words without understanding? . . . Dost thou know when the hinds bring forth? . . . Where wast thou when I set up the pillars of the earth?" I mean the thirty-eighth, thirty-ninth, and fortieth chapters of the Book of Job. The pietistic silly old man thought he was pretty good and thought God was just like him, but finally he was enlightened by an enormous lesson, a thunderous lesson in natural history and in the beauty of the natural world.

Of course natural history can be taught as a dead subject. I know that, but I believe also that perhaps the monstrous atomistic pathology at the individual level, at the family level, at the national level and the international level—the pathology of wrong thinking in which we all live—can only in the end be corrected by an enormous discovery of those relations in nature which make up the beauty of nature.

# Bibliography of the Published Work of Gregory Bateson[1]

Prepared by Rodney E. Donaldson

## I. Books, Articles, Notices, Reviews, Interviews, and Conference Remarks

1925   (With W. Bateson.) "On Certain Aberrations of the Red-Legged Partridges *Alectoris rufa* and *saxatilis.*" *Journal of Genetics* 16, no. 1 (November): 101–23. Reprinted in *Scientific Papers of William Bateson*, Vol. 2, edited by R. C. Punnett, pp. 382–404. Cambridge: Cambridge University Press, 1928. Reprint. London and New York: Johnson Reprint Corporation, 1971.

1931   "Head Hunting on the Sepik River." *Man* 31 (March): 49 (art. 48). ("Summary of a communication presented by Gregory Bateson, 13th January, 1931.")

1932a  "Further Notes on a Snake Dance of the Baining." *Oceania* 2, no. 3 (March): 334–41.

---

1. The author wishes to acknowledge the pioneering work of Vern Carroll, whose bibliography in *Steps to an Ecology of Mind* set a standard of excellence which it has been exhilarating to strive to uphold. All entries in the present bibliography have been verified with original sources, and a number of corrections and additions have been made both to Carroll's original bibliography and to the bibliography of Carroll and Donaldson in the June 1982 *American Anthropologist*. The aim being a maximally informative bibliography, certain information not at present bibliographically fashionable (month of publication, exact title punctuation, page numbers of conference remarks, etc.) has been included.

Articles marked with an asterisk appear in *Steps to an Ecology of Mind* (cf. Bateson 1972a). Articles marked with two asterisks appear in *A Sacred Unity* (cf. Bateson 1991a). As a matter of historical interest, the occasion for which each paper was prepared has been noted. Reprintings of articles very widely reprinted have been excluded. Articles primarily *about* Bateson, though incorporating interview material, have also been excluded (cf. the "About Bateson" section of the Gregory Bateson Archive, under "Miscellaneous Items"). Readers failing to find a book in this bibliography listed in a library catalog under either the volume editor's name or the volume title should try looking under the title of the conference or symposium, which is listed immediately preceding the editor's name.

Published photographs, tape recordings, records, films, and videotapes are not included in the present bibliography.

1932b   "Social Structure of the Iatmul People of the Sepik River." (Parts I–II). *Oceania* 2, no. 3 (March): 245–91.

1932c   "Social Structure of the Iatmul People of the Sepik River." (Parts III–VI). *Oceania* 2, no. 4 (June): 401–53.

1934a   "Personal Names among the Iatmul Tribe (Sepik River)." *Man* 34 (July): 109–10 (art. 130). ("Summary of a Communication presented by G. Bateson, 5 June, 1934.")

1934b   "Field Work in Social Psychology in New Guinea." In *Congrès International des Sciences Anthropologiques et Ethnologiques: Compte-rendu de la première Session, Londres, 1934*, p. 153. Londres: Institut Royal D'Anthropologie. Summary of remarks delivered July 31, 1934, to Section B: Psychology, at the first International Congress of Anthropological and Ethnological Sciences, held at London.

1934c   "The Segmentation of Society." In *Congrès International des Sciences Anthropologiques et Ethnologiques: Compte-rendu de la première Session, Londres, 1934*, p. 187. Londres: Institut Royal D'Anthropologie. Summary of remarks delivered July 31, 1934, to Section D a: Ethnography—General, at the first International Congress of Anthropological and Ethnological Sciences, held at London.

1934d   "Ritual Transvesticism on the Sepik River, New Guinea." In *Congrès International des Sciences Anthropologiques et Ethnologiques: Compte-rendu de la première Session, Londres, 1934*, pp. 274–75. Londres: Institut Royal D'Anthropologie. Summary of remarks delivered August 1, 1934, to Section F: Sociology, at the first International Congress of Anthropological and Ethnological Sciences, held at London.

1934e   "Psychology and War: Tendencies of Early Man." *The Times*, Thursday, December 13, p. 12. Letter to the editor.

1935a   "Music in New Guinea." *The Eagle* 48, no. 214 (December 1934): 158–70. ("The Eagle . . . a magazine supported by members of St. John's College, Cambridge, England. Printed at the University Press for subscribers only.")

* 1935b   "Culture Contact and Schismogenesis." *Man* 35 (December): 178–83 (art. 199). Reprinted in *Beyond the Frontier*, edited by Paul J. Bohannan and Fred Plog, pp. 187–98. Garden City, N.Y.: Natural History Press, 1967.

1936a   *Naven: A Survey of the Problems suggested by a Composite Picture of the Culture of a New Guinea Tribe drawn from Three Points of View*. Cambridge: Cambridge University Press. Reprint. New York: Macmillan Co., 1937. Excerpted, as "The Naven Ceremony in New Guinea," in *Primitive Heritage: An Anthropological Anthology*, edited by Margaret Mead and Nicolas Calas, pp. 186–202. New York: Random House, 1953.

1936b   Review of *Reports of the Cambridge Anthropological Expedition to Torres Straits, Vol. 1: General Ethnography*, by A. C. Haddon. *Man* 36 (February): 35–36 (art. 41).

1936c   "Culture Contact and Schismogenesis. (Cf. MAN, 1935, 199)." *Man* 36 (February): 38 (art. 47). Letter concerning a weakness in his formal exposition of schismogenesis.

1936d   "A Carved Wooden Statuette from the Sepik River, New Guinea. (cf. MAN, 1935, 161)." *Man* 36 (May): 88 (art. 116). Letter in reference to "A Carved Wooden Statuette from the Sepik River, New Guinea," by H. G. Beasley.

1937    "An Old Temple and a New Myth." *Djawa* 17, nos. 5–6: 291–307. Text reprinted in *Traditional Balinese Culture,* edited by Jane Belo, pp. 111–36 and Plates XVIII, XXVIII, and XXIX. New York and London: Columbia University Press, 1970. (Note: The reprint excludes five of the eight original photographs and adds two photographs which do not appear in the original but which pertain to two of the same subjects appearing in the original.)

* 1941a   "Experiments in Thinking About Observed Ethnological Material." *Philosophy of Science* 8, no. 1 (January): 53–68. Paper read at the Seventh Conference on Methods in Philosophy and the Sciences, April 28, 1940, at the New School for Social Research, New York.

1941b   Review of *Conditioning and Learning,* by Ernest R. Hilgard and Donald G. Marquis. *American Anthropologist* 43, no. 1 (January–March): 115–16.

1941c   Review of *Mathematico-deductive Theory of Rote Learning: A Study in Scientific Methodology,* by Clark L. Hull, Carl I. Hovland, Robert T. Ross, Marshall Hall, Donald T. Perkins, and Frederic B. Fitch. *American Anthropologist* 43, no. 1 (January–March): 116–18.

1941d   "Age Conflicts and Radical Youth." Mimeographed. New York: Institute for Intercultural Studies. Prepared for the Committee for National Morale.

1941e   "The Frustration-Aggression Hypothesis and Culture." *Psychological Review* 48, no. 4 (July): 350–55. Paper read at the 1940 meeting of the Eastern Psychological Association in the Symposium on Effects of Frustration. Reprinted in *Readings in Social Psychology,* edited by Theodore M. Newcomb, Eugene L. Hartley, et al., pp. 267–69. New York: Holt, 1947.

1941f   (With Margaret Mead.) "Principles of Morale Building." *Journal of Educational Sociology* 15, no. 4 (December): 206–20.

1942a   (With Margaret Mead.) *Balinese Character: A Photographic Analysis.* Special Publications of the New York Academy of Sciences, Vol. 2. New York: New York Academy of Sciences. Reprint. 1962. Excerpted, translated by Alban Bensa, as "Les Usages Sociaux du Corps à Bali," in *Actes de la Recherche en Sciences Sociales,* no. 14 (Avril 1977): 3–33.

1942b   "Announcement: Council on Human Relations (15 West 77th Street, New York City)." *Applied Anthropology* 1, no. 2 (January–March): 66–67. Excerpted, as "Invitation to Collaborators," in *American Anthropologist* 44, no. 2 (April–June 1942): 335–36.

1942c   "The Council on Human Relations." *Man* 42 (July–August): 93–94.

1942d   "Some Systematic Approaches to the Study of Culture and Personality." *Character and Personality* 11, no. 1 (September): 76–82. Reprinted in *Personal Character and Cultural Milieu,* edited by Douglas G. Haring, pp. 71–77. Syracuse, N.Y., 1948. 2nd rev. ed., pp. 110–16. Syracuse, N.Y.: Syracuse University Press, 1949. 3rd rev. ed., pp. 131–36. Syracuse, N.Y.: Syracuse University Press, 1956.

1942e   "Council on Intercultural Relations." *Character and Personality* 11, no. 1 (September): 83–84. Précised, as "The Council on Intercultural Relations," in *American Sociological Review* 8, no. 2 (April 1943): 223.

* 1942f   Comment on "The Comparative Study of Culture and the Purposive Cultivation of Democratic Values," by Margaret Mead. In *Science, Philosophy and Religion; Second Symposium* (held September 8–11, 1941, at New York).

Conference on Science, Philosophy and Religion. Edited by Lyman Bryson and Louis Finkelstein, pp. 81–97. New York: Conference on Science, Philosophy and Religion in Their Relation to the Democratic Way of Life, Inc. Reprinted widely under the title "Social Planning and the Concept of Deutero-Learning."

\* 1942g    "Morale and National Character." In *Civilian Morale*. Society for the Psychological Study of Social Issues, Second Yearbook. Edited by Goodwin Watson, pp. 71–91. Boston: Houghton-Mifflin Co. (for Reynal & Hitchcock, New York). Reprinted, with some introductory material edited out, in *Steps to an Ecology of Mind* (cf. Bateson 1972a). Excerpted, as "Formulation of End Linkage," in *The Study of Culture at a Distance*, edited by Margaret Mead and Rhoda Métraux, pp. 367–78. Chicago and London: The University of Chicago Press, 1953.

1942h    Review of *The Ageless Indies*, by Raymond Kennedy. *Natural History* 50, no. 2 (September): 109.

1942i    Note in *Psychological Bulletin* 39, no. 8 (October): 670. Note requesting "materials on the existing stereotypes and attitudes of the American people toward the cultures and the individual members of countries engaged in the present war."

1943a    "Cultural and Thematic Analysis of Fictional Films." *Transactions of the New York Academy of Sciences*, series 2, vol. 5, no. 4 (February): 72–78. An address to the New York Academy of Sciences, Section of Psychology, January 18, 1943. Reprinted in *Personal Character and Cultural Milieu*, edited by Douglas G. Haring, pp. 78–84. Syracuse, N.Y., 1948. 2nd rev. ed., pp. 117–23. Syracuse, N.Y.: Syracuse University Press, 1949. 3rd rev. ed., pp. 137–42. Syracuse, N.Y.: Syracuse University Press, 1956.

1943b    "An Analysis of the Film *Hitlerjunge Quex* (1933)." Mimeographed. New York: Museum of Modern Art Film Library. Microfilm copy made in 1965 by Graphic Microfilm Co. Reprinted, as "An Analysis of the Nazi Film 'Hitlerjunge Quex,'" in *Studies in Visual Communication* 6, no. 3 (Fall 1980): 20–55 (accompanied by still photographs from the film). Also abstracted by Margaret Mead in *The Study of Culture at a Distance*, edited by Margaret Mead and Rhoda Métraux, pp. 302–14. Chicago and London: The University of Chicago Press, 1953. (Note: The first three reels of this film—approximately forty-five minutes—with analytic titles by Gregory Bateson, are available for rent from the Museum of Modern Art Film Library, 11 West 53rd St., New York, NY 10019.)

\*\* 1943c    "Human Dignity and the Varieties of Civilization." In *Science, Philosophy and Religion; Third Symposium* (held August 27–31, 1942, at New York). Conference on Science, Philosophy and Religion. Edited by Lyman Bryson and Louis Finkelstein, pp. 245–55. New York: Conference on Science, Philosophy and Religion in Their Relation to the Democratic Way of Life, Inc. (Note: The article includes comments by Maximilian Beck, with a response by Gregory Bateson.) Reprinted, edited, in *A Sacred Unity* (cf. Bateson 1991a).

1943d    "Discussion: The Science of Decency." *Philosophy of Science* 10, no. 2 (April): 140–42.

1943e    (Collaboration.) *Melanesian Pidgin English Short Grammar and Vocabulary*, by

Robert A. Hall, Jr., with the collaboration of Gregory Bateson and John W. M. Whiting. Baltimore: Linguistic Society of America at the Waverly Press, Inc. ("This booklet is published by the Linguistic Society of America for the Intensive Language Program of the American Council of Learned Societies.") Reprinted under the title *Melanesian Pidgin Phrase-Book and Vocabulary.* Baltimore: Linguistic Society of America at the Waverly Press, Inc., 1943. ("The Linguistic Society of America and the Intensive Language Program of the American Council of Learned Societies have cooperated in publishing this booklet for the United States Armed Forces Institute.")

1943f    (Collaboration.) *Melanesian Pidgin English: Grammar, Texts, Vocabulary,* by Robert A. Hall, Jr., with the collaboration of Gregory Bateson, Phyllis M. Kaberry, Margaret Mead, Stephen W. Reed, and John W. M. Whiting. Baltimore: Linguistic Society of America at the Waverly Press, Inc. ("Identical with the edition published for the United States Armed Forces Institute, Madison, Wisconsin, by the Linguistic Society of America and the Intensive Language Program of the American Council of Learned Societies.")

1943g    Remarks in "Psychology—In the War and After, Part II: Comments on General Course in Psychology," by Louise Omwake. *Junior College Journal* 14, no. 1 (September): 20.

1944a    "Pidgin English and Cross-Cultural Communication." *Transactions of the New York Academy of Sciences,* series 2, vol. 6, no. 4 (February): 137–41. Paper read to the New York Academy of Sciences, Section of Anthropology, January 24, 1944.

1944b    "Psychology—In the War and After (VII): Material on Contemporary Peoples." *Junior College Journal* 14, no. 7 (March): 308–11.

** 1944c    "Cultural Determinants of Personality." In *Personality and the Behavior Disorders: A Handbook Based on Experimental and Clinical Research,* Vol. 2, edited by Joseph McV. Hunt, pp. 714–35. New York: Ronald Press Co.

1944d    (With Claire Holt.) "Form and Function of the Dance in Bali." In *The Function of Dance in Human Society: A Seminar Directed by Franziska Boas,* pp. 46–52 and Plates 11–19. Boas School. New York: The Boas School. 2nd ed. Brooklyn, N.Y.: Dance Horizons, [1972]. Reprinted in *Traditional Balinese Culture,* edited by Jane Belo, pp. 322–30. New York and London: Columbia University Press, 1970.

1944e    "Psychology—In the War and After (VIII): Use of Film Material in Studying Peoples." *Junior College Journal* 14, no. 9 (May): 427–29.

1944f    (With Robert A. Hall, Jr.) "A Melanesian Culture-Contact Myth in Pidgin English." *Journal of American Folklore* 57, no. 226 (October–December): 255–62. ("Dictated and Commented by Gregory Bateson; Transcribed and Translated by Robert A. Hall, Jr.")

1946a    "Discussion" [of "Some Relationships Between Maturation and Acculturation," by Arnold Gesell; "Cultural Patterning of Maturation in Selected Primitive Societies," by Margaret Mead; and "Environment vs. Race—Environment as an Etiological Factor in Psychiatric Disturbances in Infancy," by René A. Spitz and Kathe M. Wolf]. *The Journal of Nervous and Mental Disease* 103, no. 5 (May): 521–22. Remarks delivered at a joint meeting of the New York Neurological Society and the New York Academy of

Medicine, Section of Neurology and Psychiatry, and Section of Pediatrics, held January 8, 1946.

1946b    "Physical Thinking and Social Problems." *Science* 103, no. 2686 (June 21): 717–18.

1946c    "Arts of the South Seas." *Art Bulletin* 28, no. 2 (June): 119–23. Review of an exhibit held January 29–May 19, 1946, at the Museum of Modern Art, New York.

1946d    "The Pattern of an Armaments Race: An Anthropological Approach—Part 1." *Bulletin of the Atomic Scientists* 2, nos. 5–6 (September 1): 10–11. Reprinted in *Personal Character and Cultural Milieu*, edited by Douglas G. Haring, pp. 85–88. Syracuse, N.Y., 1948. 2nd rev. ed., pp. 124–27. Syracuse, N.Y.: Syracuse University Press, 1949.

1946e    "The Pattern of an Armaments Race—Part II—An Analysis of Nationalism." *Bulletin of the Atomic Scientists* 2, nos. 7–8 (October 1): 26–28. Reprinted in *Personal Character and Cultural Milieu*, edited by Douglas G. Haring, pp. 89–93. Syracuse, N.Y., 1948. 2nd rev. ed., pp. 128–32. Syracuse, N.Y.: Syracuse University Press, 1949.

1946f    Review of *Man, Morals and Society*, by John Carl Flugel. *Psychosomatic Medicine* 8, no. 5 (September–October): 363–64.

1946g    "From One Social Scientist to Another." *American Scientist* 34, no. 4 (October): 648ff. A reply to "From One Scientist (Political) to Another (Exact)," by René Albrecht-Carrié.

1946h    "Protecting the Future: Aiding the Work of Scientists Is Believed Best Safeguard." *The New York Times*, Sunday, December 8, section 4, p. 10E. Letter to the editor.

1947a    "Atoms, Nations, and Cultures." *International House Quarterly* 11, no. 2 (Spring): 47–50. Lecture delivered March 23, 1947, at International House, Columbia University.

** 1947b    "Sex and Culture." *Annals of the New York Academy of Sciences* 47, art. 5 (May 9): 647–60. Paper read to the Conference on Physiological and Psychological Factors in Sex Behavior, New York Academy of Sciences, Sections of Biology and Psychology, March 1, 1946. Reprinted in *Personal Character and Cultural Milieu*, edited by Douglas G. Haring, pp. 94–107. Syracuse, N.Y., 1948. 2nd rev. ed., pp. 133–46. Syracuse, N.Y.: Syracuse University Press, 1949. 3rd rev. ed., pp. 143–55. Syracuse, N.Y.: Syracuse University Press, 1956.

1947c    Review of *The Theory of Human Culture*, by James Feibleman. *Political Science Quarterly* 62, no. 3 (September): 428–30.

1947d    Comments on "In Quest of an Heuristic Approach to the Study of Mankind," by Laura Thompson. In *Approaches to Group Understanding* (Sixth Symposium of the Conference on Science, Philosophy and Religion, held August 23–27, 1945, at New York). Edited by Lyman Bryson, Louis Finkelstein, and R. M. MacIver, pp. 510 and 512–13. New York: Conference on Science, Philosophy and Religion in Their Relation to the Democratic Way of Life, Inc.

* 1949a    "Bali: The Value System of a Steady State." In *Social Structure: Studies Presented to A. R. Radcliffe-Brown*, edited by Meyer Fortes, pp. 35–53. Oxford: Clarendon Press. Reprint. New York: Russell & Russell, 1963. Reprinted in

*Traditional Balinese Culture,* edited by Jane Belo, pp. 384–401. New York and London: Columbia University Press, 1970. Excerpted, as a poem entitled "When the World Was Steady (after Bateson)," by David James, in *California State Poetry Quarterly* 3, no. 4 (Fall 1975): 51.

1949b    (With Jurgen Ruesch.) "Structure and Process in Social Relations." *Psychiatry* 12, no. 2 (May): 105–24. (Note: An accompanying Gregory Bateson bibliography may be found on pp. 205–6.)

1949c    Panelist comments in "An Open Forum on the Exhibition of Illusionism and Trompe L'Oeil" (held June 8, 1949, at the California Palace of the Legion of Honor, San Francisco). *Bulletin of the California Palace of the Legion of Honor* 7, nos. 3–4 (July–August): 14–35.

1949d    Remarks in "Modern Art Argument." [Report on the Western Round Table on Modern Art, held April 8–10, 1949, at San Francisco.] *Look* 13, no. 23 (November 8): 80–83. A more extensive abstract of the proceedings is reprinted in "The Western Round Table on Modern Art (1949)," edited by Douglas MacAgy. In *Modern Artists in America: First series,* edited by Robert Motherwell and Ad Reinhardt, pp. 24–39. New York: Wittenborn Schultz, Inc., [1951].

1950a    "Cultural Ideas about Aging." In *Research on Aging: Proceedings of a Conference held on August 7–10, 1950, at the University of California, Berkeley.* Social Science Research Council; Pacific Coast Committee on Old Age Research. Mimeographed. Edited by Harold E. Jones, pp. 49–54. New York: Social Science Research Council.

1950b    Conference remarks. In *Cybernetics: Circular Causal and Feedback Mechanisms in Biological and Social Systems; Transactions of the Sixth Conference* (held March 24–25, 1949, at New York). Conference on Cybernetics. Edited by Heinz von Foerster, pp. 14, 23, 57, 75, 76, 85, 89, 138, 152, 154, 157, 161, 164, 165, 181, 182, 185, 189, 200, 201, and 206. New York: Josiah Macy, Jr. Foundation.

1951a    (With Jurgen Ruesch.) *Communication: The Social Matrix of Psychiatry.* New York: Norton; Toronto: George McLeod. Reprint, with added "Preface to the 1968 Edition." New York: Norton, 1968. Reprint, with added "Preface to the 1987 Edition," by Paul Watzlawick. New York: Norton; Markham, Ontario: Penguin Books Canada Ltd., 1987. Excerpted (material from pp. 168–86 and 212–14), as "Information, Codification, and Metacommunication," in *Communication and Culture: Readings in the Codes of Human Interaction,* edited by Alfred G. Smith, pp. 412–26. New York: Holt, Rinehart & Winston, 1966.

* 1951b    "Why Do Frenchmen?" In *Impulse, Annual of Contemporary Dance, 1951,* edited by Marian Van Tuyl, pp. 21–24. San Francisco: Impulse Publications. Reprinted in *ETC.: A Review of General Semantics* 10, no. 2 (Winter 1953): 127–30. Also reprinted in *Language, Meaning and Maturity,* edited by S. I. Hayakawa, pp. 315–19. New York: Harper & Brothers, 1954. Also reprinted in *The Use and Misuse of Language,* edited by S. I. Hayakawa, pp. 187–91. New York: Fawcett World Library, 1962. Reprinted also in *Anthology of Impulse, Annual of Contemporary Dance, 1951–1966,* edited by Marian Van Tuyl, pp. 90–94. Brooklyn, N.Y.: Dance Horizons, 1969. Reprinted in *Steps to an Ecology of Mind* (cf. Bateson 1972a) as "Metalogue: Why Do Frenchmen?"

1951c    Conference remarks. In *Cybernetics: Circular Causal and Feedback Mechanisms in Biological and Social Systems; Transactions of the Seventh Conference* (held March 23–24, 1950, at New York). Conference on Cybernetics. Edited by Heinz von Foerster, Margaret Mead, and Hans Lukas Teuber, pp. 13, 26, 27, 44, 49, 78, 113, 140, 149, 150, 164, 165, 166, 169, 171, 182, 184, 185, 196, 201, 204, 222, 231, and 232. New York: Josiah Macy, Jr. Foundation.

1952    "Applied Metalinguistics and International Relations." *ETC.: A Review of General Semantics* 10, no. 1 (Autumn): 71–73.

1953a    "The Position of Humor in Human Communication." In *Cybernetics: Circular Causal and Feedback Mechanisms in Biological and Social Sciences; Transactions of the Ninth Conference* (held March 20–21, 1952, at New York). Conference on Cybernetics. Edited by Heinz von Foerster, Margaret Mead, and Hans Lukas Teuber, pp. 1–47. New York: Josiah Macy, Jr. Foundation. (Note: Additional remarks by Gregory Bateson may be found on pp. 65–66, 85, 89, 92, 95, 98, 106, 113, 114, 116, 119, 126, 137–38, 139, 140, 146, 147, 150, 152, and 158.) Excerpted in *Motivation in Humor*, edited by Jacob Levine, pp. 159–66. New York: Atherton, 1969.

* 1953b    "Metalogue: About Games and Being Serious." *ETC.: A Review of General Semantics* 10, no. 3 (Spring): 213–17.

* 1953c    "Metalogue: Daddy, How Much Do You Know?" *ETC.: A Review of General Semantics* 10, no. 4 (Summer): 311–15. Reprinted in *Psychology Newsletter* [of the Department of Mental Hygiene, State of California] 4, no. 3 (March 1962): 6–9. Mimeographed. Reprinted in *Steps to an Ecology of Mind* (cf. Bateson 1972a) as "Metalogue: How Much Do You Know?"

* 1953d    "Metalogue: Why Do Things Have Outlines?" *ETC.: A Review of General Semantics* 11, no. 1 (Autumn): 59–63.

* 1954    "Why a Swan?—A Metalogue." In *Impulse, Annual of Contemporary Dance, 1954,* edited by Marian Van Tuyl, pp. 23–26. San Francisco: Impulse Publications. Reprinted in *Anthology of Impulse, Annual of Contemporary Dance, 1951–1966,* edited by Marian Van Tuyl, pp. 95–99. Brooklyn, N.Y.: Dance Horizons, 1969. Reprinted in *Steps to an Ecology of Mind* (cf. Bateson 1972a) as "Metalogue: Why a Swan?"

* 1955a    "A Theory of Play and Fantasy: A Report on Theoretical Aspects of the Project for Study of the Role of Paradoxes of Abstraction in Communication." In *Approaches to the Study of Human Personality*, pp. 39–51. American Psychiatric Association. Psychiatric Research Reports, no. 2. Paper read (by Jay Haley) to a symposium of the American Psychiatric Association on Cultural, Anthropological, and Communications Approaches, March 11, 1954, at Mexico City. Reprinted in *Steps to an Ecology of Mind* (cf. Bateson 1972a) as "A Theory of Play and Fantasy." Also reprinted in *Play—Its Role in Development and Evolution,* edited by Jerome S. Bruner, Alison Jolly, and Kathy Silva, pp. 119–29. New York: Basic Books, Inc., 1976.

* 1955b    "How the Deviant Sees His Society." In *The Epidemiology of Mental Health*, pp. 25–31. Mimeographed. An Institute Sponsored by the Departments of Psychiatry and Psychology of the University of Utah and by the Veterans Administration Hospital, Fort Douglas Division, Salt Lake City, Utah, May 1955, at Brighton, Utah. (Note: Summaries of additional remarks by

Gregory Bateson may be found on pp. 22, 31, 32, 45, 62, and 78–79.) Reprinted, edited, in *Steps to an Ecology of Mind* (cf. Bateson 1972a) as "Epidemiology of a Schizophrenia."

1956a    Autobiographical sketch. In *Group Processes; Transactions of the Second Conference* (held October 9–12, 1955, at Princeton, New Jersey). Conference on Group Processes. Edited by Bertram Schaffner, pp. 11–12. New York: Josiah Macy, Jr. Foundation.

1956b    "The Message 'This is Play.'" In *Group Processes; Transactions of the Second Conference* (held October 9–12, 1955, at Princeton, New Jersey). Conference on Group Processes. Edited by Bertram Schaffner, pp. 145–242. New York: Josiah Macy, Jr. Foundation. (Note: Additional remarks by Gregory Bateson may be found on pp. 45, 46, 65–66, 74, 75, 77, 89, 101, 102, 105, 107, 112, 130, 131, 132, and 138.) Excerpted in *Child's Play*, edited by R. E. Herron and Brian Sutton-Smith, pp. 261–66. New York: John Wiley & Sons, 1971.

1956c    "Communication in Occupational Therapy." *American Journal of Occupational Therapy* 10, no. 4, Part II (July–August): 188.

* 1956d    (With Don D. Jackson, Jay Haley, and John Weakland.) "Toward a Theory of Schizophrenia." *Behavioral Science* 1, no. 4 (October): 251–64. Widely reprinted.

1957a    Autobiographical sketch. In *Group Processes; Transactions of the Third Conference* (held October 7–10, 1956, at Princeton, New Jersey). Conference on Group Processes. Edited by Bertram Schaffner, p. 9. New York: Josiah Macy, Jr. Foundation. (Note: Additional remarks by Gregory Bateson may be found on pp. 28, 35, 36, 40, 41, 44, 48, 49, 52, 57, 59, 61, 64, 65, 66, 67, 81, 83, 86, 89, 93, 114, 122, 124, 127, 130, 138–39, 145–46, 158, 163, 167, 169–70, 172–73, 174, 184–86, 190, 191, 206, 215, 232, 239, 241, 245, 246, 251, 263, 282, 284, 294, 296, and 302.)

1957b    Conference remarks. In *Conference on Perception and Personality*. [Report of the Conference on Perception and Personality, held April 6–7, 1957, sponsored by the Hacker Foundation for Psychiatric Research and Education, Beverly Hills, California.] Edited by Dorothy Mitchell, pp. 10, 42–43, 44, 45, 51, 62, 71, 85, 90, 92–93, 97, 112, 113, 114–15, 116, 117, 118, 119, 134, and 135. Beverly Hills, Calif.: Hacker Foundation.

1958a    *Naven: A Survey of the Problems suggested by a Composite Picture of the Culture of a New Guinea Tribe drawn from Three Points of View*, 2nd ed., with added "Preface to the Second Edition" and "Epilogue 1958." Stanford: Stanford University Press; London: Oxford University Press. Reprint. Stanford: Stanford University Press, 1965; London: Oxford University Press, 1965; London: Wildwood House, 1980. (cf. Bateson 1936a). Excerpted, as "A Selection from *Naven*," in *Anthropology of Folk Religion*, edited by Charles Leslie, pp. 261–98. New York: Vintage Books, 1960. A different excerpt, entitled "Sex Ethos and the Iatmul *Naven* Ceremony," appears in *Personalities and Cultures*, edited by Robert Cushman Hunt, pp. 204–12. Garden City, N.Y.: Natural History Press, 1967. "Epilogue 1958" is reprinted in *A Sacred Unity* (cf. Bateson 1991a) under the title "*Naven*: Epilogue 1958."

** 1958b    "Language and Psychotherapy—Frieda Fromm-Reichmann's Last Project." *Psychiatry* 21, no. 1 (February): 96–100. The Frieda Fromm-Reichmann

Memorial Lecture, delivered June 3, 1957, at the Veterans Administration Hospital, Palo Alto, California.

1958c "Schizophrenic Distortions of Communication." In *Psychotherapy of Chronic Schizophrenic Patients.* Sea Island Conference on Psychotherapy of Chronic Schizophrenic Patients, sponsored by Little, Brown & Co., October 15–17, 1955, at Sea Island, Georgia. Edited by Carl Whitaker, pp. 31–56. Boston and Toronto: Little, Brown & Co.; London: J. & A. Churchill. (Note: Additional remarks by Gregory Bateson may be found on pp. 4, 5, 7, 8, 9, 10–11, 18, 19, 20, 21, 23, 24, 65, 67–69, 72, 75, 77–78, 79, 89, 91, 97, 102, 106, 114, 115, 116, 120, 127, 131–32, 133, 139, 146, 151, 154, 155, 161, 163, 165, 166–67, 174, 175, 176, 187, 189, 190, 195, 204–5, 217, and 218.)

1958d "Analysis of Group Therapy in an Admission Ward, United States Naval Hospital, Oakland, California." In *Social Psychiatry in Action: A Therapeutic Community,* edited by Harry A. Wilmer, pp. 334–49. Springfield, Ill.: Charles C. Thomas.

** 1958e "The New Conceptual Frames for Behavioral Research." In *Proceedings of the Sixth Annual Psychiatric Institute* (held September 17, 1958, at the New Jersey Neuro-Psychiatric Institute, Princeton, New Jersey), pp. 54–71. n.p.

1959a Letter in response to "Role and Status of Anthropological Theories," by Sidney Morganbesser. *Science* 129 (February 6): 294–98.

1959b Remarks in "Memorial to Dr. Fromm-Reichmann." In *Group Processes; Transactions of the Fourth Conference* (held October 13–16, 1957, at Princeton, New Jersey). Conference on Group Processes. Edited by Bertram Schaffner, p. 7. New York: Josiah Macy, Jr. Foundation.

1959c Autobiographical sketch. In *Group Processes; Transactions of the Fourth Conference* (held October 13–16, 1957, at Princeton, New Jersey). Conference on Group Processes. Edited by Bertram Schaffner, pp. 13–14. New York: Josiah Macy, Jr. Foundation. (Note: Additional remarks by Gregory Bateson may be found on pp. 42, 46, 87, 112, 116, 129, 141, 142, 143, 144, 149, 150, 152, 154–55, 157, 166, 170, 176, 177, 178, 213, 216, and 248.)

1959d Panel Review. In *Individual and Familial Dynamics,* Vol. 2 of *Science and Psychoanalysis.* [Report of a meeting of The Academy of Psychoanalysis held May 10–11, 1958, at San Francisco.] Academy of Psychoanalysis, Chicago. Edited by Jules H. Masserman, pp. 207–11. New York: Grune & Stratton.

** 1959e "Cultural Problems Posed by a Study of Schizophrenic Process." In *Schizophrenia: An Integrated Approach.* [American Psychiatric Association symposium of the Hawaiian Divisional Meeting, 1958, San Francisco.] Symposium on Schizophrenia. Edited by Alfred Auerback, pp. 125–46. New York: Ronald Press Co. (With Discussion by Robert A. Kimmich, pp. 143–45.) Reprinted, edited, in *A Sacred Unity* (cf. Bateson 1991a).

* 1960a "The Group Dynamics of Schizophrenia." In *Chronic Schizophrenia: Explorations in Theory and Treatment.* Institute on Chronic Schizophrenia and Hospital Treatment Programs, State Hospital, Osawatomie, Kansas, October 1–3, 1958. Edited by Lawrence Appleby, Jordan M. Scher, and John Cumming, pp. 90–105. Glencoe, Ill.: Free Press; London: Collier-Macmillan.

1960b Discussion of "Families of Schizophrenic and of Well Children," by Samuel J. Beck. *American Journal of Orthopsychiatry* 30, no. 2 (April): 263–66. 36th

Annual Meeting of the American Orthopsychiatric Association, March 30–April 1, 1959, San Francisco.

* 1960c   "Minimal Requirements for a Theory of Schizophrenia." *A.M.A. Archives of General Psychiatry* 2 (May): 477–91. Second Annual Albert D. Lasker Memorial Lecture, delivered April 7, 1959, at the Institute for Psychosomatic and Psychiatric Research and Training of the Michael Reese Hospital, Chicago.

1960d   Conference remarks. In *Group Processes; Transactions of the Fifth Conference* (held October 12–15, 1958, at Princeton, New Jersey). Conference on Group Processes. Edited by Bertram Schaffner, pp. 12, 14, 20, 21, 22, 34, 35, 54, 56, 57, 61, 63, 65, 66, 96, 108–9, 120, 124, 125, and 177. New York: Josiah Macy, Jr. Foundation.

1960e   Conference remarks. In *The Use of LSD in Psychotherapy; Transactions of a Conference on d-Lysergic Acid Diethylamide (LSD-25)* (held April 22–24, 1959, at Princeton, New Jersey). Conference on d-Lysergic Acid Diethylamide (LSD-25). Edited by Harold A. Abramson, pp. 10, 19, 25, 28, 35–36, 37, 39–40, 48, 51, 58, 61, 62, 88, 98, 100, 117, 134, 155, 156, 158, 159, 162, 163, 164, 165, 183, 185, 187–88, 189, 190, 191–92, 193, 210, 211, 213, 214, 218, 222, 225, 231, 234–35, and 236. New York: Josiah Macy, Jr. Foundation.

1961a   *Perceval's Narrative: A Patient's Account of His Psychosis, 1830–1832,* by John Perceval. Edited and with an Introduction by Gregory Bateson. Stanford: Stanford University Press; London: Hogarth Press, 1962. (Paperback edition. New York: William Morrow & Co., 1974.)

1961b   "The Biosocial Integration of Behavior in the Schizophrenic Family." In *Exploring the Base for Family Therapy.* M. Robert Gomberg Memorial Conference (held June 2–3, 1960, at the New York Academy of Medicine). Edited by Nathan W. Ackerman, Frances L. Beatman, and Sanford N. Sherman, pp. 116–22. New York: Family Service Association of America. Reprinted in *Therapy, Communication, and Change,* Vol. 2 of *Human Communication,* edited by Don D. Jackson, pp. 9–15. Palo Alto, Calif.: Science and Behavior Books, Inc., 1968.

1961c   "Formal Research in Family Structure." In *Exploring the Base for Family Therapy.* M. Robert Gomberg Memorial Conference (held June 2–3, 1960, at the New York Academy of Medicine). Edited by Nathan W. Ackerman, Frances L. Beatman, and Sanford N. Sherman, pp. 136–40. New York: Family Service Association of America. (Note: A summary of an additional comment by Gregory Bateson may be found on p. 144.)

** 1963a   "A Social Scientist Views the Emotions." In *Expression of the Emotions in Man.* Symposium on Expression of the Emotions in Man (held at the meeting of the American Association for the Advancement of Science, December 29–30, 1960, at New York). Edited by Peter H. Knapp, pp. 230–36. New York: International Universities Press.

1963b   "Exchange of Information about Patterns of Human Behavior." In *Information Storage and Neural Control.* Houston Neurological Society Tenth Annual Scientific Meeting, 1962, jointly sponsored by the Department of Neurology, Baylor University College of Medicine, Texas Medical Center, Houston, Texas. Edited by William S. Fields and Walter Abbott, pp. 173–86. Springfield, Ill.: Charles C. Thomas. (Includes Discussion, pp. 184–86.) (Note: Additional shorter remarks by Gregory Bateson may be found on pp.

25, 242, 296, and 372–74.)

1963c   (With Don D. Jackson, Jay Haley, and John H. Weakland.) "A Note on the Double Bind—1962." *Family Process* 2, no. 1 (March): 154–61. Reprinted in *Communication, Family, and Marriage,* Vol. 1 of *Human Communication,* edited by Don D. Jackson, pp. 55–62. Palo Alto, Calif.: Science and Behavior Books, Inc., 1968. Also reprinted in *Double Bind: The Foundation of the Communicational Approach to the Family,* edited by Carlos E. Sluzki and Donald C. Ransom, pp. 39–42. New York: Grune & Stratton, 1976.

* 1963d   "The Role of Somatic Change in Evolution." *Evolution* 17, no. 4 (December 24): 529–39.

1964a   (With Don D. Jackson.) "Some Varieties of Pathogenic Organization." In *Disorders of Communication.* Proceedings of the Association, December 7–8, 1962, at New York. Association for Research in Nervous and Mental Disease, Research Publications, Vol. 42. Edited by David McK. Rioch and Edwin A. Weinstein, pp. 270–90. Baltimore: Williams & Wilkins Co.; Edinburgh: E. & S. Livingstone. (Includes Discussion, pp. 283–90.) (Note: Additional remarks by Gregory Bateson appear on pp. 84–85.) Reprinted (without the Discussion) in *Communication, Family, and Marriage,* Vol. 1 of *Human Communication,* edited by Don D. Jackson, pp. 200–215. Palo Alto, Calif.: Science and Behavior Books, Inc., 1968.

1964b   "Preface." In *An Anthology of Human Communication, Text and Tape,* by Paul Watzlawick, p. iv. Palo Alto, Calif.: Science and Behavior Books, Inc. Revised edition, 1974.

1964c   Patient-Therapist Dialogue with Interpretation. In *An Anthology of Human Communication, Text and Tape,* by Paul Watzlawick, pp. 36–37. Palo Alto, Calif.: Science and Behavior Books, Inc. Revised edition, 1974.

1965   "Communication Among the Higher Vertebrates (Abstract)." In *Proceedings of the Hawaiian Academy of Sciences, Fortieth Annual Meeting, 1964–1965* (held May 22, 1965, at Honolulu), p. 21. Honolulu: University of Hawaii. (Note: The abstract, though not actually written by Bateson, was based on a transcript of his talk and was approved by him for publication.)

1966a   "Communication Theories in Relation to the Etiology of the Neuroses." In *The Etiology of the Neuroses.* [Report of a symposium sponsored by the Society of Medical Psychoanalysts, March 17–18, 1962, at New York.] Edited by Joseph H. Merin, pp. 28–35. Palo Alto, Calif.: Science and Behavior Books, Inc.

* 1966b   "Problems in Cetacean and Other Mammalian Communication." In *Whales, Dolphins, and Porpoises.* International Symposium on Cetacean Research (sponsored by the American Institute of Biological Sciences, August, 1963, Washington, D.C.). Edited by Kenneth S. Norris, pp. 569–79. Berkeley and Los Angeles: University of California Press. (Includes Comments, pp. 578–79.)

1966c   "Threads in the Cybernetic Pattern." In *Proceedings from The Cybernetics Revolution Symposium* (sponsored by The Symposia Committee, Associated Students of the University of Hawaii, held February 28–March 4, 1966, at the University of Hawaii, Honolulu, Hawaii). Mimeographed. Honolulu: The Symposia Committee of the Associated Students of the University of Hawaii.

1966d   "Slippery Theories." *International Journal of Psychiatry* 2, no. 4 (July): 415–17.

Comment on "Family Interaction Processes and Schizophrenia: A Review of Current Theories," by Elliot G. Mishler and Nancy E. Waxler. Reprinted in *Family Processes and Schizophrenia*, edited by Elliot G. Mishler and Nancy E. Waxler, pp. 278–81. New York: Science House, 1969.

\* 1967a   "Cybernetic Explanation." *American Behavioral Scientist* 10, no. 8 (April): 29–32.

1967b   "Consciousness versus nature." *Peace News*, no. 1622 (July 28): 10. Synopsis by Gregory Bateson of 1968b, "Conscious Purpose Versus Nature."

1967c   Review of *Person, Time, and Conduct in Bali: An Essay in Cultural Analysis*, by Clifford Geertz. *American Anthropologist* 69, no. 6 (December): 765–66.

\* 1968a   "Redundancy and Coding." In *Animal Communication: Techniques of Study and Results of Research.* [Report of the Wenner-Gren Conference on Animal Communication, held June 13–22, 1965, at Burg Wartenstein, Austria.] Edited by Thomas A. Sebeok, pp. 614–26. Bloomington, Ind., and London: Indiana University Press.

\* 1968b   "Conscious Purpose Versus Nature." In *The Dialectics of Liberation*, edited by David Cooper, pp. 34–49. Congress on the Dialectics of Liberation, held July 15–20, 1967, at London. Harmondsworth, England; Baltimore; Victoria, Australia: Penguin Books, Pelican Books. Reprinted under the title *To Free a Generation: The Dialectics of Liberation*. New York: Macmillan Co., Collier Books, 1969.

1968c   "On Dreams and Animal Behavior." [". . . a fragment of a metalogue by Gregory Bateson which will be published in Thomas A. Sebeok and Alexandra Ramsay (Eds) *Approaches to Animal Communication*, The Hague, Mouton and Co."] *Family Process* 7, no. 2 (September): 292–98. Excerpt from "Metalogue: What is an Instinct?" (cf. Bateson 1969a).

1968d   Review of *Primate Ethology*, edited by Desmond Morris. *American Anthropologist* 70, no. 5 (October): 1034–35.

\* 1969a   "Metalogue: What is an Instinct?" In *Approaches to Animal Communication*, edited by Thomas A. Sebeok and Alexandra Ramsay, pp. 11–30. The Hague and Paris: Mouton & Co.

1969b   Comment on "The Study of Language and Communication across Species," by Harvey B. Sarles. *Current Anthropology* 10, nos. 2–3 (April–June): 215.

\* 1970a   "Form, Substance, and Difference." *General Semantics Bulletin*, no. 37: 5–13. The Nineteenth Annual Alfred Korzybski Memorial Lecture, delivered January 9, 1970, at New York. Reprinted in *Io* 14 (Earth Geography Booklet No. 3) (Summer 1972): 127–40. Also reprinted in *Ecology and Consciousness*, edited by Richard Grossinger, pp. 30–42. Richmond, Calif.: North Atlantic Books, 1978.

\* 1970b   "On Empty-Headedness Among Biologists and State Boards of Education." *BioScience* 20, no. 14 (July 15): 819. (Note: Excluded from first four printings of the Ballantine paperback edition of *Steps to an Ecology of Mind* (cf. Bateson 1972a).)

1970c   "An Open Letter to Anatol Rapoport." *ETC.: A Review of General Semantics* 27, no. 3 (September): 359–63.

\*\* 1970d   "The Message of Reinforcement." In *Language Behavior: A Book of Readings in Communication.* Janua Linguarum: Studia Memoriae Nicolai Van Wijk Dedicata, Series Maior, 41. Edited by Johnnye Akin, Alvin Goldberg, Gail

Myers, and Joseph Stewart, pp. 62–72. The Hague and Paris: Mouton & Co.

\* 1971a   "The Cybernetics of 'Self': A Theory of Alcoholism." *Psychiatry* 34, no. 1 (February): 1–18. Reprinted in *Readings in Abnormal Psychology: Contemporary Perspectives*, edited by Lawrence R. Allman and Dennis T. Jaffe, pp. 284–91. New York: Harper and Row, 1976.

1971b   "Chapter 1: Communication." In *The Natural History of an Interview*, edited by Norman A. McQuown. University of Chicago Library Microfilm Collection of Manuscripts in Cultural Anthropology, series 15, no. 95. 35 pp.

1971c   "Chapter 5: The Actors and the Setting." In *The Natural History of an Interview*, edited by Norman A. McQuown. University of Chicago Library Microfilm Collection of Manuscripts in Cultural Anthropology, series 15, no. 95. 5 pp.

1971d   Remarks on the by-products of The Natural History of an Interview research project. In "Chapter 10: Summary, Conclusions, and Outlook," by Norman A. McQuown, pp. 4–5. *The Natural History of an Interview*, edited by Norman A. McQuown. University of Chicago Library Microfilm Collection of Manuscripts in Cultural Anthropology, series 15, no. 97.

1971e   "Comment" [on "An Open Letter to Gregory Bateson," by Sheldon Ruderman]. *ETC.: A Review of General Semantics* 28, no. 2 (June): 239–40.

\*\* 1971f   "A Systems Approach." *International Journal of Psychiatry* 9: 242–44. Evaluation of "Family Therapy," by Jay Haley. Reprinted, edited, in *A Sacred Unity* (cf. Bateson 1991a).

\* 1971g   "A Re-Examination of 'Bateson's Rule.'" *Journal of Genetics* 60, no. 3 (September): 230–40.

\* 1971h   "Restructuring the Ecology of a Great City." *Radical Software* 1, no. 3: 2–3. Paper prepared for the Wenner-Gren Symposium on Restructuring the Ecology of a Great City, held October 26–31, 1970, at New York; Gregory Bateson, Chairman. Reprinted in *Io* 14 (Earth Geography Booklet No. 3) (Summer 1972): 140–49. Reprinted, edited and with an additional post-symposium section on 'The Transmission of Theory,' in *Steps to an Ecology of Mind* (cf. Bateson 1972a) under the title "Ecology and Flexibility in Urban Civilization."

1972a   *Steps to an Ecology of Mind: Collected Essays in Anthropology, Psychiatry, Evolution, and Epistemology*. San Francisco, Scranton, London, Toronto: Chandler Publishing Company. Reprint, with added "1987 Preface" by Mary Catherine Bateson. Northvale, N.J.; London: Jason Aronson Inc., 1987. (Note: The material on pp. vii–xxvi of the reprint differs in pagination from the original edition. Two items are also omitted at the end of Part I of the Bibliography in the reprint.) (Paperback editions. New York: Ballantine Books, 1972. England: Paladin, 1973, with a preface by Adam Kuper.) (Note: The first four printings of the Ballantine edition lack an index as well as the essay "On Empty-Headedness Among Biologists and State Boards of Education." The fifth and later printings [December 1976–the present] are easily identifiable by their primarily white cover [as opposed to the previous primarily blue, brown and green, or yellow covers].)

\* 1972b   "Metalogue: Why Do Things Get in a Muddle?" In *Steps to an Ecology of Mind*. (Written 1948.)

\* 1972c   "From Versailles to Cybernetics." In *Steps to an Ecology of Mind*. Lecture delivered to the Two Worlds Symposium, April 21, 1966, at Sacramento State College, California.

* 1972d   "Style, Grace, and Information in Primitive Art." In *Steps to an Ecology of Mind*. Reprinted, with additional photograph and minor editorial changes, in *Primitive Art and Society*. [Report of the Wenner-Gren Symposium on Primitive Art and Society, held June 27–July 5, 1967, at Burg Wartenstein, Austria.] Edited by Anthony Forge, pp. 235–55. New York: Oxford University Press, 1973. (Note: All printings of the American paperback edition of *Steps to an Ecology of Mind* exclude the photograph of the Balinese painting discussed in the article.)

* 1972e   "The Logical Categories of Learning and Communication." In *Steps to an Ecology of Mind*. Expanded version of "The Logical Categories of Learning and Communication, and the Acquisition of World Views," a paper given at the Wenner-Gren Symposium on World Views: Their Nature and Their Role in Culture, held August 2–11, 1968, at Burg Wartenstein, Austria. (Written in 1964, except for the section on 'Learning III,' which was added in 1971.)

* 1972f   "Pathologies of Epistemology." In *Steps to an Ecology of Mind*. Reprinted in *Transcultural Research in Mental Health*, Vol. 2 of *Mental Health Research in Asia and the Pacific*. [Report of the Second Conference on Culture and Mental Health in Asia and the Pacific, held March 17–21, 1969, at Honolulu, Hawaii.] Edited by William P. Lebra, pp. 383–90. Honolulu: The University Press of Hawaii, 1972.

* 1972g   "Double Bind, 1969." In *Steps to an Ecology of Mind*. Paper given at the Annual Meeting of the American Psychological Association, held September 2, 1969, at Washington, D.C. Reprinted in *Double Bind: The Foundation of the Communicational Approach to the Family*, edited by Carlos E. Sluzki and Donald C. Ransom, pp. 237–42. New York: Grune & Stratton, 1976.

* 1972h   "The Roots of Ecological Crisis." In *Steps to an Ecology of Mind*. Prepared for the University of Hawaii Committee on Ecology and Man as testimony before a committee of the Hawaii State Senate, March 1970, originally entitled "Statement on Problems Which Will Confront the Proposed Office of Environmental Quality in Government and an Environmental Center at the University of Hawaii." Excerpted, as "Awake!" ["Up Against the Environment or Ourselves?"], in *Radical Software* 1, no. 5 (Spring 1972): 33.

* 1972i   "Effects of Conscious Purpose on Human Adaptation." In *Steps to an Ecology of Mind*. Invitational Paper for the Wenner-Gren Symposium on the Effects of Conscious Purpose on Human Adaptation, held July 17–24, 1968, at Burg Wartenstein, Austria; Gregory Bateson, Chairman. Condensed version reprinted in *Our Own Metaphor: A Personal Account of a Conference on the Effects of Conscious Purpose on Human Adaptation*, by Mary Catherine Bateson, pp. 13–17. New York: Alfred A. Knopf, 1972.

* 1972j   "The Science of Mind and Order." Introduction to *Steps to an Ecology of Mind*.

  1972k   Comments in *Our Own Metaphor: A Personal Account of a Conference on the Effects of Conscious Purpose on Human Adaptation*, by Mary Catherine Bateson. [Report of the Wenner-Gren Conference on the Effects of Conscious Purpose on Human Adaptation, held July 17–24, 1968, at Burg Wartenstein, Austria; Gregory Bateson, Chairman.] New York: Alfred A.

Knopf. 2nd ed., with a new foreword and afterword by the author. Washington, D.C.: Smithsonian Institution Press, 1991. (Note: The book contains extensive remarks by Gregory Bateson as well as an abridged version of 1972i.)

1973a    "Both Sides of the Necessary Paradox." An interview with Gregory Bateson edited by Stewart Brand. *Harper's* 247, no. 1482 (November): 20–37. Reprinted in *II Cybernetic Frontiers,* edited by Stewart Brand, pp. 9–38. New York: Random House, 1974. (Note: The reprint contains a short additional interview.)

1973b    "A Conversation with Gregory Bateson," edited by Lee Thayer. In *Communication: Ethical and Moral Issues,* edited by Lee Thayer, pp. 247–48. London and New York: Gordon & Breach.

** 1973c    "Mind/Environment," edited by Vic Gioscia. *Social Change,* no. 1: 6–21. Lecture to Department of Psychiatry Grand Rounds, Roosevelt Hospital, New York, in 1969. Reprinted, edited, in *A Sacred Unity* (cf. Bateson 1991a).

1974a    "Observations of a Cetacean Community." In *Mind in the Waters: A Book to Celebrate the Consciousness of Whales and Dolphins,* assembled by Joan McIntyre, pp. 146–65. New York: Charles Scribner's Sons; Toronto: McClelland and Stewart.

** 1974b    "Distortions under Culture Contact." In *Youth, Socialization, and Mental Health,* Vol. 3 of *Mental Health Research in Asia and the Pacific.* [Report of the Third Conference on Culture and Mental Health in Asia and the Pacific, held March 15–19, 1971, at Honolulu, Hawaii.] Edited by William P. Lebra, pp. 197–99. Honolulu: The University Press of Hawaii.

1974c    "Gratitude for Death." *BioScience* 24, no. 1 (January): 8. Letter in response to "Permission to Die," by Eric J. Cassell.

1974d    "Energy Does Not Explain." *CoEvolution Quarterly,* no. 1 (Spring): 45. Reprinted in *Whole Earth Epilog,* edited by Stewart Brand, p. 468. Baltimore: Penguin Books, 1974.

1974e    Review of *Septem Sermones ad Mortuos,* by C. G. Jung. *Harper's* 248, no. 1487 (April): 105. Reprinted in *Whole Earth Epilog,* edited by Stewart Brand, p. 749. Baltimore: Penguin Books, 1974. Also reprinted in *The Next Whole Earth Catalog,* edited by Stewart Brand, p. 592. New York: Random House, 1980. 2nd ed., p. 592. New York: Random House, 1981.

1974f    "Conditioning." In *Cybernetics of Cybernetics.* (Biological Computer Laboratory Report No. 73.38.) Edited by Heinz von Foerster, pp. 97–98. Urbana, Ill.: The Biological Computer Laboratory, University of Illinois.

1974g    "Adaptation." In *Cybernetics of Cybernetics.* (Biological Computer Laboratory Report No. 73.38.) Edited by Heinz von Foerster, pp. 98–101. Urbana, Ill.: The Biological Computer Laboratory, University of Illinois.

1974h    "Learning Model." In *Cybernetics of Cybernetics.* (Biological Computer Laboratory Report No. 73.38.) Edited by Heinz von Foerster, p. 299. Urbana, Ill.: The Biological Computer Laboratory, University of Illinois.

1974i    "Double-Bind." In *Cybernetics of Cybernetics.* (Biological Computer Laboratory Report No. 73.38.) Edited by Heinz von Foerster, pp. 419–20. Urbana, Ill.: The Biological Computer Laboratory, University of Illinois.

1974j    Review of *Advanced Techniques of Hypnosis and Therapy: Selected Papers of Milton H. Erickson, M.D.,* edited by Jay Haley. In *Whole Earth Epilog,* edited by Stewart Brand, p. 741. Baltimore: Penguin Books. Reprinted in *The Next*

*Whole Earth Catalog,* edited by Stewart Brand, p. 581. New York: Random House, 1980. 2nd ed., p. 581. New York: Random House, 1981.

** 1974k  "The Creature and Its Creations." *CoEvolution Quarterly,* no. 4 (Winter): 24–25. Reprinted, edited, in *A Sacred Unity* (cf. Bateson 1991a).

1974l  "DRAFT: Scattered Thoughts for a Conference on 'Broken Power.'" *CoEvolution Quarterly,* no. 4 (Winter): 26–27. Paper prepared for a conference entitled "After Robert Moses, What?: an exploration of new ways of governing cities and institutions," held November 22–24, 1974, at Tarrytown, New York.

1974m  "Reading Suggested by Gregory Bateson." *CoEvolution Quarterly,* no. 4 (Winter): 28. (Note: A minor quotation regarding poets laureate may be found on the same page.)

1974n  Review of *Acting: The First Six Lessons,* by Richard Boleslavsky. *CoEvolution Quarterly,* no. 4 (Winter): 120. Reprinted in *The Next Whole Earth Catalog,* edited by Stewart Brand, p. 471. New York: Random House, 1980. 2nd ed., p. 471. New York: Random House, 1981.

1974o  Review of *Tracks,* by E. A. R. Ennion and N. Tinbergen. *CoEvolution Quarterly,* no. 4 (Winter): 123.

** 1975a  "Ecology of Mind: The Sacred." In *Loka: A Journal from Naropa Institute,* edited by Rick Fields, pp. 24–27. Garden City, N.Y.: Anchor Books. Talk delivered at Naropa Institute, Boulder, Colorado, in the summer of 1974.

1975b  "A Conversation with Gregory Bateson," edited by Rick Fields and Richard Greene. In *Loka: A Journal from Naropa Institute,* edited by Rick Fields, pp. 28–34. Garden City, N.Y.: Anchor Books.

1975c  "Introduction." In *The Structure of Magic: A Book About Language and Therapy,* by Richard Bandler and John Grinder, pp. ix–xi. Palo Alto, Calif.: Science and Behavior Books.

1975d  "What Energy Isn't." *CoEvolution Quarterly,* no. 5 (Spring): 29. A letter dated December 4, 1974.

1975e  Letter in "Counsel for a Suicide's Friend." *CoEvolution Quarterly,* no. 5 (Spring): 137. A letter dated May 27, 1973. Reprinted in *The Next Whole Earth Catalog,* edited by Stewart Brand, p. 332. New York: Random House, 1980. 2nd ed., p. 336. New York: Random House, 1981. Also reprinted in *News That Stayed News, 1974–1984: Ten Years of CoEvolution Quarterly,* edited by Art Kleiner and Stewart Brand, pp. 44–45. San Francisco: North Point Press, 1986.

** 1975f  "Some Components of Socialization for Trance." *Ethos* 3, no. 2 (Summer): 143–55. Reprinted in *Socialization as Cultural Communication,* edited by Theodore Schwartz, pp. 51–63. Berkeley, Calif.: University of California Press, 1976.

1975g  "'Reality' and Redundancy." *CoEvolution Quarterly,* no. 6 (Summer): 132–35.

1975h  (With Edmund G. Brown, Jr.) "Caring and Clarity: Conversation with Gregory Bateson and Edmund G. Brown, Jr., Governor of California," edited by Stewart Brand. *CoEvolution Quarterly,* no. 7 (Fall): 32–47.

1975i  Comments in *Edited Transcript AHP Theory Conference.* [Report of Association for Humanistic Psychology Theory Conference, held April 4–6, 1975, at Tucson, Arizona.] Edited by Rick Gilbert, pp. 12, 13, 14, 15, 16, 18–19, 43–44, and 53–54. San Francisco: Association for Humanistic Psychology.

** 1976a    "Orders of Change." In *Loka II: A Journal from Naropa Institute*, edited by Rick Fields, pp. 59–63. Garden City, N.Y.: Anchor Books. Lecture delivered August 10, 1975, at Naropa Institute, Boulder, Colorado.

1976b    (With Governor Jerry Brown.) "Prayer Breakfast." *CoEvolution Quarterly*, no. 9 (Spring): 82–84. Remarks delivered to the annual Governor's Prayer Breakfast, January 8, 1976, at Sacramento, California, with the Governor's response. Excerpted in *The Esalen Catalog* 20, no. 1 (January–June 1981): 8–9. Also excerpted in Chapter 7 of *Angels Fear* (cf. Bateson 1987).

** 1976c    "Foreword: A Formal Approach to *Explicit, Implicit,* and *Embodied* Ideas and to Their Forms of Interaction." In *Double Bind: The Foundation of the Communicational Approach to the Family*, edited by Carlos E. Sluzki and Donald C. Ransom, pp. xi–xvi. New York: Grune & Stratton. Reprinted in *A Sacred Unity* (cf. Bateson 1991a) as "A Formal Approach to *Explicit, Implicit,* and *Embodied* Ideas and to Their Forms of Interaction."

1976d    "A Comment by Gregory Bateson." In *Double Bind: The Foundation of the Communicational Approach to the Family*, edited by Carlos E. Sluzki and Donald C. Ransom, pp. 105–6. New York: Grune & Stratton. Comment on "Development of a Theory: A History of a Research Project," by Jay Haley.

1976e    (With Margaret Mead.) "For God's Sake, Margaret: Conversation with Gregory Bateson and Margaret Mead," edited by Stewart Brand. *CoEvolution Quarterly*, no. 10 (Summer): 32–44. Reprinted, with different introduction by Stewart Brand, in *News That Stayed News, 1974–1984: Ten Years of CoEvolution Quarterly*, edited by Art Kleiner and Stewart Brand, pp. 26–44. San Francisco: North Point Press, 1986. Reprinted in part as "Margaret Mead and Gregory Bateson on the Use of the Camera in Anthropology," in *Studies in the Anthropology of Visual Communication* 4, no. 2 (Winter 1977): 78–80.

1976f    "The Oak Beams of New College, Oxford." *CoEvolution Quarterly*, no. 10 (Summer): 66. Reprinted in *Organic Gardening and Farming* 24, no. 8 (August 1977): 183. Also reprinted in *The Next Whole Earth Catalog*, edited by Stewart Brand, p. 77. New York: Random House, 1980. 2nd ed., p. 77. New York: Random House, 1981.

1976g    "Invitational Paper." *CoEvolution Quarterly*, no. 11 (Fall): 56–57. Paper prepared for the Mind/Body Dualism Conference, held July 27–30, 1976, at Marin County, California; Gregory Bateson, Chairman.

** 1976h    "The Case Against the Case for Mind/Body Dualism." *CoEvolution Quarterly*, no. 12 (Winter): 94–95. A reply to "The case FOR Mind/Body dualism," by Charles T. Tart.

** 1977a    "The Thing of It Is." In *Earth's Answer: Explorations of Planetary Culture at the Lindisfarne Conferences*, edited by Michael Katz, William P. Marsh, and Gail Gordon Thompson, pp. 143–54. New York: Lindisfarne Books/Harper & Row. Talk delivered to a Summer 1975 Lindisfarne Conference.

** 1977b    "Epilogue: The Growth of Paradigms for Psychiatry." In *Communication and Social Interaction: Clinical and Therapeutic Aspects of Human Behavior*, edited by Peter F. Ostwald, pp. 331–37. New York: Grune & Stratton. Talk delivered November 17, 1976, to the Langley Porter Clinic, San Francisco. Reprinted in *A Sacred Unity* (cf. Bateson 1991a) as "The Growth of Paradigms for Psychiatry."

** 1977c    "Afterword." In *About Bateson: Essays on Gregory Bateson*, edited by John

Brockman, pp. 235–47. New York: E. P. Dutton. Reprint. London: Wildwood House, 1978. Reprinted, edited, in *A Sacred Unity* (cf. Bateson 1991a) as "This Normative Natural History Called Epistemology."

1977d   "Play and Paradigm." [Keynote Address, delivered April 8, 1977, at the Third Annual Meetings of The Association for the Anthropological Study of Play, held at San Diego. Transcribed, edited, and annotated by Phillips Stevens, Jr.] *The Association for the Anthropological Study of Play Newsletter* 4, no. 1 (Summer): 2–8. Revised, with the assistance of Gregory Bateson, and reprinted in *Play: Anthropological Perspectives* [1977 Proceedings of the Association for the Anthropological Study of Play], edited by Michael A. Salter, pp. 7–16. West Point, N.Y.: Leisure Press, 1978. A still differently edited version appears in *Play and Culture* 1, no. 1 (February 1988): 20–27.

1978a   "Towards a Theory of Cultural Coherence: Comment." *Anthropological Quarterly* 51, no. 1 (January): 77–78. Remarks delivered to a symposium on Sepik Politics: Traditional Authority and Initiative, at the 75th annual meeting of the American Anthropological Association, held November 17–21, 1976, at Washington, D.C.

1978b   "A Conversation with Gregory Bateson Conducted by John Welwood." *Re-Vision* 1, no. 2 (Spring): 43–49.

\*\* 1978c   "Intelligence, Experience, and Evolution." *Re-Vision* 1, no. 2 (Spring): 50–55. Adapted from a lecture delivered March 24, 1975, at Naropa Institute, Boulder, Colorado. Readapted from the original tape recording for publication in *A Sacred Unity* (cf. Bateson 1991a).

1978d   "Number is Different from Quantity." *CoEvolution Quarterly*, no. 17 (Spring): 44–46.

1978e   "Protect the Trophies, Slay the Children." *CoEvolution Quarterly*, no. 17 (Spring): 46. Reprinted in *News That Stayed News, 1974–1984: Ten Years of CoEvolution Quarterly*, edited by Art Kleiner and Stewart Brand, pp. 45–46. San Francisco: North Point Press, 1986.

\*\* 1978f   "The Double-Bind Theory—Misunderstood?" *Psychiatric News* 13 (April 21): 40–41. Reprinted with minor editorial changes as "Theory versus Empiricism," in *Beyond the Double Bind: Communication and Family Systems, Theories, and Techniques with Schizophrenics*, edited by Milton M. Berger, pp. 234–37. New York: Brunner/Mazel, 1978. Reprinted, again with minor editorial changes, in *A Sacred Unity* (cf. Bateson 1991a).

\*\* 1978g   "The Birth of a Matrix, or Double Bind and Epistemology." In *Beyond the Double Bind: Communication and Family Systems, Theories, and Techniques with Schizophrenics*, edited by Milton M. Berger, pp. 39–64. New York: Brunner/Mazel. Address delivered to a conference entitled "Beyond the Double Bind," held March 3–4, 1977, at New York. (Note: Additional shorter remarks by Gregory Bateson appear on pp. 81–82, 97–99, 113, 116, 191–92, 242, and 243 of the same volume.) Reprinted, with minor editorial changes, in *A Sacred Unity* (cf. Bateson 1991a).

1978h   "Bateson's Workshop." In *Beyond the Double Bind: Communication and Family Systems, Theories, and Techniques with Schizophrenics*, edited by Milton M. Berger, pp. 197–229. New York: Brunner/Mazel.

1978i   "The Pattern Which Connects." *CoEvolution Quarterly*, no. 18 (Summer): 4–15. Excerpt from a draft of the Introduction to *Mind and Nature: A Necessary Unity* (cf. Bateson 1979a).

1978j    "Nuclear Addiction: Bateson to Saxon." *CoEvolution Quarterly*, no. 18 (Summer): 16. Letter dated July 15, 1977, from Gregory Bateson to David Saxon, President of the University of California.

1978k    "Bateson to Ellerbroek." *CoEvolution Quarterly*, no. 18 (Summer): 16–17. Letter dated March 14, 1978, from Gregory Bateson to W. C. Ellerbroek, M.D.

1978l    "Breaking Out of the Double Bind," an interview edited by Daniel Goleman. *Psychology Today* 12 (August): 42–51.

** 1978m    "Symptoms, Syndromes and Systems." *The Esalen Catalog* 16, no. 4 (October–December): 4–6.

1979a    *Mind and Nature: A Necessary Unity.* New York: E. P. Dutton; London: Wildwood House; Sydney: Bookwise; Toronto, Vancouver: Clarke, Irwin & Co. Paperback edition. New York: Bantam; Glasgow: Fontana/Collins, 1980. Trade paperback edition. New York: Bantam, 1988. Introduction excerpted, as "Mind and Nature," in *Omni* 1, no. 9 (June 1979): 54–56, 106.

** 1979b    "The Science of Knowing." *The Esalen Catalog* 17, no. 2 (April–July): 6–7. Reprinted, edited, in *A Sacred Unity* (cf. Bateson 1991a).

1979c    Letter in "Gregory Bateson on Play and Work," by Phillips Stevens, Jr. *The Association for the Anthropological Study of Play Newsletter* 5, no. 4 (Spring): 2–4.

1979d    "The Magic of Gregory Bateson." *Psychology Today* 13 (June): 128. Excerpts from an address delivered to a conference entitled "From Childhood to Old Age: Four Generations Teaching Each Other," held March 1979, at Southfield, Michigan. (Note: Excerpts from the same lecture may be found, edited, in *Angels Fear* (cf. Bateson 1987).)

1979e    "Nuclear Armament as Epistemological Error: Letters to the California Board of Regents." *Zero* 3: 34–41. (1979f and the first letter in 1980g.) Reprinted in *Lomi School Bulletin* (Summer 1980): 13–15.

1979f    "Letter to the Regents of the University of California." *CoEvolution Quarterly*, no. 24 (Winter): 22–23. A memorandum entitled by Bateson "Formal and Educational Aspects of the Arms Race."

1979g    "Profile: Gregory Bateson," by C. Christian Beels. An interview with Gregory Bateson. *The Kinesis Report* 2, no. 2 (Winter): 1–3 and 15–16. Reprinted, as "Entretien avec Gregory Bateson (1979), par C. Christian Beels," in *La Nouvelle Communication*, edited by Yves Winkin, pp. 283–90. Paris: Editions du Seuil, 1981.

1980a    "Syllogisms in Grass." *The London Review of Books* 2, no. 1 (January 24): 2.

** 1980b    "Seek the Sacred: Dartington Seminar." *Resurgence* 10, no. 6 (January–February): 18–20. Extract from a discussion with Henryk Skolimowski and others at Dartington Hall, England, in October 1979. Reprinted, edited, in *A Sacred Unity* (cf. Bateson 1991a).

1980c    "Health: Whose Responsibility?" *Energy Medicine* 1, no. 1: 70–75. Keynote Address delivered to Governor's Conference, May 3, 1979, at Berkeley, California. Excerpted in *The Esalen Catalog* 19, no. 2 (May–October 1980): 4–5. (Note: The *Energy Medicine* article is accompanied by a self-portrait sketch.) (Portions of the article, often heavily adapted, appear in several chapters of *Angels Fear* (cf. Bateson 1987).)

1980d    (With Paul Ryan.) "A Metalogue." *All Area*, no. 1 (Spring): 46–67.

1980e    (With Robert W. Rieber.) "Mind and Body: A Dialogue." In *Body and Mind:*

*Past, Present, and Future,* edited by Robert W. Rieber, pp. 241–52. New York: Academic Press. Reprinted, with minor changes, in *The Individual, Communication, and Society: Essays in Memory of Gregory Bateson,* edited by Robert W. Rieber, pp. 320–33. Cambridge: Cambridge University Press, 1989.

** 1980f   "Men Are Grass: Metaphor and the World of Mental Process," edited by Mary Catherine Bateson. *Lindisfarne Letter,* no. 11. Address to the Lindisfarne Fellows annual meeting, June 9, 1980. Reprinted in *Gaia: A Way of Knowing,* edited by William Irwin Thompson, pp. 37–47. Great Barrington, Mass.: Lindisfarne Press, 1987. Excerpted (differently edited) in "Bateson's Last Tape," by Stewart Brand, in *New Scientist* 87, no. 1214 (14 August 1980): 542–43.

1980g   "In July, 1979. . . ." *The Esalen Catalog* 19, no. 3 (September 1980–February 1981): 6–7. Two letters from Gregory Bateson relating to nuclear armaments and the University of California, written to fellow Regents Vilma S. Martinez and William A. Wilson.

1980h   Letter in "An Exchange of Letters between Maya Deren and Gregory Bateson." *October* 14 (Fall): 18–20.

1980i   Comments in *Language and Learning: The Debate Between Jean Piaget and Noam Chomsky.* [Report of a conference held in October, 1975, at Abbaye de Royaumont near Paris.] Edited by Massimo Piattelli-Palmarini, pp. 76, 77, 78, 222, 262, 263–64, 266, and 269. Cambridge, Mass.: Harvard University Press. (Note: References to Bateson's comments on the part of the editor or another speaker may be found on pp. 53, 56, 84, 153, 230, 257, and 323.)

1981a   "The Manuscript." *The Esalen Catalog* 20, no. 1 (January–June): 12. A poem written October 5, 1978. Reprinted, edited, in *Angels Fear* (cf. Bateson 1987).

1981b   "Allegory." *The Esalen Catalog* 20, no. 1 (January–June): 13. An allegory written May 12, 1979. Reprinted in *CoEvolution Quarterly,* no. 35 (Fall 1982): 42–43.

1981c   "Paradigmatic Conservatism." In *Rigor and Imagination: Essays from the Legacy of Gregory Bateson.* [Report of a conference in honor of Gregory Bateson, held February 15–18, 1979, at Pacific Grove, California.] Edited by Carol Wilder and John H. Weakland, pp. 347–55. New York: Praeger. (Note: A transcription of a 1954 discussion between Bateson, John Weakland, Jay Haley, and Don D. Jackson appears on pp. 56–63 of the same volume, in "One Thing Leads to Another," by John H. Weakland.)

1981d   Excerpt from a letter to Bradford P. Keeney. In "Gregory Bateson: A Final Metaphor," by Bradford P. Keeney. *Family Process* 20, no. 1 (March): 1.

1981e   "The Eternal Verities." [Excerpted from a presentation made to the Jungian Institute of San Francisco on March 14, 1980, and edited by Kai Erikson and Mary Catherine Bateson from a set of original notes and from a transcript of the San Francisco lecture.] *The Yale Review* 71, no. 1 (Autumn): 1–12. Reprinted, edited, in *Angels Fear* (cf. Bateson 1987).

1981f   Letter in "Editors' Note: Sociobiology: A Paradigm's Unnatural Selection Through Science, Philosophy, and Ideology," by Anthony Leeds and

Valentine Dusek. *The Philosophical Forum: A Quarterly* 13, nos. 2–3 (Winter–Spring 1981–1982): xxix–xxx.

1982a    "Foreword." In *St. George and the Dandelion: 40 Years of Practice as a Jungian Analyst,* by Joseph B. Wheelwright, pp. xi–xiii. San Francisco: The C. G. Jung Institute of San Francisco, Inc.

1982b    "Difference, Double Description and the Interactive Designation of Self." In *Studies in Symbolism and Cultural Communication* (University of Kansas Publications in Anthropology No. 14), edited by F. Allan Hanson, pp. 3–8. Lawrence, Kans.: University of Kansas. Lecture delivered by long-distance telephone to a class of Hanson's at the University of Kansas, April 18 and 20, 1978; title chosen by Hanson.

1982c    "They Threw God Out of the Garden: Letters from Gregory Bateson to Philip Wylie and Warren McCulloch," edited by Rodney E. Donaldson. *CoEvolution Quarterly,* no. 36 (Winter): 62–67.

1986    "The Prairie Seen Whole." In *Prairie: Images of Ground and Sky,* by Terry Evans, p. 12. Lawrence, Kans.: University of Kansas Press.

1987    (With Mary Catherine Bateson.) *Angels Fear: Towards an Epistemology of the Sacred.* New York: Macmillan Publishing Company. Paperback editions. New York: Bantam Books, 1988. London: Rider (Century Hutchinson Ltd.), 1988. (Note: The subtitle of the British edition is *An investigation into the nature and meaning of the sacred.*)

1989    (With Carl Rogers.) "Dialogue Between Gregory Bateson and Carl Rogers." In *Carl Rogers: Dialogues,* edited by Howard Kirschenbaum and Valerie Land Henderson, pp. 176–201. Boston: Houghton Mifflin Company. A public dialogue between Bateson and Rogers, held May 28, 1975, at the College of Marin, Kentfield, California. (Note: Pages 176–78 contain editorial remarks about Bateson, and a follow-up correspondence between Rogers and Bateson follows the dialogue, on pp. 199–201.)

1991a    *A Sacred Unity: Further Steps to an Ecology of Mind,* edited by Rodney E. Donaldson. San Francisco: HarperCollins.

** 1991b    "From Anthropology to Epistemology." In *A Sacred Unity.* Remarks delivered to an American Association for the Advancement of Science Symposium entitled "Fifty Years of Anthropology," honoring Margaret Mead, held February 1976 at Boston. Previously unpublished. Originally entitled "Summary: From Anthropology to Epistemology."

** 1991c    "Our Own Metaphor: Nine Years After." In *A Sacred Unity.* A letter to daughter Mary Catherine Bateson written June 26, 1977, as a potential afterword for a new edition of *Our Own Metaphor* (cf. 1972k). (Note: In the Bateson Archive this article is listed as "Dear Cathy (1977).") Previously unpublished.

** 1991d    "The Moral and Aesthetic Structure of Human Adaptation." In *A Sacred Unity.* Invitational paper for the Wenner-Gren Symposium on The Moral and Aesthetic Structure of Human Adaptation, held July 19–28, 1969, at Burg Wartenstein, Austria; Gregory Bateson, Chairman. Written November 5, 1968. Previously unpublished. Edited.

** 1991e    "'Last Lecture.'" In *A Sacred Unity.* Draft written September 29, 1979, for distribution to the press, of a lecture delivered October 28, 1979, at the Institute of Contemporary Arts, London. Previously unpublished.

## II. Minor Published Items: Short Quotations and Miscellania*

1971aa Excerpts from letters to Arthur Koestler dated April 6 and July 2, 1970. In *The Case of the Midwife Toad,* by Arthur Koestler, pp. 24, 51, 82, and 121. London: Hutchinson. Reprint. New York: Random House, 1972. (Paperback editions. New York: Vintage Books, 1973. London: Pan Books, 1974 (pp. 13, 42, 76, and 119).)

1975aa Quotation regarding "Sagan's Conjecture." *CoEvolution Quarterly,* no. 6 (Summer): 7.

1975bb Quotation regarding wrapping up water in a Christmas package. *CoEvolution Quarterly,* no. 6 (Summer): 22.

1975cc Quotation regarding statisticians. *CoEvolution Quarterly,* no. 6 (Summer): 151.

1975dd Quotation regarding a church he would start. *CoEvolution Quarterly,* no. 7 (Fall): 51. Reprinted in *The Next Whole Earth Catalog,* edited by Stewart Brand, p. 593. New York: Random House, 1980. 2nd ed., p. 593. New York: Random House, 1981.

1976aa Quotation regarding Isak Dinesen on co-evolution. *CoEvolution Quarterly,* no. 9 (Spring): 90.

1976bb Answers to watershed quiz. *CoEvolution Quarterly,* no. 12 (Winter): 12.

1977aa Tank log, 28 October 1973. In *The Deep Self: Profound Relaxation and the Tank Isolation Technique,* by John C. Lilly, p. 185. New York: Simon and Schuster. (Paperback edition, p. 189. New York: Warner Books, 1978.)

1977bb Quotation from Bateson's first meeting with the University of California Board of Regents. *CoEvolution Quarterly,* no. 13 (Spring): 143.

1978aa Quotation regarding bosses. *CoEvolution Quarterly,* no. 17 (Spring): 90. [From 1973a.]

1979aa Response to inquiry regarding magazines. *CoEvolution Quarterly,* no. 21 (Spring): 75.

1981aa Short excerpt from a letter to Oliver Caldecott. In "Introduction to the Wildwood Edition," by O. Caldecott. *Life and Habit,* by Samuel Butler. London: Wildwood House Ltd.

1985aa Excerpt from a letter to William Coleman dated December 1, 1966. In *Alfred North Whitehead: The Man and His Work, Volume I: 1861–1910,* by Victor Lowe, pp. 206–7. Baltimore and London: The Johns Hopkins University Press.

# Index

Crime, 203, 233

Crookes, William, 218

Cultural change, 5, 17, 64, 70; positive, 192, 207, 209

Cultural contrast, 75; between England and America, 19–20; 30–33

Cultural determinism, 3–5, 24–25

Cultural deviance, 12–14, 18, 114

Cultural diffusion, 4–6, 7, 37, 89

Cultural diversity, 34

Cultural evolution, 4–5, 7, 89, 183–84

Culture: an abstraction, 4, 37; definition of, 41; in a double bind, 112–13, 116, 119; and human dignity, 29–34; and learning, 24, 42–43; and personality, 9–25,; and sex, 35–48

Culture contact, 17, 69–71

Cybernetics, 50, 52, 90, 198, 237, 307; and aesthetics, 255, 257; and the behavioral sciences, 111; and control, 202; and double-bind theory, 148; and epistemology, 215; first model in, 154; and individual psychology, 259; and learning theory, 60; Macy Conferences on, 55–56, 90; and occurrence graphs, 253; and Norbert Wiener, 271. *See also* Communications theory; Games, theory of; Information theory; Systems theory

Darwin, Charles, 4, 77, 171, 193, 228; and mind and matter, 236; and Wallace, 153.

Darwinism, 90, 100, 216, 218, 227, 279. *See also* Biological evolution

Death, 67, 112–13, 227, 286, 309; of ideas, 265

Deduction, 47, 135; and double-bind theory, 186, 191; and science, 115, 150, 232; traps in anthropological, 38

Delancey Street, 203

Democracy, 33–34

Descartes, René, 175–76, 178, 195, 196, 305, 308

Description, 50, 61–67, 182, 221–22; of character, 197; and double-bind theory, 107, 215; and enlightenment, 177; and explanation, 148; of a flowering plant, 195; and observers, 74, 99; parsimony of, 73; and "stability," 283–89; and theories of description, 177–78; total, 166. *See also* Language

Design, 228. *See also* Paley, William; Purpose

Deutero-learning, 53–54, 60, 63, 90, 118; and contingencies of relationship, 129; and double-bind theory, 149, 197–98, 209; and search patterns, 141; and the unconscious, 168. *See also* Learning

Dickens, Charles, 184

Difference(s), 152–54, 161–66, 178–81, 188–90, 199–202, 218–22, 232–33, 273, 276–77, 286–87, 309, 311. *See also* Time

Dignity, 29–34

Dimensions: inversion of, 180; rule of, 62, 238

*Ding an sich,* 165–66, 182, 219, 226, 287

Dionysian culture, 10–11, 14

Discipline, 212, 268

DNA, 177–80, 183

Dolphins, 75, 207–9. *See also* Porpoises

Dominance-submission, 17, 19, 32, 33, 58, 112

Donkey, 303

Dormitive principle, 76, 135, 170–72

Double bind(s), 106–9, 112–13, 116–21, 130–31, 224; cannot count, 188; and evolution, 102, 106, 211, 227, 279; and hypnosis, 207; and "levels," 221; and perception, 205–6; theory, 147–50, 186–87, 191–98, 215–16, 259; therapeutic, 206–13; and wisdom, 281. *See also* Schizophrenia

Downs, the South, 69–70

Dream, 129–30, 266, 267, 301; and double-bind theory, 148, 150; and randomness, 227

Dualism. *See* Body/mind problem

Ecology, 90, 196; and evolution, 276; and fractionation, 69–70; of ideas, 256; of mind, 187, 265–66, 278; perception of change by the, 154; pollution, 211

"Economic determinism," 3–4

Economics: and culture, 7, 36; and explanation, 4, 50, 134; of flexibility, 100–101, 107, 137–38, 209–10; and money, 95, 297; and objectivity, 246; of sex behavior, 41

Education, 231, 233, 254, 295; and epistemology, 308–13

Ego, 260; false cult of the, 224

Eidos, 46–47, 50, 63

Elephant, 232, 300

Eliot, T. S., 226, 292–93, 307

Embryology, 178–81, 232, 240, 241, 310; and a theory of family homeostasis, 115

Emotions, 23–24, 127–31, 171, 267. *See also* Feelings

Empathy, 76–77, 248, 291